THE OXFORD
ILLUSTRATED HISTORY OF
WESTERN PHILOSOPHY

Congradulations Amy !
We hope this will be a
helpful introduction to
some ideas. Come visit
us soon !

Love,
George & Colleen
6-21-97

THE OXFORD ILLUSTRATED HISTORY OF
WESTERN PHILOSOPHY

Edited by
ANTHONY KENNY

OXFORD UNIVERSITY PRESS
1997

Oxford University Press, Great Clarendon Street, Oxford OX2 6DP

Oxford New York
Athens Auckland Bangkok Bogota Bombay
Buenos Aires Calcutta Cape Town Dar es Salaam
Delhi Florence Hong Kong Instanbul Karachi
Kuala Lumpur Madras Madrid Melbourne
Mexico City Nairobi Paris Singapore
Taipei Tokyo Toronto
and associated companies in
Berlin Ibadan

Oxford is a trade mark of Oxford University Press

Published in the United States by
Oxford University Press Inc., New York

First published 1994
First issued as an Oxford University Press paperback 1997

British Library Cataloguing in Publication Data
Data available

Library of Congress Cataloging in Publication Data
The Oxford illustrated history of Western philosophy/edited by
Anthony Kenny
p. cm
Originally published: 1994.
Includes bibliographical references and index.
1. Philosophy–History. I. Kenny. Anthony John Patrick
B72.08 1997 190–dc20 96–41967
ISBN 0–19–285335–X

1 3 5 7 9 10 8 6 4 2

Datacapture by Alliance Typesetters, Pondicherry, India
Text processing by Oxford University Press and Selwood Systems
Printed in Great Britain
on acid-free paper by
Butler and Tanner Ltd
Frome, Somerset

PREFACE

An illustrated history of philosophy must differ from other illustrated histories for two reasons. First, it is plain from the outset that the abstract matters with which philosophy deals cannot be pictorially represented in a historical text in the way that siege engines and farm implements can be pictured in a military or agricultural history. Second, and less obviously, the history of philosophy, even when unillustrated, differs in kind from the history of any other pursuit. This is because philosophy itself is a discipline without a peer, resembling both the sciences and the arts, but belonging with neither.

Philosophy resembles a science in that the philosopher, like the chemist or the meteorologist, goes in pursuit of truth, and hopes to make discoveries. Yet classics in philosophy are not antiquated by succeeding research in the way that the works of even the greatest scientists become dated in time. No one would now read Ptolemy to learn about the planets, but one need not be an antiquarian to read Plato.

In this respect, philosophy resembles the arts rather than the sciences: when we read Homer and Sophocles it is not in order to find out what quaint ideas people used to have in far-off days. Yet when we read Aristotle we raise the questions which we would ask of a scientist rather than a poet: are his conclusions true, and are the arguments he offers for them valid?

Because philosophy is unique, the history of philosophy is unique. A historian of medicine does not, *qua* historian, practise medicine; but one cannot write the history of philosophy without philosophizing. The interpreter of a past philosopher is bound to present and offer reasons for his thoughts, and to expound and evaluate his arguments. But offering reasons for philosophical conclusions, and evaluating the logic of philosophical arguments, is itself a full-blooded philosophical activity. Hence, while a historian of painting need not be a painter, a historian of philosophy cannot but be a philosopher.

Of all disciplines which claim to be the fruit of human reasoning, philosophy is the most contentious; and if philosophy is contentious, so must its historiography be. Disagreements, even among philosophers, have their limits; and if you ask any member of the profession to name the six greatest writers in the Western philosophical tradition, four names are sure to figure in the reply: Plato, Aristotle, Descartes, and Kant. But there is unlikely to be consensus about filling the two remaining places. My own candidates would be Aquinas and Wittgenstein; but others, with equal confidence, will put forward the names of Augustine, Locke, Leibniz, Hume, Hegel, Marx, Frege, and half-a-dozen others. The differing rankings of philosophers reflect disagreements not just about the genius of the individual writers, but about the nature of philosophy itself.

This volume reflects both the consensus and the divergence to be expected from historians of philosophy. All the philosophers I have just mentioned, and all philosophers who are likely to figure in anyone's list of the twelve all-time greatest, are discussed, at respectful length, somewhere in the book. On the other hand, the several contributors have been given a free hand in the method of treatment of the major figures and in the choice of minor figures to be included.

All the contributors belong broadly to the Anglo-American analytic style of philosophy, in the sense that they have been trained in, or have taught in, that tradition. But none of them, I imagine, would think of themselves as typical practitioners of the school; several of them, I know, pride themselves on having healthily distanced themselves from its mainstream. The reader will notice quite significant variations of emphasis and interpretation between different contributors and no editorial attempt has been made to make the contributors agree with one another or with the editor. In Chapter 5, the sections on Wittgenstein are by David Pears; the remainder was written by myself.

The pictorial representation of philosophical ideas does indeed present a special challenge. Like any history, a history of philosophy must contain portraits—whether authentic or imaginary—of significant contributors to the history; and it can contain photographs of places and objects closely associated with those contributors. Again, like any history of written texts, it must contain some illustrations of those texts. But beyond that, it is not immediately obvious what kinds of picture provide fit material to adorn a philosophical narrative.

In fact, artists in many periods have striven to render philosophical ideas in visible and tangible form. This is most obvious in the case of the ideas of ethics and political philosophy, and its practice was most obviously fashionable in the Middle Ages and the Renaissance. But artists in later ages have continued to interest themselves, in more sophisticated if less explicit form, in the personification of virtues and vices and the representation of civic ideal and political horror. In our own century, artists have striven to give visual immediacy to concepts drawn even from epistemology and metaphysics.

The interrelation between the abstractions of the intellect and the images of the senses or the fancy has indeed been an enduring theme of philosophy. The nature of representation itself—the internal relationship between thought, image, and reality—has preoccupied philosophers from Plato's allegory of the cave up to Wittgenstein's picture theory of the proposition. Rationalists and empiricists have contested whether, in the book of the mind, priority should be assigned to the texts provided by the intellect or the illustrations provided by the senses. Thus philosophy, throughout its history, has been fascinated by the interweaving of words and images; and the illustrated text that follows will, we hope, provide a congenial medium for the narration of that history.

A.J.P.K.

Oxford
November 1993

CONTENTS

LIST OF MAPS   ix

LIST OF COLOUR PLATES   xi

1. ANCIENT PHILOSOPHY   1
Stephen R. L. Clark

2. MEDIEVAL PHILOSOPHY   55
Paul Vincent Spade

3. DESCARTES TO KANT   107
Anthony Kenny

4. CONTINENTAL PHILOSOPHY FROM FICHTE TO SARTRE   193
Roger Scruton

5. MILL TO WITTGENSTEIN   239
David Pears and Anthony Kenny

6. POLITICAL PHILOSOPHY   275
Anthony Quinton

AFTERWORD   363

CHRONOLOGICAL TABLE   371

FURTHER READING   379

ACKNOWLEDGEMENTS   393

INDEX   395

LIST OF MAPS

The eastern Mediterranean in antiquity   2

Europe in the fourteenth century   96

Europe in the eighteenth century   159

LIST OF COLOUR PLATES

Where Do We Come From? What Are We? Where Are We Going? by Paul Gauguin   *facing page* 20
    Tompkins Collection; reproduced by courtesy of the Museum of Fine Arts, Boston

Socrates, wall-painting from hill-house in Ephesus   21
    Selcuk Museum, Turkey; photo: Erich Lessing/Magnum

The School of Athens by Raphael: four details believed to represent Parmenides,
Heraclitus, Pythagoras, and Socrates   52
    Stanze di Raffaello, Vatican; photo: Scala

Diogenes of Sinope, Urbino istoriato dish   53
    Private collection; photo: Christie's, London

St Catherine of Alexandria, c.1520, detail from diptych, Danube School   84
    Private collection; photo: Christie's, London

Hippocrates and Galen, from the medical texts of Hippocrates with commentaries
of Galen, in version of Constantinus Africanus of Monte Cassino   84
    Osterreichische Nationalbibliothek, Vienna: codex 2315, folio 1^r; photo: Erich
    Lessing/Magnum

The Lady Philosophy appears to Boethius in a dream, from a fifteenth-century folio
edition in the Library of Congress   85

Thomas Aquinas, by Justus of Ghent, fifteenth-century   116
    Louvre, Paris

St Bonaventura and Franziskus, detail from a wing of an altarpiece   116
    Wallraf-Richartz-Museum, Cologne; photo: Rheinisches Bildarchiv

The Virgin Mary by Ingres   117
    Louvre, Paris

Constantine Huygens and his Clerk, 1627, by Thomas de Keyser   180
    National Gallery, London

The Five Senses, 1640, by Simon de Vou   180
    Private collection; photo: Christie's, London

Italian manuscript, fourteenth-century, showing Socrates, Aristotle, Plato, and
Seneca   181
    Musée Condé, Chantilly; photo: Bridgeman Art Library, London

Marcus Aurelius, statue in Piazza del Campidoglio, Rome   212
    Photo: Scala

Karl Marx, statue in Berlin   213
    Photo: Thomas Koepker/Magnum Photos

Wittgenstein in New York, 1965, by Eduardo Paolozzi   244
    Editions Electo, New York; photo: Bridgeman Art Library, London

The Treason of Images by René Magritte   245
    Los Angeles County Museum of Art; photo: Giraudon, Paris. © ADAGP Paris/DACS
    London 1994

Self portrait, *c.*1640, by Salvatore Rosa   245
    National Gallery, London

Illustration from a fifteenth-century text of Aristotle   276
    Bibliothèque Nationale, Paris; photo: Bridgeman Art Library, London

The Emperor Justinian, mosaic in S. Vitale, Ravenna   276
    Photo: Ancient Art and Architecture Collection

Machiavelli's writing-desk during his exile in Sant' Andrea, Perussino, Italy   277
    Photo: Erich Lessing/Magnum

1

Ancient Philosophy

STEPHEN R. L. CLARK

The Very Beginnings

THE curtain of history rises on a world already ancient, full of ruined cities and ways of thought worn smooth. Currently respectable theory suggests that there were people physically much like ourselves a hundred thousand years ago. Stone artefacts and paintings date from forty millennia BC, and were probably long preceded by woven baskets, sand paintings, and dramatic art. The experience of present-day primitives suggests that, even if our ancestors lacked our technical abilities, they normally had little difficulty in providing for their everyday needs, and had time to play or fantasize or argue. It may be, as some moderns have proposed, that they talked mostly about kinship, telling stories to authenticate and justify their rules of intermarriage, but also about hospitality and predation. Maybe, as an earlier generation of speculative palaeoanthropologists proposed, their stories of hero, damsel, dragon were coded messages about the sun and stars. But merely by talking, they ensured that their stories were not only about kinship, nor only about the sky.

Like other social animals we signalled to each other, marked out our favoured routes, played with children, established hierarchies, and listened to the experienced elders (not wholly credulously). The earliest tales we have seek to explain why non-human animals no longer speak in human tongues, why the sky no longer rests upon the earth, why brothers and sisters must no longer mate, why we age and die (which was not so, we said, in the beginning), and why there is anything. There were warriors then, and gardeners, builders, weavers, nurses, cooks, craftsmen, and magicians. There were probably also people with a reputation for recounting marvels, bringing messages from the sky or from our remembered ancestors. Some told more elaborate stories to accommodate what seemed to be mistaken, while their rivals, maybe, sought to loosen their stories' hold upon the people by other stories, or by less narrative distractions.

In other words, for however long it was that people lived in small and roaming bands, or settled to build gardens in the waste, they behaved like people. They explained their worlds to themselves, and wondered about differences, and used their verbal powers to confute or entertain. When they encountered other bands of talking beasts they tried to reach some mutual understanding, even if only to identify their enemies. Some of them began to think that there was a god in their speech, something that could outlast its mortal speakers and connect each new generation of mortality back to the forgotten sky, the way things really were. They became, in brief, philosophers, and the mythologies we find recorded by later, literate thinkers are the distorted record—Aristotle was later to say—of past philosophy. The peoples around the Mediterranean basin who, by convention, constitute the ancient world (ignoring other peoples clustered around the Yangtse, the Ganges, or innumerable forgotten lakes and rivers) elaborated stories to explain both what they did and what they saw being done. No one was really content to say: we do it because we always did, and things happen thus and so because they do ('because it's a law of nature'). We all wanted to make sense of things, to know why things weren't as we suspected they had been and should be.

Something like this is true, but it would be rash to go much further and expound the speculations of pre-literate, pre-historic peoples, or even be sure that we had wholly understood the words of historical and literate ones. Some commentators have proposed great fables: think how our ancestors spread from Africa to wonder at and at long last displace the products of an earlier emigration (remembered now as elves and ogres); think how we bred ourselves to be obedient, playful beasts; think how a settled population grew in Europe to serve

THE EASTERN MEDITERRANEAN was the cradle of Western philosophy. Almost every one of the major philosophers of the ancient world lived on its islands or its coastlines.

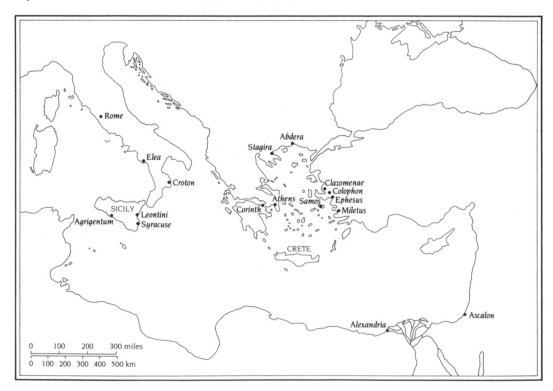

the Earth Mother and her attendant spirits till displaced hordes of horse-men serving the Sky Father disrupted ancient harmonies, and installed patriarchy and a priesthood in the hearts of their successors. These make pleasant stories, but the evidence for them is quite small. Something was being thought back then, and people developed reasons for what they did and thought, but what those thoughts and reasons were, who knows? Archaic philosophizing certainly existed—unless we suppose that the philosophic temperament is a recent and unprincipled mutation—but attempts to describe it show more about us than them. Some of the stories—and especially those that blame 'the Greeks' or Plato (*c*.430–347 BC) for deserting the Earth Mother—show our ignorance of what those same Greeks, and Plato, thought. 'The land', he said, 'is [our] ancestral home and [we] must cherish it even more than children cherish their mother; furthermore, the Earth is a goddess and mistress of mortal men, and the gods and spirits already established in the locality must be treated with the same respect.'

Life is easier for the curious historian when the stories were written down in ways more readily intelligible to outsiders. In oral cultures, stories change with every telling, and there is no real pressure to demand that every story be obviously consistent with all others. The dead lie underground, but also in the dream-world and a distant heaven; the sun is a celestial ball rolled up the arch of heaven by a dung-beetle, but also a boat that carries the King himself across the sky. Arguments that we might reckon invalid if we saw them written down may serve quite well in oral debate—because our memories rewrite what went before (as they do still in parliaments and courts).

Arguments and stories can of course be 'written down' even in oral cultures: the local landscape is inscribed, for those who remember, with our local history; every symbol of authority, every relic of past endeavour, is a message to the future. Some messages, perhaps, were such as any hominid could read (scents or scratches or piled rocks); others, as the hominids began to be human, could only be read by those already initiated in the special histories of each local tribe (the sigil of a remembered individual, or the branch of a tree where something striking happened not too long ago). Writing in the sense intended nowadays allowed strangers and the young to be initiated in more abstract ways (although it was still a secret art for many years). What was thus written down, in cuneiform or hieroglyphic, had been spoken and remembered and embodied in secret images long since. By writing it down our ancestors embarked upon the process that has led to formal argument, universally decipherable messages, abstract imagination. We no longer need to be told what a particular set of symbols means: they can be deciphered from a knowledge of the meaning of elementary symbols. The powers who used to be 'written in the landscape', as they still are for peoples who rely on memory, were persons because they changed with each new telling of the story, seeming to respond to the story-teller and the audience; the powers who were written into literal texts became less personal because they changed much less. People who read stories from the landscape are reminded of the stories they know in unpredictably different ways: people who read stories from books have at least some chance of reading it the same way today as yesterday (though actually all our readings change a little). The god that used to be in speech, the inspired utterance of the selected few which changed and multiplied as it leapt from mouth to mouth, now takes up residence in the written word, meaning 'the very same' whoever reads it—except that of course it doesn't. After the age of prophets comes the age of scribes.

The earliest written stories that we know combine political realism and 'fantasy' in ways we now find strange: though the gods no longer (as the story says they did in days gone by) share one world with us, they are regular visitors, and the heroes may cross over into that other world more easily than shamans. We incline to think that their authors 'must have known' they were writing fantasy, or allegory. The gods did not 'really' battle around Troy, nor did Pheidippides encounter the god Pan upon the road from Sparta. The gods who engendered royal dynasties must 'obviously' have been artefacts, pretentious ways of saying both that the new king was to be feared and 'Who *his* father was, God knows'. We react, in fact, a little like one who holds that, say, Picasso's *Guernica* distorts the truth, merely because we would not think we saw such things in the village street. The truth is that we do not actually see what we now think we see: our visual field is fractured and delusive, and only our 'reason' tells us that ghosts, will-o'-the-wisps, and monsters don't exist, and that associated meanings and evaluations aren't 'out there' in the world.

The two chief morals of that speculative opening are these: first, that the pursuit of knowledge through the exchange of ideas is something that we must assume we have been about since we were talking beasts; second, that we cannot assume too ready an acquaintance with the world our ancestors explained, as if they had only to 'look and see' that things were as we now say they are. It is all too often assumed that 'ancient Greeks' were the first to speculate, and reason, about the world, the first to exchange and criticize each other's thoughts. 'The achievements which some attribute to the barbarians belong to the Greeks, with whom not merely philosophy but the human race itself began,' according to Diogenes Laertius, who wrote his *Lives of the Philosophers* in the early third century AD. Clement of Alexandria, a second-century Christian, on the other hand, was sure the Greeks had borrowed from the barbarians. It is also all too often assumed that they were reasoning about the world *we* find. The philosophic temperament, on the available evidence, is found throughout the world and may be assumed to have been present throughout the hundred thousand years of human being, whether or not particular tribes admired it (is it admired now?). But precisely because, on the available evidence, most of those millennia were lived under conditions very unlike our own, we cannot take it for granted that our ancestors saw exactly what we say we do, and differed from us only in the explanations that they invented. Such an assumption blinds us to the way they reasoned, and incidentally saves us from any radical critique of our own present thoughts.

But is there after all a sense in which it was the Greeks who began it? There were two features of those Greeks who rediscovered writing after the long collapse of Minoan and Mycenaean culture that were distinctive: their preference for impersonal explanations, and their readiness to offer reasons. The two may be associated but are logically distinct. Where other peoples found it acceptable to say that trees and cities fell or winter followed summer because

ZEUS, the chief of the Greek pantheon, was both a sky god and an embodiment of superhuman law: his thunderbolts enforce divine justice. Here, in a painting contemporary with the beginnings of Greek philosophy, he is subduing the monster Typhon, who represents disorder and devastation.

the gods were squabbling, or a witch ill-wished them, some Greeks began to appeal to 'Law' instead. At first that Law was simply Destiny: that nothing is allowed to grow too high, that everything has limits, that winter follows spring. Even Zeus, the greatest of the gods, is subject to Destiny, which remains half-personal because so clearly moralistic. But if Zeus does not, or cannot, by his arbitrary choice, subvert that Law, perhaps we can do without him. Things happened as they did because there were timeless, and unintended, relationships between different, and discoverable, factors. Where other peoples found it easiest to defend particular stories by appeal to the authority of chosen texts or prophets, some Greeks began to demand that they be given reasons for endorsing one theory or another that could, in principle, be checked by anyone prepared to work at it. They invented—or discovered—a world no longer arbitrary, ruled by changing purposes; they insisted that no special gifts—beyond the gift to follow arguments—were needed to uncover it. That is the world enlightened people have inherited, although there are plenty of archaizers with us still, content to appeal to scriptural authority or charismatic prophecy to defend their moralizing account of how things are.

The story appeals to us, as do all Whiggish histories that trace the line of progress to our own condition. Those most convinced by it, of course, are compelled at once to admit that the Greeks quite quickly sinned and fell away. Plato remoralized the world, suggesting that things happened because they should, or something very like them should. Even Aristotle—conventionally depicted as Plato's opponent—thought that whatever helped us to see God was best. Even the Stoics, though they cultivated logic and 'the natural sciences', are now best remembered for their 'stoicism', their moral commitment to the divine presence. Few were the philosophers who rejected ordinary religious practice or wholly abandoned the authority of traditional story. Some of them (Epimenides the Cretan, for example, who said, epi-grammatically, that all Cretans were liars, about 600 BC, or Iamblichus of Syria in the early fourth century AD) behaved like witch-doctors, or seemed to approve of similar cleansing rites. The whole Greek experiment, so modernists suppose, succumbed to mystifying Platonism and occult practice, and even unbelievers, because they had lost confidence in the

ANAXIMANDER OF MILETUS, like other sixth-century thinkers, was a primitive scientist no less than a primitive philosopher. He believed that all living things originated in slime, and that mankind had evolved from a species of less complex organisms. This Roman mosaic shows him holding a sundial.

power of reason to uncover truth, were happy to sing along with their ancestral pieties. The bits of past philosophizing that such moderns choose to praise are only might-have-beens, momentary anticipations of the true philosophy. Hear Thomas Sprat, first historian of the Royal Society:

The poets of old to make all things look more venerable than they were, devised a thousand false Chimaeras; on every Field, River, Grove and Cave they bestowed a Fantasm of their own making: With these they amazed the world. . . . And in the modern Ages these Fantastical Forms were reviv'd and possessed Christendom. . . . All which abuses if those acute Philosophers did not promote, yet they were never able to overcome; nay, not even so much as King Oberon and his invisible Army. But from the time in which the Real Philosophy has appear'd there is scarce any whisper remaining of such horrors. . . . The cours of things goes quietly along, in its own true channel of Natural Causes and Effects. For this we are beholden to Experiments; which though they have not yet completed the discovery of the true world, yet they have already vanquished those wild inhabitants of the false world, that us'd to astonish the minds of men.

It is difficult to see, in that case, why we should bother to discuss the ancient texts. It may be historically important to recognize that the Greeks were well aware—at least since Pythagoras—that the earth was round (such recognition might prevent some gross distortions of Columbus' later venture), but no one expects to find new details of the earth's circumference by reading Eratosthenes (*c.*284–192 BC), who calculated it, quite accurately, by comparing the noon-shadows at Aswan and Alexandria. Nor do we expect Empedocles of Agrigentum (484–424 BC) to offer us a serious rival to Darwinian evolutionary theory, even though, after the event, we can detect a resemblance.

The practice of interpreting the writings of our predecessors as lisping attempts to speak a truth we understand more clearly than did they is not without merit. Aristotle himself described the earlier philosophers as ones who were groping for the distinctions he expounded—notably, the distinction between four sorts of explanation (material, efficient, formal, and final). He may have misrepresented them—though the evidence that he did is largely drawn from his account of them: if we entirely doubt his word, we have almost no evidence of what they thought. If he did misrepresent them, it does not follow that we will do much better: our knowledge of that past is fragmentary and distorted. Where are the 232,808 lines of Theophrastus, Aristotle's first successor, or the 705 works of the great Stoic Chrysippus (*c.*280–207 BC)? They would have been many fewer if he had quoted less, so his detractors said. Not every serious thinker wrote a book—we have but one book by a slave, and none by any woman; not every book was copied often enough to have much chance of lasting; many books were destroyed, deliberately or not, by fire; many that survive have strayed so far beyond their context as to be unintelligible; even those we think we understand have lost whole realms of context, commentary, and implication. In the end, the account we give of past philosophy will always represent a present self, and therefore change from one year to the next. 'Socrates' names any number of distinguishable philosophers: Plato's Socrates and Xenophon's, Diogenes' and Aristotle's, Pyrrho's and Plotinus', or even Plotinus' Plato's

'KNOW YOURSELF', a saying attributed to the Seven Sages, was inscribed on the temple of Apollo at Delphi.

Socrates. Each age, each individual, sees in the texts what they can understand, for good or ill. We usually end up by arranging thinkers into schools, and intellectual genealogies, even though experience should teach us that a philosopher's pupils do not usually go on where he left off, and that actual influences cross centuries and thousand-miles without affecting anything in between.

To say that the truth is not, or need not be, what we suppose assumes two things that have, of late, been questioned: that there is a truth of the matter, and that we might find it out, if only to the extent of finding what it isn't. The assumptions have been questioned—and were so in the ancient world, most rigorously by the Sceptical philosophers whose arguments are summarized by Sextus Empiricus (*fl.* AD 200). As they recognized, we cannot—without contradiction—declare either of them *false*: if we say there is no truth, then in that at least we are liars; if we cannot find the truth, what right have we to say we can't? The best we can manage, by way of abandoning the Way of Truth, is to sink back into the Way of Seeming (on which I shall have more to say below), without ever saying that we are right, or correct, to do so. It is a path that many of us, from the beginning, have found easy. The philosophical temperament, we may agree, is found everywhere; but not everyone is even tempted to philosophy. Before the question of its 'truth' is raised, the world of our experience is just that, the realm of what is obvious; if we first raise the question and then find no answer we may well revert to that most obvious condition, when we found everything obvious—including the army of King Oberon. It is that struggle between Seeming and Reality that serves as a golden thread to follow through the past.

Inspired Thinkers

The earliest stories that we have embody questions about our lives and deaths, and about the stories to be read in the flights of birds, the growth of flowers, and the shifting streams. They usually embody somewhat weary answers, as of a world grown old: it is best not to hanker after immortality, but to obey the gods of our time and station; best not to expect marvellous results from the twin passions of love and war; best to be honest if we can't be lucky; strength is good, but cleverness is better; the world of light and order is marooned in everlasting darkness, and those who leave the light do not return unchanged. All new growth would be cut back at last, and only the heavens were for ever. The aphorisms attached to the sixth-century sages (seven, ten, or seventeen of them according to different tastes) were 'philosophical' in the vulgar sense (i.e. depressed): know yourself; nothing too much; never go bail; recognize your opportunity; most people are bad. At the same time, the very fact of being brought up among the ruins could impress some people with the thought that they at least were young. Whatever had been achieved before, and lost, there was perhaps a moment when the world was new and could reinvent or rediscover glory. According to Pindar, 'A shadow in a dream is man, but when god sheds a brightness then shining light is on earth and life is sweet as honey.'

According to the poets who were the first to speak for Greece, Something came out of Nothing and became, through slow degrees, the world of human, Greek experience: mortals stumbled through the world in fear of beautiful or horrid presences, but not without their mortal dignity. The powers who had formed the world, mere selfish impulses, were now in balance beneath the all-seeing Sky, which demanded that people keep their promises and offer hospitality to all (or at least to anyone who was someone). Some had been imprisoned in the dark below the earth; others had been reborn as loyal—or fairly loyal—Olympians: Metis, for example, who is crafty wisdom, is swallowed by Zeus and reinvented as Athena. Zeus Xenios, Zeus Horkios (God of Strangers, God of Oaths) would not leave treachery unavenged, nor allow mere mortals to rise up too high. Back in the age of Kronos we did what we desired, but now live under discipline. The stories the poets told were also scandalous, as though the powers were vast and lustful children, shaped in the imagination of those who thought success would be to conquer their enemies and feast in comfort. Later Platonists were to allegorize the stories (as I just did), and thereby inspire Philo, a first-century Alexandrian Jew, to find new, philosophical, meanings in the Torah. Plutarch, a first-century Boeot-

THALES OF MILETUS (*fl.* 585 BC) is often regarded as the earliest Greek philosopher. Only brief sayings have survived, such as 'all things are full of gods'. This is a Roman representation of him from the Sala dei Filosofi in the Museo Capitolino.

ian who served as a priest at Delphi (and incidentally provided Shakespeare with many of his plots), found similar profundities in Egyptian tales of Isis and Osiris. Xenophanes of Colophon (570–478 BC), like Clement, despised such myths: the power that ruled the world could not really be in the shape of just one of its dependent creatures, but rather be complete in itself. No image of Zeus as manlike, bull-like, or a golden rain could be acceptable, and nor could Zeus be moved by lusts and angers of a lesser kind. Elsewhere on the Mediterranean shore, similarly indignant prophets denied that God had any picturable shape, or rose from Nothing. That God could only be known as the God of Justice, and the people of Israel were self-defined as his alone, while the other nations served, at best, his servants: demons unless they were obedient to him.

Later generations were to acknowledge the Hebrews as a 'nation of philosophers', self-

THE NAKED TRUTH. The Greek word for Truth (*aletheia*) was often etymologized as 'the unhidden' or 'the uncovered'. Hence the long artistic tradition of representing truth as nude—as here, in Botticelli's 'Calumny'.

dedicated to living as philosophers should, by God's laws, not the king's nor any mob's commands. But it was not obvious at first that Greek philosophers were saying the same as Hebrew prophets. Xenophanes' principle has had its effect: on the one hand, the Thing from which the world takes shape cannot itself be shaped as one of its derivatives; on the other, nothing can be trusted as a true account of that same Thing that too obviously owes its origin to the special character of those who give the account. But of course a Thing that is utterly unlike any particular thing is indescribable in any common terms; and a Thing whose true description must owe nothing to the characters of those who describe it is beyond our reach: whatever we find it plausible to say It is will be what *we* find plausible. If it is absurd to think that the Thing is azure-haired and bearded (as it is), must it not also be absurd to think it rational? If Thales of Miletus (a sixth-century man of affairs who came to seem to be a philosopher) was right to say that *Water* was the root of things, it was not *watery* water, common water, that he meant. Maybe he only meant, like Heraclitus, that 'everything flows'; maybe he only sought the most obvious image for that Being 'in which we live and move and have our being'. The poets had known that the gods 'took shapes' that were not essentially their own, that they spoke another language, breathed a different air, and yet were not entirely alien: Xenophanes, in honouring the god and exclaiming against scandal, made them utterly unknown.

The point was not 'merely theological', as though there were a different realm of reason where such problems did not arise. Theology, in the earliest sense, was only talking about the inscrutable, incomprehensible powers and reasons of the world (which is why I spoke of the Thing and not of God). From being obvious, a realm of human tracks and traces, the world became mysterious. Truth lies in the depths, so Democritus of Abdera (*c.*460–357 BC) declared. The aphorism is one that now itself seems obvious: how things really are and how they seem to us, to anyone, are not necessarily, or at all, the same. It was not obvious then, and the aphorism is deliberately paradoxical. The Greek word that we translate as 'truth' is *Aletheia*, and a stream of puns makes clear that the Greeks could, if they chose, hear this as 'the Unhidden', or 'the Unforgotten'. Its actual etymology is probably quite different. The Truth that lies in the Democritean depths is paradoxical because 'the Truth' should rather be what does not hide, the obvious. The Truth is what we cannot forget because it never sets, because there is no other thing than Truth to take its place (as darkness replaces light)—as Heraclitus of Ephesus (*fl. c.*500 BC) said. The Truth is the all-seeing sky in which—and not just under which—we live.

And yet it hides. Really, Democritus declared, we know nothing; all that we perceive is only 'conventionally true', true by custom. Different customs generate different sense-worlds, different stories, but the truth overall is only 'atoms and the void'. In a later age this 'atomism' can be hailed as a brilliant anticipation of physical theory: Plato, his detractors said, never dealt directly with Democritus (who'd visited Athens in Socrates' lifetime), because he was afraid of genuine, able opposition. Modern physicalists also speak as if the common human world were a complete illusion (sometimes even denying that there is anything to which the illusion appears). In which case, of course, the words and writings that propound the theory

DEMOCRITUS OF ABDERA is best known in the history of philosophy for his anticipations of the atomic theory. In the literary and artistic tradition he was represented as 'the laughing philosopher' convulsed at the spectacle of human folly. Both his physical and moral philosophy are alluded to in this painting by Terbrugghen.

are an illusion too (more obviously so because they depend upon particular human languages to be perceived at all). Democritus was perhaps more careful, acknowledging that the very reasons that he had for thinking that the senses did not show us Truth were drawn from what the senses showed us. His atomism was less a physical theory than a mystical conclusion. Like other, earlier sages he is said to have travelled widely in the East, and frequented graveyards, as did Buddhist monks, to contemplate, no doubt, his dissolution. Persons (like taste, temperature, and colours) exist 'by convention': 'really' there are only atoms and the void. All ordinary objects are composed, without remainder, of atomic simples. Because there could be no infinite regress of parts, there must be unrestricted, simple singulars (*atoms*), without the characters that were the province of their complex products. As before, the real world, the explanans, could not possess the characters it was invoked to explain.

It is this gap between Appearance and a hypothesized Reality that will constitute the central thread of philosophical speculation in the ancient (and many another) world. But one philosopher went so far as to deny that there were multiple truths at all, or any sort of untruth. 'It is necessary', said Parmenides, 'to say and think that Being Is.' One possible interpretation amounts to no more than the duty of being truthful, that of what is we should say

PYTHAGORAS OF SAMOS was a philosopher and polymath of the sixth century: he made discoveries in music and geometry and to this day the theorem determining the area of the hypotenuse of a right-angled triangle bears his name. Here he appears in a relief by Lucca della Robbia on the Campanile of the Duomo of Florence.

that it is, of what is not we should say that it is not. Even this, though it has the air of truism, is significant: why, after all, not lie, tell stories, hide away from truth? That the truth imposes its own burden on us, that we *can* hide but shouldn't, tells us something of its nature (notably that it is not, as later thinkers have pretended, value-free). But Parmenides had more to conclude than that. Amongst the 'truths by convention' things we agree are true but really aren't are claims about change and possibility. Other things than are might be; other things than are are not; some things come to be and others cease. How can this be? What *isn't*, isn't, and so cannot be spoken or described. There can be no void, no Nothing; nor can there be nothings, fictions; nor can things come to be or ever have been Nothing. Parmenides did not conclude that there were, in a way, things that did not exist (which, after all and commonsensically, there are), but rather that there could be neither void, nor change, nor difference. The Way of Truth requires us to think that Being Is, and never could be otherwise.

'Parmenides' inspiration': this was, indeed, exactly as he presented it. He was a native of Elea, in the sixth century BC, and was later said to have been a pupil of Xenophanes, and to have taught Pythagoras (on whom more below). He chose to represent his thought in verse, as the revelation of a goddess. Others, like his disciple Zeno of Elea, might argue that there were irresoluble contradictions in the Way of Seeming, and Parmenides himself might focus—certainly Plato supposed he did—on rational argument for his conclusion. But the text he wrote begins as revelation. Just so, amongst the Hebrews, teachers might, eventually, argue about the properties (so to miscall them) of the Lord, but began with a shattering revelation of the One that Is. The poets and philosophers were wrong—Parmenides and the prophets said—to think that Nothing preceded Everything: there was, and is, no Nothing. There is Something that must be; which is the only Truth we grope to express in all our utterances. Any little truth is 'true' only by convention, because we agree to count it so. The Truth is neither contingent (as if there might be nothing true), nor incomplete (as if there were something else as true which was needed to explain it), nor differentiated into this little truth or that. If (for the sake of argument) 'Pythagoras was born in Samos' is true, and so is 'John died in Ephesus', then Pythagoras' being born in Samos and John's dying in Ephesus are as identical as Hesperus and Phosphorus (both being—as either Parmenides or Pythagoras his teacher found—the planet Venus). They are not *different* truths, for there can only be one truth: nothing that names a different truth is a true name of anything.

Much of this now looks to us like sophistry, as it did to Plato, who spelt out the ways in which, after all, we might intelligibly utter falsehoods, and how what didn't 'exist' might still be thinkable. Sophistries are not without their uses: they enable us to make the distinctions that we need to make if we are to cope with living in the everyday. Though Seneca, for example (a Roman Stoic notorious for having tutored—or failed to tutor—Nero), thought it ridiculous to spend time on fallacies (as that 'mouse' is a syllable and mice eat cheese, so at least some syllables eat cheese), that very absurdity (less easily detectable without the crutch of inverted commas) amounts to the important thesis that a map is not the territory, *our* words at any rate are not the world. But Parmenides' Being has a longer history, even as an idea, than merely to identify some problems with the copula (that is, the grammatical form uniting subject and predicate: . . . *is* . . .). If he was right, then the Truth which loves to hide is even more distant from the Way of Seeming than Democritus supposed. If we know nothing about reality (as Democritus said), how can we claim that it is composed of individual simples scattered across space and moving over time? Once we close our eyes to seeming, we have no reason left to think that there are several things at all, or that Space and Time are more than ways we seem to see. If we *can* know a truth—as Parmenides said we could—it could not be on the basis of sensory appearance. Reason alone declares what Is. The truth open only to the divine intellect is what the intellect declares it to be: there can be no division between Being and Thought. This, for Parmenides, is the One.

His disciple Zeno's aim was to make the alternatives to Parmenides' account still less acceptable: it certainly sounded strange to say that there could be no change, no difference. Heraclitus' dictum, that everything changes, seems at first more plausible. But the very notion of change, so Zeno argued, involved inescapable paradox. To change completely it was necessary to change half-way: and each half-way stage could then be treated as something to be completed, and there be another half-way stage to achieve first. Achilles could never overtake the tortoise since the latter would always have moved on when Achilles arrived where the tortoise had been before; the arrow could never reach its target, nor ever move at all, since at any instant it occupied no greater space than its own length, and whatever occupies a space equal to itself must be at rest. Zeno's Paradoxes, which still fascinate the puzzle-minded, were devised to show that, despite appearances, there could not be any such thing as change or difference, that really there was only One. There is an irresoluble conflict between the demands of reason and of sense. All differentiation (and not just temporal change) involves a contradiction. Consider any supposed distinction between A's being x and not-x (as it might be a change from hot to cold, or else a spatial difference between being red and green). Consider the last instant (or furthest point) at which A is x: is this the same or a different instant from the first at which it is not-x? If it is the same, then there is a point or instant where A is x and not-x; if it is not, then there is a gap (who knows how long?) when A is neither x nor not-x. Either way the laws of contradiction or excluded middle fail. Which is absurd. In order to loosen our grip on common sense Zeno, it was said, invented dialectic: that remained, as we shall have cause to see, its secret purpose. Zeno, by the way, was one of those who perished as philosophers were meant to do: defying a tyrant with such courage that, after his murder, the tyrant was overthrown.

It is possible, after all, that Parmenides' poem was only gloss, that he did not really owe his thought to inspiration. Two other figures of the Sicilian and South Italian group are less amenable to redescription, namely Pythagoras (*fl. c.*530) and Empedocles (*fl. c.*450). Both made important contributions to our science, and both were professed prophets, even shamanic seers. Both claimed to remember the past lives that one tradition of archaic thought had postulated. Both claimed (or it was claimed on their behalf) to be embarked for godhead. At the same time Pythagoras laid the basis for deductive geometry, and Empedocles investigated natural happenings more imaginatively than any before Aristotle. A Pythagorean or 'Orphic' Platonism was the final state of Greek philosophy before it blended for a thousand years or so into the Jewish, Christian, and Islamic stream: a state which Enlightened people call a 'fabulous, formless darkness': on which more below. But it was Pythagoras who showed (at least to some) how the unseen Reality, the Truth, could be discerned. The language that the gods speak to themselves is that of number. We no longer need to depend on failing sight to learn new truths: they can be deduced from mathematical principle, and the same patterns can be discerned in marvellously different ways. Much Pythagorean, or sub-Pythagorean, speculation on the subject was mere numerology, dependent on the magic properties of simple numbers; many paths were blocked—as they were in later ages—by a fear of the supposed irrational. The story went that the disciple who discovered, by a simple application of the theorem still known as Pythagoras', that the square root of 2 was an infinite surd, was drowned—by pure mischance—at sea. The gods at times spoke gibberish. But the hope remained that we could see Truth plain, by disregarding what could not be counted. Pythagoras was more astute than some who held the same faith later on: why, after all, should we be able to learn the gods' language if we were not gods ourselves? If we are not, how could we expect to know more than our senses tell us? The God of mathematicians was born, and the thought that mathematicians could aspire to godhead. Even Aristotle, who was far less enamoured of numbers than was Plato, said 'as sight takes in light from the surrounding air, so does the soul from mathematics'.

The Sophistic Movement

The inspired thinkers I have just described, who directed their attention to a hidden Truth, were also, and often openly, reformers. Heraclitus anticipated later moralists by spurning the delights of Ephesus, and ended his days, it was said, as a grass-eating misanthrope. Others attempted to discover or imagine how societies, especially civil societies, had formed, and how they might be better managed. Democritus, whose physical theories inspired the early atomists, could far more plausibly be counted as the founder of contract theory: just as there were individual singulars, the atoms, so were there—at least by convention—individual persons, frightened and attracted into larger masses. Pythagoras of Samos, whose numerology and geometry gave hope to mathematical cosmologists, was also the ascetic reformer of the Greek city of Croton (his death too was violent, apparently in a coup). Most philosophers gradually concluded, as had Heraclitus, that there was no general hope, that the fall of cities, the decay of morals, were a universal fate; only small groups of friends, or even solitaries, could live as they should. But even in that despair they offered guidance. It was absurd to spend much time on logic, Seneca said, when our souls were at stake: the object of philosophizing was to cure the soul. Perhaps we should remember Epictetus' warning (a slave of one of Nero's nastier henchmen, and a better Stoic than Seneca) that one who pretends to 'teach philosophy' without the knowledge, virtue, and the strength of soul to cope with distressed and corrupted souls, 'and above all the counsel of God advising him to occupy this office', is a vulgarizer of the mysteries, a quack doctor.

The affair is momentous, it is full of mystery, not a chance gift, nor given to all comers. . . . You are opening up a doctor's office although you possess no equipment other than drugs, but when or how these drugs are applied you neither know nor have ever taken the trouble to learn. . . . Why do you play at hazard in matters of the utmost moment? If you find the principles of philosophy entertaining sit down and turn them over in your mind all by yourself, but don't ever call yourself a philosopher.

The lessons that philosophers ought to rehearse, so Epictetus said, to write down daily and to put into practice, are the primacy of individual moral choice, the relative unimportance of body, rank, and estate, and the knowledge of what is truly their own and what is permitted them. The slave (which is Epictetus) here agreed with the emperor (Aurelius): it was our own souls only that we can save, and our souls alone.

Plato's attacks upon the fourth-century Sophists (a title that once meant only 'experts') left his successors sure that 'sophistry' (the technique of Sophists) was evil—a pastime of quack doctors. He may have been right to think so, because he saw in their pretence to persuasive speech a consciously amoral technique, neglectful of real values. Some later scientists, asserting that there is no knowledge (no scientific knowledge) of true value, thence conclude that they have no duty to consider values. Those who profess themselves prepared to serve *all* masters who will pay them well can hardly be surprised to be distrusted—even by those who buy them. But though Plato had a point, it may also prove to be the case that the Sophists did as well.

Inspired and evangelical thinkers may set out to change the world, but even less pretentious folk may have a mission. Some Sophists, no doubt, were only what they said they were:
teachers of useful arts, and mostly those that were useful in competition. Where the prize was
a man's life or livelihood, as it might be in the courts, such arts were at once desirable and
dangerous. The civil peace is delicate: how many contests can it take, and how readily can it
assign advantages to those rich enough to pay? Learning to defend oneself and learning to
suborn a jury or destroy an enemy may not be very different. Consider how we feel about
mercenary soldiers, ready to teach anyone how to fight a war: their art may be real, and some
of their causes just, but do they really know which ones are just, or why? Do they entirely
care? And even if the cause is just, will civil war achieve it? Gorgias of Leontini, who also
figures as a moral and epistemological sceptic in later commentaries, was probably just such
a well-meaning teacher. Later biographers decided he had been a pupil of Empedocles, and
himself taught Antisthenes the Cynic (of whom more below). There is a certain justice in the
story (from magician to illusionist to disillusionist), but it is probably only a product of the
impulse to discover schools and lines of intellectual descent. Like many other philosophers
(not that he called himself one), he served on an embassy to foreign powers (in his case,
Athens, in 427 BC).

The two greatest Sophists were something more than mercenaries or illusionists: namely
Protagoras (*c*.481–*c*.411 BC) and Socrates (469–399 BC). Plato was at pains to distance his
friend Socrates from any 'sophistic movement', but his contemporaries could have seen little

difference, except that Socrates was an Athenian patriot, and the others were deracinated foreigners. Sophists, typically, travelled, and sought pay for their efforts; Socrates stayed in Athens and relied on private means—and on his friends. All seemed to take great pleasure in subverting ancestral certainties. Aristophanes composed *The Clouds*, an unsuccessful comedy that maybe helped to poison men's minds against Socrates. He places in his characters' mouths a number of metaphors that took centre stage in Plato's most serious dialogues. The Socratic thinker 'looks away' from earthly things to contemplate eternal entities that are not the city's gods, but also practises a spiritual midwifery, encouraging his acolytes to give birth to new ideas—the Platonic addition being that midwives take it upon themselves to judge which infants can be reared.

The idea most closely tied to the historical Socrates is the Socratic paradox that no one does wrong willingly: to act at all is to do what one thinks good, or thinks will have a better effect than any known alternative. If one none the less does ill, it must be through ignorance. It follows that 'wrongdoers' need only be taught their error, and that no one should be spared that teaching. To avoid punishment for one's wrongdoing is like avoiding necessary medicine, or wilfully preferring error. True friends should denounce each other. Socrates seems to have assumed that it is always better not to be deceived, and that even the pain of realizing that one was deceived (but that one still has no better notion of the truth than that one hasn't found it) is good. His interlocutors did not always agree, but perhaps were coaxed into a more tolerant frame of mind than when they took it for granted that they had things right.

Protagoras, more obviously a successful Sophist, denied that there was any Truth beyond what people said. 'Man is the Measure of all things,' he said; this amounts to a rejection of the Democritean revelation. Truth, once again, is obvious, but what is thus obvious to one need not be so to another. The choice between conflicting 'truths' must be made on other grounds than that one side was 'truer'. His aim, it seems, was to enable people to maintain a 'better' peace, to find some laws and doctrines that they could all maintain. Such a consensus would not have greater claims to being 'true', but would at any rate avoid the pains of war. The civil peace was best maintained by mutual persuasion, not by any caste or clan that had an undisputed line to God. The story is told that one pupil agreed to pay him for his teaching when he had won his first court case. When the pupil delayed payment, Protagoras threatened court proceedings, pointing out that if the pupil lost, he would have to pay by the court's judgement, and if he won, he would have to pay by the agreement. The reply, perhaps apocryphally, was that if the pupil won he need not pay, but if he lost he also need not pay (by the court, and the agreement respectively). The story sounds like satire, but is revealing: persuasive arguments can start from either of two contradictory premises, and can always be turned round. What matters in the end is what is settled by agreement.

So the effect of Socrates and Protagoras alike was to diminish the conviction that we 'know' the Truth. If all we know is our own ignorance, then maybe we can concentrate instead on finding what we most desire for now (without insisting that we know what will be good for us). The rejection of such absolutes may seem to have an 'antinomian' effect, a

THE BEGINNING OF PHILOSOPHY, according to Aristotle, is the wonder that is natural to human beings. Paul Gauguin's *Where Do We Come From? What Are We? Where Are We Going?* depicts the expression of this wonder among a pre-literate people.

ΣWΚΡΑΤΗΣ

refusal to be bound by laws of justice (as Plato perhaps considered), but it could also be argued that it was the antinomians who more professed an absolute, objective knowledge. When the retired Athenian general Thucydides, writing a history of his country's downfall in the wars of the late fifth century BC, described the arguments used by the Athenian envoys to the doomed island of Melos (which Athens was to conquer and despoil), he attributed to them the old division between the laws of nature and of custom: it was natural that the strong should rule the weak, and acknowledge no discipline of equal justice. Custom alone, and fictions about the gods, demanded any respect for those without defence: realists understood that no one had any motive but his own success, and must be expected to do anything at all that might secure it. The Athenians assumed, in short, that they knew what 'success' was, and that all exchanges must be zero-sum games, with winners and losers. If this is false, then Athenian realism was misguided, and a better way, less likely to go wrong, would be to find ways of being that everyone affected would find acceptable.

Socrates and Protagoras both, by this account, were advocates of tolerance and consensuality, and concerned to disillusion those who thought they had a path to truth so certain that they could afford to ignore tradition and the opinion of their friends. The better 'truth' was what we could, for a while, agree upon. It may be only accident that Socrates has come to seem the defender of more ancient ways, the rule of those best fitted to rule, while Protagoras has seemed to be the theoretician of democracy. It is often now imagined that it is 'objective moralism', the belief that there are real truths of value, which must lead to 'expert rule', and that 'democracy' depends upon the assumption that the 'right road' merely means the one that most of us approve. In fact there seems no reason for this view. Protagoras professed to help cities achieve a 'better' state, one they could approve, and Socrates reminded them of the simple rules they actually would use in ordinary life when choosing between builders, cobblers, doctors, and the rest. Socrates, in effect, asked people to trust their common sense in deciding between their would-be rulers, and not to obey them merely because they claimed to know the truth. Protagoras suggested that the best rulers would be the ones best able to convince the populace to keep the peace. It does not follow that the Socratic choice would be for aristocracy, the Protagorean for democracy. The reverse might be true. The weak are best protected by an *ancient* order that the strong may think they can afford to lose. That Socrates was a defender of the ruling élite, and Protagoras of all the struggling masses, is absurd: Socrates, on the contrary, attacked the élite, and Protagoras sold them weapons. Both, so it seems, offended powerful parties, and were respectively killed and banished by the city of Athens (as was Anaxagoras of Clazomenae (500–428 BC), nicknamed the Mind, who first suggested that Reason, despite appearance, ruled the world, and that the sun was a heated lump of metal, not a god). Both might not unreasonably claim to have intended to do good, if only by relieving people of error.

SOCRATES, the most revered of philosophers, is known to posterity mainly through the dialogues of his pupils Plato and Xenophon. Here he is seen through Roman eyes, in a wall-painting from Ephesus.

Divine Plato

No history of ancient thought can avoid the mountain mass of Plato. It is true that in his day the massiveness of what he was and did was far less obvious. There were many other post-Socratics, variously acting out the role that Socrates had created or transformed. Phaedo of Elis, so it seems, carried on the logical enquiries that have since delighted myriads of puzzle-solvers. Aristippus of Cyrene sought to identify true pleasures more delightful and long-lasting than those of fashionable Athens. Antisthenes, and after him Diogenes the Cynic, whom Plato described as Socrates run mad, followed Heraclitus' lead by rejecting civilization in favour of the wild (except that they stayed in cities just to shame them). Pyrrho of Elis tried to 'strip himself of human nature' so far as not to agree that anything that happened to him was either good or bad. In the end these radicals captured the name of 'true philosophers', although it was Plato's theories that they, in the end, purveyed.

Plato himself was chiefly responsible for re-creating Socrates as one who has made himself immortal by his contact with true Beauty, and later commentators have disagreed about the accuracy of his portrayal, even about the extent to which Plato presented 'his own' philosophy in his dialogues (dramatized discussions between Socrates, or some other, and a younger friend—or stooge). The letters attributed to Plato, especially the second and seventh, deny that any of Plato's writings describe his own philosophy, but rather because such philosophical truths can never be conveyed in the written word than because Plato himself disowned the views he attributed to Socrates. The presently conventional account is that the early dialogues, typified by a relative simplicity of diction and uncertain outcome, may show us something of the 'real' Socrates, a man devoted to the demolition of misplaced certainties and the pursuit of truth. Typically, he enquires what people mean by 'courage', 'piety', 'friendship', or 'virtue', and rejects their usual attempt to answer him, which is to give examples of each kind. Without some principle, he suggests, we cannot understand how to extend the list of examples, say, of courageous action. When they respond by offering a criterion for the disputed kind, he answers by adducing other examples that are recognizably, say, courageous but do not fit the criterion, or recognizably not, but do. The dialogue will then conclude with the rueful admission that we don't know what we mean. It may often seem that there is an unadmitted contradiction in this methodology: if we can recognize an act of courage even before we can give form to a criterion, and use that recognition to rebut a hypothesized criterion, then it seems clear that we don't, after all, need to articulate what we know very well. In his dialogue with Euthyphro, Socrates can easily be made to seem corrupt: Euthyphro is sure that his father has indeed committed a grave wrong—and most of us may well agree that he has (namely, throwing an offending labourer into a ditch to die). Socrates subverts his certainties by raising doubts about the way, at Socrates' behest, Euthyphro ('Mr Straight-thought') explains himself.

In the middle period, in dialogues that remain the triumphant apex of philosophical literature (such as *Meno*, *Phaedo*, *Symposium*, and *Republic*), Plato himself subverts some apparently Socratic axioms. First, he devises a psychology that makes it possible that people

PLATO's appearance is unknown; only idealized representations survive.

should do wrong although they know it's wrong. Human action can stem from other roots than reason, and it is not ignorance only that produces ill. In the schematic psychology of Buddhism, Anger, Lust, and Ignorance are to blame—and Plato thought so too (though extending 'anger' to cover false ambition). Second, he noticed Socrates' reliance on an unarticulated knowledge of what counts as courage, justice, and the rest. We can assess the accuracy of a suggested criterion because we can already discriminate, rather as we can say whether a suggested name is the one that we've forgotten. Third, he spoke more firmly of the kind of being such kinds must have (and thereby also gave an answer to the Parmenidean puzzles). In brief, he outlined what has since been called the theory of forms (though we need not think that there was ever a single, well-formed theory), which I shall sketch below. Fourth, he admitted—what is indeed implied in the Socratic practice—that 'right opinion' and a sound upbringing may spare the city many evils that 'free-thinkers' bring. During this middle period he also tried to play a practical part in the politics of Syracuse, and failed—with what effect on his morale, who knows?

Third-period dialogues (identified by a new stylistic complexity and the gradual elimination of the dramatic Socrates) employ a new technique of definition-seeking: homing in on a disputed concept by successive, and often rather strange, dichotomies. A statesman, for example, is at one point defined as a sort of herdsman of tame, gregarious animals, specifically those land-dwelling, walking, hornless, non-interbreeding, and bipedal animals that we call human. The very nearest thing to the statesman is the swineherd. A slightly different cut might instead have identified us as featherless bipeds, and the statesman's nearest kin, by unspoken analogy, as a craneherd or gooseherd. This sort of dichotomizing definition was much mocked in comedy of the period, and more seriously criticized by Aristotle (as indeed, implicitly, by Plato). Diogenes Laertius, typically, chooses to represent Plato chiefly as one who drew up complex lists: three kinds of good, five forms of civil government, three species of justice, three of science, five species of medicine, three kinds of philanthropy, and five of wisdom. Some later commentators have concluded that Plato at last abandoned any theory of forms he may ever have held, and also at last betrayed the radical, free-thinking spirit of his master. Socrates, it is said, would certainly have been convicted by the thought police of Plato's last imaginings, in *The Laws*. Atheists, he suggests, and those who think that the gods don't care about us, are enemies of civil peace, and should be taught otherwise, exiled or killed.

The idea that Plato radically changed his mind and methods, and became, in his last days, at once an analytical philosopher and an inquisitor, is too modern a thought to be entirely convincing. Earlier critics saw few signs of any change of heart, even if the details of the exposition changed. That we owe obedience to the laws of our land as to our parents and originals is an idea to be found from the (early) *Crito* to *The Laws*. That the statesman is a sort of herdsman is an idea attributed to Socrates himself by Xenophon, a retired mercenary soldier and another author of 'Socratic dialogues'. Socrates was never praised as a 'free-thinker', bent on his own way, but as an obedient servant of the gods. The possibility that kings might become philosophers is as much to be hoped for at the end as at the beginning, and as little to be

ANTRVM PLATONICVM.

PLATO'S CAVE. In the *Republic* Plato summed up his epistemology in an allegory. Prisoners chained in a cave watch on its inner wall the shadows of statues carried along a wall behind them. These represent the majority of mankind, who take their opinions, even about worldly matters, at second hand. The painful, and initially blinding, process of emerging from the darkness has three stages: first, to see the objects of this (cavernous) world as they really are; then to see the forms which transcend the imperfect objects of the present world; and finally to see the Form of the Good, which is the source of all truth and reason. The vision of the Good corresponds to emergence from the cave into the sunshine. Here we see a sixteenth-century representation of the allegory.

expected. Even the 'unwritten doctrines' that are sometimes adduced to show that Plato changed his mind do not establish this, because—to state the obvious—they are unwritten, and unknown.

But there is, after all, an issue about the forms. Those forms, and the associated Immortality of the Soul, are what is usually meant by Platonism, and it is not uncommon for historians and theologians alike to depict that Platonism as a dreadful error somehow to be expected of the Greeks (who were, such theologians and historians 'know', contemptuous of the physical and historical world). It is all the fault of Platonism, and the Greeks, that the modern industrial complex ravages the earth and patriarchalists despise the womanly sentiments. Even a brief acquaintance with Platonism's critics might reveal that it was actually they who despised the sentiments, and offered reasons to despise the earth and our fellow denizens. Platonists, historically, have usually been the ones to consider our duties to those not of our species. It was said of Xenocrates, the third head of the Academy, that when a sparrow took refuge with him from a hawk, he stroked it and let it go, declaring that a suppliant must not be betrayed. Platonists have found corporeal nature sacramental. Plotinus, greatest of pagan Platonists, was vegetarian, refused medicines made from animal research, cared honourably for orphans, and denounced those 'gnostics' who despised the earth. Porphyry, his pupil, was until recently the only 'professional philosopher' to write at length in favour of 'the rights of beasts'.

So what is 'the theory of forms'? It has at least three roots: in speaking of what there is, of how we know it, and of what we should do. First, it is an answer to the challenge posed by the twin hypotheses that everything changes and that nothing does. The answer is that there must be unchanging forms if anything is to change at all. If nothing at all were ever 'the same' from one instant to another, or 'the same' in different places, there could not even be instants or those different places. Rationality requires that there be real beings present at many different points in space and time. Even if such samenesses were *only* immanent, possessed by those several points and never to be found outside them, they would be quite real (the term *eidos* is sometimes reserved for immanent forms, *idea* for the transcendent). All efforts to exclude such realism rest, for their coherence, on exactly the same thought: even to say that there is nothing in common between This and That except that we employ the *same* name for it (say, 'dog') implicitly assumes both that there is a speaker who is the *same*, and that there is a word that is the *same* in many instances. Nominalism, as it was later called, is a literally unspeakable doctrine. Platonic realism differs from more immanent varieties in admitting that there are unrealized entities, kinds such that there are no particular instances, and that—once again—there must be if we are to think. The mathematical entities that Pythagoras discerned cannot be equated with their images in sand or stone. Truths about circles and triangles would still be true even if there never had been particular geometric figures, and even though the ones there are aren't altogether what those truths decree. Most working mathematicians are probably still Platonists at heart, even though modern philosophers may say they shouldn't be.

As to how we know these things, or any others: Plato saw (as above) that we must already know a great deal that we cannot wholly say. He saw in particular that we could never find evidence for any thought at all unless we already knew what counted as evidence and what as true. How could you reliably recognize a picture of Antisthenes if you have never met him in the flesh? The question then arises: How? How is it that creatures such as we should have devices for discovering truths, or ever be able to articulate them? Modern attempts to suggest that evolutionary theory can explain it fail: natural selection cannot, in its nature, ever select for creatures able to look aloft, cloud-watchers, and to get things right. Maybe it can select for creatures able to avoid immediate danger or recognize advantages: there is an immediate pay-off there. But even if—*per incredibile*—a variation capable of accurate cloud-watching did appear (and how?)—it would not be preferred to the far more practical ground-watchers. The comic anecdote about Thales was right: watching the sky he fell into a well. The other anecdote, that by watching the sky he could predict a bumper olive crop, is far less plausible, and quite irrelevant. Such long-distance gains have little effect on evolution. Plato's answer seems the only hope: we have the capacity to see such truths because we carry the image of truth in us, and we do so not by chance and natural selection, but from our origin, which is also the world's origin. We could never work out truths by sense alone, and we have the wherewithal to work them out because we are offspring of the selfsame intellect that engenders the ordered universe. The thought dominated the next thousand years and more.

And what should we do? The forms themselves are what is to be admired, and constitute the standards of all judgement. There are no forms of disease or devilry except the forms of health and righteousness, from which the unhealthy and malicious deviate: to be diseased is simply not to be healthy, in however many ways it might be possible to fall ill or fail. The standards to which particulars approximate are the ways in which pure Beauty can be known; the goals for which we yearn are the ways pure Good is matched to our particular beings. The truth of ethical propositions is as unchanging as the truth of mathematics, but far more difficult to identify—except that even the truths of mathematics actually depend on those of ethics. Only if it is *true* that mathematical elegance is a form of beauty, that beauty is a standard to which we ought to bend, will it prove true (in any but a trivial sense) that Pythagoras' Theorem (or any other) is a truth to be obeyed. And why should we concern ourselves with beauty? That, said Aristotle, is a blind man's question. However abstract or pedantic Platonic forms may seem, especially when they are identified with Numbers, it is essential to remember that they are properly the object of a passionate love. They are beauty in its several forms, or else they derive their being from the Good Itself. That Good lies even 'beyond being', as the One lies beyond intellect: Plato's public lecture on the Good Itself surprised his audience because it seemed to be about arithmetic. 'The Good' and 'the One' are different names for It, for something that makes it possible for anything to be or to be thought, which cannot itself be the object of any rational thought.

The soul, or at any rate the mind, shares in the eternal being of the forms. That is to say, so some have supposed, we can regard the most important part of ourselves as indestructible precisely because it has no content save the eternal objects that it contemplates. By identifying myself with eternal truths I know myself, that self at least, immortal. What matters about Plato, what he minded about, must be for ever. More metaphysically, the immortal mind in me is just the same as the immortal mind in you (a thought also attributed to Aristotle, and to later philosophers). That mind, in fact, is God—though the way a particular corporeal being thinks is only intermittently, and waveringly, the immortal mind. We do not always think the truth: when we do, there is one thought in each of us. This may be all that Plato's actual arguments for immortality could show (if they show this much), but it is difficult to doubt that he really wanted more, that he believed—as Pythagoras had done—that there were real immortal, individual souls who were condemned to live our earthly lives until they had sufficiently purified their thought. Perhaps the conviction rested on his belief that there were 'forms of individuals': Socrates was not a figment, real only as a passing reflection of the one eternal mind, but a real, active form, forever to be distinguished from the immortal form of Critias or Dion (though not necessarily from the form of every other mortal, who might after all be another incarnation of the selfsame spirit, as Pythagoras claimed to have been Hermes' son Aethalides). In the absence of forms, neither sort of immortality (the general or the specific) makes much sense; the only further question is whether the forms need bodies to be actual. In the absence of forms no sort of personal identity makes sense: once allow that there are such real identities, why must they be manifest continuously?

So why, if the theory has so many and so great advantages, did anyone dismiss it? One unimportant reason (unimportant because entirely arbitrary) is doubtless only that some people do not wish to think that there are unchanging standards by which we can be judged. More seriously, some have thought that there was a contradiction in the usual idea of forms. This argument, habitually known as the Third Man, is found in Plato's dialogue *Parmenides*, as well as in Aristotle's writings: it was, in short, a commonplace. Suppose, the argument goes, that we postulate a form for every class of things that are rightly called by the same name (as it might be the Ideal Human); such a form will itself be Human (if it were not, what could be?), and there will 'therefore' be a further form, the Ideal Human*, in parallel with the newly enlarged class composed of all the particular humans and the Ideal Human. The argument is then repeated to create the Ideal Human**, and so for ever. Better, obviously, not to begin, but what is the beginning? The conventional claim is that Plato seems to have committed himself to two conflicting notions: first, that every real class of things must manifest or share or imitate one form which is distinct from any or all of that class (Monroe was beautiful, but was not beauty); second, that such a form itself—paradigmatically—is of the same class as its avatars or mimics. In other words:

(1) Nothing that is predicatively *f* is identical with the form it manifests.
(2) The form manifested by any such particulars itself is *f*.

It is unnecessary (indeed it is fatal) to abandon the idea that the Form itself is *f* (if justice itself is not just, what could be just?). Nor is it necessary (indeed it is fatal) to abandon the idea that there is an *F* that every *f*-thing manifests (if there is no justice, what could be just?). The fallacy in the argument is to assume that 'being *f*' must always be 'being predicatively *f*'. Everything derivatively moist, by an analogy, is such because it's covered in a thin film of liquid: is liquid itself moist, and what is the hyperliquid film that covers it? The simple answer is that liquid is moist essentially: liquid is, identically, moisture. Just so the Ideal Human (whom a later age would identify with Intellect) is essentially and identically Human, and we particular beings manifest It. We 'are', by partial participation, what It *is*.

The Aristotelian Synthesis?

Aristotle of Stageira (384–322 BC) is another giant figure, and one much abused. Elementary histories of science, when not being rude about the 'Greek' disdain for getting their hands dirty, identify that dreadful bogy Aristotle, who could not even count his own wife's teeth correctly, and wished on medieval Europe a grotesque tale of stones that longed to be at rest in earth, falling more quickly the heavier they were, and species that were created quite distinct and never to be lost or mingled. Worst of all, he conditioned people to believe that only what was written in the texts was true, and that ordinary observation and experiment alike

ARISTOTLE. This head is believed to be a copy, made in the time of the emperor Claudius, of a statue set up in the philosopher's lifetime.

were vain. Science rescued us from Aristotle by successive stages: light and heavy stones turned out to fall at the same speed; the earth revolved around the sun; species lost their essential, hard-edged quality; and living things were no longer moved by 'animal spirits', but by lever and sinew mechanisms. It was vital for seventeenth-century scientists and philosophers to disown the Aristotelian synthesis, and scientists since—with rare and praiseworthy exceptions—believe all that they read.

Aristotle himself, the son of a medical household, student in the Academy, tutor of Alexander, and indefatigable gatherer of information, would hardly recognize the distorted picture drawn of him. The Aristotle of the later Middle Ages, embellished by pagan and Islamic commentaries and at last acclimatized by Thomas Aquinas to his Christian role, was also a greater figure than the adolescent Enlightenment pretended, but that shape is not my present concern. The strangest use of Aristotle, of course, was to enlist him to expound the Eucharist; hardly less strange to ask him to defend biological essentialism, the idea that each member of a biological species is conformed to one unique and unambiguous essence and that there are no hybrids, deviations, or ancestral types. The truth is both that Aristotle would have thought 'transubstantiation' ludicrous (because what a thing *is* is what it perceptibly *does*), and that 'transformism' is an integral part of his biology.

Aristotle's chronology is less easily defined than Plato's. By founding his own school when he returned from a tutoring job in Macedon (while a native Athenian ruled Plato's Academy) he became the father of a different line of philosophers, the Peripatetic. But later Platonists considered him a Platonist who created formal logic and corrected, or sought to correct, Plato's own divisions of language and the world. That the best life, for Aristotle as for Plato, was to contemplate and serve the God which was eternally identical with the objects of pure thought was undisputed. That our characters needed to be trained as well as our minds educated was also common doctrine. That something divine and beautiful could be discerned in even the most trivial of natural entities was implicit in Plato, explicit in Aristotle. In later ages Aristotle, conveyed through the Islamic commentators to Western Europe, provided an alternative to Platonism by emphasizing personal being against what seemed a mystical extravagance. But even then no one supposed that Aristotle was the enemy of Plato. He held that, where both are friends, true piety prefers the Truth to Plato—but Plato had said just the same, and Aristotle really meant that Plato was indeed his friend. In the Renaissance Plato became a rallying-cry against Aristotle, insinuating after all that human beings had share enough of the divine to intuit real truths, when medieval Aristotelians had been content to save the phenomena by models and might-bes. In this century it has seemed obvious that Aristotle himself began as a Platonist, a loyal defender of personal immortality and real Forms, but gradually transferred his attention to the world of everyday: to achievable goods, and detailed accounts of what had happened where. The truth is probably much closer to the ancient view, that Aristotle disagreed with Plato sometimes (and maybe was less willing to abandon common sense), but agreed upon the most important things.

It may be that Aristotle, of a medical family, had more natural sympathies than Plato with the staunch empiricism expressed in certain authors of the Hippocratic Corpus, a body of

ARISTOTLE'S RESEARCH ASSISTANTS. Aristotle was the founder of scientific biology. Alexander the Great, on his campaigning journeys, sent him specimens of rare organisms. This assistance to his former tutor was embellished in Hellenistic and medieval legend, as illustrated in this medieval illumination of Alexander exploring the sea-bed in a glass diving-bell.

texts from various dates recording the thoughts and diagnostic notes of Hippocratic healers. The author, for example, of *Ancient Medicine* (usually dated sometime in the early fourth century) spoke scornfully of theorizing as a route to medical truth. What mattered were the individual cases, not the Ideal Form. It is a necessary response to exaggerated hopes of modelling a complex universe by thought alone. It may be the effect of family tradition also that Aristotle was so insistent that even the most trivial and vulgar creature could show something wonderful, something divine, if it were examined honestly. His fascinated attempts to find some order in the sprawling complexity of biological nature were constantly modified by observation, even though he also hung on tight to methodological aphorisms like 'Nature does nothing to no purpose'.

At the furthest remove, it seems, from natural history, Aristotle created formal logic, specifically the systematic study of syllogistic reasoning. He identified the valid forms of syllogism, by example and by argument. The first mode combines two premises with a shared middle term (functioning as predicate in the minor and subject in the major premiss: as it might be, 'All humans are mortal and all poets human', thence concluding, in what was later called 'Barbara', that 'All poets are mortal'). The second mode, with the shared term as the predicate in each premiss, can only, in its valid forms, have a negative conclusion (e.g. 'If no philosophers mind about money and all professors do, then no professors are philosophers':

PLATONISM AND ARISTOTELIANISM. Especially since the Renaissance, philosophical tradition has liked to represent Plato and Aristotle as polar opposites. Here Raphael, in *The School of Athens*, shows Plato, holding a work of cosmology, pointing heavenwards, while Aristotle, holding a work of ethics, makes a gesture which expresses his commitment to the life of every day. In fact Plato was neither as other-worldly, nor Aristotle as worldly, as the traditional contrast makes out.

which is in Cesare). The third, with the shared term as the subject in each premiss, can never result in either an affirmative or a negative universal conclusion (e.g. in Ferison: 'If no non-human animals have duties and some non-human animals have rights, then some things that have rights do not have duties'). The fourth mode, merely converting the conclusion of the first mode (so: 'Some mortal things are poets'), was actually added later, for completeness' sake. These jolly transformations were the bread and butter of medieval logic, and used then for very much the same reasons as originally they were, in dialectical contests. Aristotle, in short, decided to regularize and discipline the art of rhetoric as practised in the courts and in the schools.

In classifying arguments Aristotle acted in what came to be thought his character. So also in biology, where he attempted cogent classifications of the various sorts of animal, from mussels, fish, birds, and quadrupeds to humankind. But biological classes could not be deduced or demonstrated, and neither were they rigidly separate. On the contrary, 'nature abhors discontinuities' as much as nature abhors a vacuum. Between every two identifiable classes there will be intermediates; many kinds can most easily be understood as variations, deformations of a wider kind (as seals are 'deformed quadrupeds', or flatfish 'twisted' from the norm). There is even some suggestion that all animals there are can be explained as variations from an ancestral type to be identified with the 'least specialized, best balanced, most complete of kinds', the human. Classes are conveniences of description, but such biological species should not be thought to be mere mirrors of distinct forms. It is not the species that is transmitted in procreation, but exclusively the father's individual form, more or less well replicated in maternal matter. In brief, the later notion that distinct species leapt from the mind of God and never were (nor should be) mixed is wholly un-Aristotelian.

Discontinuous classes are linguistic figments, in that the reality we seek to describe is always continuous. Aristotle answered the conundrum that I posed before, in speaking of the Eleatic Zeno, by denying that there were truths 'at an instant'. There is no first nor last instant or point when A is x: the instant or point is only a mark upon the ever-changeful real. He attempts a more complex answer to an argument that was to affect the Stoics, but one in the same spirit. 'If anything is now true of what will be (and therefore has been true from everlasting), and if we cannot now affect, for good or ill, what has been true, then neither can we affect what follows from that truth.' Accordingly, we can determine nothing—yet, as Aristotle insisted—we demonstrably can. His answer again is that we cannot allow logical laws to tempt us into denying experienced facts. Better agree that we can affect the past than be squeezed into denying that we affect the future. The real world is changeful and continuous, and is not adequately described in the static, discontinuous terms of formal reasoning.

So surely there is some truth in the conviction that Aristotle distrusted Plato's theories? His political theories, requiring that the statesman balance opposing interests in the hope of peace, are seamless developments from Plato's later writings. His ethical theories, which identify the human good as one to be achieved within community, in the pursuit of what is good and beautiful, do little more than shift an emphasis. His epistemology does not overtly rest on any notion that we already 'know' or 'half-remember' fundamental truths, but rec-

THEORY AND EXPERIMENT. Aristotle believed that the speed of free fall was proportionate to the weight of the body falling. This remained the dominant mechanical theory until Galileo refuted it by making use of the leaning tower of Pisa for experiments on the velocity of falling bodies.

ognizes intellectual intuition as the source of vital principles, things that must be known already before any demonstration is possible. He relied, perhaps, much more than Plato did on what we could ordinarily perceive, but he was confident that we 'perceived' more than we strictly saw, heard, or touched. Colours and translucencies are special objects of sight, perceived—one might conceive—because our eyes could 'become' them. But shapes, sizes, times, and the like (the properties later called primary) are not special to any one sense: we perceive them, common sensically, because our minds (not our eyes only) can become such forms. It is in his metaphysics that the difference lies—but it is exactly in his metaphysics that Aristotle is least clear.

He begins from individual substances, like people: these are the primary subjects of predication, things that endure through time and change, that cannot be taken apart and put together again, nor broken up into more of the same kind (as stones can be broken into stones). A person may be pale or tanned; weigh ten stone or eleven; be in the town or country, at morning or evening; be father and/or son; be cloaked or cloakless; lying down or standing; acting and being acted on (which concludes the list of ways that Aristotle thought an entity could be 'categorized'). In all those separate ways a person could change and yet be the same person. What that person was essentially, what it was for that person to be at all, was not equivalently 'present in' the person (as if she could endure through losing it). To know the person properly is to know what it was for her to be. That nature, in turn, could—accidentally—be predicated of the matter which constitutes the person: that lump, one might say, is Critias (but there is no lump at all except that Critias is there). This radical individualism turns Plato on his head. For Plato it was the thing that remained the same, that was shared by many instances, that more truly was an entity, and not the shifting sands in which those figures were drawn. Aristotle insisted that it was the individuals that carried the shared properties, that it was they that were the real entities that did not depend on other things, on properties, for their existence. Without individuals to be red there could be no redness; whereas a red thing might be blue or colourless without extinction.

Unfortunately, a merely individual, unrepeated instance cannot be described at all. Individuals cannot be known in their own individuality: only a shared form is knowable (even if the form is only potentially shared). And the individual substances in which Aristotle put his trust already are more than instants, punctiform particulars: if Critias can be present, being Critias, on more than one occasion, it can only be because the 'what it is for Critias to be' (which is, what Critias *qua* Critias does) is possessed by successive moments of material nature. Properties are predicated of real substances—but the essence of those substances is predicated of an underlying stuff. That stuff, by successive arguments, begins to look like the primary matter, the sheer substance, that troubled later thinkers: it is the ultimate subject of all predication, and has all properties, but it actually *is* nothing. It is the receptacle, unbeing, the nothing on which the form of life is cast. And because it is nothing (and there is nothing for it to be precisely because it—predicatively—is everything) we cannot know it at all. Only the forms are knowable (which is where we began, with Plato).

And yet there is a difference between the giants. Aristotle preferred experience, in the end, to any logical deduction (or rather, he employed those logical deductions to cast doubt upon the premisses that led to unacceptable results). It is for that very reason that Renaissance science disowned him. The notion that heavy and light things fall at different speeds is actually confirmed by ordinary experience (try dropping a piece of paper and a book at the same time). It was not experience but logic that persuaded Galileo that the truth was otherwise, that paper and book fell at different speeds only because of factors other than their weight. Two one-pound weights would weigh the same as one two-pound weight: how fast should they fall, all three? Would the two weights fall faster if there was a string around them? Would it have to be tied tight? It was, in short, because Galileo was a Platonist, trusting his reason rather than his fallible sense, that he broke free into a larger world than that with which Aristotle was, in the end, content.

No one, we may reasonably suspect, since Aristotle, has had such a compendious grasp of so many fields of human intellectual endeavour. Few have suffered so much misrepresentation by their friends and foes alike. His ethical theories are sometimes denounced, either because he is thought to have defended slavery for those who could not live by their own choices, or because he is thought to have neglected the primary importance to human existence of, exactly, choice. The former charge is justified (though his thought carried the liberating implication that masters-at-law could actually be slaves); the latter, sometimes expressed as the thought that it is human nature not to have a given nature, is actually far better expressed by Aristotle himself. The good life for human beings is one that those same human beings must choose and live: our life is one of deliberate action, and it is that we must get right.

Stoics, Epicureans, and Wandering Sages

In 323 BC King Alexander died (and, on the same day it's said, Diogenes the Cynic), and Aristotle hurriedly left Athens—lest, as he said, the Athenians sin *twice* against philosophy. In the following year he died himself, and so—according to the practice of too many undergraduate courses—did philosophy, until one René Descartes determined to start again. The truth is that it was in the following centuries that philosophy most clearly became what, in ordinary language, it still is: a way of coping with a world at war. How did this happen?

Part of the answer must be Socrates, even though he had precursors. After his life and death, as it was portrayed by his indignant friends, the feeling that, not being Socrates, one should still *wish* to be Socrates, is definitive of true philosophers till a century or two ago. It seems an alarming prospect. Epictetus himself confessed that he and his disciples were, as it were, Jews in word but not in deed, 'not dyed-in-the-wool Jews', very far from applying the principles they taught: 'so although we are unable even to fulfil the profession of man, we take on the additional profession of the philosopher'. So high an account of mere philosophy is bound to produce misgivings, summed up in Descartes's aphorism: 'Philosophy teaches us to speak with an appearance of truth on all things, and causes us to be admired by the less learned.' But however pretentious the post-Socratic vision may be, and however often it has been betrayed, we cannot ignore its influence. Many a Cynic, literally 'doggish', was doubtless no more than a tramp—but every age and nation but our own has recognized that many

CRATES OF THEBES is shown here as a typical Cynic philosopher, careless of convention and wearing tattered clothes. The painting is by Domenico Fetti.

ZENO OF CITIUM, the founder of Stoicism, shown here in a Hellenistic marble bust from the Louvre.

a tramp may be a wandering sage. When Alexander's expeditions (and his successors') acquainted the Greeks with Indian gymnosophists (which is to say, with 'naked sophists') they did not, it seems, learn much of Hindu thought (translated as it was through several intermediaries), but they were not wrong to think that such 'gymnosophists' were not unlike 'philosophers', busy about the elimination of desire.

So who were these sages? Diogenes, formerly of Sinope but long resident in Corinth (c.404–c.323 BC), is known through anecdotes: as that, asked by a momentarily respectful Alexander what he, Alexander, could do to help, he replied 'Get out of my light'. Many of the anecdotes are crude; many are by now incomprehensible; what survives is the image of freedom. Amongst his followers was Crates, who'd abandoned a rich inheritance to live the Cynic's life (accompanied by a similarly devoted wife, Hipparchia). He left his fortune in trust, with instructions that his sons, if ordinary men, should have the money, and if philosophers, it should be given to the people, as they, his sons, would have no need of it. A merchant from Citium in Cyprus, another Zeno, happened on Xenophon's account of Socrates at an Athenian bookstall and asked where he could find a man like that: the bookseller pointed to Crates, and Zeno abandoned trade for good, eventually establishing himself in the Painted Portico, the Stoa. Those early Stoics, it seems, were almost as shameless as the Cynics, acknowledging no merit in traditional distinctions and taboos. Why not have sex in temples, eat one's dead parents, and reckon other people's property one's own? The gods, after all, own everything; friends have everything in common, and only the wise are really friends of the gods: so the wise own what they please, though being wise they will not use it to satisfy escapable desires. These strictures were not put in practice, and later theorists gradually toned down their effect. A Stoic philosopher was only one whose behaviour would not change from state to state, being governed by nature, not the spurious 'laws' decreed by foolish rulers: but the real laws turned out to be the ones demanded by traditional ideas of justice. Private property, in one sense, was absurd, since the whole world was available for all—but actual property rights must be respected, just as a seat in the theatre is in one way public and in another reserved for the one who sits there. Stoicism requires one to to remember what is really in one's power: I cannot always prevent tyrants (or petty villains) robbing, torturing or killing me, but they in turn cannot prevent my doing what God-and-nature means me to. My inescapable needs are few: if I ensure I want only what I can get, and remember that 'the door is always open' (i.e. I can always kill myself), I am immune to bribery and threat alike. Only so can I be 'free': only the wise are free, and only they are sane.

Stoic ethics are, they said, the albumen of philosophy, but they also practised logic (the shell) and natural philosophy (the yolk). Their logical analyses constitute one of the most creative periods in the history of logic, as they advanced from Aristotle's syllogistic (now mostly seen as a fragment of predicate calculus) to what is now known as propositional calculus, and the discussion of natural and conventional signs. Their natural philosophy, in turn, was a profound and challenging exploration of a rigorously deterministic, naturalistic universe. Amongst the greatest names, now known to us only through fragments, are Chrysippus and Posidonius (135–51 BC), of whom the latter seems to have adopted a more nearly Platonic realism, while the former established the monistic materialism that was mainstream Stoicism. Nothing had any causal powers, the Stoics said, except corporeal individuals, and those causes could not have any effects but those they did have. Everything that happens—including human actions—is strictly inevitable, the outflow of the principles, the principle, which is their immanent God. God is not now quite obvious—at least to ordinary folk—but there will be a time when God is all in all, when everything is obviously full of God, the 'conflagration' at the end of the world age. Each following age, as God again withdraws from open view, will unfold exactly as the former did: wisdom lies in welcoming that repetition. Particular maverick Stoics (of whom Aristo of Chios, a third-century pupil of Zeno's, was the chief) realized rather more of the implications of the general doctrine. Some denied, in short, that there would be any special conflagration (since God already ruled the whole), and that there was any value at all in the things we ordinarily desired (food, drink, sex, and shelter). The majority preferred to agree that it was not now obvious that all was well, and that such morally indifferent things (as food, drink, sex, and shelter: for after all, no one is 'really' a more admirable person just because he has such things) were still what nature made us to pursue. Good Stoics chose the 'preferable indifferent' while still reminding themselves that it really made no difference to what really mattered ('virtue').

Such Stoicism has had a bad press in more sentimental times: good people, we are prone to think, must mind a lot about what happens to friends and especially to children. Detachment is no longer much admired. The response is understandable, but it is worth emphasizing that the Stoics' theory of moral consciousness (and the practice of their major sages) rested upon the love of children. The 'rights of future generations', which modern moralists argue about, were never in doubt in Stoic thought, even if—as Cicero reports—they expressed the moral (more aptly) in terms of our duties. 'As we feel it wicked and inhuman for men to declare that they care not if when they themselves are dead, the universal conflagration ensues, it is undoubtedly true that we are bound to study the interest of posterity also for its own sake.' Sentimentalism, not sentiment, was their enemy: when Epictetus counselled a tearful father who was too upset to nurse his fevered son he drew attention to the way the father's 'pathetic' nature was getting in the way of love. 'Apathy', detachment, is not apathetic in the modern sense, but simply not pathetic.

If Stoics have sometimes been (mis)represented as too harsh, Epicureans have suffered from the opposite libel, that they care only for their pleasure. In fact the pleasures that Epicurus (341–270 BC) advocated are those that bring no pain, and are chiefly those of friendship and a quiet life. Pleasures can be guaranteed if we restrict desire, and pains endured until they are unendurable, when 'the door is open'. Epicurus was born in Samos (like Pythagoras), but by 306 he was established in a garden outside Athens, and his disciples simply called the Friends. Seneca tells us: 'Epicurus says you should be more concerned to inspect whom you eat and drink with than what you eat and drink. For feeding without a friend is the life of a

LUCRETIUS THE EPICUREAN. A page from an illuminated manuscript of the philosopher's great poem *De Rerum Natura*. This is the opening of book one, a paean to Venus, the personification of sexual love.

NEADVM G
ENITRIX H
OMINV DI
VVM qʒ uoluptaˢ

A Lma venuſ cœli ſubter Labentia ſigna
Q uæ mare nauigeruin quæ terraſ frugiferantiſ
C oncelebraſ perʼ te quoniam genʼomeʼ ʒmatum
C oncipitur inſitque exortum Luminis ſoliſ
T e dea te fugiunt venti te nubila cœli
A duentumque tuum tibi ſuauiſ dædala teʒ
S ummittit floreſ tibi rident æquora poʒ
P Lacatumque nitet diffuſo Lumine cœleʒ
N am ſimulac ſpecies patefacta eſt verna diei
E t reſerata uiget genitabiliſ aura fauoni
A eriæ primum uolucreſ te diua tuumque
S ignificant initum perculſæ corda tua uiʒ
I nde feræ pecudeſ perſultant pabula Læta
E t rapidoſ tranare amniſ ita capta Lepore
T e ſequitur cupide quocumʒ inducere pergis
D eniʒ per maria ac monteſ fluuioſʒ rapaciſ

lion and a wolf.' He might agree that Pleasure was what counted (where the Stoics mentioned Virtue), but there might be little difference in practice between one and the other. Roman administrators (indeed like Cicero) could reasonably feel that Stoic insistence on our duty to family, friends, and country was more useful than an Epicurean readiness to cultivate one's garden, but radical Stoics were as irritating as radical Epicureans could be agreeable. Radical Stoics after all (even if they no longer suggested eating parents) might urge us to abuse the emperor, while Epicureans would prefer to leave the court alone. Once again, we have little but fragments to go on—and the greatest single work of philosophical poetry, Lucretius' *Nature of the Universe*. That poem, written in the last days of the Roman republic, opens with an appeal to Venus to calm down the god of war, but is in its essence a rigorously materialistic, atheistic sermon. It ends with a detailed account of the great plague that helped to ruin Athens four hundred years before: perhaps, in brief, it ends in the collapse of hope.

The centre of Epicurus' creed was ethical, but he too (and his followers) made natural philosophy his base. In his account the Democritean vision reasserts itself: reality is 'atoms and the void', and the seeming substances of everyday (and also the visionary forms of deities) were only aggregates of atoms, having no enduring substance. The Stoic view that there was in the end One Substance only, the whole world, was mirrored by the Epicurean, that there were innumerable substances, but not our selves. The monistic view that human individuals are only parts of the one substance and the atomistic that they are only aggregates of lesser bits both urge us to discount our own identities. All that can matter (if anything can matter) is the state of everything (whether that be one or many). Enlightenment is the discovery that I don't exist.

Lest that conclusion seem abrupt: the *Questions of King Milinda* (which is Menander, ruling in the second century BC in north-west India) will usually feature only in histories of Indian or Buddhist thought, but they have as much right here. Their influence was lessened in the West for centuries, but the same can be said of many texts that had their greatest influence in a later age. Nagasena explains to Menander that no complex entity is anything but the confluence of its parts: better still, such words as seem to name that complex entity are but convenient designations for what has no substantial being. 'Nagasena' itself is 'but a way of counting, term, appellation, convenient designation, mere name for the hair of the head, hair of the body. . . . brain of the head, form, sensation, perception, the predispositions and consciousness. But in the absolute sense there is no ego to be found.' Later Buddhists dissolved even the elements to which the complex entities had been reduced, at the same time as they identified desire as the sole cause of everything. Buddhists, like the Hellenistic sages, wished to save 'us' from distress, and do so, in their various ways, by creating the conviction that there is no one to be saved.

Epicureans and Stoics both insisted (unlike most Buddhist schools in this) that corporeal beings were the only causes. For Epicureans there was no overall plan, no destiny, no fear of divine wrath, no reason for human action save to achieve a little tranquillity. Stoics thought otherwise: although corporeal beings were the only causes, they had their effects in virtue of an everlasting law, the immanent divinity. Things as they are are as they should be, and tranquillity is achieved by identifying our own purposes with God's. The more radical, and root-less, sages known as Cynics shared many of the Stoics' moral attitudes, but had abandoned any attempt to ground their conduct on the way things were. Instead they achieved tranquillity (if they did) by forgoing the dangerous advantages of cosmological reason. What we need to know is only how to live here-now, reducing our wants to what can easily be achieved, and entertaining no opinions about how things happen. Diogenes, found masturbating in the market-place, remarked that it was a pity hunger could not be assuaged so easily. In this they mirrored, wordlessly, something of the attitude that Pyrrhonian Sceptics offered: suspending judgement about what was really true, and binding themselves instead to nature, custom, impulse, and the discipline of such crafts as they wished to practise. Where the Cynics despised custom because they did not see that it mattered, Pyrrhonian Sceptics followed it because they did not see that it mattered. Such Sceptics, of course, had no general reason to abandon civilized ways, as Cynics did, but equally they had no reason to think it wrong to do so. Their scepticism was a reasonable response to all the theories which, in effect, denied that we had any reason to respect our own truth-seeking faculties. If all that we think is what corporeal elements require us to, whether by chance or by the operation of a biophysical law, what reason have we to trust those thoughts to be, at root, veridical? One might as easily expect that sea-slugs carry a map of Athens on their bellies as think that this little 'perspiration of the brain called thought' (as a later sceptic, David Hume, described it) was a model of the universe. Tranquillity must lie in giving up such dreams. The Stoics insisted that our reason was indeed the presence of God in us: the law of the universe was indeed inscribed, in secret, on the minds of the wise. Such wise men were the equals in nature of God himself—if only we could find them. If, as the Stoics said, most people are not wise, what value have our guesses about what wise men say? If, as the Stoics say, all that we do is predetermined, what obligation can we have to come to other conclusions than in fact we do? Stoic enlightenment is to realize that God is already everything, and that what had seemed errors in our thought (including thoughts impossible for truly enlightened minds) were always what they should be.

The conclusion—if conclusions remain possible—must be that Epicurean thought allowed no room at all for being right about the world (save by a mad coincidence), and Stoic thought allowed no room for any obligation to abandon ancient errors. Equivalently, Epicureans thought every impression they had was 'true' (that is, that it occurred), and Stoics that only the wise could tell the truly reliable impressions. Cosmology began to become what Clement called it, fabulous stories to soothe children's fears, which really lead on to despair.

Why, in the name of Truth, do you show those who have put their trust in you that they are under the dominion of flux, and motion and fortuitous vortices? Why, pray, do you infect life with idols, imagining winds, air, fire, earth, stocks, stones, iron, this world itself to be gods? Why babble in high-flown language about the divinity of wandering stars to those men who have become real wanderers through this much-vaunted—I will not call it astronomy, but—astrology? I long for the Lord of the winds, the Lord of fire, the Creator of the World, He who gives light to the sun. I seek for God himself, not for the works of God.

From Doubt to Dogma

Clement's assault on the 'inherited conglomerate' of civic custom and philosophy invoked Plato as an ally, and it was Platonism, in a variety of forms, that shaped the serious thought of the early centuries AD. Our appreciation of this obvious truth has sometimes been

PHILO OF ALEXANDRIA was one of the first writers to attempt a reconciliation of Platonism and Judaism. Here he is represented in the seventeenth-century frieze that runs around the upper reading room of the Bodleian Library in Oxford.

muffled: the distinction drawn by Christians and by pagan polemicists between philosophy and superstition (each claiming the high ground for their own) has its descendant in the professional distinction between patristic scholars and students of late antique philosophy. The truth is that, however important their disagreements, Philo of Alexandria (Jewish), John the Evangelist and Clement (Christian), and Plotinus (Pagan) shared a world. Nor is it a world that we can happily ignore. Renaissance Europe rediscovered Plato, and was inspired to scientific as to literary effort. Nor was that just an accident. Platonic tools remain of vital importance to the rationalist and realist endeavour, as they do to an honest piety.

So what line connects Athens, Alexandria, Jerusalem, and Rome? There is this much truth in Clement's remarks about the influence of 'barbarians', and later speculations about the 'Semitic' cast of (for example) Stoic thought, or the 'Eastern' nature of later mystical philosophy, that some of the most brilliant thinkers of the Hellenistic and the Roman worlds came out of 'the East'. There is no need to indulge faintly racist speculation about the (possibly) Phoenician ancestry of Zeno, or the (certainly) Phoenician ancestry of Porphyry (pupil and biographer of Plotinus; his name, at first, was Malchus): their racial, or even their cultural, background need have been no different from any pure-born Athenian's for them to have had exactly the methods and conclusions that they did. The point is rather that the Mediterranean world was one, although its languages were many (ranging from Latin, through Greek, to Aramaic). One important moral of this truism is that intertestamental Judaism, and Christianity, were Hellenistic creeds, and their intellectuals contributed to the philosophic stream as equals (not always recognized) of those pagans who remained in full communion with the gods of Greece.

Plato's immediate successors as heads and leaders of 'the Academy' were more recognizably 'academics' than any previous philosophers. They might make contributions to political life, and were expected to set good examples. It was expected that they might have had a conversion to philosophy: Polemo, for example, the fourth head of the Academy till 276 BC, had in his youth secreted cash around the city so that he could always have the wherewithal to buy himself a pleasure (the inventor, so to speak, of the cash-dispenser), but was transformed by a meeting with the great Xenocrates (the third head, who died in 314 BC). Their ways of life, and death, were scrutinized for signs that their philosophical pretensions were hypocritical. But they were for the most part settled and secure, retiring scholars seeing no need to go the Cynic way or raise a wider populace to the light eternal. As head succeeded head the connection with Plato grew more tenuous: Arcesilaus, though Diogenes Laertius thinks it worth mentioning that he had copies of Plato's works, directed the Academy in more eristic directions, setting himself and his successors to subvert the dogmatists', especially the Stoics', certainties (he was head from 273 to 242 BC). Such 'Academic Scepticism' could find inspiration in the memory of Socrates, knowing only that he knew nothing, and the contest between Stoic and Academic Sceptic served to keep their minds alive. Carneades (retired 137, died 129 BC), especially, contributed to the discussion of Stoic ethics and their influence on Rome, but, like Socrates and other sages both before and since, wrote nothing down. When he visited Rome in 156 BC he gave a public lecture in defence of justice, to general applause. On the next day, he gave a public lecture in defence, instead, of injustice: Cato the Censor (who was to demonstrate his own commitment to 'justice', of a sort, by procuring Carthage's destruction) objected to such philosophers because they upset the young. 'Platonic tolerance' was made vain ('and vain all Doric discipline') many years before the Passion. Academic Sceptics, like academics everywhere, did not perhaps entirely 'live' their creed: Pyrrhonian Sceptics abandoned any faith even in dialectic, and did not claim to know even that they knew nothing. What they found themselves doing they did, and that was that (but of course 'that' might be dialectic).

Antiochus of Ascalon (*fl.* 87 BC) returned the Academy to Platonism, though in a shape that cannot be identified in Plato's published works. Antiochus was from Palestine, from an area that contributed a number of late Hellenistic intellectuals (the neighbourhood of Gadara, or Gerasa, might even have had a school, though it was probably only a habit). In Antiochus' synthesis things hinted at before took definite shape: his master Philo of Larisa (head of the Academy from 110 to 79 BC), he said, was wrong to think (as far too many practising philosophers in British universities have thought) that there was an unbroken line of analytical and undogmatic thought from Socrates through Plato to the contemporary academy. There were after all truths that we could count upon. Socrates had turned his back (for a while) on truths that nature veiled in mystery, but Plato had established a single enterprise conducted in two co-operating schools, the Academic and Peripatetic, under Xenocrates and Aristotle. That in turn was in agreement with the most important doctrines of the Stoa, developed by Zeno under Polemo. It seems that Antiochus conceded more to the Stoics in denying the intelligibility of 'immaterial substance' than any genuine Platonist could stomach, but his chief endeavour was to identify the criterion of truth and the end of action in the face of naïve scepticism. The forms (though we are hampered by the lack of direct citations on the point) turn out to be the eternal thoughts of God (as probably they had been for Xenocrates).

The central theses of what amounts to the 'perennial philosophy' (the belief that there is a truth that we can partly grasp if we reform our souls), as it developed in the hands (perhaps) of Posidonius, Antiochus, Philo of Alexandria, and at last Plotinus, are these. Although we do not always see things straight, we can, in good health and our wits about us, take hold of some immediate realities. Those who deny the claim, the Stoics pointed out, must really be relying on it: no argument is valid against the possibility of a secure grip on truth since any such argument needs its conclusion to be securely true. Unless we let ourselves be distracted by emotional attachments and misleading memories (which either are or are caused by demons), we can uncover real patterns in the world, which exist unchangingly in the mind of God. That God, the Divine Intellect, is—as Aristotle said—identified eternally with its own objects, the eternal forms. Although eternal it is not the primary source, the One. Only a few of us, or even only one, can hope to be, to embody, the Mind and Word of God (and thereby be identified, in Philo's vocabulary, as the Son of God). The rest of us can hope to be the children of the Word—which is to say, of a healthy revelation—and share the life of the

ST PAUL'S SERMON ON THE AREOPAGUS in Athens—here represented by Raphael in a cartoon for a tapestry—was the earliest recorded contact between Christianity and Greek philosophy.

Soul, the immanent God. By constantly recalling ourselves (being recalled) to the Word we are saved from all the mistakes and vices regularly symbolized as beasts (by Epictetus, Clement, and Spinoza amongst many). In short, recognizable notions of the Divine Trinity (the One, the Word, the Soul) and of the Divine Humanity pervaded the early centuries of our era. Disputes about the details of those doctrines became, within the Christian Churches, occasions for denouncing heresy—a term itself derived from the Greek for 'philosophical school' (*hairesis*)—but they were familiar questions, at least as familiar as disputes about the detail of evolutionary theory in the late twentieth century.

Philo's system was 'subordinationist', precisely in that he distinguished between those who could only take instruction from the Word, from the Torah and Divine Philosophy ('sons of the Word'), and those who were 'self-taught', the embodied Word, 'sons of God'.

We must not indeed reject any teaching that has grown grey with age . . . but when God causes the young shoots of self-inspired wisdom to spring up within the soul, the knowledge that comes from teaching must straightway be abolished and swept off. God's scholar, God's pupil, God's disciple, call him what you will, cannot any more suffer the guidance of mortals.

Amongst such sons of God, incarnate Logos, were Melchizedek, the High Priest, and, especially, Moses. Plotinus too distinguishes those who reach only as far as Intellect, and those who are brought into the 'Cloud of Unknowing', where all words fall silent. For Christians, in so far as they denied the possibility of *another* incarnation, the distinction did not matter: the incarnate Word is the *only* way for us, and therefore is not a second-best route upwards but the *only* one. No one has seen the Father, nor any adequate account of him: only the Word declares him.

The identification of the Word with Moses, or with the dramatic figure of Moses—for Philo is not always confident that there was, or that it mattered if there was, an actual historical figure who led the Israelites from slavery—also appears in Samaritan thought. The universe itself was made for Moses' sake, for the one being who was and is the embodied Word. Christians, who thought that Jesus was and is that Word, adopted the same language, and with it the same problems. Philo speaks of the Word as a First-born Son, and (equivalently) of Wisdom as first-born daughter, but he also follows scriptural precedent in thinking of the Word as a thing God makes, and not necessarily eternally. There is, in fact, no other pattern than the Word as it is, for the universe and for human reason—but God 'might' have acted otherwise. Making is an act of will, not of necessity. As Eusebius of Caesarea was to say during the debates that culminated at Nicaea: 'nothing is from [God's] *ousia* (His Being), but all things coming into being by his will, each one exists just as it came into being'. This way of putting the relation of God and the Word, which is known to Church historians as the Arian heresy (to which Eusebius and his master, the emperor Constantine, were sympathetic), lays us open to the standard arguments culled from Plato's *Euthyphro*, that if God 'might' have ordered us to hate each other, or to rob and lie, it 'might' have been the case that wickedness was righteous after all. The orthodox reply has been that the Word does not stem, as such, from God's *arbitrium* (his will), but from his very being. The Word, exactly, is not arbitrary, since there could never have been another Word than there is. Indeed the very notion that it is made by God's will and reason is absurd—the Word *is* God's will and reason.

The good news that the Word had dwelt, does dwell, among us was what one sect of wanderers took round the world. Those wanderers, whom we now identify as Christian missionaries, would have seemed to most of their contemporaries just another sort of Cynic. There are indeed many echoes of Cynic conversation in the gospels (as one might expect from a native of a heavily Hellenized Galilee). But the doctrine of the gospel was 'Platonic' in its essence. Later polemicists, of course, either derided it as 'Plato for the masses' or attacked what they said were distortions of an honest theory. Pagan attacks on Christian dogma, indeed, read very much like Christian attacks on pagans. As so often in such feuds each side accuses the other of the same offences. 'How could God be mingled with base matter? How could he suffer and die? How could sensible people take rites seriously that involved such simple things as bread and wine? Such things were excuses for depraved behaviour.' It is easy to see that pagans might think Christians guilty here: the point is that all three questions, and the concluding jibe, are raised by Clement against pagan thought and practice. Orthodox theologians remain convinced that 'Platonists' despised or were weirdly ignorant of time and matter. Their orthodoxy is in fact Platonic.

Hebrew, Samaritan, and Christian thought, when properly understood, are no fabulous darkness. On the contrary, such thinkers rightly saw themselves to stand for reason against the dark. According to the famous historian of ideas A. O. Lovejoy,

the primary and most universal faith of man [is] his inexpugnable realism, his twofold belief that he is on the one hand in the midst of realities which are not himself nor mere obsequious shadows of himself, a world which transcends the narrow confines of his own transient being; and on the other hand that he can himself somehow read beyond those confines and bring those external existences within the compass of his own life yet without annulment of their transcendence.

A third inexpugnable belief is that we do indeed exist, and are not to be dissolved in atoms or the unchangeable. Our century, like the early centuries of what is called the present era, has seen an assault on Truth, Reason, and the Self. The Platonizing synthesis with which our predecessors aimed to defeat despair did serve them well, in whatever little sect they found themselves.

The Pagan Possibilities

The centuries to follow were Hebraic in their chief inspiration, though pagan schools continued to recruit new pupils at Athens and Alexandria, even after Justinian closed the Academy. Modern commentators sometimes speak as if the Hebraists betrayed philosophy by bowing to what could be confirmed from the scriptures. The truth is that they thereby proved themselves realists: is it really better to 'follow the argument' wheresoever it leads, when we have good reason to think that we already know some unexpected truths? Jewish, Muslim, and Christian scholars and philosophers determined what the direction of philosophy should be. That outcome, they would all have been convinced, was providential: there was no real chance that Julian 'the Apostate' would halt the advance in the generation after Constantine, and restore a 'pagan' Platonism. Perhaps they were right, but it is still worth concluding with a sketch of what might have happened if one of the last—and probably the greatest—of firmly Hellenic sages had had the last word. This was, uncontroversially, Plotinus, whose friend and disciple Porphyry coaxed into writing (without notes and without revision) his considered views on almost everything. Plotinus was from Upper Egypt, and was taught at Alexandria by one Ammonius, who also, almost certainly, taught Origen, one of the most philosophical of Church Fathers (and eventually judged to have been dangerously close to heresy). Porphyry records that when Origen turned up at Plotinus' lecture, Plotinus halted, blushing, on the grounds that the hearers had nothing to learn. Plotinus'

JULIAN THE APOSTATE. This painting by the Victorian artist Edward Armitage represents the emperor observing with amusement a group of quarrelling Christian scholars.

working life was at Rome, where he professed to follow Plato. The term 'Neoplatonism' was only coined a century or so ago: till then no one much doubted the continuity of Platonism.

How different would the future have been if a pagan Plotinism had won? The first thing to notice, of course, is that Julian himself was influenced by philosophers far less respectable than Plotinus (though Iamblichus (d. *c.* AD 330), whose writings were perhaps to be the scriptures of a reborn 'pagan church', is not as foolish as his reputation). The armies of King Oberon swarmed everywhere. In the absence of any deep conviction that there was a single way to Truth, people were confronted once again by what was 'obvious'. Epicureans said all impressions were true, as being what they were; Stoics said that all of us, since we weren't wise, were mad, and therefore had no escape—except in fantasy—from our convictions; Sceptics of whatever school agreed that, because we did not know we knew the Truth, we were bound up in seemings. The conclusion, so far from being, as Whiggish writers think, a triumph for materialistic common sense, released all manner of seemings in the intellectual world. Memories of triumph and heartbreak, ancient stories, seemingly (and therefore inescapably) meaningful occurrences are all 'obvious'. In the absence of an actual, universal agreement about what, in detail, it was that was obvious, people had better stick to their ancestral creeds, and certainly not proselytize. That was, to Julian's eye, the Christians' greatest crime, that they abandoned 'the gods of their fathers'.

Similarly, in the absence of any deep conviction that there was a 'real self' our multiple obsessions and emotions became as real as any. Fractured memories, discordant motives, concealed causes are not anomalies: they are the ordinary human condition, and only the saint, hero, or philosopher has tamed and transformed the squalling horde of impulses so far as to 'know herself' as single. The rest of us do not know why we do things, are not 'the same' from one foolish moment to the next, and constantly misidentify even our most 'present' and 'immediate' feelings. It does not follow that there is no single self to be uncovered. It is an important step in self-knowledge to be made to realize (most easily perhaps at three in the morning) just how fluid and uncontrolled our ordinary thinking is. 'Whence came the soul,' asks Philo, 'whither will it go, how long will it be our mate and comrade? Can we tell its essential nature? . . . Even now in this life, we are the ruled rather than the rulers, known rather than knowing. . . . Is my mind my own possession? That parent of false conjectures, that purveyor of delusion, the delirious, the fatuous, and in frenzy or senility proved to be the very negation of mind.'

In brief, the state of intellectual affairs in Julian's day was much like ours. Some serious thinkers, including the ones that Julian esteemed, devoted themselves to the control of 'demons' (which are the memories, 'projections', and fragmentary selves I have described) by ritual, aiming to harness Oberon. Reason, they said, was not enough: there must also be 'god-working' (theurgy) in open view—precisely because most of us were not equipped to reason our way to truth. They sought to re-create, in a wider world, the Olympian *tour de force*, to tame the demons, the mad impulses, the hideous memories, within a dramatic representation of what they took to be real relationships, as told them by the prophets. The rites that brought God's Word into the living imagination of believing Christians were not, perhaps, so unlike those that pagan enthusiasts employed for the sake of peace, except that the Christians, like more orthodox Plotinists, abjured blood sacrifice (as Julian did not). Christians 'spoke in tongues' (though cautioned not to think the practice very important); pagans wrote out screeds of gibberish. Both felt themselves thereby to be bypassing Babel, recovering the 'really obvious', the day when the gods were with us.

Plotinus did not quite approve: we should not trouble ourselves with demons, but only with the '*daimon*' that was our better self, the voice of the divine intellect whom Christians identified with Christ. It would be one thing to agree that there were demons, and that they must be bound by Zeus' chain or swallowed up in Kronos (depending on what myth was allegorized); it is quite another to imagine that they are at one's beck and call, that the powers that rule the world are ours to command at will—or ours to serve. Just so, it was one thing to agree, as Plotinus did, that the world of sense-experience was not ideal, and quite another to despise it. Plotinus most probably thought of 'Christians' as included amongst the 'gnostics' that he scorned: people who claimed so peculiar a grasp of the divine as to be relieved of any normal duties, including those of intellectual coherence. It is an irony of history that, on this, unknowingly, he agreed with them. Although popular religion has always found it easier to speak as if there were *two* worlds (this inferior version, and the heavenly other), no Platonist could quite agree with that. It is not that there are two real worlds, any more than there are two real things (the soul and the body). The body, so a later Platonist declared, is that part of the soul that is visible to the five senses. The 'flight of the alone to the Alone' of which Plotinus spoke was, as he said, 'no journey for the feet'! Coming to see things straight is seeing things as they are, the visible impress of the divine beauty. Porphyry, who wrote more fiercely and more directly against Christians (which is one reason why we have so little of his work), would also have found himself agreeing with them, rather than with an emperor who took blood sacrifice to be a literal duty.

Two errors, by Plotinian and orthodox Christian standards, were equivalent. The first is to suppose that the world is utterly evil, and that nothing worldly can be trusted or esteemed. If that were so, we should not trust even our intellect, or our response to revelation. The second is to think that just as it is the world deserves our worship, that the world, the sense-world, is unambiguously God. If that were so, we could not rise above it, nor expect any higher standard than 'the way things are'. The middle way is to agree that the world is fallen, or we are fallen in it; that the world does owe its being to the soul that suffuses it (for without that there is as good as nothing, without any boundaries or form) but that this soul is our Sister, not our Mother (as being another image of the one divine Soul). We owe her respect, but never worship. Julian tried to re-create a civil society that would do what the Christian Churches did, namely provide both meaning and a living to the struggling peoples of his day. Christians, of course, were not the only ones to care for the defenceless. Plotinus himself was trusted as the guardian of many orphaned children: like Crates, he kept their possessions safe in case they did not become philosophers. But the Christian Churches offered the only organized and ecumenical charity. Julian hoped to emulate this virtue, but could not shake free from the other features of pagan tradition. His attempt to reinstate, for example, oracles and blood sacrifice at Daphne (near Antioch in Syria, by the Castalian spring) in AD 362, was attacked by Christians in something like the terms that any Enlightenment thinker might deploy— except that the Christians gave most credit for the oracle's failure to the bones of the martyred Babylas.

Suppose Julian, instead of following the 'theurgic school' that sprang from Iamblichus' teachings, had been content with Plotinus or Porphyry? Could there have been a 'pagan' Platonic Empire? In such a world the Divine would have been known as Three Hypostases: the

THE SCHOOL OF ATHENS. Raphael's fresco in the Stanza della Segnatura in the Vatican is the most spectacular Renaissance representation of Greek philosophy. The figures in these four details probably represent (*clockwise from top left*) Parmenides, Heraclitus, Pythagoras, and Socrates.

DIOGENES OF SINOPE. The Cynic philosopher's request to Alexander to move out of his light was a favourite topic for artists working in several media. Here it appears in a maiolica dish from Urbino.

One, the Intellect, the Soul, in descending order, allegorized as Ouranos, Kronos, Zeus. The human being embodying Intellect would not have been a mythical Pythagoras, but either a Platonic Socrates, or Plotinus himself. Our saints would have been sages: joyfully ascetic in their lives, and in their occasional martyrdom. Matter would have been sacramental, and the sun at once 'a red-hot mass of metal' and the visible image of the divine. There would have been no more blood sacrifices, not only because such sacrifices fed inferior spirits but because the creatures sacrificed would have been recognized as friends. Platonic concern for our fellow creatures, unfortunately for them, was not adopted by the Christian Church, whose doctors decided (weirdly) that to care for animals must be to care for the demons represented by wild beasts. A more Platonic, or Plotinian, empire would have been kinder. When Porphyry thought of suicide (which Platonists thought less honourable than the Stoics did) Plotinus turned up unannounced to point out that the decision sprang from mere melancholy, not from reason. The Delphic Oracle, consulted about Plotinus, is said to have said the gods often set him on the right track again, that he was granted a vision transcending 'the bitter waves of this blood-drenched life'. In brief, he seemed to his friends to have lived out the project defined by Epictetus: 'the affair is momentous, it is full of mystery, not a chance gift, nor given to all comers'. Plotinus managed it, but once he'd 'gone aloft' how could his followers cope? A more strictly Plotinian Empire would have made clear an absolute division between (perhaps a more civilized) Custom, for the masses, and an ascetic Wisdom for the few (which is how things happened in the Buddhist world). Julian's Empire would have lost all sense that ancient Custom could be criticized at all. He ruled, in fact, that Christians might not teach the classic texts, because they did not think them true. It is possible that it was this ruling which compelled Gregory of Nyssa to abandon the classics for theology, and a bishopric. For all its faults the notionally Christian Empire that succeeded Julian insisted that it was not sages only who could aspire to the light, that there were 'ordinary' saints as well as sages. Philosophers were not the only friends of God, and no one was to be seen as less deserving of existence than another. The thought had been there before, and even before Plotinus: Aristotle, taunted with having given charity to the undeserving, replied that he pitied the man, not his character. Practice surpassed doctrine among many pagans (as doctrine surpassed practice among many Christians).

Put otherwise: we were all to be, like the Hebrews, a nation of philosophers. The long experiment of Christendom is, maybe, failing, as may that other inheritor of Hebraic Platonism, Islam. If they fail, our descendants may find themselves once more in a world our forefathers knew well: the world of hopeless custom, caste, and confusion. On the other hand, we have been here before. The very fact of being brought up among the ruins may yet impress some people with the thought that they at least are young. Whatever has been achieved before, and lost, there is perhaps a moment when the world is new and can reinvent or rediscover glory.

2

Medieval Philosophy

PAUL VINCENT SPADE

THE most prominent feature of medieval philosophy is that it was conducted within the context of Christian doctrine. This is not to deny the importance of Jewish and Muslim contributions, but in the main stream of later European philosophy it was the medieval Christian tradition that was most influential. Medieval philosophy, then, may be taken to begin when thinkers started measuring their philosophical speculations against the requirements of the Christian faith. In fact, in terms of the distinction between philosophy and theology, as it was drawn, for example, in the thirteenth century, most of those nowadays regarded as important medieval 'philosophers' would not have regarded themselves as philosophers at all, but as theologians.

This close connection between philosophy and Church doctrine in the Middle Ages makes it easy to dismiss medieval philosophy as nothing but a thinly disguised apologetic for Christianity. But that is naïve. To take a parallel situation, it sometimes happens in the late twentieth century that highly respected philosophers claim (rightly or wrongly, it does not matter) that standard logic itself must be changed because it conflicts with certain results of quantum theory. Philosophy, it seems, rarely proceeds in an ideally autonomous manner. There is almost always some 'given' to be preserved—a theological doctrine, a scientific theory that gets the right experimental results no matter what real conceptual difficulties are involved, or some other factor. Still, in the Middle Ages just as today, the pressure of these external 'givens' is often more stimulating than stifling to philosophy. And just as today there are many areas of philosophy where one may speculate freely without fear of trespassing on science, so too in the Middle Ages there were many areas of philosophy where one could speculate freely without trespassing on theological ground. The situations are quite parallel.

Setting the beginning of medieval philosophy as early as suggested above has the consequence that late ancient and early medieval philosophy chronologically overlapped. Proclus (c. AD 410–85), for example, the last major exponent of ancient pagan philosophy, was much younger than St Augustine (354–430).

At the other end of the period, medieval philosophy is generally taken as ending sometime before 1500. No one event marked its passing, but certainly by 1450 the forces of humanism had introduced recognizably new themes. Medieval philosophy, then, occupies roughly half the entire history of Western philosophy.

In a single chapter it is impossible to treat all the major figures and topics from this long period, even granted that certain whole centuries offer little of philosophical interest. For such detail, the reader is referred to one of the admirable surveys of medieval philosophy cited in the Further Reading. Instead, the present chapter will concentrate on a few persons and themes. Other matters will be treated more briefly, as 'connecting tissue'. But many important topics will be omitted entirely; one cannot do everything.

The picture of medieval philosophy presented in this chapter is a tentative one. An enormous number of medieval philosophical texts have never been critically edited; many survive only in manuscripts, often very corrupt ones. This is true not only for minor works by insignificant authors, but also for some writings known to be important and for many others the significance of which no one is yet in a position to assess. The matter is aggravated by the fact that manuscripts from after about 1200 are usually written in a highly compressed system of abbreviations that takes special training to decipher. This situation is quite unlike that in ancient, early modern, or more recent philosophy, where for the most part the major surviving texts are readily available, and the remaining task is primarily one of interpretation. Despite the labours of many dedicated scholars, the history of medieval philosophy is still known only very incompletely.

The Influence of Greek Philosophy

Medieval philosophy was a mixture of two main influences, Christian doctrine and the Greek philosophical heritage. With respect to the latter, it is important to realize that after the early centuries of the Christian era, most Greek philosophy exerted its influence on the West only indirectly, at least until the twelfth century. The original Greek texts were lost to the Latins, in the sense that few people could read them even if they had access to manuscript copies. The knowledge of Greek rapidly declined in the West, and by the sixth century it was a rarity.

From Plato, the Middle Ages possessed only part of the *Timaeus* (up to 53c) in a Latin translation by Chalcidius (late third/early fourth century AD). A few other works were translated too, but did not circulate widely. It was not until Marsilio Ficino (1433–99) that the whole of Plato became available to the Latins. For Plotinus, the situation was even worse. His writings were almost completely unknown. Marius Victorinus in the fourth century may have translated some of the *Enneads* but if so, those translations disappeared very soon. Aristotle suffered a better fate. Most of his logical writings were translated by Boethius around the turn of the fifth and sixth centuries, although only the *Categories* and *De interpretatione* were in general circulation before the twelfth century. Between the mid-twelfth and mid-thirteenth centuries, virtually all the remaining works of Aristotle were translated and became readily available. This 'recovery' of Aristotle marks a watershed in medieval philosophy. A few other translations of lesser authors were done from time to time. But except for Aristotle, the primary texts of Greek philosophy were mostly unavailable to the Middle Ages.

Nevertheless, the medievals managed to have a fair second-hand knowledge of at least some aspects of Greek philosophy. They learned it in part from Latin pagan authors such as Cicero and Seneca, who did read Greek and passed on much information about the philosophical past. In part too, they learned it from some of the Latin 'Church Fathers' such as Ambrose and Boethius, who discussed Greek doctrines in some detail.

During the early Middle Ages, Platonic, Neoplatonic, and broadly Stoic influences dominated philosophical thinking. This situation lasted until the recovery of Aristotle in the twelfth and thirteenth centuries. Hence it is quite wrong to think of medieval philosophy as mainly a slavish parroting of Aristotle, as it has sometimes been portrayed. For most of the Middle Ages by far, Aristotle was of decidedly secondary importance.

Augustine

The term 'patristics' or 'patrology' refers to the study of the 'Fathers of the Church', early Christian writers who were taken to represent authentic tradition. The patristic period is regarded as lasting as late as Gregory the Great (*c*.540–604) or Isidore of Seville (*c*.560–636) in the Latin West, and John Damascene (*c*.675–*c*.729) in the Greek East.

Without question, the most important author of the patristic period was St Augustine. He was born of a pagan father and a Christian mother in 354 at Thagaste in North Africa (now Souk Ahras, Algeria), near Carthage. Although he was raised a Christian, he lived his youth in uninhibited fashion. He was trained in rhetoric, and in 373 read Cicero's (now lost) *Hortensius*, which inspired him to philosophy. For a while he was strongly influenced by the Manichean religion. In 383 he went to Rome to teach rhetoric, and later to Milan. There he came under the influence of St Ambrose and Neoplatonism. After a long inner turmoil, he was converted to Christianity and baptized in 387. Returning to Africa, he was ordained in 391, and consecrated Bishop at Hippo Regius (modern Annaba, or Bône, Algeria) in 395 or 396. He filled this position for some thirty-four years, dying in 430 as the Vandals were besieging the city. Augustine's literary output was enormous. It includes over a hundred books and treatises on various topics, more than five hundred sermons, and over two hundred letters.

It is arguable that Augustine is the most influential philosopher who ever lived. His authority has been felt much more broadly, and for a much longer time, than Aristotle's, whose role in the Middle Ages was comparatively minor until rather late. As for Plato, for a long time much of his influence was felt mainly through the writings of Augustine. For more than a millennium after his death, Augustine was an authority who simply had to be accommodated. He shaped medieval thought as no one else did. Moreover, his influence did not end with the Middle Ages. Throughout the Reformation, appeals to Augustine's authority were commonplace on all sides. His theory of illumination lives on in Malebranche and in

Descartes's 'light of nature'. His approach to the problem of evil and to human free will is still
widely held today. His force was and is still felt not just in philosophy but also in theology,
popular religion, and political thought, for example in the theory of the just war.

It is therefore ironic that Augustine was not really a philosopher at all by training or profession. He was a 'rhetor', a rhetorician and teacher of rhetoric. A rhetor might be asked to
deliver orations on ceremonial occasions, but was also expected to be able to plead cases in a
court of law. Rhetoric is the study of the practical use of language, 'how to do things with

words', including how to shape people's minds and characters. It was a corner-stone of classical pedagogy, and indeed much of classical society. But rhetoric is not exactly philosophy in the modern sense, and one ought not think of Augustine as primarily a philosopher in that sense at all.

Augustine's rhetorical training explains the flavour of his writing. There is little precise, systematic argumentation. Sometimes, Augustine maintains conflicting views in different works. In other cases, it is unclear what exactly his views are. Augustinianism, then, may best be viewed as a matter of broad themes and tendencies rather than strict theories.

This style of philosophy prevailed until the time of St Anselm in the eleventh century. Philosophers were people trained in classical culture and the liberal arts, speculating about their religion and about philosophical topics in a loose but often by no means shallow way. Much of this speculation consisted of presenting a vision of reality and exploring it, without any rigorous argument for its truth. In Anselm's time, this style began to change dramatically.

Augustine's Hierarchical World

In the best Platonic manner, Augustine views the world as hierarchically arranged. The principle of ordering is one of intrinsic value. Thus the better or more worthy something is, the higher it stands in the hierarchy of things. God is at the top (like Plato's form of the good), physical objects occupy a very low position, and human souls are somewhere in between, the souls of good people higher than those of wicked ones. Good angels reside below God but above the souls of good people, while fallen angels are somewhere between the souls of wicked people and mere material objects.

So far this ordering is innocuous. It is simply an arrangement of things according to how Augustine assesses their value. But the hierarchy has ontological implications. For Augustine put great emphasis on Exodus 3: 14, where God tells Moses 'I am who am' and instructs him to tell the Israelites that 'He who is' sent Moses to them. Augustine interpreted this passage as implying that God is a being *par excellence*, the most real thing of all. Hence the hierarchy of value becomes also a hierarchy of reality, so that it makes sense to speak of 'degrees of being'. Physical objects, which are very low on the hierarchy, and indeed all creatures when compared to God, are '*prope nihil*' (= 'next to nothing'). They are not altogether nothing, of course, but they are by no means fully real; that is reserved for God alone.

There are many consequences of this way of regarding reality. First, note that change or becoming is another striking case where one finds things that exist but are not fully real. What changes or comes to be is real in some sense; it is not absolutely nothing, after all. But it is not yet *fully* real; it is only 'on the way', 'coming to be'. In fact, this intermediate status seems to be characteristic of change or becoming, and is what makes it so hard to grasp philosophically, as people have known since Parmenides. Hence, creatures, which exist but not fully, are linked with change and becoming. In short, *mutability is a mark of a creature*; only God is strictly immutable.

Creatures, changeable things, are not fully but only 'partially' real. This way of speaking (as well as the philosophical analysis of change derived ultimately from Aristotle) implies that creatures are metaphysically composite: they have parts. On the other hand, Augustine accepted the Neoplatonic identification of the One with the highest Good, so that the hierarchy of reality not only involves degrees of goodness and degrees of being, but also degrees of unity. God, therefore, the supreme good and supreme being, is also supremely one and has no composition or parts whatever. Like mutability, *composition is a mark of a creature.*

If degrees of goodness are identified with degrees of being, it follows that there can be nothing purely evil, possessing no degree of goodness whatever. If there is no goodness at all in a thing, then there is no reality in it either, and it simply does not exist. Thus there is no place in Augustine's universe for a force of pure evil, a polar opposite to God on the hierarchy. (This marks a sharp break with the dualist Manicheanism, which attracted Augustine before his conversion.)

If there is no such thing as pure evil, then the lesser worth of creatures cannot be explained as a kind of 'dilution' of pure goodness by mixing it with its opposite. Hence, Augustine not only denies a pure form of evil, he also denies that things below God on the hierarchy are somehow *mixtures* of good and evil. Everything on the hierarchy, which is to say everything in reality, is good in varying degrees; nothing on the hierarchy is evil. Evil is of course a fact that has to be accounted for; the author of the *Confessions* knew too much about evil to deny that. But his account does not proceed by saying that some things are evil simply in virtue of what they are. He denies what is sometimes called the theory of 'metaphysical evil', the theory that anything falling short of the highest good (God) is to that extent 'imperfect' and so evil by its very nature.

Good and Evil

For Augustine, it is not the case that the less good something is, the more evil it is. Good and evil are not related as positive and negative, so that a certain degree of evil may be defined as simply the absence of a certain degree of goodness. Something with only a low degree of goodness is not thereby automatically evil. It is evil only if it ought to have a higher degree of goodness and does not. To think otherwise, Augustine says, is like blaming the earth because it is not the heavens (*On Free Choice of the Will*, iii. 5). Evil, therefore, is not simply an 'absence' of good; it is the 'privation' of good. It is the absence of a good that *ought* to be present.

The main link between this notion of 'ought' and the metaphysical goodness built into Augustine's hierarchy seems to be this (*On Free Choice of the Will*, i): Higher things ought to 'govern and rule' (have power over) lower ones; never the other way around. If one wants to put this in terms of causality, causal influence ought to run down the hierarchy, never up. (Readers familiar with Descartes will here be reminded of his claim that there must be at least

ST AUGUSTINE IN HIS STUDY as imagined in the fifteenth century by Botticelli.

as much reality in a cause as in its effect.) When things are in fact as they ought to be, the higher ruling the lower, then they are arranged 'in order', or 'justly'; otherwise they are 'dis-ordered' or 'unjustly' arranged. As the final link in the chain, Augustine regards 'evil' as injustice or disorder, when lower things have power over the higher, reversing their proper order. Evil then is not an entity on the hierarchy of reality; it is an arrangement of things on that hierarchy otherwise than they ought to be arranged. To ask how evil arises in the world is to ask how it comes about that lower things have power over higher ones.

The Responsibility for Evil

God created the world 'justly' in the sense described, so that the higher has power over the lower, not the reverse. Nevertheless, that order somehow got overturned. How is this poss-ible? Who or what is able to upset the order God has established? Augustine's answer is: Human beings do it (and, earlier, certain angels did), and they do it through free will. The world as God created it was, and remains, justly and properly arranged; he is not responsible for evil. On the contrary, human beings (and fallen angels) bear that responsibility, since they are the ones who unjustly give lower things power over higher ones.

Lower things never have power over higher ones, since that is the way God has arranged them according to his eternal law. Yet sometimes they do have such power, since that is the way human beings have arranged them. Do they have that power then or do they not? It begins to appear that Augustine is trying to have it both ways and has fallen into outright contradiction.

Although Augustine discusses the problem of evil many times in many contexts, this air of contradiction is never wholly eliminated. But that is not surprising. There is at the outset something at least apparently paradoxical about free will. If free will is responsible for evil, then one can expect evil to seem paradoxical in the same way.

For example, in love between two persons, each one takes on an importance in the other's eyes that he or she did not have before. Wishes become laws; requests become commands. Each person freely bestows on the other a power that is real enough to determine one's behaviour, and yet is really no power at all; each party remains strictly free to act otherwise.

This at least sounds like a paradox involving free will and the bestowing of power. No doubt it is only apparent in the end, but note that it is exactly the kind of paradox involved in Augustine's account of evil. Recall the ancient Greek and biblical notion (e.g. Romans 6: 16) that one is a slave to the things in which one places one's ultimate values. The just person places his ultimate values in what are really the highest things, so that he is subject to the things to which he ought to be subject; he 'orders' his priorities correctly. The unjust person gets it all mixed up, so that he allows lower things to affect him, even though there is a strict sense in which they do not have the power to do so.

Nowhere in Augustine's writings does he ever successfully remove the paradoxical flavour either of evil in a properly ordered world or of human free will. What he does do, however, is to reduce the former paradox to the latter. The result is that one has no less reason for accepting the presence of evil in a divinely ordered world, even if one does not know how to resolve the apparent paradox that results, than one has for accepting the existence of free will, even though one does not know how to resolve the apparent paradox that results in that case either. In fact, the two apparent paradoxes are ultimately the same. Now Augustine is quite certain human beings have free will, and in fact thinks he can prove this (*On Free Choice of the Will*, i). If he is correct, then his proof has the corollary that free creatures can be responsible for evil in a world arranged by a just and perfectly good God. If everything works out, then Augustine is in the peculiar situation of having shown that the problem of evil is no good reason for abandoning the faith, even though he never 'resolves' that problem by completely eliminating the paradox it involves. It is an ingenious approach.

Scepticism

Augustine had been attracted for a while by the scepticism of the late Platonic Academy. Indeed, one of the first writings he undertook after his conversion was an attack on scepticism, his *Against the Academics*. He returned to the topic in other writings as well.

Many of the sceptical arguments Augustine considers are standard arguments from sensory illusion. He is for the most part happy to accept these arguments and to agree that, while in practice we must rely on the senses, they are ultimately fallible. But he does not think wholesale scepticism follows from this. In *Confessions*, x, Augustine distinguishes between things present to the mind directly or immediately and those present to the mind only indirectly, through a representation. The difficulty with sensation is that it presents us with objects only in the latter way, through a representation or sense-image of them. All the usual problems with representational theories of knowledge follow at once. One could be certain that the representation is accurate only by comparing it with the reality itself and seeing that they match. But, by hypothesis, sensation yields only representations, never the realities themselves, so that one is never in a position to make the comparison.

In this familiar situation, Augustine makes the familiar moves. As long as one says only 'There appears to be a bent oar in the water', and does not go on to say 'There really is a bent oar in the water', one is on safe ground. Incorrigible error can arise only when one goes beyond the representation, which is directly given, to infer something about the object represented, which is not directly given. In general, the mind can have absolute and certain knowledge only about what is directly and immediately present to it. This will be an important theme for Augustine's theory of illumination (see below).

Augustine is not maintaining here that the mind is infallible about whatever is directly given to it, or that the only source of error is the presence of an intermediary (a sense-image or other representation) between the mind and the object of judgement. One can err even about things directly present to the mind, if one is careless or not paying attention. But that kind of error can be discovered and corrected by being more careful and paying closer attention. It is only in the case of representational awareness of objects that one is presented with an *insuperable* barrier to certitude.

The alert reader will recognize that there is a remaining problem, a more radical one. How can one ever determine that one has paid enough attention, that one has been careful enough? In short, how can one formulate infallible criteria for knowledge, and know that one has satisfied them? But Augustine was not trying to formulate such criteria. He was concerned only to point out that there are certain things (those present directly to the mind) about which, when one takes reasonable care and pays reasonable attention, one is justified (in some moral sense) in placing absolute credence in one's judgements. By contrast, there are other things (those present to the mind only indirectly, such as the external objects of sensation) about which, even if one does take reasonable care, one is never justified in placing such absolute credence in one's judgements.

What things did Augustine think are directly present to the mind, so that in principle they can be known with certainty? Sensory representations (although not the external objects sensed), to be sure, but other things as well. The mind knows itself without intermediary, Augustine thinks, and likewise it knows that it exists and is alive. It also knows that it wants to be happy, and that it wants to avoid error. All of this will remind modern readers of Descartes, as well it should. Indeed, there is a passage in Augustine's *On the Trinity*, xv. xii.

VISUAL ILLUSIONS AND SCEPTICISM. Philosophers in all ages have been fascinated by visual illusions, and have often drawn sceptical conclusions about the deceptiveness of the senses. The illusions exhibited in this diagram will be familiar to most modern readers. Ancient writers such as Augustine considered real-life examples such as the apparent bending of an oar in the water.

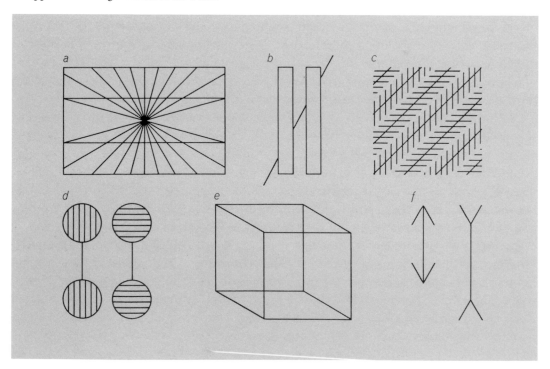

21, where the parallel with Descartes's First Meditation is plainly more than coincidental. Augustine there considers sceptical arguments based on sensory illusion, dreams, and madness, and says many of the same things Descartes says about them.

There are important differences, however. Augustine, like Descartes, finds that the mind can have certain knowledge not only of itself, its acts, and its sensory images, but also of other truths that are in no sense 'mental' truths or 'facts about the mind' and that we cannot have got through the senses. For example, truths of mathematics and (for Augustine but not Descartes) certain a priori truths about values, such as 'Good is to be preferred to evil' (*On Free Choice of the Will*, ii). For Descartes, such knowledge is obtained through 'clear and distinct ideas', which (like all ideas) are representations. All the problems with representational knowledge re-emerge, and Descartes is faced with the notorious problem of justifying his reliance on clear and distinct ideas. For Augustine, however, such 'non-mental' certainties are not known by representation; that is ruled out by the discussion in *Confessions*, x. Instead such truths of mathematics and values are present to the mind directly, without intermediary. How does this work? That is the topic of Augustine's theory of 'illumination'.

Divine Ideas and the Theory of Illumination: The General Theory

The theory of illumination is in effect Augustine's version of Plato's theory of 'reminiscence' or 'recollection', or of Descartes's later theory of 'innate ideas'. All three theories address a common set of problems. Augustine's theory has two forms, a stronger one and a weaker one. Texts supporting both versions may be found in Augustine's writings from throughout his life.

The stronger version maintains a general claim: Illumination, something like Platonic reminiscence, is required for all human knowledge. The weaker version maintains only a special case of the more general claim: Illumination is required for certain kinds of human knowledge that cannot be got any other way.

The stronger or general theory is motivated as follows. Knowledge worthy of the name is something very exalted, a kind of ideal cognitive state, fixed and immutable. (This attitude is already present in Plato's distinction between knowledge and opinion, and in Aristotle's notion of the universal and necessary character of science.) Thus, since fixed and immutable knowledge cannot be had of fleeting and mutable things, the *objects* of knowledge must likewise be exalted, ideal things, like the Platonic forms. (Aristotle rejected this step.) Now the human mind is able to know in this exalted way only objects that are directly present to it. (This 'principle of acquaintance' is a consequence of the discussion of scepticism, above.) Finally, since human minds do sometimes have real knowledge in this exalted sense, it follows that they must occasionally come into direct contact with those ideal objects of knowledge.

For Plato, since the world around us is far from ideal, it follows that this direct contact occurred before this life, and that the knowledge we have now is only recollection. This of course implies the pre-existence of human souls or minds, before their entry into the body in this life. Descartes, by contrast, in effect abandons the principle of acquaintance. His theory of innate ideas, which yield real knowledge in the highest and most exalted sense, has them built into our very nature, put there by God, without our necessarily having had any direct cognitive contact with the objects of those ideas. As a result, Descartes is not committed to the pre-existence of souls, as Plato is. But for both Plato and Descartes, the knowledge we have by reminiscence or by innate ideas is knowledge by representation. The recollection of a direct encounter with a Platonic form is not itself that direct encounter; an innate idea, even if implanted by God, is still only an idea of its object, not an immediate encounter with it.

That is not enough for Augustine; for him, certain knowledge is immediate knowledge, not knowledge by representation. Hence he cannot accept either the old Platonic theory of

THE TOMB OF ST AUGUSTINE, rebuilt in the fifteenth century, in the church of S. Pietro in Ciel d'Oro in Pavia.

reminiscence or the later, Cartesian theory of innate ideas. When one has real knowledge, one is in direct contact with the ideal objects of that knowledge.

What are those objects? Since they are immutable, they must be divine; mutability, recall, is characteristic of creatures. Augustine interprets such objects as thoughts in the mind of God, 'divine ideas'. In effect, they are the old Platonic forms moved into God's mind. Philo of Alexandria (= Philo the Jew, d. *c.* AD 40) and others before Augustine had already made this move. It is a good question how the plurality of divine ideas is compatible with the simplicity of God.

The general theory of illumination, therefore, starts with such an exalted notion of knowledge and its objects that knowledge becomes strictly the prerogative of God. Creaturely minds are too changeable to be able to achieve the firm and abiding state of real knowledge under their own natural powers. If human beings nevertheless do sometimes have such knowledge, it is only because it has been gratuitously bestowed upon them by God. Such knowledge somehow involves a glimpse into the divine mind itself.

The Special Theory of Illumination

The weaker or special theory of illumination, by contrast, does not depend on Augustine's hierarchical view of reality or on such a lofty notion of knowledge. Even if Augustine was wrong about all that, there still appear to be certain kinds of knowledge human beings have that cannot be accounted for by their own powers. Such knowledge involves ideal concepts, limiting notions. These concepts are encountered most obviously in two main areas: (1) mathematics and geometry, including mathematicized physics or philosophy of nature (e.g. the concepts of perfect circle, geometrical point, Euclidean plane, frictionless surface, ideal gas, etc.), and (2) values (perfect justice, ideal beauty, etc.). Not coincidentally, it is in these two areas that different forms of Platonism have historically always been most appealing.

There is a difficulty in explaining how human beings have such concepts, and so any propositional knowledge involving such concepts. For plainly these concepts are not acquired by simply recording what is found in the empirical world around us. That world falls conspicuously short of such ideals; there is no perfect justice and there are no perfect circles exhibited in the familiar world. Moreover, it is hard to see how one could produce such ideal concepts by combining, somehow changing, or in general *doing* something to non-ideal concepts derived from the empirical world in the normal way.

One cannot, for example, form the notion of a perfect circle by observing various imperfectly circular coins and dinner plates, and then somehow mentally 'removing' their imperfections. One could not recognize that there is any imperfection to remove unless one already had the notion of a perfect circle, against which measure coins and dinner plates are found to fall short. For the same reason, neither can one simply say that the mind just 'recognizes' the shape these coins and dinner plates are approximating, or somehow just 'discerns' the limit toward which they are all converging. No doubt the mind does this, but how it *can* do this without already having the concept of the ideal to which the others are approximating or converging—that is the question. Nor can one plead that, while there are perhaps no perfect circles or true Euclidean planes in nature, there certainly are things perceptually indistinguishable from those ideals, so that the mind can derive ideal concepts directly from experience after all. For if there are observable things perceptually indistinguishable from those ideals, they are also perceptually indistinguishable from slightly lopsided circles or slightly lumpy planes. What does the mind do to distinguish the one pair of concepts from the other? Moreover, the 'indistinguishability' theory is not even initially plausible for values. Ideal justice, alas, is very definitely distinguishable from anything experience offers.

These considerations are perhaps not decisive. But they do indicate that there is at least a serious difficulty in explaining how one comes to have ideal concepts, and therefore any knowledge involving such concepts, in virtue of anything human beings can do themselves. Yet humans plainly do have such knowledge. Hence something like a theory of recollection (Plato), of innate ideas (Descartes), or of illumination (Augustine) seems to be called for. If one accepts the Augustinian view that the objects of any certain knowledge must be present to the mind directly, not merely through a representation, then recollection or innate ideas will not suffice and immediate contact with ideal objects will be needed. Once again, Augustinian illumination gives us a glimpse of the divine ideas.

Problems for the Theory of Illumination

The theory of illumination, in either form, raises perhaps as many problems as it solves. The first problem applies only to the general form of the theory: In what sense is knowledge by illumination 'human' knowledge? Who does the knowing? Knowledge is, at least in part, an *act* of a knowing mind. But on the general theory of illumination, the human mind is passive

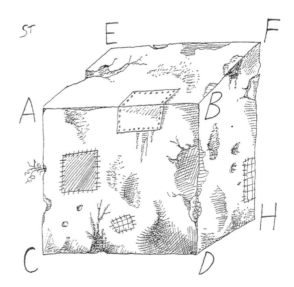

IDEAL AND ACTUAL. Platonists, like Augustine, see the objects of this world as imperfect approximations to a reality belonging to a world of pure intelligence. In this cartoon Sol Steinberg wittily relates the perfect cube of the geometer to the messiness of the everyday world.

ST AUGUSTINE'S THEORY OF ILLUMINATION owed much to the mystical passages in the Epistles of St Paul. This painting by Jacopo Amigoni shows Paul blinded by divine light on the road to Damascus.

and receptive; it is only the divine mind that acts and illuminates it. Again, if the human mind is passive in knowledge, then why is it one has to work so hard to get what little knowledge one possesses—years of schooling, study, and wide reading? In short, the general theory as it stands needs to be supplemented by an account that gives some active role to the human mind.

A second problem arises for both versions of the theory. If illumination involves a direct glimpse of the divine ideas, and if God's simplicity means there is no distinction between him and his ideas, then how does illumination differ from the direct encounter with God, the 'beatific vision' that is supposed to be reserved for the blessed in the next life? Illumination appears to put God's mind into direct contact with ours. We see 'face to face', not 'as in a glass darkly' (1 Corinthians 13: 12); the latter would be a mere representation, and spoil the point of the theory. Again, Augustine describes the direct vision of God as the ultimate goal of mankind (e.g. *On the City of God*, xix). But surely that goal cannot be reached in this life by anyone who cares to do a little mathematics or geometry. Salvation ought not to consist in adding a column of figures.

Third, who is illumined? Illumination looks a lot like the beatific vision. But apart from the problem when that vision is supposed to occur (namely, in the next life), it is also supposed to be reserved for the blessed, the saints. Yet even the most degenerate reprobate can learn a little geometry, an activity that requires illumination if anything does.

In effect, these problems are ones of 'nature' versus 'grace'. God gives a creature some things by nature; they are built into its very structure. But he gives some creatures more than that. He gives them supernatural things, things over and above what they get by nature. Such gifts are 'gratuitous', given by 'grace'. In this framework, the theory of illumination makes knowledge (some or all of it) a matter of supernatural grace. But supernatural knowledge, knowledge we have but could not get by means of our own natural power, is called 'revelation', is it not? In short, the theory of illumination tends to assimilate what appears to be purely natural knowledge, some or all of it, to revelation. Yet the ancient Greeks, who did not have the benefits of revelation, were strikingly good at mathematics and geometry, where illumination is required even on the weaker or special theory. How can this be?

All of this only shows that Augustine did not leave the theory of illumination as a finished theory. Further refinements and distinctions needed to be made. Later thinkers in the Augustinian tradition were left with much to do.

Boethius

Nothing of note happened in Latin philosophy between the time of Augustine and Boethius. Boethius was born *c*.480 into a distinguished old Roman family, the Anicii. His father died while Boethius was still young, and the child was adopted by the equally distinguished Symmachus (a descendant of the earlier Symmachus who tried to revive paganism in the 370s). By this time the old Roman families, including Boethius', were orthodox Christians, but the Ostrogothic administration of Rome under Theodoric was not; they were Arian Christians, whom the orthodox regarded as heretics. Despite this tension, Boethius rose to the position of *Magister officiorum* under Theodoric. There is no good modern equivalent of this office, but it was definitely a powerful post, combining both military and civil functions. Boethius was eventually entangled in political intrigue and charged with treason. He was put in prison and sentenced to death. While awaiting execution, he wrote his most famous work, *The Consolation of Philosophy*, in which he claims he was innocent; most scholars have been willing to believe him. Guilty or innocent, Boethius was executed in 524 or 525.

Boethius knew Greek, both the language and the intellectual heritage, and is one of the most important conduits through which Greek learning passed into the Latin West. In addition to the *Consolation* and several other works, he produced translations of Aristotle's *Categories* and *De interpretatione*, and of the *Isagoge*, an introduction to Aristotle's *Categories* by Porphyry, the pupil and biographer of Plotinus. Boethius seems to have translated other Aristotelian logical works too, but those translations did not circulate widely until much later. In addition, he wrote commentaries and several independent treatises on logical matters. Except for part of Plato's *Timaeus* (translated by Chalcidius) and the writings of a Pseudo-Dionysius the Areopagite (see below), the works translated by Boethius were the only primary texts of Greek philosophy generally available in the West until the twelfth century.

The Consolation of Philosophy

Boethius' *Consolation* is in effect a meditation on evil and the unreliability of fortune. Not surprisingly, there is much of Augustine in it. Boethius accepts Augustine's view both that evil is not an entity in its own right, but instead the privation of a good, and that creatures' free will is ultimately responsible for evil. Although he talks about all this at length in the *Consolation*, that is not what really bothers him there. His main concern is a slightly different

BOETHIUS THE PATRICIAN with his father-in-law Symmachus; an illustration from a ninth-century manuscript of Boethius' treatise on arithmetic.

question: Given all that, why is it that evil people in this world seem to prosper and the good suffer? Even if Augustine is right about the nature of evil and the responsibility for it, still why is nothing done about it? What Boethius is really asking in this work is 'Why am I in prison?'

Foreknowledge and Free Will

Philosophically, perhaps the most significant part of the *Consolation* comes in book v (the last book). There Boethius acknowledges that if creatures' free will is going to account for evil in the world, then their free will had better be compatible with God's advance knowledge of how they are going to behave. In short, it is the classic puzzle: If God knows in advance what one is going to do, then how can one have any free choice in the matter?

Augustine had already addressed this problem in *On Free Choice of the Will*, iii, but Boethius's treatment greatly advances the discussion. He clearly recognizes (as Augustine did not) that the question is not one of *causality*, whether the prior knowledge causes the future action or conversely. Instead, for Boethius, it is purely a matter of the logical relations between necessity, time, and knowledge.

One of the most frequently cited parts of Boethius' discussion makes the distinction between the necessity of a conditional and what might be called necessity 'under a condition'. In Latin as in English, to say 'If it is known that p, then necessarily p' is ambiguous. It can mean that the conditional 'If it is known that p, then p' is a necessary one—which is true (since one cannot know a falsehood), but in no way prevents its being a contingent matter of free will that p. Or it can mean that if it is known that p, then it is a necessary fact that p—which *would* imply that it is not a contingent matter of free will that p, at least not while it is known. But while the latter claim would indeed make foreknowledge incompatible with free will, there seems to be no reason to believe it is true in general.

Certainly any serious treatment of the problem must be clear about this distinction. But Boethius does not stop there. For there is something odd about the future. I do not know, for example, whether it will rain one year from today or not (in my locale); that is beyond my ken. But I do know, even now, that *either* it will rain then *or* it will not. The former is a matter of a contingent fact about the future (at least as far as I know); but the latter is a necessary fact.

The point can be generalized. What can be known about the future—not just predicted with confidence, but actually 'known'—seems to be confined to what is necessary. Thus, where p is a proposition about the future, it appears that we have not only the innocuous necessity 'If it is known that p, then p', but also the stronger, 'If it is known that p, then it is a necessary fact that p'. And in that case, foreknowledge is incompatible with free will after all.

Boethius meets this problem with an ingenious device. He moves God outside time. He was not the first to adopt this strategy, but in the Latin tradition he was the first prominent author to do so in the context of this problem. God, the theory goes, does not see events unfold one after another, as we do. He sees them all at once, in a kind of 'eternal present'. The ordering of events is preserved in God's perspective (he knows what precedes and what follows), but he does not *experience* them in sequence; they are all simultaneously 'present' to him. Just as, therefore, I can know present contingent facts as they occur, without in any way interfering with their contingency, so too God can know even our future free acts without in any way interfering with their contingency.

Boethius' solution has become a classic one, but its success is uncertain. If it works, it must be possible to translate, without loss of content, all propositions about past, present, and future (propositions that can change their truth value over time) into propositions about 'before', 'simultaneous with', and 'after' (which do not change their truth value over time). Whether this can in fact be done is a question for tense-logic; the outcome is not promising.

Universals

The problem of universals is the problem whether our general concepts correspond to general entities ('universals') in reality. If they do, then the philosopher is faced with the metaphysical problem of explaining what those entities are and how there can be such things. If they do not, then he is faced with the epistemological threat that our general concepts seem not to correspond with reality, so that any general knowledge of the world is impossible.

Boethius was the first Latin philosopher to discuss this problem in a serious way. He addresses it in several works, and there may in fact be more than one theory of universals in Boethius' writings. Probably the most influential discussion occurs in his longer commentary (the second of two) on Porphyry's *Isagoge*.

In the *Isagoge*, Porphyry systematically treated the notions of genus, species, difference, characteristic property, and accident. But in a prologue, he informed the reader that he would not be considering certain questions that are too difficult for an introductory work. In particular, he would not ask (1) whether genera and species are real entities or merely mental figments; (2) if they are real, whether they are corporeal or incorporeal; and (3) whether they are separated from sensible things (like Platonic forms) or built into them (like Aristotelian natures).

In this situation it was inevitable that commentators would feel obliged to say more about the questions Porphyry raised but conspicuously declined to answer. Boethius takes up the challenge. In the course of his discussion, he offers an admirable description of a universal. A universal is an entity shared by many things (*a*) as a whole, not part by part as, for example, a pie is shared by all those who take a slice; (*b*) simultaneously, not one after another as, for example, a used car may have many successive owners throughout its useful life; and (*c*) in such a way as to enter intimately into the metaphysical make-up of the things that share it, not in the merely external way in which, for example, an entire audience shares a public event as a whole and simultaneously. (Note that separated Platonic Forms appear not to be universals according to this description, in virtue of clause (*c*).)

Throughout the Middle Ages, this passage was taken to give one of the standard definitions of a universal. But it was not the only definition in circulation. At the beginning of *De interpretatione*, 7 (which Boethius translated), Aristotle had said: 'By "universal" I mean that which is apt to be predicated of many.' Predication, to be sure, is primarily a verbal relation. But in the Middle Ages authors often took that verbal relation to be based on a more fundamental metaphysical relation, which could also be called 'predication'. In terms of the Aristotelian definition, then, the problem of universals becomes: Are there entities that are 'metaphysically' predicated of many, or are there not?

The problem of universals was discussed in both its Boethian and its Aristotelian forms in the Middle Ages. Although there is no antecedent reason to think that one who believes in universals in the one sense must also believe in them in the other sense, in fact this was most often the case in the Middle Ages. But there were some interesting exceptions—for example, Peter Abelard in the twelfth century (see below).

Boethius himself, in his commentary on the *Isagoge*, adopts a view sometimes known as 'moderate realism'. (He says he is taking this theory from Alexander of Aphrodisias, the famous third-century AD commentator on Aristotle.) He denies that universals are real, but argues that this does not compromise general knowledge of the world. Our general concepts are based in reality, even though they are not based on general *entities* in reality. The device for making this work is in effect a theory of abstraction (what Boethius calls 'division'). The difficulty for Boethius, as for all moderate realist theories, is to explain clearly just how this abstracting (or dividing) works. On this, he has little to say.

Boethius returns to the problem of universals in other passages, among them several in a series of works known collectively as the *Theological Tractates*. Some of these passages supplement what he said in the commentary on Porphyry. But there are others, especially in his *On the Trinity*, that suggest a theory allowing universal realities after all. All these passages were widely read later in the Middle Ages, and spawned a great variety of later medieval theories of universals.

Pseudo-Dionysius and John Scottus Eriugena

The disintegration of Graeco-Roman culture, which had begun long before Boethius, continued and even accelerated after his death. Europe entered a long period of intellectual torpor, when learning in general and philosophy in particular were not widely cultivated. With one conspicuous exception, this state of affairs lasted until after the turn of the millennium. The exception was the 'Carolingian Renaissance' associated with Charlemagne (768–814) and his successors.

Charlemagne encouraged monastic and cathedral education throughout his realm, and gathered an international group of scholars at his own court. Among them was Alcuin of York (*c*.730–804), who turned the palace school into a serious educational institution. But perhaps the most distinguished figure of this renaissance was John Scottus Eriugena (*c*.810–77), who was at the court of Charlemagne's grandson Charles the Bald by 850.

As his name suggests, Eriugena was Irish by birth and education. At that time Ireland was called Scotia Major; hence the 'Scottus' in his name. He is sometimes called 'John the Scot', but is by no means to be confused with John Duns Scotus, who lived much later (see below).

In most of Western Europe, knowledge of Greek had virtually disappeared by the Carolingian period. But for some reason, it never wholly died out among the Irish monks. Eriugena knew Greek well enough to be thoroughly influenced by late Greek thought, including some of the Greek Church Fathers, and to translate Greek writings into Latin.

Among them were the works of a certain Pseudo-Dionysius the Areopagite. Eriugena's was neither the first nor the last medieval translation of this important author's works, but it was the most influential. The *Corpus Areopagiticum* consists of ten letters and four treatises: *On the Divine Names*, *The Mystical Theology*, *On the Celestial Hierarchy*, and *On the Ecclesiastical Hierarchy*. The first two treatises are the most important for philosophy.

The true identity of Pseudo-Dionysius is a mystery. He lived in the Near East, probably in the late fifth century, to judge by his philosophical views. But the man's real identity is not so important as his assumed identity. For the works ascribed to him claim to have been written by the Dionysius who heard St Paul preach on the Athenian Areopagus, and who, unlike the other philosophers gathered there, did not laugh at Paul but believed him (Acts 17: 33–4).

These writings were taken very seriously in the Latin West once they became generally known. Their putative author was an immediate disciple of the Apostle himself, so that their authority was second only to that of scripture. There was a certain awkwardness in this, since the doctrine contained in the writings is sometimes of dubious orthodoxy and on occasion quite discordant with the prevailing Augustinian tradition in the West. Their inauthenticity had been suspected from the very beginning, but not definitely established until the late nineteenth century.

For the Latin West, Pseudo-Dionysius is the proximate source of the familiar doctrine that there are three ways of speaking about God: (1) the *via affirmativa*, in which predicates are affirmed of God; (2) the *via negativa*, in which predicates are denied of him; and (3) the *via eminentiae*, which reconciles the first two ways and in which predicates are affirmed of God only with an indication of some kind of supereminence. Thus (1) we may call God 'good' in so far as he is the source or cause of all the goodness we find in creatures; but (2), if we wish to speak about God as he is in himself, not as he is related to creatures, we must deny all predicates of God, since he is not like any of the familiar things language is used to describe. In that sense then, God is not good, and in fact does not even exist! But the *via negativa* does not amount to outright atheism, as (3) shows. God in himself is not good and does not exist. But this does not mean that he is less than good or less than existing; rather he is 'super-good' or 'hyperexisting'—more than good, more than a being.

To say that God is 'above being' in this Neoplatonic way has epistemological implications. Given the traditional equation of being and intelligibility (as early as Parmenides' fragment 2), it means that God is strictly unknowable. As a result, in that part of the Western mystical tradition stemming from Pseudo-Dionysius, the direct encounter with God in mystical experience is described not in terms of light and intellect, but of darkness and the will (which can love even what it does not understand). Familiar phrases like 'cloud of unknowing' and 'dark night of the soul' are characteristic of this tradition. This is quite unlike the Augustinian view described above, which—on the authority of Exodus 3: 14—regards God not as above being but as the most real and therefore most intelligible being of all. Accordingly, when this latter tradition describes a direct encounter with God, it is in terms of intellect and light: a blinding flash, a 'beatific vision', even 'illumination'. The authority of Augustine and the supposed authority of Pseudo-Dionysius meant that neither viewpoint could be disregarded altogether. They maintained a sometimes uneasy coexistence throughout the Middle Ages.

Eriugena, Pseudo-Dionysius' translator, was strongly influenced by him and by other late Greek authors. As a result, his works often seem exotic and bizarre to those familiar only with the main Latin tradition. They seemed that way in the Middle Ages as well. Two of his treatises, *On Predestination* and *On the Division of Nature*, were condemned as heretical—the former twice during his own lifetime. Eriugena has been called everything from a pantheist to a great free-thinking rationalist. The correct assessment of his views is still a matter of dispute.

On the Division of Nature is no doubt Eriugena's *magnum opus*. It is a long dialogue in five books, offering a vision of reality that combines the Augustinian tradition with Neoplatonic themes from Pseudo-Dionysius and others. Despite the uncertainty of interpreting it, the work is probably the most systematic presentation of an overall philosophical view that the Middle Ages had yet produced. Nevertheless, although it was not entirely unused by later authors, it does not appear to have been widely influential.

Anselm of Canterbury

The Carolingian Renaissance was only temporary. It was not until after the turn of the millennium that Europe entered a new and prolonged period of cultural and social development. Philosophy participated in this general revival. Before about 1050 the significant medieval philosophers can be counted in single digits. But after that time the important, profound, and influential philosophers become so numerous one cannot keep track of them. Moreover, the style of philosophy changed as well. It became much less a 'visionary' enterprise, a matter of simply offering an interpretation of reality, and much more an argumentative discipline.

We see this already in St Anselm of Canterbury (1033–1109). Anselm was Italian by birth. But he later entered the Benedictine abbey of Bec in Normandy, and after the Norman Conquest became abbot there when the previous abbot, Lanfranc, became Archbishop of Canterbury. Eventually, Anselm himself went to England and succeeded Lanfranc at the see of Canterbury.

Anselm's emphasis on reasoned argumentation is appealing and familiar to present-day philosophers. At the same time, his writing has not yet acquired the layers of highly technical scholastic terminology that make later medieval philosophy so forbidding. For the non-specialist interested in reading primary texts, Anselm is thus perhaps the most readily accessible author.

Anselm wrote several important works, most of them at Bec. The most important of them

THE DEBT OF LATIN MEDIEVAL PHILOSOPHY to its Greek and Arabic forerunners is shown in this manuscript illustration portraying Averroes (*left*) and Porphyry.

are the *Monologion*, a systematic discussion of the existence and nature of God; the *Proslogion*, a much briefer discussion of many of the same topics, including Anselm's famous 'ontological argument' (see below); and *Cur deus homo* ('Why did God Become Man?', written while Archbishop of Canterbury), a dialogue on the Incarnation.

Anselm is interested in finding 'necessary reasons' for the truths of the faith. Thus, he not only tries to demonstrate the existence and nature of God in the *Monologion* and *Proslogion*, but in the former he even endeavours to find 'necessary reasons' for the Trinity, and in *Cur deus homo* to find 'necessary reasons' for the Incarnation. In all these cases, the 'necessary reasons' involved are available to our purely natural powers. In contrast to Augustine, in Anselm there is relatively little appeal to Scripture or the authority of the Fathers.

Although Anselm was criticized for this novel and extreme appeal to reason in religious matters, his was the way of the future. Later scholastic authors came more and more to view theology not simply as a matter of 'wisdom literature' but as a scientific discipline. But two things should be noted about Anselm's use of reasoning. First, he was not trying to prove the truths of theology as though they were otherwise subject to doubt. His purpose was not to shore up a faith that might otherwise falter, but rather simply to explore what he already firmly believed. His attitude is summed up near the beginning of the *Proslogion* in a famous statement: 'I believe in order to understand' (*Credo ut intellegam*). Second, Anselm did not think his appeal to reason excluded the realm of mystery in religion. In the *Monologion*, for example, he thinks he can prove that God is a Trinity of persons, but he does not think he can explain just how this works (see ch. 64).

Doubtless Anselm's most enduring contribution to philosophy is his so-called 'ontologi-

ANSELM'S PROSLOGION
in a twelfth-century
manuscript copy.

cal argument' for the existence of God. (The title is a later neologism.) In the introductory chapter of his *Proslogion*, Anselm tells us that after he had written the *Monologion*, he began to wonder whether it was possible to find a single argument that could accomplish in one fell swoop what the *Monologion* had laboriously established by a network of intricate reasonings. Finally, he hit upon the following ingenious argument (here reduced to its essentials): (1) By 'God', we mean 'that than which no greater can be thought'. (2) Suppose for *reductio* that than which no greater can be thought does not really exist. Nevertheless, (3) it can be *thought* to exist in reality. Now (4) that than which no greater can be thought is greater if it really exists than if it does not. Hence (5), from (3)–(4), it is possible to think of something greater than that than which no greater can be thought. Since (5) is contradictory, the hypothesis in (2) is false, so that by *reductio* (6) that than which no greater can be thought— that is, God—really exists after all. The premisses of this argument are (1), (3), and (4). (3) seems innocuous enough, and (1) is simply a definition that does express a unique property of, even if it does not exhaust, what we normally mean by 'God'. The real work of the argument is done by step (4).

Much ink has been spilled attacking or defending Anselm's argument. Too often it has been criticized without actually looking carefully at what it says. In fact, it has often been conflated with an entirely different kind of 'ontological argument' put forth by Descartes and others. Anselm does not say, for example, that 'existence is a perfection'; there is no talk of 'perfection' here at all. He does not say that everything that exists is *ipso facto* greater than everything that does not, or even that everything is *ipso facto* greater if it exists than *it* is if it does not; all he says is that the latter claim holds for the one very special thing he is talking about. The argument does not secretly presuppose, as is sometimes charged, that the notion of God is a consistent one (which premiss would presuppose it?), although of course if the argument is sound it *follows* that the notion of God is consistent, *ab esse ad posse*. Again, Anselm's argument does not depend, for all its talk of 'greatness', on any theory of absolute or objective 'greatness' or value. For the formal structure of the argument is exactly the same whether 'greater' means 'absolutely greater' or 'greater according to my own personal idiosyncratic ranking'. And it is surely possible to rank my private priorities in a way that verifies the premisses. Hence even if Anselm otherwise believed in a theory of absolute 'greatness' or value, as he no doubt did, assuming such a theory in no way affects his argument as it stands.

Finally, Anselm's argument has frequently been rejected on the grounds that it illicitly moves from the realm of pure concepts (the 'relations of ideas', as Hume called it) to the realm of actual existence ('matters of fact'). And that, it is said, simply cannot be done; otherwise, one could infer the existence of all sorts of spurious things from the mere fact that one can conceive them. But this refutation is frivolous. It in no way follows from Anselm's argument that one can infer the existence of just anything whatever from its mere concept. It only follows that one can do this in a certain special case, for the reasons given in the argument itself. Furthermore, it is not as if we can tell nothing at all about actual existence by inspecting concepts. One can quite correctly infer from the concept of a square circle, for example, that such a thing does *not* exist. Why should it be possible to infer the non-existence of things from their concepts, but not their existence? That would seem oddly asymmetric. In a word, this type of 'refutation' of the ontological argument seems nothing but a dogma that would try to refute the argument without actually taking the trouble to look at it.

Nevertheless, it appears there is *something* wrong with Anselm's argument. And it appeared so, to some at least, even in Anselm's own day. For a contemporary of Anselm's—a certain Gaunilo, a monk at Marmoutier—read Anselm's *Proslogion* and wrote a reply to it. Anselm had addressed his 'ontological argument' to the biblical Fool who 'says in his heart "There is no God"' (Psalm 14: 1). Gaunilo accordingly entitled his reply 'In Behalf of the Fool'. Of course Gaunilo no more seriously doubted the existence of God than Anselm did. But he thought he recognized a bad argument when he saw one.

Gaunilo's text is difficult and remarkably obscure. But one passage stands out. Gaunilo in effect claims that if Anselm's argument were sound, similar arguments could be used to prove the existence of ideally great things of any kind whatever. For example, he remarks, it is said that somewhere in the ocean there is an island than which no greater island can be conceived—called, for obvious reasons, 'The Lost Island'. Such an island is of course greater if it exists than if it does not, and so by Anselm's reasoning must really exist after all. The arguments are exactly parallel. Since the example is meant to be generalized, the implicit conclusion is that because arguments like Anselm's can be constructed to prove the reality of all sorts of bogus things, there must be something wrong with it.

Anselm wrote a reply to Gaunilo, and it is curious to look at his response to the Lost Island argument:

Now I say boldly that if anyone should find for me anything existing either in actual fact or in thought alone, except that than which a greater cannot be thought, to which he can fit the logic of this argument of mine, I will find and give him that Lost Island, not to be lost any more.

And that is all Anselm says about it! In other words, the Lost Island argument is *not* parallel to his own.

Nevertheless, it seems Anselm is mistaken. Gaunilo's argument is formally exactly like Anselm's. He merely restricts the domain of discourse; instead of discussing all thinkable things whatever, his argument is only about thinkable islands. But any argument that is valid within a wider domain of discourse remains valid within a narrower range of discourse. And since Gaunilo's argument, like Anselm's, does not presuppose any absolute or objective ranking of things, it is possible to verify the premises of Gaunilo's argument by a suitable choice of priorities of 'greatness'. In short, if Anselm's argument works, so does Gaunilo's. Since Gaunilo's plainly does not, neither does Anselm's.

But while Gaunilo has shown that something is wrong with Anselm's argument, he has

IBN SINA OR AVICENNA, as he was known in the Middle Ages, was a physician living in Iran who left more than a hundred works, some in Persian but mostly in Arabic, including influential commentaries on Aristotle. This is a page of a translation of his *Canon of Medicine*, illustrating urinoscopy.

done nothing to reveal where its failure lies. For that, thinkers must still exercise their utmost ingenuity. Anselm's argument remains one of the most intriguing and puzzling arguments of all time.

The Twelfth Century

By the time of Anselm's death in 1109, the revival of European culture and learning had acquired considerable momentum. Indeed, the twelfth century is another of those periods sometimes described as a 'renaissance'.

One occurrence in particular during the century changed the entire subsequent course of European intellectual life. Greek and Arabic writings began to be translated in great number, in Sicily, occasionally in Constantinople, and especially in Spain where Archbishop Raymond of Sauvetât (d. 1151) had set up a kind of school of translators at Toledo. The translations from these places included works of mathematics, medicine, and philosophy. By the early thirteenth century this wealth of newly available material began to act as a bracing shock to Western Europe. Suddenly learning was no longer just a matter of preserving a tradition; it was also a matter of dealing with new and sometimes quite unfamiliar ideas. For philosophy, the decisive translations were of course the remaining texts of Aristotle. By the end of the century most of his works were available in Latin, and in the early thirteenth century they were circulating widely. In addition, the writings of the great Arabic philosophers became available, most importantly Avicenna (Ibn Sina) (980–1037) and Averroes (Ibn Rushd) (1126–98)

Peter Abelard

Peter Abelard (1079–1142) had finished his career before the effects of these new texts were felt. Indeed, he is the last major medieval philosopher to do so. And a major philosopher he certainly was! Abelard's thought is exceptionally rich and original. He did important work in theology, ethics, and especially logic, but perhaps his most widely discussed views are those in metaphysics, especially the problem of universals.

Abelard discussed this problem in several different contexts; the most familiar of them occurs in the glosses on Porphyry's *Isagoge* contained in Abelard's *Logica 'Ingredientibus'*. There he discusses and argues against several contemporary theories before setting out his own. The first is a strongly 'realist' theory held by Abelard's teacher William of Champeaux, at one time master of the cathedral school at Paris and later of the monastic school at the abbey of St Victor outside Paris. William held in effect that Socrates, for example, is a kind of metaphysical 'layer-cake', built up of successive metaphysical ingredients: substantiality, bodiliness, life, animality, humanity, Greekness, and so on—each subsequent ingredient narrowing or specifying its predecessors. The individual, Socrates, is the sum total of all these ingredients. What makes this a 'realist' view, in terms of the definition of a universal given in Boethius's second commentary on Porphyry, is the claim that if one begins with

ABELARD AND HELOISE. Peter Abelard studied at Paris about 1100 before setting up his own school. His love affair with Heloise led to his being castrated by her uncle. Later he became Abbot of St Gildas in Brittany; he left behind a remarkable autobiography, *The Story of My Adversities*.

Socrates and Plato, say, and mentally removes all the ingredients after 'humanity', one ends up with *one* humanity common to Socrates and Plato—not two humanities, one for each of them.

Abelard rejects this theory as metaphysically incoherent. There is an important textual problem in this part of Abelard's discussion, but it appears that his arguments are inconclusive. They seem to depend on another claim of William's, that in the traditional schema of definition in terms of genus and difference (e.g. man = animal + rational), the difference-term contains an implicit reference to the genus (thus, rational = rational *animal* = man).

But William could surely have abandoned this latter semantic claim without compromising the fundamental realism of his theory.

Whatever the merits of the case, Abelard claims in his *Story of My Adversities* that as a result of his ingenious arguments, William was forced to abandon his theory and adopted instead another theory, according to which if one mentally removes all the ingredients of Socrates and Plato after 'humanity', one ends up with *two* humanities. The two are exactly alike, to be sure, but they are numerically two, not one.

Abelard goes on to report that he attacked William's second theory too, with the result that William was forced to abandon the problem of universals altogether, and his 'lectures bogged down in carelessness'. It was then that William retired to St Victor.

Abelard's main objection to William's second theory is not that it is incoherent; on the contrary, Abelard's own theory is quite similar. Rather his objection is that the theory is not a realist theory at all in the Aristotelian sense of there being non-linguistic entities that are 'predicated of many'. Abelard considers several variations on William's second theory, and in each case asks what it is on such a theory that is 'predicated of many' in this non-linguistic way. He can find no acceptable answer. Apparently the proponents of these theories thought of themselves as being realists in this Aristotelian sense. Abelard argues that they are not.

The correct interpretation of Abelard's own theory of universals is a matter of considerable disagreement. But on at least one plausible reading, he splits the difference. There *is* some metaphysical ingredient common to Socrates and Plato after all, as William's first theory had said. It is what Abelard calls the *status* of man, and is expressed by the infinitival phrase 'to be a man' (not by 'humanity'). This metaphysical ingredient, he insists, is not a 'thing', which seems to mean that it cannot be predicated and so does not fall into the recognized Aristotelian categories. (This qualification presumably disarms his own objections to William's first theory.) Nevertheless, it is real and serves as the metaphysical correlate of the general term 'man'. This theory saves the objectivity of our general claims about reality. It is 'realist' in postulating general entities that fit Boethius' description of a universal in his second commentary on Porphyry. But it is not realist in the Aristotelian sense; it does not allow that any non-linguistic entity is 'predicated of many'. Thus Abelard's theory eliminates any easy and simple connection between ontology and predication.

There are many complicating factors. In particular, Abelard links this entire account to a subtle theory of 'signification' and the psychology of language. It is impossible to rehearse these matters here, but they repay careful study.

Universities

During the twelfth century, the forms of medieval education developed and changed in important ways. Monastic schools, like Anselm's at Bec and William of Champeaux's at St Victor, had been responsible for the education of young monks and others assigned to their care since at least the time of Cassiodorus (*c.*477–*c.*570). In addition, from about 1050 or so, schools associated with individual teaching 'masters' were sometimes set up. Such masters

ST CATHERINE OF ALEXANDRIA was regarded during the Middle Ages as the patron saint of philosophy. According to her legend, the Emperor Maxentius (d. 312), who wished to marry her, summoned fifty philosophers to convince her of the errors of Christianity; but she vanquished them all in disputation, before being broken on the wheel by the enraged emperor. The disputation and martyrdom are here illustrated (*left*) in a diptych of the Danubian school, *c*.1520.

PHILOSOPHY AND MEDICINE were closely interwoven in the thought of Galen (AD 129–99) who was the most influential physician of the ancient world. In this French manuscript of the early fourteenth century (*below*) he is shown lecturing on the texts of the semi-legendary founder of Greek medicine, Hippocrates.

Carmi/
na qui
quon//
dā ſtu
dio flo
rēte p/
egi·
Flebi/
les heu
meſtos

cogor mire modus · Ecce michi la
cere· dictant ſcribenda camene ·

Et vꝛis elegi· flecibus oꝛa rigant
An vꝛeugꝺ ſcreef ic wi
len eer· Wat ic dichte
hets laes al ſeer Dus
es vꝛkeert dat eerſte ſcri
uē· dat ic desmoet mijn oghe wꝛiuē
Er eeren ende loue ons ꝓxꝛel
ven itꝛeſu xpꝛſti· ſiner liewer
moeder alle des ghꝛſinde wan
hꝛemelꝛike· emmer gods ende
haꝛer alder gꝛacie ende hulpe
lꝛoꝛen aenghꝛeꝛoupen Alſe
dat plato in ſine loue van tꝩ
meo leert te doene · So wil

A &

often moved from place to place, taking their students with them. Abelard ran such an individual master's school for a while (*c.*1104) at Melun.

Both these kinds of institution declined in importance after about 1150, although monastic schools survive to this day. Meanwhile, other kinds of school were developing at cathedrals, for the education of those entering the secular clergy. When Abelard studied under William of Champeaux, it was at the cathedral school of Paris. He also studied theology at another such cathedral school at Laon, under a master Anselm (not Anselm of Canterbury). These cathedral schools flourished between roughly 1000 and 1200.

The later medieval universities frequently grew out of such cathedral schools by the granting of a royal or ecclesiastical charter. The first universities began in Italy around 1150, and in France by about 1200. Oxford and Cambridge were somewhat later. It is worth remarking that the university is one of the few great medieval institutions (along with the Church and Parliament) to have survived more or less intact to the present day.

Once universities were firmly established, philosophy became an increasingly specialized academic discipline, increasingly distinct from theology. Philosophy was taught in the Faculty of Arts, which offered a kind of 'undergraduate' course of studies all students had to complete before going on to one of the 'higher' faculties. But theology, which appealed not only to reason but also to scripture, the Fathers, and the Church Councils, was taught in the separate Faculty of Theology as a kind of 'graduate programme'.

It is important to realize that much (but by no means all) of what is regarded as the best of late medieval philosophy is in fact the work of theologians. If one finds them appealing to scripture or Church dogma, it is not that they are illegitimately importing matters of faith into an argument that ought to be conducted on the basis of reason alone. On the contrary, they are simply doing their job as theologians. The modern reader must recognize that to read such texts with an eye to only their philosophical content is to adopt an artificially selective standpoint and to some extent to do violence to their authors' intentions. Still, having acknowledged this, there remains much good pure philosophy to be found in these theological texts.

The strictly academic context of late medieval philosophy is also responsible for an important change of style. A highly precise and technical scholastic vocabulary grew up, and a characteristic '*quaestio*' format for discussing issues was established that required an author to survey a sometimes quite long series of arguments on both sides of a question before giving his own opinion and replying to the preliminary arguments. (The *quaestio* format was used not only in writing but in live academic debate as well.) These factors make late medieval philosophy much more difficult for the non-specialist, and are what Renaissance humanists

THE CONSOLATION OF PHILOSOPHY of Boethius records how the lady Philosophy appeared to him in a dream. The page here reproduced is from the fifteenth-century folio edition of the work. On the lady's dress are embroidered the names of the seven liberal arts which formed the elementary curriculum of the medieval university: arithmetic, music, geometry, astronomy, grammar, rhetoric, and logic.

had in mind when they ridiculed scholastic 'pettifoggery' and obscurantism. But their complaints should not deter more patient readers.

Universities by their very nature bring many scholars together. Thus is it not surprising to find that the number of important philosophical thinkers after about 1200 grows enormously.

New Developments in Logic

Of Aristotle's remaining works (those apart from the *Categories* and *De interpretatione*, already known in Boethius' translation), the logical writings were among the first to be made newly available in the twelfth century in Latin translation. In particular, Aristotle's *Sophistic Refutations* began to circulate shortly after 1125. This little work had a great impact on the development of medieval logic.

Aristotle's treatise is a survey of fallacies of various kinds, how they arise and how to avoid them. Although there is a certain structure imposed on the discussion, it is clear even to the first-time reader that Aristotle's treatment is not exhaustive and could well have been organized differently. Moreover, when the work began to be known in Latin, thinkers were already very concerned about fallacies, which threatened to arise especially in discussions of the Trinity and the Incarnation, where great care must be taken to avoid outright inconsistency.

The theory of syllogistic (apart from modal syllogistic, which puzzled everyone—and does so to this day) was, with the exception of some minor points of detail, effectively exhausted by Aristotle himself; there was little that remained to be done there. The theory of demonstration developed in the *Posterior Analytics* was so difficult that it was only later that the medievals felt comfortable with it. Aristotle's *Topics* was such a miscellaneous grab-bag that there was little for medieval thinkers to do there either. But the *Sophistic Refutations* suggested much work remaining to be done on a timely topic the medievals could deal with without having already mastered the other intricacies of Aristotle's thought.

As a result of all these factors, there was a new emphasis on the logic of fallacies beginning in the mid-twelfth century. This concern seems to be responsible for many of the characteristically medieval contributions to logic. Thus, a genre of treatises *De sophismatibus* developed, in which various kinds of tricky reasoning were illustrated, discussed, and sorted out. Again, a genre *De syncategorematibus* developed to investigate the logical force of various puzzling expressions in language, like 'inasmuch as', 'except', 'only', and others. These treatises went far beyond anything that had previously been known in the history of logic.

Yet again, a cluster of logical genres grew up to deal with logico-semantical factors such as reference, tense, modality, equivocation, truth-conditions, and so on. These factors were collectively known as the 'properties of terms'. The logic that was developed to deal with them is known as 'terminist' logic. The main medieval contributions in this area were all in place by about 1350, although much interesting work continued to be done to the end of the Middle Ages.

The Augustinian Doctrinal Complex

In the thirteenth century, there was a loose cluster of doctrines that at first appear to be entirely independent of one another, yet in fact are often found together in the same authors—especially St Bonaventure and his Franciscan followers after mid-century. (Bonaventure will be discussed more fully below.) Such a grouping of doctrines has been called a 'doctrinal complex', and in the present case the doctrines involved are all broadly 'Augustinian'. But much had happened to them since the time of Augustine. They were affected and shaped not only by Boethius, Anselm, and others in the Latin tradition, but in the twelfth century by Avicenna and other authors who were translated then, especially a certain Solomon Ibn Gabirol (*c*.1021–*c*.1058).

Ibn Gabirol (= Avencibrol, Avicebron, and other variants) was a Spanish Jew who wrote in Arabic. As a result, many Latins thought he was a Muslim. He was the author of an influential *Fons vitae* ('The Fountain of Life'), which shows broad Neoplatonic influences. Such influences affected Augustine too, which no doubt accounts for the fact that so much of Ibn Gabirol's thought was readily incorporated into the basically Augustinian Latin framework.

Among the recurring themes in this 'Augustinian' doctrinal complex are realism with respect to the problem of universals, the theory of illumination, and a pair of doctrines called 'universal hylomorphism' and 'plurality of forms'.

The last two theories were constantly conjoined in medieval authors. The first of the pair claims that, with the single exception of God, everything is a composite of matter and form. This view is based on the twin principles that: (1) only God is absolutely simple, all creatures are in some way composite; and (2) composition is always a case of matter and form, something relatively or completely indeterminate and something else that determines it. It follows that all creatures contain some kind of matter. Physical objects have 'corporeal matter', but 'spiritual' creatures (e.g. angels or the soul) have a kind of matter too—'spiritual matter'. Augustine, as noted above, had already maintained that composition is characteristic of creatures. The term 'spiritual matter' likewise appears in Augustine (e.g. *Confessions*, XII. xvii. 25), although the notion is not developed there into a full theory.

This odd doctrine appears to assume a view of language and thought according to which whatever one can truly and affirmatively say about a thing reflects some real ontological property that determines the thing, apart from which property the thing is to that extent indeterminate. But what is indeterminate is 'material' with respect to 'form', which is what determines it. (Note that Pseudo-Dionysius' *via negativa* is a corollary: God's utter simplicity prevents one's truly affirming anything of him.) If these considerations do underlie universal hylomorphism, the fact explains why that doctrine was so often associated with the correlative theory of 'plurality of forms'. For there are in general many things one can truly affirm of a given object, and so many forms inhering in it.

Nevertheless, the term 'plurality of forms' is most often used in a more restricted sense, to refer to the kind of 'nesting' of forms that can be illustrated by the following series of predications (all referring to the same thing): 'This is a substance', 'This substance is corporeal',

'This corporeal substance is animate', 'This animate corporeal substance is sensate', 'This sensate animate corporeal substance is rational', and so on. In such a case, the sequence of predicates proceeds by genus and difference, each predicate answering to a distinct form inhering in the individual referred to. Thus if one defines man as a rational animal—that is, as a rational sensate animate corporeal substance—it is clear that man, by definition, has several distinct forms. Once the terminology of 'substantial form' came into circulation with the recovery of Aristotle's metaphysical writings, the theory of 'plurality of forms' was taken to be the claim that an individual substance has several substantial forms at once, nested according to the hierarchy of genus and difference.

Note that if the human soul has a kind of spiritual matter of its own, even after death when it exists apart from the corporeal matter of the body, then it seems that the soul is a complete Aristotelian substance in its own right. It is thus hard to see how it can reside in the body like an Aristotelian substantial form in uninformed matter, producing a single unified substance; for the soul is *already* a substance. Hence the hylomorphist view tends instead to regard the relation of soul to body in Platonic–Augustinian 'two-substance' fashion, as one substance's somehow inhering in another 'like a captain in his ship' or 'like a ruler in his city'.

If the soul is a substance in its own right, it must have its own proper activity, just as any substance has. Moreover, if it is a fully constituted substance even after death, it must be able to exercise its proper activity apart from the body. Such activity plainly cannot be physical activity, but rather a spiritual one—in short, knowing. Universal hylomorphism thus tends to favour a theory of knowledge that minimizes the role of sensation, and so to lead naturally to some version of the theory of illumination.

The alert reader will no doubt recognize in all this an uneasy mixture of Aristotelian ideas and vocabulary with traditional Augustinian themes. He will also recognize that the connections sketched among the various ingredients of this doctrinal complex do not amount to logical entailments but rather to pressures and tendencies. Different authors found different ways of working out the details.

Thomas Aquinas

For modern readers, St Thomas Aquinas (1224/5–74) is surely the most well-known thinker of the High Middle Ages. His reputation has been perhaps artificially enhanced by the fact that Pope Leo XIII, in his 1879 encyclical *Aeterni patris*, called Thomas 'the chief and master among all the scholastic doctors', and urged that 'thoughtfully chosen teachers apply themselves to introducing the doctrine of Thomas Aquinas into the minds of students and set its soundness and excellence clearly ahead of others'. Not surprisingly, such words led for a time to an exaggerated emphasis on Thomas's thought and to some distortion of both its originality and its content. To recognize this fact is by no means to minimize Aquinas' genuine importance.

Thomas was Italian by birth, although the most important parts of his career were spent at the University of Paris, which by that time had become the premier institution of learning in all Christendom. He joined the Dominicans in the early days of that order's existence, a fact that no doubt contributed to his becoming for subsequent generations the Dominicans' primary spokesman on matters of philosophy and theology.

The Assimilation of Aristotle

Aquinas has a well-deserved reputation for making Aristotle acceptable to Christian thinkers. The newly available translations of Aristotle came as a challenge to reflective and informed Christians. The theory of illumination, as it had left the hands of Augustine, had never quite succeeded in clearly distinguishing full-fledged knowledge, which required illumination, from revelation. Yet here was Aristotle, who plainly knew a great deal of importance and yet was a pagan without benefit of revelation. The situation was complicated by the fact that Aristotle's views were sometimes heterodox. He maintained the eternity of the world, for example, and his verdict on the immortality of the soul was at best ambiguous. Moreover, there was nothing in Aristotle's scheme of the cosmos corresponding to the Christian provident God. Note that the medievals did not have a comparable problem with Plato, since they did not possess any of his actual writings (apart from a portion of the *Timaeus*) and so knew about him only through the 'baptizing' filter of Augustine and other Church Fathers.

In this situation some authors concluded that Aristotle's errors just showed what could happen if one tried to reason without the help of revelation. Others, like Bonaventure, an almost exact contemporary of Aquinas, definitely knew and appreciated Aristotle, but nevertheless sided with the conservative Augustinian cause.

Aquinas was among the first to champion the new Aristotelianism and to break with, or at least to reinterpret radically, many of the doctrines that had come to be associated with traditional Augustinianism.

The Rejection of Universal Hylomorphism and Plurality of Forms

Throughout his career, for example, Aquinas resolutely rejected the twin doctrines of universal hylomorphism and plurality of forms. The latter he regarded as confusing substantial with accidental forms. As Thomas interpreted Aristotle, once a thing has a substantial form it is a substance, and any subsequent forms it might possess have to be forms of the kinds that inhere in already established substances—i.e. accidental forms. The notion that a substance might have several substantial forms at once is simply incoherent for Thomas; it misconstrues what a substantial form does. On his view, for example, a human being does not possess a plurality of substantial forms or souls: a 'vegetative soul', which makes him an organism and gives him life and the ability to grow, take in nourishment, and reproduce; a 'sensitive' soul, which adds sensation and the other powers associated not with organisms in general but with animals in particular; and a 'rational' soul, which adds rationality and so makes him specifically a rational animal or man. On the contrary, for Thomas a human being has a single, rational soul, which acts as the one substantial form and bestows vegetative and sensitive powers in addition to rational ones. Note how this theory departs from the view of predication and language that links the doctrine of plurality of forms with universal hylomorphism; for Thomas, language is not always a reliable guide to ontology.

The situation with hylomorphism is more complicated. For Thomas, claims (1) and (2) of the universal hylomorphist theory (that only God is absolutely simple, all creatures are in some way composite; and composition is always a case of matter and form) conflict with an important thesis of Aristotelian epistemology: (3) matter obstructs knowledge. This means two things for Aquinas. First, it means that matter on the part of the object of knowledge prevents the object's being known. It is form that is the principle of intelligibility, so that before anything can be understood about a material object, its matter must be mentally separated from its purely formal features. But second, it also means that matter on the part of the knower prevents its knowing. Aristotle had remarked (*De anima*, 3. 4. 429ª24–5) that the mind or knowing part of the soul cannot be 'mixed with the body'. Thomas interpreted this to imply that the knowing power must be the power of an utterly immaterial agent. Combined with the hylomorphist view that all creatures have some kind of matter, this thesis has the result that (4) only God is a knower, a conclusion that is plainly false. Even the most dedicated adherents to the Augustinian 'complex' would allow that human beings do have real knowledge, even if they need illumination from outside to help them achieve it.

In this situation, traditional 'Augustinians' rejected (3), at least as Thomas interprets it. For some of them, it is not just any matter that impedes knowledge, but only corporeal matter. Aquinas argues against this in *On Being and Essence*, and is unwilling to compromise (3) at all. For him, human souls are entirely immaterial in their inner structure, even though they are joined to the material body in this life.

Still, Aquinas grants the hylomorphists (1), that only God is absolutely simple and without composition. He holds this in part because he accepts the view, found in Avicenna and others, that any composition—whether of matter and form, of essence and accident, or whatever—requires an agent cause to put the components together. Indeed, that is what an agent or 'efficient' cause does: combines things. Thus, since God is a first cause, uncaused by anything further, he must be absolutely simple; but creatures, all of which are created by God as their efficient cause, are all composite. Aquinas must therefore find some other way, besides the composition of matter and form, for creatures to be composite. In short, his only way to avoid (4) is to deny the hylomorphists' (2). This he does for several reasons, not all of them involving his response to universal hylomorphism.

Existence

For Thomas, in order to have a composite creature, one does not need to have a composition of matter and form. That is one kind of composition, to be sure, but there is another, more basic kind, the composition of a thing's essence with its existence (*esse*). The distinction between essence and existence is absolutely crucial to understanding Aquinas' metaphysics.

ALBERT THE GREAT AND HIS PUPIL THOMAS AQUINAS are here shown greeting Dante and Beatrice in Giovanni di Paolo's illustrations to the *Paradiso*. Below are seated representatives of wisdom, including the Venerable Bede, St Ambrose, Isidore of Seville, Dionysius the Areopagite, Solomon, Boethius, Gratian, Peter Lombard, Richard of St Victor, and Siger of Brabant.

Although Aristotle had distinguished the question what a thing is (its essence) from the question whether it is (its existence), and although other authors (notably Avicenna) had built on this distinction, it was Aquinas who developed the notion of existence into an importantly new metaphysical factor.

For Aquinas, the existence of a thing is not of course its matter, since immaterial things exist too. But neither is existence a form. For in that case it would have to be either an essential form, so that one could no longer distinguish the question what a thing is from the question whether it is, or else an accidental form. But accidental forms are ontologically dependent on an already existing substance. Thus existence cannot be reduced to any of the recognized Aristotelian categories or principles; the notion of existence introduces an entirely new ontological dimension.

Material substances, for Aquinas, have an essence composed of prime matter and substantial form. But in addition there is another composition in them, between the composite essence and the act of existence. These two must in some sense be 'really' distinct, not a mere product of the mind's thinking, or else one could not really know what a thing is without knowing whether it is. Spiritual creatures, on the other hand, do not have an essence composed of matter and form; they are essentially immaterial. Nevertheless, there is still the composition of essence and existence in them. Only in God is there no composition at all; his essence is purely and simply his act of existing. God is '*ipsum esse subsistens*' (subsistent existence itself).

Aquinas' theory of existence has important applications throughout his thought. For example, existence plays the role of a principle of 'identity'; it is what makes an individual the individual it is. Thus, an individual human being is essentially a composite of body and soul. Yet after death, his individual soul survives apart from the body. Is there one individual or two here? For Aquinas, the separated soul is the same *individual* as the material human being, because the same act of existence is involved in both cases. But it is not the same *substance*, since the human being essentially has a body, whereas the separated soul is an immaterial substance. This is why it makes sense, for example, to pray to the saints—why the separated soul of St Peter that exists now is the same *individual* as the flesh and blood human composite *substance* that was destroyed long ago.

Although their theological import is patent, it would be a mistake to think that Aquinas' views on these matters are grounded solely on theological considerations. On the contrary, he has a remarkably large number of purely philosophical arguments to support the conclusions required by his theological convictions. This was plainly a matter to which Aquinas had devoted considerable thought.

Of course, many nuances and subtleties are required. For example, if God's essence is strictly identical with his existence, then presumably it is impossible to know what God is without knowing whether he is. Does this mean that Aquinas accepts Anselm's ontological argument? Again, if each individual has an act of existence distinct from its essence, and if God is just a pure act of existence, as Aquinas holds, then does this mean that the divine act of existence is also the existence built into creatures? If not, what could distinguish them? If so, then since existence is the principle of identity, would this not mean that everything that exists is ultimately the same individual—namely, God? A stronger version of pantheism can hardly be imagined. Aquinas addresses these questions and resolves them. But a complete account is beyond the scope of this chapter.

Bonaventure

Bonaventure (1221–74), like Thomas, was Italian by birth but spent the most important part of his career at the University of Paris. Whereas Thomas entered the Dominicans, Bonaventure became a Franciscan and eventually rose to the position of Minister-General of that order. Like Thomas, Bonaventure had a formidable mind. But unlike Thomas, who championed Aristotelianism and sought to incorporate it into Christian theology as much as possible, Bonaventure was profoundly suspicious of Aristotle and defended the more traditional Augustinian views. But Bonaventure's conservatism was by no means uninformed or reactionary. On the contrary, he definitely knew his Aristotle and was quite happy to adopt what he could of Aristotelian thought. But he regarded Aristotle has having made serious mistakes.

Aristotle's basic error, for Bonaventure, came in rejecting the Platonic forms. Bonaventure did not have the original texts of Plato, of course, and—like Philo of Alexandria, Augustine, and virtually everyone afterwards—interpreted Platonic forms as thoughts in the mind of

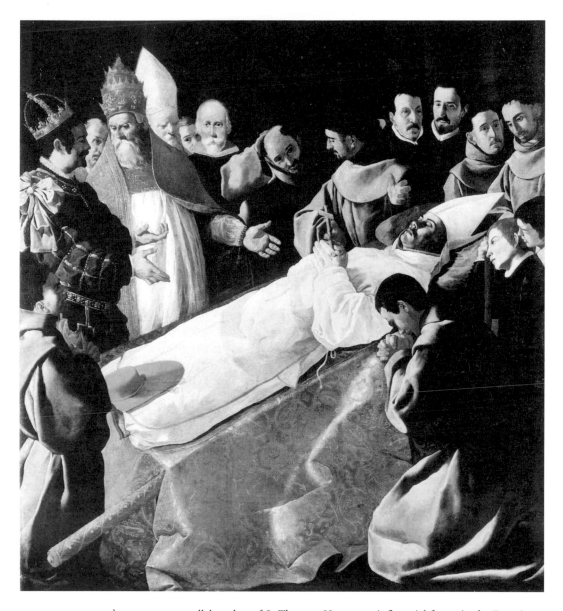

ST BONAVENTURE's career ran parallel to that of St Thomas. He was an influential figure in the Franciscan Order as St Thomas was in the Dominican Order. Both studied Aristotle, but Bonaventure took a more unfriendly and conservative attitude to his philosophy. Bonaventure's death, here portrayed by Zurbaran, took place in the same year as Aquinas'.

God (divine ideas). By rejecting these, Bonaventure thought, Aristotle committed himself to several further errors.

First, there is no providence.

Second, the world is eternal, without beginning or end. It is perhaps hard to see how this follows from the denial of divine ideas, but in any case Aristotle certainly held it. Note that

Bonaventure thought he could prove philosophically that the world had a beginning in time. Aquinas argued that the question could not be decided philosophically either way, although theologically the case was clear.

Third, since the world—and therefore presumably the human species—was without beginning, there can be no personal immortality of the soul. Either souls do not survive death at all, or else there must be some 'sharing' of souls, as in theory of transmigration or in the Arab version of Aristotelianism, according to which the mind or intellect is (in whole or in part) a single, separated entity shared by all men. The reasoning here is based on the quite straightforward Aristotelian view that there cannot exist an actual infinity of things. But if the succession of human generations has been going on from all eternity, and if each human being has his own individual soul that is immortal, then it follows that there are an infinite number of human souls now existing.

Fourth, if there is no personal immortality, then there is no personal reward or punishment after death.

These are not small matters. Bonaventure put his finger on exactly those features of Aristotelianism that were the most difficult for Christian thinkers to deal with. Moreover, one must be very careful about selectively rejecting certain of Aristotle's doctrines while accepting the rest. A philosopher's views tend to be related and interconnected. Bonaventure thought that in the rejection of Platonic forms, he had found Aristotle's fundamental mistake, the one that tied the others together.

The Later History of the Theory of Illumination

As described above, Augustine left the theory of illumination unfinished, with many ambiguities and unanswered questions. Bonaventure did a great deal to clarify the situation. He agreed with Augustine that real knowledge was fixed and immutable, and so were its objects. He likewise agreed that nothing in the created world could provide such exalted objects of knowledge. Only the 'eternal reasons' (divine ideas) were as immutable as that. Hence we need something like Augustine's 'illumination' in order to have knowledge.

Everyone recognized that 'illumination' is a metaphor. Bonaventure wanted to understand what the metaphor really meant. He considered three ways of interpreting the Augustinian theory.

1. On one interpretation, the divine ideas are the 'sole and entire reason' for human knowledge. Besides the divine ideas and the human mind, nothing else is needed and nothing else will help. On this view, the divine ideas are the *objects* of knowledge, since nothing else is involved. But this interpretation, Bonaventure observes, conflates ordinary knowledge in this life with the beatific vision, the 'face-to-face' knowledge of God that is supposed to be reserved for the blessed in the next life. It confuses knowledge by reason with knowledge by revelation, knowledge by our natural powers with knowledge by supernatural grace. We have seen all these difficulties before.

2. For these reasons, Bonaventure considers a second interpretation. This time, the divine ideas are not the objects of knowledge, but nevertheless play a necessary role in man's having knowledge, just as the light from the sun plays a role in seeing things even when one is not looking directly at the sun itself. Although some recent scholars have argued this is the correct way to interpret Augustine, Bonaventure claims one has to distort the texts to get them to support such an interpretation. Moreover, on this view, what exactly is the 'necessary role' of the divine ideas? Bonaventure calls it an 'influence', a kind of concurrence of the divine ideas with the human mind. He considers two sub-theories about what this might be.

a. Is it simply a particular case of God's general contribution to the natures of things? God is a prime mover and creator, and so 'influences' his creatures by the mere fact of giving them the natures they have. But if this is all illumination involves, then man's purely natural cognitive faculties are sufficient for real knowledge after all, contrary to Augustine's plain intent. This is in effect to abandon the theory of illumination altogether.

b. Yet if the divine role in illumination goes beyond the general influence of God on the natures of things, then it is a 'supernatural' influence, and many of the problems with interpretation (1) return. (Not all of them. Interpretation (2*b*) does not conflate the beatific vision with knowledge in this life.)

If the theory denying that the divine ideas are objects of knowledge is unacceptable, and so is the theory that affirms this and goes on to say that nothing else is needed, then perhaps the acceptable solution is the one Bonaventure himself adopts, that (3) divine ideas are indeed objects of knowledge in illumination, but they are not the only such objects. In addition, there is the creaturely object, which the mind grasps through a concept produced by ordinary, natural human powers. (This and the fact that the mind's view of the divine ideas is not a 'clear' one are what distinguish illumination from the beatific vision.) In knowledge by illumination then, there is a legitimate and necessary role for human cognitive powers; they are just not sufficient.

Bonaventure's discussion clarifies many of the issues, but it is not certain that his own theory will work. First, it seems to be false as a matter of experience that the mind has two objects before it in real knowledge, a divine one and a created one. But second, it seems that the problems with (2*b*) (and so some of the problems with (1)) have still not been adequately addressed.

Authors after Bonaventure continued to struggle with these problems. But even in Bonaventure's own day, Thomas Aquinas had in effect abandoned the theory of illumination altogether, as would John Duns Scotus shortly afterwards. (On Scotus, see below.) For Thomas, the theory of illumination was an attempt to explain how man's purely natural powers are insufficient to account for his purely natural knowledge—that is, for knowledge acquired by using only purely natural powers. No wonder there were difficulties! Nevertheless, rather than abandon the authority of Augustine altogether, Thomas was willing to describe as 'illumination' the purely natural activity of that part of the mind Aristotelians

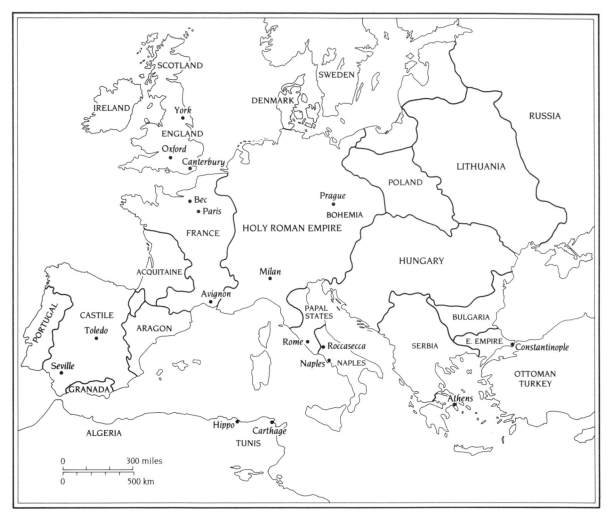

EUROPE IN THE FOURTEENTH CENTURY. This represents the configuration of Europe at the height of medieval philosophical activity in the years just before and just after 1300.

called the 'agent intellect'. (Aristotle himself had used the terminology of light in this context.) Scotus later did the same thing. In effect, Thomas and Scotus were adopting interpretation (2*a*) above.

Universals, Individuation, Unity, and Distinction

In the thirteenth and fourteenth centuries, the problem of universals and related questions were discussed with a seemingly infinite variety of nuances and opinions. Aquinas adopted what is sometimes called a 'moderate realist' theory, rather like (if one does not press the point) the view Boethius propounded in his second commentary on Porphyry's *Isagoge*. Other opinions ranged from the strongly realist theory of Walter Burley (*c.*1275–1344/5), reminiscent perhaps of the view Abelard reported as William of Champeaux's first theory, to an uncompromising rejection of real universals altogether by William of Ockham. (On Ockham, see below.)

These views are complicated and subtle, and it is impossible in a small space to rehearse even the most important of them without over-simplification and distortion. What can be done, however, is to point out some of the new forms the discussions took and some of the new factors that influenced those discussions.

For example, sometimes the metaphysical status of universals was not treated directly, but only indirectly in the context of the correlative 'problem of individuation'. There are several forms of the latter, not always clearly distinguished by medieval authors any more than they are today. Thus, the problem of individuation can mean, among perhaps other things: (1) What is it that makes something an individual (rather than a universal)? (2) What is it that makes an individual the individual it is? (This was called the 'principle of identity' above.) (3) What is it that allows there to be more than one individual in the same species? Aquinas' answer to (2) and perhaps also to (1) is to be found in his notion of existence or *esse*, but his answer to (3) appeals to matter and in particular to what he calls 'designated' matter, a remarkably obscure notion.

But perhaps the most striking new feature of the discussions in the High Middle Ages is the extent to which questions of unity and distinction have entered the picture. In earlier centuries, the problem of universals was generally asked in terms of the *being* of universal entities: With respect to Boethius' definition of a universal in his second commentary on Porphyry, what is it, if anything, that is metaphysically 'common to many' in the way Boethius describes? With respect to the Aristotelian definition of a universal in terms of predication, what is it (apart from mere words or concepts) that is 'predicated of many'? The problem of universals was still discussed in these forms with great sophistication in the thirteenth and fourteenth centuries, to be sure, but in addition new questions were asked involving unity and distinctness. For example, what is the connection, the 'unity', between a universal and its particulars?

Such questions, in their medieval form, can seem remarkably obscure and foreign to present-day philosophers as much as to present-day laymen. Perhaps the following illustration will help. Consider a pile of three bricks, *ABC*, as in the accompanying figure. One can regard

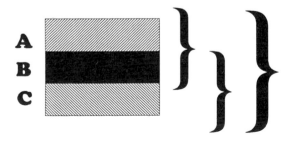

A QUESTION OF UNITY. In the pile of bricks ABC, B is common as a whole, simultaneously, and in a metaphysically constitutive way, to AB, BC, and ABC. Why then is it not a Boethian universal?

them as in a sense a single entity; they are, after all, one pile of bricks. Nevertheless, it is equally legitimate to consider the sub-pile *AB* and the distinct sub-pile *BC* as single entities too. Notice that, in apparent accordance with Boethius's definition of a universal, brick *B* is 'common' to *AB*, to *BC*, and to *ABC* 'as a whole', 'simultaneously', and in such a way that *B* enters into the 'metaphysical make-up' of *AB*, *BC*, and *ABC*. Yet it would seem that brick *B* is hardly what philosophers mean by a universal; it is just an ordinary brick, after all.

The example illustrates a general question: What is the difference between the kind of unity a mere pile or heap has and the kind of unity a genuine 'individual' is supposed to have? To get clear on this difference is to get clear on the difference between the way in which something can be a part of several wholes at once and the way (if any) in which a universal is supposed to be 'common' to several individuals at once. And to do that is an indirect way of getting clear on what one thinks about universals.

The Influence of Avicenna

This new emphasis is due in part to the influence of Avicenna, newly available in Latin translation. Avicenna had maintained that universals or 'common natures' possess a kind of ontological status of their own. They are certainly not completely nothing in themselves, since there are important philosophical jobs for them to perform. Yet they are not full-fledged beings in the way individuals are. On their own they have a kind of lesser being—an *esse essentiae*, the kind of being essences have, as distinct from individuals. Nevertheless, with respect to the question whether these universals or 'common natures' were in themselves one or many, Avicenna had said that the question simply did not arise. In effect, he had allowed degrees of 'being', but not degrees of 'unity'.

When this view was translated into the Latin West, it of course conflicted with the Augustinian equation of being and unity. If one accepted the Avicennian theory of a 'lesser being' for universals, one would therefore be required to contrive a theory of 'degrees' of unity and distinction as well. To be sure, authors familiar with Augustine's hierarchy of being were, in virtue of the same equation, already familiar with the notion of degrees of unity too. But it had not previously been directly applied to the problem of universals.

John Duns Scotus

Some of the most original and exciting work in this area was done by the Franciscan John Duns Scotus (*c*.1265–1308). Corresponding to the lesser grade of being common natures have, Scotus distinguished a 'real minor unity' or identity for them, 'real' because it is not merely the work of the mind, but 'minor' because it is less than the strict unity or identity of an individual. Individuals, in the usual scholastic terminology, were said to have 'numerical' unity or identity, to be 'numerically' one. The criterion for such unity is 'indiscernibility': Individuals *A* and *B* are numerically identical if and only if whatever is true of the one is true of the other. But universals or common natures do not have this kind of unity. For example,

JOHN DUNS SCOTUS teaching, as represented in an illuminated letter at the beginning of a manuscript of his *Ordinatio* from Rovigo.

the animality in Socrates is a rational sort of animality, but the animality in Browny the donkey (a favourite medieval example) is an irrational animality. Hence the animality of the one and the animality of the other cannot be numerically the same animality. Yet Scotus thought there must be some sense in which animality *is* the same in Socrates and Browny. Hence, real minor unity. (Plainly, many additional steps needed to forestall objections have been omitted here.)

Along with the real minor unity common natures have, Scotus distinguished a correlative kind of non-unity or distinction. This is the justly celebrated 'formal' distinction. It is notoriously difficult to state this distinction precisely in a way that accommodates all the relevant texts of Scotus, and indeed at different times in his career Scotus appears to have intended two quite different versions of it. The details are still subject to scholarly debate.

If the formal distinction is one of Scotus' best-known legacies, the notion of 'haecceity' or 'thisness' is another. Oddly, the actual term 'haecceity' is perhaps not Scotus' own (the manuscript evidence is not clear), but the theory itself is certainly his. In brief, haecceity is Scotus' answer to the 'problem of individuation'. Three forms of the problem of individuation were distinguished above. The theory of haecceity seems to be addressed primarily to the second of them: What is it that makes an individual the individual it is? (Depending on one's interpretation of Scotus, it may also answer the other forms as well.)

Just as the specific difference is what 'contracts' a genus to a species, so too an 'individual difference' is what contracts a lowest species to an individual. For example, it is what is added to *man* to get Socrates. Scotus argues that such an individual difference must, among other requirements, (1) be something positive, not merely the absence or negation of something; (2) combine with the specific nature to form a substantial unity, not a loose, merely accidental unity; and (3) be something that is not 'conceivable' by the mind. This last does not mean that the mind cannot grasp it at all. It means rather that the intellect has only a kind of 'job description' for an individual difference (clauses (1)–(3) are parts of that description); the mind knows what an individual difference does, but because for Scotus the proper object of the intellect is common natures, the intellect does not have any direct grasp of what it is that satisfies that job description. 'Haecceity' or 'thisness' is simply the name for whatever does that job.

It is worth pointing out that, although of course the details are very different, haecceity plays a role for Scotus much like the role of existence for Aquinas. Each is at the very heart of its author's views, each is mysterious in the sense that there is no proper concept to be had of it (for Aquinas, this is because the intellect knows forms and *esse* is not a form), and each is responsible for making an individual the individual it is. With such striking similarities, it is all the more important to sort out the differences.

William of Ockham

William of Ockham (*c.*1285–1347) was, like Scotus, a Franciscan. But on philosophical matters, and many theological ones, they were poles apart. Ockham uncompromisingly rejected the existence of real universals or common natures, whether in Scotus' version or in anyone else's. He thought they were theoretically unnecessary and, at least in some versions, conceptually incoherent. He defended these views with a large number of powerful arguments. And in this, he thought he was following the true teaching of Aristotle against others who had adulterated Aristotelian doctrine with foreign elements from Plato or the Arabs.

Ockham's theory of universals has been called 'nominalism' on the grounds that only names (including concepts, which for him counted as 'names' in a mental language) are for him truly 'predicable of many'. Only they satisfy the Aristotelian definition of a universal in terms of predictability. Nothing whatever satisfies the Boethian definition of a universal in terms of being 'common to many'.

For Ockham, the long-standing search for a 'principle of individuation' was simply so much wasted effort and ink. Things do not need to be 'individuated'; they are individual from the outset—they simply come that way. What needs to be explained instead is, given that there is absolutely nothing common between one individual and another, how the mind can nevertheless form universal or general concepts that somehow correctly apply to several individuals at once. In short, one does not need a metaphysical 'principle of individuation'; one needs an epistemological 'principle of universalization'. On this, Ockham is honest enough to admit that he simply does not know the answer. In forming universal concepts, he says, 'nature works in a hidden way'. Nevertheless, it is clear that the focus has been shifted in Ockham from a metaphysical question to an epistemological one.

There is another theme in Ockham that has sometimes also been called a kind of 'nominalism', even though it is entirely independent of his denial of universal entities. (Indeed, 'nominalism' is a term used for a wide variety of claims, and one ought always to be quite explicit about what one means by using it.) This other, independent theme is Ockham's programme of reducing the list of ontological categories to two only: substance and quality.

WILLIAM OF OCKHAM. A sketch on the last leaf of a manuscript in Gonville and Caius College, Cambridge, dated 1341. The inscription reads 'Frater Ockham iste'.

Ockham thought and argued that the other eight traditional Aristotelian categories could be eliminated in favour of these two alone. They were simply abbreviated manners of speaking about substances and qualities. This part of Ockham's philosophy is a matter of some dispute. Although he repeatedly claims that such reductions are in principle possible, it is striking that he does not provide even a single satisfactory example of such a reduction. The examples he does offer are all of incomplete reductions; propositions containing terms in the other Aristotelian categories are parsed in terms of other propositions, but those other propositions do not by any means contain only substance and quality terms (and logical particles). This odd situation has made some modern scholars wonder whether Ockham's ontological programme has not perhaps been misunderstood.

Although there is no doubt Ockham was a monumental and influential thinker, his influence is not always to be found where one has been told to look for it. For example, his logical writings have been regarded as influential, and indeed decisive, in shaping late medieval logic. But his influence in this respect has been grossly exaggerated. Sometimes indeed his logical views have been associated with his metaphysics, so that one hears of Ockham's 'nominalist logic'.

Nothing could be further from the truth. To be sure, much of what Ockham says about logic is found in later authors as well. But in almost every such case, Ockham is not being original in those passages, and is simply repeating common doctrine. For example, his account of 'personal supposition'—that is, the kind of reference a term has when it refers to things of which it can be truly predicated (despite the name, these things need not be 'persons')—has sometimes been described as a vehicle for Ockham's nominalist programme against universals because it appeals only to individuals and not to any common natures. Yet a view that works almost exactly the same way (in some cases the correspondence is almost verbatim) was held by Walter Burley (*c*.1275–1344/5), who was a realist about universals. (In other respects, to be sure, Ockham and Burleigh disagreed strongly.)

Contrariwise, where Ockham does hold idiosyncratic logical views that were not common coin of the realm, those views are typically *not* the ones that caught on and were influential afterwards. For example, his theory that propositions with tenses other than the present, or with explicit modal words like 'possibly' or 'necessarily', are ambiguous and need to be read in one of two distinct senses differs from the more common theory that such propositions have a univocal reading involving the disjunction of those two readings, which is quite another thing altogether. There are many other differences of terminology and doctrine as well.

None of this of course is to deny the importance of Ockham's thought, or its subtlety. It is only to raise doubts about claims of influence where they do not appear to be warranted.

Beyond Aristotle

Aquinas, Scotus, and Ockham have traditionally been the 'big three' figures in accounts of later medieval philosophy. But certainly a great many others were active too during this late

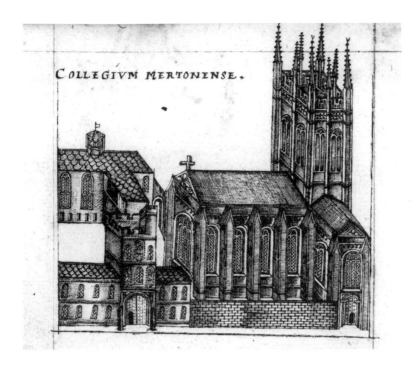

COLLEGIVM MERTONENSE.

period, and many deserve serious consideration. Nevertheless, only a few can be mentioned here, and they only very briefly.

As early as the late thirteenth century, and certainly by the mid-fourteenth, the main outlines of Aristotelianism had become familiar enough to the Latins that some authors began to find not just theological problems with Aristotle's views but straightforward philosophical problems as well. It was no longer only a matter of conservatives defending traditional views against Aristotelian novelties; in some cases it was a matter of going beyond Aristotle in altogether new directions.

At Merton College, Oxford, for example, a group of logicians and philosophers of nature began after *c.*1320 to develop the physics of motion and change in ways that went far beyond Aristotle, often applying mathematical techniques to solving physical problems. This practice would have a distinguished future, and indeed some direct influence, as early modern science developed in later centuries. Mathematical techniques were so characteristic of Mertonian physics that these authors were sometimes referred to as the 'Calculators'. On the Continent, John Buridan (*c.*1295/1300–after 1358) and others were responsible for other non-Aristotelian developments in physics, including the 'impetus' theory of projectile motion.

Again, there were difficulties with the Aristotelian theory of knowledge. For Aristotle's metaphysics, individual substance was the primary and most basic kind of being. Thus, given the equation of being with intelligibility (an axiom accepted by virtually all medievals, as it had been by the Greeks), it ought to follow that individual substances are the most fully intelligible of all entities. Yet Aristotelian epistemology, as the medievals understood it, emphasized that the object of the intellect was the universal, not the individual. Aristotle of course was thinking primarily of demonstrative 'science' in his very strict sense, but the fact remains that he offered no good account of how the mind can have any knowledge of individuals that goes beyond mere sensation. Aquinas had discussed this problem to some extent, but it was not until Scotus and Ockham and their theories of 'intuitive cognition' that a sustained effort was made to deal with it.

Some authors made a more radical break with Aristotle. Thus at Paris Nicholas of Autrecourt (*c.*1300–after 1350) rejected Aristotelianism entirely. He had not found a single demonstration in all of Aristotle, he declares, that is really certain! Nicholas wanted to ground all our natural certitude (as distinct from the certitude of faith) on the principle of non-contra-

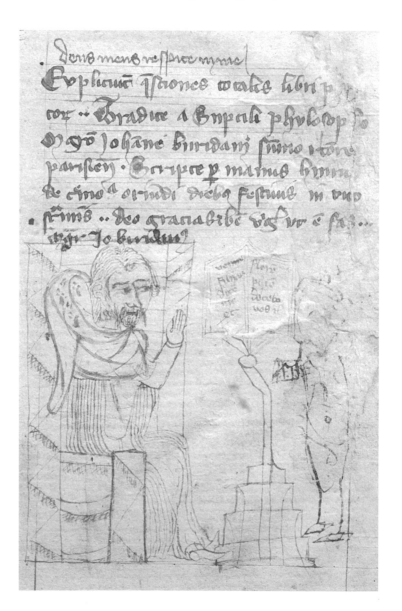

JOHN BURIDAN TEACHING. From a Paris manuscript of *c.*1370. The inscription in the open book reads, in translation, 'Come, sons, hear me and I shall teach you the flower of philosophy'.

diction, supplemented it seems by experience. (Some of his arguments simply make no sense without the supplement.) He went on to argue that there is no sufficient reason to believe in Aristotelian substances and that it is impossible to demonstrate the existence of God philosophically. Indeed, contrary to the Aristotelian ideal of demonstrative science, Nicholas stated that it is impossible ever to demonstrate the existence of one thing from the existence of something else. As a result, he is sometimes (recklessly) called 'the medieval Hume'. Nicholas's views were not widespread, and indeed his main work was condemned at Avignon in 1346. But they do indicate that the intellectual climate was definitely changing.

After about 1350, for reasons not yet fully understood, the level of philosophical work in England declined dramatically. Certainly the plague had something to do with it, but that cannot be the whole story. Relatively few names of philosophical authors are known from this period. What little is known of their work indicates that, while it is sometimes sophisticated, it is generally derivative and unoriginal. There are a few exceptions, the most prominent of which is John Wyclif (*c*.1330–84). Wyclif's views were highly idiosyncratic, and are only beginning to be understood. He was a staunch realist about universals, although his views on the question are perhaps not as extreme as his rhetoric about it. Wyclif appears to have had a considerable influence in England and, because of his link with John Hus, in Bohemia.

On the Continent, things were different. Buridan's numerous students continued his work, and in the late fourteenth and fifteenth centuries there was a flourishing of interest in Italy in the work of earlier English philosophers, particularly the Mertonian 'Calculators'. Again, at Paris and elsewhere there was for a time a very spirited and subtle debate over the problem of 'future contingents' and the related issues of free will and predestination. Much of this work is very good, and some of it is original. Still, it is not ground-breaking. Certainly there was no one in these twilight years of the Middle Ages with the stature of an Aquinas, a Scotus, or an Ockham.

3

Descartes to Kant

ANTHONY KENNY

THE writings of the classical philosophers of the seventeenth and eighteenth centuries in Europe form a continuous and coherent chapter in the history of philosophy. Despite the many differences of doctrine between them, the major philosophers between the time of Descartes and the time of Kant address a broadly similar agenda by broadly similar methods. When Descartes wrote, the Aristotelian tradition had come to the end of the productive development of the Middle Ages; after Kant's death, European philosophy began to fragment into schools which barely communicated with each other. But in the period between Descartes and Kant the differences between 'empiricist' philosophers in Britain and 'rationalist' philosophers on the Continent were minor in comparison to their shared presuppositions and goals.

On the surface, however, the philosophy of the seventeenth and eighteenth centuries was less homogeneous than the philosophy of the Middle Ages had been. In Western Europe, medieval philosophers wrote entirely in Latin: now, though a number of classic works, such as Descartes's *Meditations* and Spinoza's *Ethics*, appeared first in Latin, philosophers began to produce major works in the national languages of their own country. A scholar who wishes to read the great works of this period in the original must know English, French, and German as well as Latin.

There are other contrasts between medieval philosophy and this early modern philosophy. Medieval philosophy, like medieval architecture, had been the work of a tradition. Individual scholars built on the work of previous generations and presented even their most original ideas in the form of commentary on the writings of their predecessors. In the modern period, the history of philosophy, like the history of architecture, becomes a procession of outstanding individuals, each with a personal style, each proud of marking an epoch. All the major philosophers of the High Middle Ages were firmly based in educational institutions, such as monasteries or universities; but the best-known philosophy texts in the two centuries before Kant were the work of authors who were not university teachers. In

FRANCISCI
DE VERULAMIO,
Summi Angliæ
CANCELLARIJ,
Instauratio
magna.

Multi pertransibunt & augebitur scientia.

Anno

LONDINI
Apud Joannem Billium
Typographum
Regium.

1620

this period the typical philosopher is as likely to be found in an embassy or at court as in a college.

Medieval philosophers were professionals who produced their voluminous works for other professionals; they employed technical language and wrote in structured formats. The great philosophers of the early modern period could write brief and polished treatises to catch the attention of the general reader, female as well as male. The printing press had made it possible for a thinker to communicate with a public much larger than the colleagues and pupils of a lecturer in a medieval school. Only with Kant shall we encounter a front-rank philosopher whose whole life was lived in a university, and whose favoured output was the academic lecture, even though those lectures turned into printed books which were read world-wide.

The philosophy of the early modern period is no longer clerical. Medieval philosophers were, without exception, bishops, priests, monks, or friars: henceforth almost all the major philosophers are laymen. George Berkeley, to be sure, was a bishop, but in his day even bishops lived at some remove from religious enthusiasm.

As a result of the Reformation and the wars of religion there was a new relationship between philosophy and theology. Not that philosophers ceased to believe in God: of the major figures of the period only Hume was an atheist, and the concept of God plays a fundamental role in the philosophies of Descartes, Spinoza, and Berkeley. What had changed was the attitude to ecclesiastical hierarchy. No longer was the teaching authority of the Catholic Church regarded as supreme. Britain and northern Europe had rejected it in favour of various forms of Protestantism. The effect of the split in Christian Europe was to permit philosophical speculation to enjoy greater liberty from theological constraint.

It was not that individual Christian denominations necessarily became more tolerant of dissent. On the contrary, the thought control exercised by the Counter-Reformation in the seventeenth century was more thorough and rigid than anything in force in medieval Christendom. In Protestant countries too philosophers had to be on guard against charges of heresy, as Descartes and Spinoza were to experience; and as late as 1793 Kant was forbidden by his king to write on religious topics. What was important was that philosophers on different sides of the religious divisions could read each other's works and could communicate with each other. They were thus constantly made aware of the limits of religious consensus.

The authority of scripture, though almost universally acknowledged, was weakened by the variety of interpretations imposed by different authorities. Those who studied the Bible most seriously approached it from a literary or mystical standpoint rather than treating it as a source of illumination on philosophical topics. The dangers of doing otherwise were shown in the case of Galileo. The Inquisition condemned him on the grounds that his teaching that the earth went round the sun was in conflict with texts of the Old Testament. This condemnation of heliocentrism quickly became a dead letter, among Catholics as well as Protestants.

FRANCIS BACON's life (1561–1626) and writings illustrate the secularization of philosophy in the seventeenth century. No cleric, but a lawyer and politician, he had a great faith in empirical methods of observation and experiment. The front page of his *Novum Organum* (1620)—whose title throws down a challenge to Aristotle— shows the ship of knowledge setting sail onto the new ocean of science.

Throughout the Middle Ages the unquestioned scientific authority had been Aristotle; for St Thomas Aquinas he was *the* philosopher; for Dante he was 'the master of those who know'. In the first half of the seventeenth century this situation was changed, for ever, by the man who came to be known as the father of modern philosophy, René Descartes.

Descartes

Descartes was born in Touraine in 1596, at about the time Shakespeare was writing *Hamlet.* Though he was born and died a Catholic he spent most of his life in Protestant Holland rather than in his native country, Catholic France. He was educated by the Jesuits, and fought, briefly, in the wars of religion. He was a layman in both the ecclesiastical and the professional sense. He was a man of the world, a gentleman of leisure living on his fortune; he never lectured in a university and commonly wrote for the general reader. His most famous work, the *Discourse on Method,* was written not in the Latin of the learned world, but in good plain French.

Descartes was a man of quite extraordinary genius. Nowadays it is his philosophical works which are most read: in his own time his reputation rested as much on his mathematical and scientific works. He was the founder of analytical geometry, and the Cartesian co-ordinates that every schoolchild learns about derive their name from the Latin form of his name, Cartesius. In his thirties he wrote a treatise on dioptrics which was a substantial contribution to the science of optics, the result of careful theoretical and experimental work on the nature of the eye and of light. He also composed one of the first scientific treatises on meteorology, and he has a claim to have been the first to discover the true nature of rainbows.

The culmination of his early scientific work was a treatise called *The World.* In it he set out to give an exhaustive scientific account of the origin and nature of the universe, and of the working of the human body. Like Galileo he adopted the then unusual hypothesis that the sun, and not the earth, is the centre of our universe. As he was completing his work he learnt of Galileo's condemnation; he decided not to publish his treatise, and kept it in his files until his death. By the time he was 40, he had acquired a reputation among a circle of friends as something of a genius, but he had still not published a word.

In 1637 he decided to publish his dioptrics, his geometry, and his meteorology; and he prefaced these works with a brief *Discourse on Method.* The three scientific treatises are now read only by specialists in the history of science; but the preface is reprinted every year, has been translated into more than a hundred languages, and is still read with pleasure by millions.

In the first place, it is a delicious piece of autobiographical writing: vivid, urbane, ironic. A few extracts will give its flavour.

GALILEO's belief that the earth went round the sun was shared by Descartes. But after learning of Galileo's condemnation, Descartes kept this opinion to himself. (Portrait by J. Susterman.)

as soon as my age allowed me to pass from under the control of my instructors, I entirely abandoned the study of letters, and resolved not to seek after any science but what might be found within myself or in the great book of the world. So I spent the rest of my youth in travel, in frequenting courts and armies, in mixing with people of various dispositions and ranks and in collecting a variety of experience.

from college days I had learnt that one can imagine nothing so strange and incredible but has been said by some philosopher; and since then, while travelling, I have realised that those whose opinions are quite opposed to ours are not, for all that, without exception barbarians and savages; many of them enjoy as good a share of reason as we do, or better.

it is by custom and example that we are persuaded, much more than by any certain knowledge; at the same time, a majority of votes is worthless as a proof, in regard to truths that are even a little difficult of discovery; for it is much more likely that one man should have hit upon them for himself than that a whole nation should. Accordingly I could choose nobody whose opinions I thought preferable to other men's; and I was as it were forced to become my own guide.

The *Discourse* presents, in an astonishingly small compass, a summary of Descartes's scientific views and of his philosophic method. He had the gift of presenting complicated philosophical doctrines so elegantly that they appeared fully intelligible on first reading and yet still provide matter for reflection to the most advanced specialists. He prided himself that his

PHILOSOPHICAL MEDITATION. In the *Discourse on Method* Descartes describes his philosophical vocation as having come to him in 'an oven'. A late riser, throughout his life he was much concerned with keeping warm during his waking hours. This sketch in a letter to a friend illustrates a philosophical method of preventing a chimney from smoking.

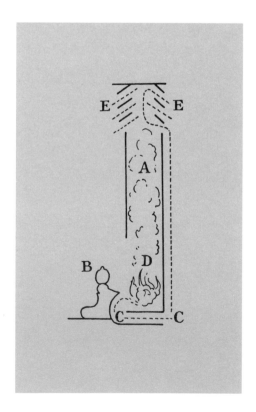

works could be read 'just like novels'. Indeed, his main ideas can be so concisely expressed that they could be written on the back of a postcard; and yet they were so revolutionary that they changed the course of philosophy for centuries.

If you wanted to put Descartes's main ideas on the back of a postcard you would need just two sentences: man is a thinking mind; matter is extension in motion. Everything, in Descartes's system, is to be explained in terms of this dualism of mind and matter. Indeed, we owe to Descartes that we think of mind and matter as the two great, mutually exclusive and mutually exhaustive, divisions of the universe we inhabit.

For Descartes, a human being is a thinking substance. In the tradition of Aristotle, a human is essentially a composite of soul and body; disembodied existence, if possible at all, is a maimed and incomplete human existence. For Descartes, man's whole essence is mind. In the present life our minds are intimately united with our bodies but it is not our bodies that make us what we really are. Moreover, mind is conceived in a new way: the essence of mind is not intelligence but consciousness, awareness of one's own thoughts and their objects. Humans are the *only* conscious animals; all other animals, Descartes believed, are merely complicated, but unconscious machines.

For Descartes, matter is extension in motion. By 'extension' is meant what has the geometrical properties of shape, size, divisibility, and so on; these were the *only* properties which Descartes attributed, at a fundamental level, to matter. He offered to explain all of the phenomena of heat, light, colour, and sound in terms of the motion of small particles of different sizes and shapes. Descartes is one of the first systematic exponents of the idea of modern Western science as a combination of mathematical procedures and experimental methods.

Both of the great principles of Cartesian philosophy were—we now know—false. In his own lifetime phenomena were discovered which were incapable of straightforward explanation in terms of matter in motion. The circulation of the blood and the action of the heart, as discovered by the English physician John Harvey, demanded the operation of forces for which there was no room in Descartes's system. None the less, his scientific account of the origin and nature of the world was fashionable for a century or so after his death; and his conception of animals as machines was later extended by some of his disciples who claimed, to the shocked horror of their contemporaries, that human beings too were only complicated machines.

Descartes's view of the nature of mind endured much longer than his view of matter: indeed, throughout the West, it is still the most widespread view of mind among educated people who are not professional philosophers. It was later to be subjected to searching criticism by Kant, and was decisively refuted in the present century by Wittgenstein, who showed that even when we think our most private and spiritual thoughts we are employing the medium of a language which cannot be severed from its public and bodily expression. The Cartesian dichotomy of mind and body is, in the last analysis, untenable. But it is a measure of the enormous influence of Descartes that even those who most admire Wittgenstein think that his greatest achievement was the overthrow of Descartes's philosophy of mind.

Descartes said that knowledge was like a tree, whose roots were metaphysics, whose trunk was physics, and whose fruitful branches were the moral and useful sciences. His own writings, after the *Discourse*, followed the order thus suggested. In 1641 he wrote his metaphysical *Meditations*, in 1644 his *Principles of Philosophy* (an edited version of *The World*), in 1649 a *Treatise on the Passions*, which is largely an ethical treatise. The 1640s were the final, most philosophically fruitful, decade of his life.

Methodical Doubt

One way in which Descartes profoundly influenced later philosophy was by his insistence that the first task for the philosopher is to rid oneself of all prejudice by calling in doubt all that can be doubted. This gives epistemology, that is to say the methodical study of what we can know and how we can know it, pride of place in philosophy. The second task of the philosopher, having raised these doubts, is to prevent them from leading to scepticism. This

THE TREE OF KNOWLEDGE was not an idea invented by Descartes. Here is an illustration from a scholastic textbook which shows the tree of knowledge growing under the guidance of those pre-Cartesian gardeners Aristotle and Aquinas.

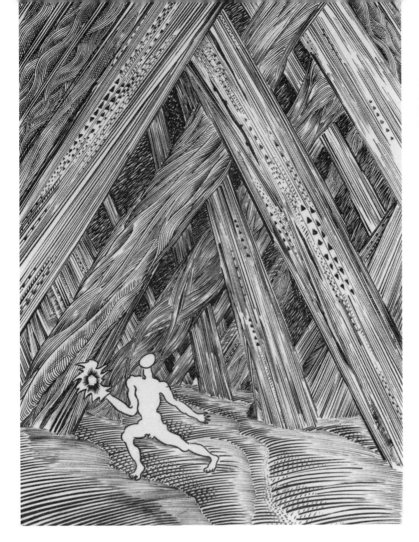

DESCARTES IN THE
FOREST OF DOUBT as
imagined in the engravure
of Roger Vieillard.

strategy comes out clearly in Descartes's *Meditations*. Here are some extracts from the First Meditation, in which the sceptical doubts are raised.

What I have so far accepted as true *par excellence*, I have got either from the senses or by means of the senses. Now I have sometimes caught the senses deceiving me; and a wise man never entirely trusts those who have once cheated him.

But although the senses may sometimes deceive us about some minute or remote objects, yet there are many other facts as to which doubt is plainly impossible, although these are gathered from the same source; e.g. that I am here, sitting by the fire, wearing a winter cloak, holding this paper in my hands, and so on.

A fine argument! As though I were not a man who habitually sleeps at night and has the same impressions (or even wilder ones) in sleep as these men do when awake! How often, in the still of the night, I have the familiar conviction that I am here, wearing a cloak, sitting by the fire—when really I am undressed and lying in bed!

Well, suppose I am dreaming . . . Whether I am awake or asleep, two and three add up to five, and a square has only four sides; and it seems impossible for such obvious truths to fall under a suspicion of being false.

But there has been implanted in my mind the old opinion that there is a God who can do everything, and who made me such as I am. How do I know he has not brought it about that, while in fact there is no earth, no sky, no extended objects, no shape, no size, no place, yet all these things should appear to exist as they do now? Moreover, I judge that other men sometimes go wrong over what they think they know perfectly well; may not God likewise make me go wrong, whenever I add two and three, or count the sides of a square, or do any simpler thing that might be imagined? But perhaps it was not God's will to deceive me so; he is after all called supremely good.

I will suppose, then, not that there is a supremely good God, the source of truth; but that there is an evil spirit, who is supremely powerful and intelligent, and does his utmost to deceive me. I will suppose that sky, air, earth, colours, shapes, sounds and all external objects are mere delusive dreams, by means of which he lays snares for my credulity. I will consider myself as having no hands, no eyes, no flesh, no blood, no senses, but just having a false belief that I have all these things. I will remain firmly fixed in this meditation, and resolutely take care that, so far as in me lies, even if it is not in my power to know some truth, I may not assent to falsehood nor let myself be imposed upon by that deceiver, however powerful and intelligent he may be.

These doubts come to an end when Descartes produces his famous argument to his own existence. However much the evil genius may deceive him, it can never deceive him into thinking that he exists when he does not. 'Undoubtedly I exist if he deceives me; let him deceive me as much as he can, he will never bring it about that I am nothing while I am thinking that I am something.' 'I exist' cannot but be true when thought of; but it has to be thought of to be doubted; once this is seen it is indubitable.

Cogito ergo sum

Descartes's argument is usually presented in the terser form in which he elsewhere presents it: *Cogito ergo sum*: 'I think, therefore I exist'. With these few words he brings his doubt to an end, and from these few words he seeks to discover the nature of his own essence, to demonstrate the existence of God, and to provide the criterion to guide the mind in its search for truth. No wonder that every word of the *cogito* has been weighed a thousand times by philosophers.

'I think'. What is 'thinking' here? From what Descartes says elsewhere, it is clear that any form of inner conscious activity counts as thought. How important is the 'I' in 'I think'? In ordinary life he used 'I' to talk about the human being René Descartes; is he entitled to use 'I' in a soliloquy when he doubts whether there is anybody answering to that name? Should he really have said only 'There is thinking going on'? If he had, would he have been able to reach his conclusion?

'Therefore'. This word makes the *cogito* look like an argument from a premiss to a conclusion. But elsewhere Descartes speaks as if his own existence is something he intuits immediately, not something he infers indirectly. Probably he intended it to be an inference, but an

THE ANGELIC DOCTOR (*left*). This portrait of Aquinas, by Justus of Leiden, is the one with the best claim to be an actual likeness of the saint.

THE BRETHREN OF ST FRANCIS (*right*). The Order of Friars Minor, or Franciscans, produced many of the best philosophers of the Middle Ages, including St Bonaventure (shown here with the founder St Francis), John Duns Scotus, and William Ockham.

immediate inference, not one which presupposes some more general principle such as 'Whatever thinks exists'.

'I exist'. If the premiss should have been 'Thinking is going on', should the conclusion be only 'Existing is going on?' Critics have argued that the doubting Descartes has no right to conclude to an enduring, substantial self rather than to a fleeting subject for a transient thought. How can he assume that the 'I' revealed by the Cartesian doubt is the same as what, unpurified by doubt, he called 'René Descartes'? Once the link has been severed between body and mind, how can we be certain of the identity of the thinker of the *Meditations*?

This question was later to be pressed home by Kant. Let us waive it for the present, and ask, with some of Descartes's contemporary critics, how 'I think, therefore I am' differs from 'I walk, therefore I am'. Descartes's answer is that as an argument one is as good as another; but the premiss of the first is indubitable, whereas the premiss of the second is vulnerable to doubt. If I have no body, then I am not walking, even if I believe I am; but however much I doubt, then by the very fact of doubting, I am thinking.

Sum res cogitans

In the rest of the *Meditations* Descartes proceeds to answer the question '*What* am I, this I whom I know to exist?' The immediate answer is that I am a thing which thinks (*res cogitans*). 'What is a thing which thinks? It is a thing which doubts, understands, conceives, affirms, denies, wills, refuses, which also imagines and feels.' 'Think' is being used in a wide sense: for Descartes, to think is not always to think *that* something or other. For him, it is consciousness that is the defining feature of thought. 'I use this term to include everything that is within us in such a way that we are immediately conscious of it. Thus, all the operations of the will, the intellect, the imagination and the senses are thoughts.'

An unclarity runs through Descartes's account. It is not clear whether, in a conscious thought, thought and consciousness are identical (my thought is a form or species of consciousness), or whether consciousness is something which accompanies thought (I don't just *have* the thought, I am *conscious* of having it). The ambiguity has consequences for Descartes's epistemology, since he was hoping to find indubitable certainty in the immediacy of thought. If thoughts are a form of consciousness, then there are some thoughts (e.g. pains) which are neither true nor false. If consciousness is an accompaniment of thought, then the possibility seems open for the consciousness to occur in the absence of the appropriate thought and thus be false. (If, for example, I think I understand a piece of geometry

THE MYSTERY OF FAITH. A major concern of medieval thinkers was to effect a reconciliation between classical philosophy and Catholic theology. One of the most remarkable results of this was the theory of transubstantiation, which used the Aristotelian notions of substance and accident to express the doctrine that in the Eucharist the bread and wine turn into the body and blood of Christ. Thomas Aquinas was a leading proponent of the Eucharistic piety represented in this nineteenth-century painting by Ingres.

DESCARTES' PORTRAIT was painted several times in his lifetime. The best-known portrait is that by Frans Hals in the Louvre; this less-known one by Bourdin shows an older, and perhaps less self-confident, sitter.

when in fact I do not.) What Descartes needs is something which *can* be true and *cannot* be false.

The thing which thinks is a thing which 'understands, conceives'. Apart from volitions, that is to say the acts of the will, Descartes says that all modes of thought can be called perceptions or operations of the intellect. Perceptions which are both clear and distinct are the operations of the intellect *par excellence*. Understanding the proposition '2 + 2 = 4' would be an instance of perception; but making the judgement that the proposition is true, asserting that two and two are indeed four, is an act not of the intellect but of the will. The intellect provides the ideas which are the content on which the will is to judge. It is, as it were, the intellect which provides the unasserted propositions, and the will which affirms or denies them. In many cases, the will can refrain from making a judgement about the ideas which the intellect presents; but this is not so when the intellectual perception is clear and distinct. A clear and distinct perception is one which forces the will, a perception which cannot be doubted however hard one tries. Such is the perception of one's own existence produced by the *cogito*.

In addition to understanding and perceiving, then, a thinking being affirms and denies, wills and refuses. The activity of the will consists in saying 'yes' or 'no' to propositions (about what is the case) and projects (about what to do). Descartes attributed to the human will two key properties: one was infinity and the other was freedom. 'The will, or freedom of choice, which I experience in myself is so great that the idea of any greater faculty is beyond my grasp.' In humans it is the will which is the especial image and likeness of God.

We must distinguish, however, between two kinds of freedom. One kind of freedom (sometimes called 'liberty of indifference') is the ability to choose between alternatives; another kind of freedom (sometimes called 'liberty of spontaneity') is the ability to follow one's desires. Descartes valued the latter much more than the former. Clear and distinct perception, which leaves the will with no alternative but to assent, takes away liberty of indifference but not liberty of spontaneity. The human mind is at its best when assenting, spontaneously but not indifferently, to the data of clear and distinct perception.

Finally, the *res cogitans* 'imagines and feels'. Imagination and sensation are understood by Descartes sometimes broadly and sometimes narrowly. Taken in the broad interpretation, sensation and imagination are impossible without a body, because sensation involves the operation of bodily organs and even imagination was conceived by Descartes as being the inspection of images in the brain. But taken in the narrow sense—as they are in the definition of the *res cogitans*—sensation and imagination are nothing other than modes of thought. As Descartes puts it, as he emerges from his doubt: 'I am now seeing light, hearing a noise, feeling heat. These objects are unreal, for I am asleep; but at least I seem to see, to hear, to be warmed. This cannot be unreal, and this is what is properly called my sensation.'

The upshot of the Cartesian doubt and the *cogito* is Descartes's conclusion that he is a thing that thinks, a conscious being. But is that *all* he is? Well, at this stage, this is all that he is certain of. 'There is thought: of this and this only I cannot be deprived. I am, I exist; that is certain. For how long? For as long as I am thinking; maybe if I wholly ceased to think, I should at once wholly cease to be. For the present I am admitting only what is necessarily

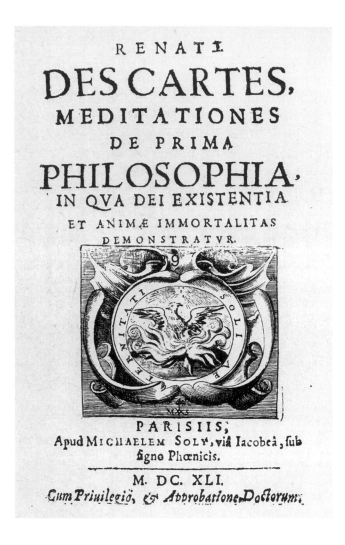

true; I am, with this qualification, no more than a thinking thing.' Later, Descartes concludes 'my essence consists solely in the fact that I am a thinking thing'.

It is fallacious to argue from

It is not known for certain that I have any essence other than thought

to

It is known for certain that I do not have any essence other than thought.

Critics of Descartes are to this day undecided whether or not he committed this fallacy. What is certain is that his eventual conclusion—that he does indeed have a body as well as a mind—is reached only by a roundabout route, involving an appeal to the existence and truthfulness of God. And even after drawing this conclusion Descartes continues to believe that mind and body are separable from each other: he can clearly conceive each of them separately, and whatever he can think apart, God can set asunder.

Mind and Body

Human beings in this world are, Descartes agrees, compounds of mind and body. But the nature of this composition, this 'intimate union' between mind and body, is one of the most puzzling features of the Cartesian system. The matter is made even more obscure when we are told, in the Sixth Meditation and in *The Passions of the Soul*, that the mind is not directly affected by any part of the body, except the pineal gland in the brain. All sensations consist of motions in the body which travel through the nerves to this gland and there give a signal to the mind, which calls up a certain experience.

The transactions in the gland, at the mind–body interface, are highly mysterious. Is there a causal action of matter on mind or of mind on matter? Surely not, for the only form of material causation in Descartes's system is the communication of motion; and the mind, as such, is not the kind of thing to move around in space. Or does the commerce between brain and mind, like intercourse between one human being and another, take place through messages and symbols? If so, then the mind is in effect being conceived as a homunculus, a man within a man. The mind–body problem is not solved, but merely miniaturized, by the introduction of the pineal gland.

These difficulties in Descartes's system were quickly noted in his own day. One of his most perceptive critics was Princess Elizabeth of the Palatine, the niece of King Charles I. 'How can soul move body?', she asked. Surely motion involves contact, and contact involves extension, and the soul is unextended. In reply, Descartes told her to think of gravity, of the heaviness of a body which pushes it downward without there being any surface contact involved. But this notion of gravity, as Elizabeth was quick to point out, was one which Descartes himself regarded as a scholastic muddle.

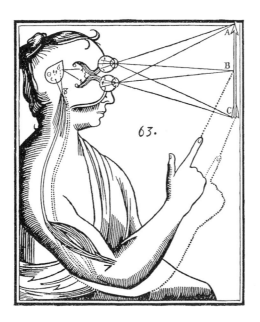

THE PINEAL GLAND in the brain, according to Descartes, is where body and mind interact. The physiological diagrams in his works show how perception and motion in the body are all controlled by this gland.

THE SOUL AS HOMUNCULUS. Medieval artists quite explicitly represented the soul as a small human body inside a large human body, as in this mosaic of the creation of Adam in S. Marco in Venice. Descartes's theory of the transactions between the soul and the pineal gland is guilty of the same fallacy in a more subtle fashion.

'I could more readily allow', she wrote, 'that the soul has matter and extension than that an immaterial being has the capacity of moving a body and being affected by it.' Descartes told her to feel free to do so, since to attribute matter and extension to the soul was simply to conceive it as united to the body. But this answer was hardly fair. Extension as defined by Descartes could not be a genuine attribute of soul as defined by Descartes: the one is divisible and the other indivisible.

Elizabeth undoubtedly had the better of this exchange, and the great philosopher was reduced to telling her not to bother her pretty head further about the problem. It was very harmful, he told her, to occupy one's intellect too much with meditating on the principles of metaphysics, which interfered with the leisure to exercise one's imagination and senses.

It is difficult to reconcile Descartes's dualism with his insistence, in the face of some of his academic critics, that in the present life mind and body are a single thing. It is only because he trusts in the truthfulness of God that he can be certain even that he has a body. This means that the establishment of God's existence is a crucial step in the construction of his philosophical system.

The Existence of God

In the *Discourse on Method* Descartes argues for God's existence in the following manner:

I saw quite clearly that, assuming a triangle, its three angles must be equal to two right angles; but for all that I saw nothing that assured me that there was any triangle in the real world. On the other hand,

PRINCESS ELIZABETH, the niece of Charles I of England, dressed as a huntress. Her correspondence with Descartes shows that she was able to take accurate aim at the weak points of his system.

going back to an examination of my idea of a perfect being, I found that this included the existence of such a being, in the same way as the idea of a triangle includes the equality of its three angles to two right angles, or the idea of a sphere includes the equidistance of all parts (of its surface) from the centre; or indeed in an even more evident way. Consequently it is at least as certain that God, the perfect being in question, is or exists, as any proof in geometry can be.

Descartes clearly thought that theorems could be proved about triangles, whether or not there was actually anything in the world that was triangular. Similarly, therefore, theorems could be stated about God, without begging the question whether there was a God or not. One such theorem is that God is a totally perfect being, that is, he contains all perfections. But existence itself is a perfection; hence, God, who contains all perfections, must exist.

One of Descartes's contemporary critics, the mathematician Pierre Gassendi, objected that existence could not be treated in this way.

Neither in God nor in anything else is existence a perfection, but rather that without which there are no perfections . . . Existence cannot be said to exist in a thing like a perfection; and if a thing lacks existence, then it is not just imperfect or lacking perfection; it is nothing at all.

Descartes had no ultimately convincing answer to this objection. The non-question-begging way of stating the theorem about triangles is to say: if anything is triangular, then it has its three angles equal to two right angles. Similarly, the non-question-begging way of stating the theorem about divine perfection is to say that if anything is divine, then it exists. That may perhaps be true: but it is perfectly compatible with there being nothing that is divine. But if nothing is divine, then there is no God, and Descartes's proof fails.

The argument which we have just presented and criticized seeks to show the existence of God by starting simply from the content of the idea of God. Elsewhere, Descartes seeks to show God's existence not just from the content of the idea, but from the occurrence of an idea with that content in a finite mind like his own. Thus, in the Third Meditation, he argues that while most of his ideas—such as the ideas of thought, substance, duration, number—may very well have originated in himself, there is one idea, that of God, which could not have himself as its author. I cannot, he argues, have drawn the attributes of infinity, independence, supreme intelligence, supreme power from reflection on a limited, dependent, ignorant, impotent creature like myself. But the cause of an idea must be no less real than the idea itself; only God could cause the idea of God, so God must be no less real than I and my idea are.

The argument here seems to be vitiated by an ambiguity in the notion of 'reality' here (as in 'Zeus was not real, but mythical' versus 'Zeus was a real thug'). The fallacy in the Third Meditation argument seems to be related to the question-begging nature of the Fifth Meditation argument, though the precise relationship between the two arguments continues to puzzle students of Descartes. What is clear is that both arguments are designed to be deployed while Descartes is still in doubt whether anything exists besides himself and his ideas.

This is an important matter, since the existence of God is an essential step for Descartes towards establishing the existence of the external world. It is only because God is truthful

PIERRE GASSENDI (1592–1655) wrote a set of objections to Descartes's *Meditations* in which he made himself the spokesman of materialism.

that the appearances of bodies independent of our minds cannot be wholly deceptive. Because of God's veracity, we can be sure that whatever we clearly and distinctly perceive is true; and if we stick to clear and distinct perception, we will not be misled about the world around us.

The Cartesian Circle

Descartes's friend Antoine Arnauld thought he detected a circle in the argument here. 'We can be sure that God exists, only because we clearly and evidently perceive that he does; therefore, prior to being certain that God exists, we need to be certain that whatever we clearly and evidently perceive is true.'

There is not, in fact, any circularity in Descartes's argument. To see this we must make a distinction between particular clear and distinct perceptions and the general principle that what we clearly and distinctly perceive is true. Individual intuitions—as, that I exist, or that two and three make five—cannot be doubted as long as I continue clearly and distinctly to perceive them. But though I cannot doubt something I am here and now clearly and distinctly perceiving, I can—prior to proving God's existence—doubt the general proposition that whatever I clearly and distinctly perceive is true.

Again, propositions which I have intuited in the past can be doubted when I am no longer adverting to them. I can wonder now whether what I intuited five minutes ago was really true. Simple intuitions can only be doubted in a roundabout way: they cannot be doubted in any way which involves advertence to their content. It is only in connection with the general principle, and in connection with the roundabout doubt of the particular propositions, that appeal to God's truthfulness is necessary. Hence Descartes is innocent of the circularity alleged by Arnauld.

Descartes nowhere offers an argument to prove the truth of an immediate intuition. He regarded intuition as superior to argument as a method of attaining truth. To use an argument to validate an intuition would be like using a (possibly defective) telescope to look at what was in plain view nearby. In Descartes's validation of reason there is no circular *argument*. Undoubtedly, however, in the *Meditations* the mind is *used* to validate itself. But that kind of circularity is unavoidable, and properly understood it is harmless: no fallacy is involved.

Descartes's publications brought him fame throughout Europe. He entered into correspondence and controversy with most of the learned men of his time. Some of his friends began to teach his views in universities; and the *Principles of Philosophy* was designed as a textbook. Other professors, seeing their Aristotelian system threatened, subjected the new doctrines to violent attack. However, he did not lack powerful friends and so he was never in real danger.

Out of his correspondence with Princess Elizabeth grew the last of his full-length works, the *Passions of the Soul*. When it was published, however, it was dedicated not to Elizabeth but to another royal lady who had interested herself in philosophy, Queen Christina of Sweden.

Against his better judgement Descartes was persuaded to accept appointment as court philosopher to Queen Christina, who sent an admiral with a battleship to fetch him from Holland to Sweden.

Descartes had immense confidence in his own abilities and still more in the method he had discovered. He thought that given a few more years of life, and sufficient funds for his experiments, he would be able to solve all the outstanding problems of physiology, and learn thereby the cures of all diseases. Perhaps he never knew how chimerical was this hope; for his life was cut short by his ill-advised acceptance of the position at the Swedish court. Queen Christina insisted on being given her philosophy lessons at 5 o'clock in the morning. Under this regime Descartes, a lifelong late riser, fell victim to the rigours of a Swedish winter and died in 1650 of one of the diseases whose cure he had vainly hoped was within the grasp of his methods. There was a strange and ironic fittingness about the epitaph which he had chosen as his own motto.

> No man is harmed by death, save he
> Who, known too well by all the world,
> Has not yet learnt to know himself.

QUEEN CHRISTINA OF SWEDEN is here represented listening to Descartes giving an early-morning philosophy lesson—the activity which led to his premature death in 1650.

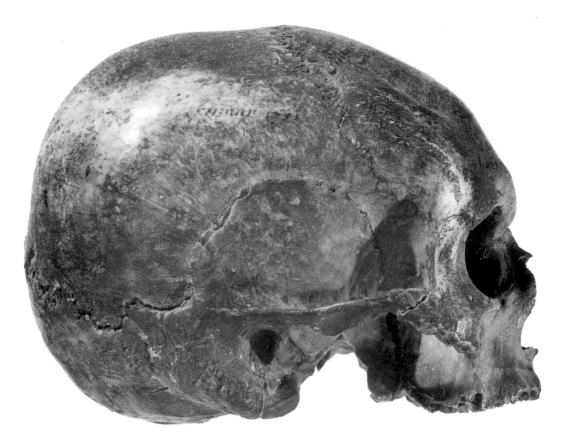

THE SKULL OF DESCARTES, preserved in the Musée de l'Homme in Paris.

Locke and Innate Ideas

One of the doctrines for which Descartes was famous after his death was the notion that some of our ideas are implanted in us from birth. Thus he wrote in a letter that an infant in its mother's womb 'has in itself the ideas of God, itself, and all truths which are said to be self-evident; it has these ideas no less than adults have when they are not paying attention to them, and it does not acquire them afterwards when it grows up'. But later he qualified this; 'I have never written, nor been of opinion, that the mind needs innate ideas in the sense of something different from its faculty of thinking.' Ideas were innate, he explained, in the sense in which gout might be hereditary in a family.

Despite these qualifications, belief in innate ideas came to be regarded as the hallmark of Cartesian rationalism in contrast to the empiricism of other seventeenth-century philosophers such as the Englishman John Locke.

Locke was a generation younger than Descartes: he was born in 1632. After education at Westminster School he took his MA at Christ Church, Oxford, in 1658. He qualified in medicine and became physician to Lord Shaftesbury, a member of the inner cabinet of King

Charles II. Shaftesbury led the Whig party which sought to exclude Charles's Catholic brother James from the succession; he had to flee the country after being implicated in a plot against the royal brothers in 1683. Locke accompanied him to Holland, and devoted the years of his exile composing his greatest philosophical work, the *Essay Concerning Human Understanding*. In 1688 the 'Glorious Revolution' drove out James II and replaced him with William of Orange, whom Locke followed to England. His *Essay* was published in 1689, and in the next few years he published a number of political tracts, *A Letter Concerning Toleration* and *Two Treatises of Government*. He worked at the Board of Trade in the 1690s, and died in 1704.

Locke and Descartes are often thought of as the founding fathers of two opposing schools of philosophy, empiricism and rationalism, one basing knowledge on the experience of the senses, the other trusting to the speculations of reason. In fact, the presuppositions that these two thinkers share are more important than the issues that divide them. They have a great deal in common, as we shall see.

Locke is forever talking about 'ideas'. His 'ideas' are very similar to Descartes's 'thoughts'. In each case there is an appeal to immediate consciousness: ideas and thoughts are what we meet when we look within ourselves. In Locke's notion of 'idea' as in Descartes's notion of 'thought' there lurks a confusion between the object of thought (what is being thought about) and the activity of thinking (what thinking itself consists in or amounts to). Locke says that an idea is 'whatever it is which the mind can be employed about in thinking'. The ambiguity is present in the phrase 'what the mind is employed about', which can mean either what the mind is thinking of (the object) or what the mind is engaged in (the activity). This ambiguity infects Locke's philosophy of mind just as it infected Descartes's.

There are indeed differences between Locke's empiricism and Descartes's rationalism, and the answers which Locke gives to philosophical questions often conflict with those given by Descartes. But though the answers differ, Locke's questions are Descartes's questions. Are animals machines? Does the soul always think? Can there be space without matter? Are there innate ideas?

This last question much preoccupied Locke, and disbelief in innate ideas is often taken as the hallmark which distinguishes empiricism from rationalism. But the question 'Are there innate ideas?' can have several meanings, and once we break the question down the contrast between Locke and Descartes no longer seems sharp.

First, the question may mean 'Do infants in the womb think thoughts?' Both Descartes and Locke believed that unborn infants have simple thoughts, since they reckoned among 'thoughts' or 'ideas' such things as pains and sensations of warmth. Neither Descartes nor Locke believed that infants had complicated thoughts of a scientific or metaphysical kind.

Secondly, the question may be taken to concern not the activity of thinking, but simply the capacity for thought. We may ask whether there is an inborn, general, capacity for understanding which is specific to human beings. To this question, both Descartes and Locke give an affirmative answer.

Thirdly, we may raise a question not about the general faculty of understanding, but about assent to some particular propositions, e.g. 'That one and two are equal to three' or 'That it is impossible for the same thing to be, and not to be'. Both Descartes and Locke are willing to agree that our assent to truths such as these depends not on experience but on their self-evidence. Locke will insist, however, that a process of learning must precede the grasp of these propositions. And Descartes will claim that not all innate ideas are principles assented to as soon as understood: some of them take laborious meditation to bring to clarity and distinctness.

Fourthly, we may ask whether there are any principles which command universal assent. Locke is at pains to argue both that universal consent would not be sufficient to prove innateness—the explanation might be a common process of learning—and that one cannot in fact assume universal consent to any theoretical or practical principles. But there is nothing here with which Descartes need disagree: universal consent does not entail innateness, and innateness does not entail universal consent, since some people, perhaps most, may be prevented by prejudice from assenting to innate principles.

In fact, to a great extent the arguments of Locke and Descartes pass each other by. Locke insists that innate concepts without experience are insufficient to account for the phenomena of human knowledge; Descartes argues that experience without an innate element is insufficient to account for what we know. It is possible for both views to be correct.

There was much philosophical confusion involved in the seventeenth-century debate which asked which of our ideas are innate, and which are acquired. This broke up into two problems, one of which was psychological (What do we owe to heredity and what do we owe to environment?) and the other epistemological (How much of our knowledge is a priori and how much a posteriori?). As happens with philosophical questions, the process of clarification led to the transformation of philosophical questions into non-philosophical ones. The question of heredity versus environment was handed over, for better or worse, to experimental psychology; it is no longer a philosophical question. The question how much of our knowledge is a priori and how much a posteriori was a question not about the acquisition of knowledge, but about its justification, and that, after this first split, remained within philosophy.

But that problem, too, propagated by fission into a set of questions which were philosophical and a set of questions which were not philosophical. The philosophical notions of a priori and a posteriori ramified and refined into a number of questions, one of which was 'Which propositions are analytic and which are synthetic?' The notion of analyticity was in the end given a precise formulation in terms of mathematical logic, and in the end the question 'Is arithmetic analytic?' was given a precise mathematical answer. But that is a later story.

Locke claimed that the arguments of his rationalist opponents would lead one 'to suppose all our ideas of colours, sounds, taste, figure, etc. innate, than which there cannot be anything more opposite to reason and experience'. Descartes would not have regarded this conclusion

JOHN LOCKE, in the portrait by Sir Godfrey Kneller, which now stands in the hall of his Oxford college, Christ Church.

as at all absurd—and that for a reason which Locke would himself whole-heartedly accept, namely that our ideas of qualities such as colours, sounds, and taste are entirely subjective.

Primary and Secondary Qualities

Locke divided the qualities to be found in bodies into three categories. The first group are the *primary qualities*: these are such things as solidity, extension, figure, motion, rest, bulk, number, texture, and size, etc.; these qualities, he says, are in bodies 'whether we perceive them or no'. The second and third group are both called *secondary qualities*, but some of these secondary qualities are immediately perceived (colours, sounds, tastes, etc.), while others are bare powers or secondary qualities mediately perceived (these are powers to vary other bodies, such as the power of the sun to blanch wax, or of fire to melt lead). In one sense all qualities, according to Locke, are mediately perceived, since the immediate object of perception is for him always an idea. What really makes the difference between primary and secondary qualities turns on the question whether ideas resemble their objects. As Locke put it: 'The ideas of primary qualities of bodies, are resemblances of them, and their patterns do really exist in the Bodies themselves; but the ideas, produced in us by these secondary qualities, have no resemblance of them at all.'

There are many precursors of Locke's distinction. The Aristotelian tradition distinguished between those qualities like shape which were perceived by more than one sense ('common sensibles') and those like taste which were perceived by only a single sense ('proper sensibles'). Locke's distinction had also been anticipated by Galileo, but the closest precedent occurred in Descartes himself. Descartes made a fundamental distinction between dimensions, shapes, and motions on the one hand (which were genuine properties of matter), and colours, smells, and tastes, on the other hand (which were 'merely sensations existing in my thought').

Descartes offered a number of arguments for the subjectivity of secondary qualities, none of them convincing. First, he pointed to the fact, already recognized by Aristotle, that the secondary qualities were perceptible only by a single sense. That fact, however, does not preclude objectivity, provided that judgements about colours and smells and tastes can be intersubjectively validated by various people using the same senses (as they are, for example, by interior decorators and wine-tasters). Secondly, Descartes ridiculed the alternative scholastic theory that colours and the like were accidents inhering in substance. The notion of a real accident, he claimed, was a contradiction in terms; but his ridicule depended on confusing the concept of 'real' with that of 'substantial'. Thirdly, he argued that whereas for primary qualities we can give quantitative analysis and prove a priori theorems (e.g. in geometry) nothing of the kind is possible in the case of secondary qualities. The contrast he draws is only very partially accurate. With the progress of science many forms of quantitative analysis are possible in the case of secondary qualities; and is it only by experience that we know that nothing can be red and green all over? Finally, Descartes argues that a physiological account of perception need involve only primary qualities as explanatory factors: what goes on in our bodies when we see or hear or taste is nothing more than motions of shaped matter. Even if this had turned out to be true, it would not have entailed that secondary qualities were subjective.

Locke's arguments deserve fuller consideration. His first claim is that only primary qualities are inseparable from their subjects: there cannot be a body without a shape or a size, as there can be a body without a smell or a taste. What are we to make of this argument? It may be true that a body must have some shape or other, but any particular shape can surely be lost, as a piece of wax may cease to be cubical and become spherical. And surely the case is the same with some at least of the secondary qualities, such as heat: a body may cease to be hot, but it must have some temperature or other. We might say that objection involves a misunderstanding. Locke was thinking of heat not as a point on a continuum—even though a thermometer scale had been established by Hooke in 1665—but as a felt sensation. But what Locke says of heat might be said also of some of the primary qualities. Motion is a primary quality, but a body may be motionless. It is only if we think of motion and rest as a pair of possible values on a single axis of 'mobility' that we can say that here we have a quality which is inseparable from bodies.

Locke says that secondary qualities are nothing but a power to produce sensations in us. Let us grant that this is true. It does not mean that secondary qualities are not genuine properties of the objects that possess them, or that they are merely subjective properties. To be poisonous is simply to have a power to produce a certain effect in an animal; but it is an objective matter, a matter of ascertainable fact, whether something is poisonous or not. We may agree with Locke that secondary qualities are defined by their relationship to human perceivers; but a property can be relational while being perfectly objective. 'Being taller than de Gaulle' is a relational property; but it is a straightforward question of fact whether or not Churchill was taller than de Gaulle.

Locke claims that the vehicle of the power to produce ideas in us is nothing but the primary qualities of the object which has the power. The sensation of heat, for instance, is caused by the corpuscles of some other body causing an increase or diminution of the motion of the minute parts of our bodies. But even if primary qualities alone figure in the corpuscularian explanation, why should one conclude that the sensation of heat is nothing but 'a sort and degree of motion in the minute particles of our nerves'? Why should the secondary qualities figure in the causal explanation? Only, it seems, if one accepts the archaic principle that like causes like. But what reason is there to accept this principle? Can a substance not be poisonous without itself being sick?

Locke claims that secondary qualities do not exist unperceived. But this consorts ill with his view that secondary qualities are powers. Powers may exist when they are not being exercised (I may have the ability to speak French though I am not actually speaking it). The secondary qualities are powers which are not exercised save when the qualities are perceived. The matter was more clearly put in the Aristotelian tradition which Locke is deserting. According to Aristotle, the activity of a secondary quality is one and the same thing as the activity of the appropriate sense-faculty: a piece of candy's tasting sweet to me is one and the

THE HAND PLACED IN THE FIRE (which feels heat and pain together) recurs constantly as a philosophical example among the British empiricists. Did they have in mind the Roman hero Mutius Scaevola—familiar from their classical schooldays—who placed his hand in the fire to show his indifference to death?

same thing as my tasting the sweetness of the candy. But the sense-quality and the sense-faculty are two different powers, each of which continues to exist in the absence of the other. Locke claims that objects have no colours in the dark; but this is a conclusion from, not an argument for, his thesis.

Locke says that the ideas caused by secondary qualities do not resemble the qualities in the bodies themselves. But this argument for the subjectivity of secondary qualities rests on a false analogy between ideas and images. If perceiving something can be called having an idea of it, then there is no reason to expect having an idea of colour to be like being coloured, any more than there is reason to expect eating a potato to resemble a potato or knowing how to play the piano to resemble a piano.

Finally, Locke argues from an analogy between feeling and sensation. If I put my hand in the fire, the fire causes both heat and pain; the pain is not in the object, why should we think that the heat is? Once again, the analogy is being drawn in the wrong way. The fire is painful as well as hot. In saying it is painful no one is claiming that it feels pain; equally, in saying it is hot, no one is claiming that it feels heat. If Locke's argument worked, it could be turned against himself. When I cut myself on a knife, the motion of steel causes pain: is motion then a secondary quality?

Locke is correct in thinking that secondary qualities are powers to produce sensations in human beings, and he has arguments to show that the sensations produced by the same object will vary with circumstances (lukewarm water will appear hot to a cold hand, and cold to a hot hand; colours look very different under a microscope). But from the fact that the secondary qualities are anthropocentric and relative it does not follow that they are subjective or in any way fictional. In a striking image suggested by Robert Boyle, the secondary qualities are keys which fit particular locks, the locks being the different human senses.

The Idea of Substance

In both Aristotelian and Cartesian philosophy great play is made with the notion of substance. Locke says that the notion of substance arises from our observation that certain ideas constantly go together. No man has any clear idea of substance in general but 'only a supposition of he knows not what support of such qualities, which are capable of producing simple ideas in us'—such as the simple ideas of the secondary qualities.

The ideas of particular kinds of substance such as *horse* or *gold* are called by Locke sortal ideas: collections of simple co-occurrent ideas plus this general confused idea of a something, we know not what, in addition to its observable qualities. (It is not quite clear whether Locke thinks that the idea of the support or substratum is entailed by each sortal, or whether the notion is an uncertain hypothesis.)

Particular substances are concrete individuals which belong to these different sorts or species. They fall into the two general categories of material and spiritual: material substances which are characterized by the primary qualities, and substances which are characterized by the possession of intellect and will and the power to cause motion.

Substances such as humans and trees have essences: to be a man, or to be an oak, is to have the essence of man or the essence of oak. But there are, for Locke, two kinds of essence. There is the nominal essence, the right to bear a particular name. Nominal essences are the creation of the human mind; for it is human language which, often arbitrarily, sorts items in the world under different sortal nouns. But things also have real essences, structures that are the work of nature, and are commonly quite unknown to us, at least in advance of experimental enquiry.

The notion of substance, as presented to us by Locke, is impenetrably obscure. He seems to maintain that substance itself is indescribable because propertyless: but can one seriously argue that substance has no properties because it is what *has* the properties? He tells us that substance is unknowable: but what would it be to know and characterize a propertyless entity? What, according to Locke, is the origin of the confused general idea of substance? Is it a priori? Is it derived from experience? Is it formed by abstraction? The relation between substance and essence also remains obscure. It seems that the substance itself is in principle unknowable; but the real essence of a thing, though commonly unknown, is something which is capable of penetration by scientific investigation.

Later philosophers in Locke's tradition were to decide that the concept of substance was dispensable; but what they dispensed with was not the notion of substance as employed in common life, or in scholastic or even Cartesian philosophy, but a chimera of Locke's own creation. For Locke, substance is postulated because of the need of a subject for inherence. But what, in his system, does the inhering? Shall we say 'qualities'? But qualities, in Locke's system, are imperceptible because ideas place a veil between them and the perceiver. Shall we then say 'ideas'? But ideas already have something to inhere in, namely the mind of the perceiver. The trail is laid for Berkeley's idealist criticism of the notion of material substance.

In the Aristotelian tradition there was no such thing as propertyless substance, a something which could be identified as a particular individual without reference to any sortal. Fido is an individual substance only so long as he remains a dog, only so long as the sortal 'dog' can be truly applied to him. All identity is relative identity, in the sense that we cannot sensibly ask whether *a* is the same individual as *b* without asking whether *a* is the same individual *F* as *b*, where '*F*' holds a place for some sortal. (*a* may be the same book as *b*, but a different edition; or the same edition, but a different copy.) Locke's confused doctrine of substance led him into insoluble difficulties about identity and invividuation; but it also stimulated some of his most interesting philosophical writing, in his discussion of the problem of personal identity.

Personal Identity

There are many different contexts in which there arise philosophical problems about personal identity. For instance, many religious doctrines present such contexts. Can any of us survive the death of our body? If an immortal soul outlives death, is it still a human being? Can a single soul inhabit two different bodies in succession? If so, do we have two different human beings or a single one in two incarnations? Can two souls or spirits inhabit the same body at the same time, as in alleged cases of devil possession?

Not only religious but scientific and medical contexts present problems for theories of personal identity. When a single human body, at different periods, exhibits different cognitive capacities and contrasting patterns of behaviour, it is natural to talk of split or dual personality. But can a single body really be two different persons at two different times? If the link is cut between the left and right hemispheres of a single brain, the capacities and behaviour of the two halves of a single body may become dissociated. Is this a case of two persons in a single body at one and the same time? Problems like this call for reflection on the concepts of body, soul, mind, person, and on the criteria for identification and reidentification which go with each concept.

Locke was not the first thinker to discuss these problems. They were posed in crucial form by a number of specifically Christian doctrines which had exercised theologians for centuries. Christians believed that the dead would rise again on the last day: what was the link between a body now dead and turned to clay and a future body gloriously risen? According to the doctrine of the Trinity, a single God could be three persons, and according to the doctrine of the incarnation, a single person could be both man and God: what concept of personal identity can be reconciled with these two dogmas?

Between death and resurrection, so Catholics believed, individual disembodied souls rejoiced in heaven or suffered in hell or purgatory. Christian Aristotelians strove to reconcile this with their philosophical belief that matter is the principle of individuation. According to this thesis, two peas, however alike, are two peas and not one pea because they are two different parcels of matter. But since disembodied souls are immaterial, what makes the disembodied soul of Peter distinct from the disembodied soul of Paul?

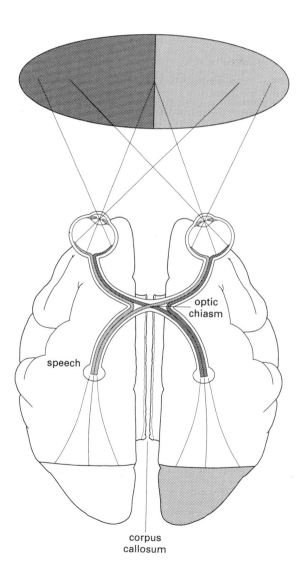

THE SPLITTING OF THE BRAIN. When the corpus callosum, which links the two hemispheres of the brain, is severed, co-ordination between speech and vision is impaired. Split-brain patients have difficulty in describing stimuli in the left visual field because of the disconnection between the right hemisphere (which receives these visual stimuli) and the left hemisphere (where the speech centre is located). Psychologists are accordingly tempted to talk of multiple personalities in the manner of Locke.

optic chiasm

speech

corpus callosum

Despite his confused account of substance, Locke saw clearly that the problems of personal identity could only be resolved if one accepted that identity was relative: that *a* can be the same *F* as *b* without being the same *G* as *b*. A colt, he says, growing up to be a horse, sometimes fat, sometimes lean, is all the while the same horse, though not the same mass of matter. 'In these two cases of a Mass of Matter, and a living Body, *Identity* is not applied to the same thing.'

The identity of plants and animals consists in continuous life in accordance with the characteristic metabolism of the organism. But in what, Locke asks, does the identity of the same *Man* consist? (By 'man', of course, he means 'human being' including either sex). A similar answer must be given.

He that shall place the *identity* of man in any thing else, but like that of other animals in one fitly organized Body taken in any one instant, and from thence continued under one Organization of Life in several successively fleeting Particles of Matter united to it, will find it hard, to make an *Embryo*, one of Years, mad and sober, the same Man, by any Supposition, that will not make it possible for *Seth, Ismael, Socrates, Pilate, St Austin* and *Caesar Borgia* to be the same Man.

If we say that soul alone makes the same man, we cannot exclude transmigration of souls and reincarnation. Man is an animal of a certain kind, indeed an animal of a certain shape. (It is not sufficient to define humans as rational animals, because for all we know there could be a rational parrot.) So 'the same successive Body not shifted all at once, must as well as the same immaterial Spirit go to the making of the same *Man*'.

But Locke makes a distinction between the concept *man* and the concept *person*. A person is a being capable of thought, reason, and self-consciousness; personal identity is identity of self-consciousness. 'As far as this consciousness can be extended backwards to any part Action or Thought, so far reaches the Identity of that *Person*; it is the same *self* now it was then; and 'tis by the same *self* with this present one that now reflects on it, that that Action was done.'

Here Locke's principle is that where there is the same self-consciousness, there there is consciousness of the same self. But the passage contains a fatal ambiguity. What is it for my present consciousness to extend backwards?

If my present consciousness extends backwards for so long as this consciousness has a continuous history, the question remains to be answered: What makes *this* consciousness the individual consciousness it is? Locke has debarred himself from answering that *this* consciousness is the consciousness of *this* human being.

If, on the other hand, my present consciousness extends backwards only as far as I remember, then my past is no longer my past if I forget it, and I can disown the actions I no longer recall. Locke sometimes seems prepared to accept this; I am not the same person, but only the same man, who did the actions I have forgotten, and punishment should be directed at persons, not men. However, he seems unwilling to contemplate the further consequence that if I erroneously think I remember being King Herod ordering the massacre of the innocents then I can justly be punished for that.

According to Locke I am at one and the same time a man, a spirit, and a person, that is to say, a human animal, an immaterial substance, and a centre of self-consciousness. These three entities are all distinguishable, and in theory may be combined in a variety of ways. We can imagine a single spirit in two different bodies (if, for instance, the soul of the wicked emperor Heliogabalus passed into one of his hogs). We can imagine a single person united to two spirits: if, for instance, the present mayor of Queensborough shared the same consciousness with Socrates. Or we can imagine a single spirit united to two persons (such was the belief of a Christian Platonist friend of Locke's who thought he had inherited the soul of Socrates).

More complicated combinations are possible. Locke invites us to consider that the soul of a prince, carrying with it the consciousness of the prince's past life, might enter and inform the dead body of a cobbler: this, he says, would be a case of one person, one soul, and two men. For Locke Socrates awake is not the same person as Socrates asleep, nor is Socrates drunk the same person as Socrates sober; but they are all the same man; indeed the infant Socrates and Socrates after the resurrection of the body are the same man. So in these cases we have two persons, but one spirit and one man.

What are we to make of Locke's trinity, of spirit, person, and man? There are difficulties, by no means peculiar to Locke's system, of making sense of immaterial substance, and few of Locke's present-day admirers employ the notion. But the identification of personality with self-consciousness remains popular in some quarters. The main difficulty with it, as pointed out long ago by Bishop Butler, arises in connection with the concept of memory.

If Smith claims to remember doing something, or being somewhere, we can, from a common-sense point of view, check whether this memory is accurate by seeing whether Smith in fact did the deed, or was present on the appropriate occasion; and we do so by investigating the whereabouts and activities of Smith's body. But Locke's distinction between person and human being means that this investigation will tell us nothing about the person Smith, but only about the man Smith. From within, as it were, there is no way for Smith to distinguish between genuine memories and present images of past events which offer themselves, delusively, as memories. The way in which Locke conceives of consciousness makes it difficult to draw the distinction between veracious and deceptive memories at all. The distinction can only be made if we are willing to join together what Locke has put asunder, and recognize that persons are human beings.

Berkeley and Abstract Ideas

Locke's influence on British scientists and thinkers was great. Among philosophers, his most important heir was George Berkeley, who was born in Ireland in 1685, just at the time when the *Essay Concerning Human Understanding* was being written. Berkeley's own main philosophical works were written in his twenties, shortly after Locke's death and after his own graduation from Trinity College, Dublin. His *New Theory of Vision* appeared in 1709, *Principles of Human Knowledge* in 1710, and *Three Dialogues* in 1710. In 1713 he came to England

and became a member of the circle of Swift and Pope; he travelled about Europe as tutor and chaplain to noblemen. He was much interested in missionary activity, and crossed the Atlantic in an abortive attempt to set up a college in the Bermudas. He became Bishop of Cloyne in 1734 and died in retirement in Oxford in 1752; he is buried in Christ Church Cathedral. A college at Yale and a university town in California are named after him.

Berkeley's importance in philosophy is largely as a critic of Locke. His principal criticisms focus on three heads: the notion of abstract general ideas, the distinction between primary and secondary qualities, and the concept of material substance. Locke's empiricism, shorn of the features attacked by Berkeley, turns into a unique form of idealism.

According to Locke's theory of language, words have meaning in virtue of standing for ideas, and general words, such as sortals, correspond to abstract general ideas. The ability to form abstract general ideas, Locke suggests, is what makes the difference between humans and dumb animals.

Berkeley extracts from Locke's *Essay* several different accounts of the meanings of general terms. One, which we may call the representational theory, is that a general idea is a particular idea which has been made general by being made to stand for all of a kind, in the way in which a geometry teacher draws a particular triangle to represent all triangles. Another, which we may call the eliminative theory, is that a general idea is a particular idea which contains only what is common to all particulars of the same kind: the abstract idea of man eliminates what is peculiar to Peter, James, and John, and retains only what is common to them all: colour, but no particular colour, stature, but no particular stature, and so on. Berkeley's particular target is a passage in which Locke combines features of the two theories, where he explains that it takes pains and skill to form the general idea of a triangle 'for it must be neither oblique nor rectangle, neither equilateral, equicrural nor scalenon; but all and none of these at once'.

There are two principal errors embedded in Locke's account. It is wrong to think that the possession of a concept (which is standardly manifested by the ability to use a word) is to be explained by the having of images. To use a figure, or an image, to represent an *X*, one must already have a concept of an *X*. And concepts cannot be acquired simply by stripping off features from images. Apart from anything else, there are some concepts to which no image corresponds: logical concepts, for instance, such as those corresponding to the words 'all' and 'not'. There are other concepts which could never be unambiguously related to images, for instance arithmetical concepts. One and the same image may represent four legs and one horse, or seven trees and one copse.

Berkeley's criticism takes a different form. 'The idea of man that I frame myself must be either of a white, or a black, or a tawny, a straight, or a crooked, a tall, or a low, or a middle-sized man. I cannot by any effort of thought conceive the abstract idea.' Here, Berkeley's criticism shares the ambiguity of Locke's terminology. Like Locke, Berkeley will use the word 'idea' to mean indifferently a sense-experience, an image, a secondary quality, or a concept.

BISHOP BERKELEY in this contemporary engraving is shown with two of his works: *Alciphron*, a defence of Christianity against free-thinkers, and *Siris*, which promotes the virtues of tar-water. No mention is made of the works on which his reputation now rests, the *Essay towards a New Theory of Vision*, the *Principles of Human Knowledge*, and the *Three Dialogues*.

Dr GEORGE BERKELEY BISHOP OF CLOYNE

J. Lathem Pinx.

J. Brooks Fec.

THE HOLY BIBLE.

MINUTE PHILOSOPHER
SIRIS

This Plate is Inscrib'd to his Lordship as a mark of Gratitude by his Lordships most Obe.^t Servant John Brooks

It is unclear whether his criticism is a piece of logic or of introspective experimental psychology. What does seem clear is that here he is attacking not the passage from image to concept, but the description of the image itself.

If Berkeley is denying the possibility of abstract images, he seems to be mistaken. Mental images do not need to have all the properties of that of which they are images, any more than a portrait on canvas has to represent all the features of the sitter. A dress pattern need not specify the colour of the dress, even though any actual dress must have some particular colour. A mental image of a dress of no particular colour is no more problematic than a non-specific dress pattern. There would, indeed, be something odd about an image which had all colours and no colours at once, as Locke's triangle had all shapes and no shape at once. But it is unfair to judge Locke's account by this single rhetorical passage.

Berkeley is correct in thinking that one can separate the mastery of language from the possession of abstract general images; wrong in thinking that the way in which names have meaning is that they 'signify indifferently a great number of particular ideas'. Once concept-possession is distinguished from image-mongering, mental images become philosophically unimportant. Imaging is no more essential to thinking than illustrations are to a book. It is not our images which explain our possession of concepts, but our concepts which confer meaning on our images.

Berkeley's arguments against abstract ideas are most fully presented in his *Principles of Human Knowledge*; his other criticisms of Locke are most elegantly developed in his *Three Dialogues between Hylas and Philonous*. Berkeley's own thesis is encapsulated in the motto *esse est percipi*: for unthinking things, to exist is nothing other than to be perceived. There are four main elements in the development of the system in the *Three Dialogues*. First, he argues that all sensible qualities are ideas. Secondly, he launches an onslaught on the notion of inert matter. Thirdly, he proves the existence of God. Fourthly, he reinterprets ordinary language in terms of his own metaphysics, and takes the necessary steps to defend the orthodoxy of his conclusions.

Ideas and Qualities

The strategy of the first dialogue is to begin by using Locke as an ally in arguing for the subjectivity of secondary qualities, and then to turn the tables against Locke by using parallel arguments for the subjectivity of primary qualities. Starting from the Lockean premiss that only ideas are immediately perceived, Berkeley reaches the conclusion that no ideas resemble objects.

The two characters in the dialogue are Hylas, the Lockean friend of matter, and Philonous, the Berkeleian spokesman for idealism. Hylas mocks Philonous for disbelieving in the reality of sensible things; but Philonous insists that they must enquire what is meant by 'sensible things'. There are some things which we come to know by the senses, but only indirectly, through symbols, or effects. But these are not what Hylas means; 'by sensible things', he says, 'I mean those only which are perceived by sense; and that in truth the senses perceive nothing which they do not perceive immediately: for they make no inferences'. Hylas goes on to show that he is only a half-hearted friend of matter; for he accepts without argument that we perceive, not material things in themselves, but only sensible qualities: 'sensible things are nothing else but so many sensible qualities'.

At this stage, however, Hylas wishes to maintain the objectivity of sensible qualities, and in order to destroy this position Berkeley makes Philonous expound the line of argument used by Locke to show the subjectivity of heat. There are, as we have seen, a number of fallacies in the argument. Cunningly, it is in the mouth of Hylas that Berkeley places many of the false moves.

Thus, at the beginning Hylas claims that qualities such as heat have a being 'distinct from, and without any relation to, their being perceived'. A shrewder defender of the objectivity of qualities might have admitted that they may have a relation to being perceived, while still insisting that they are distinct from perception.

Stripped of its dialogue form, the argument goes as follows. All degrees of heat are perceived by the senses, and the greater the heat, the more sensibly it is perceived. But a great degree of heat is a great pain; material substance is incapable of feeling pain, and therefore the great heat cannot be in the material substance. It is vain to try to escape this conclusion by distinguishing between the heat and the pain, because on putting one's hand in the fire, only a single uniform sensation is felt. All degrees of heat are equally real, and so if a great heat is not something in an external object, neither is any heat.

Like all fallacious philosophical arguments, this one can be disarmed if we pay careful

THE RELATION BETWEEN HEAT AND PAIN felt simultaneously in the hand fascinated Berkeley, as it had done Locke. Both of them studied the problem from a purely introspective point of view; unlike Descartes who, as this drawing from his *Treatise on Man* shows, was more interested in the physiology of the matter.

attention to words and make clear distinctions wherever there is ambiguity. When Philonous asks 'Is not the most vehement and intense degree of heat a very great pain?' Hylas should reply: 'The *sensation* of heat is a pain, maybe; the heat itself is a pain, no. It is true that unperceiving things are not capable of feeling pain; that does not mean they are incapable of being painful.'

Again, when Philonous asks 'Is your material substance a senseless being, or a being endowed with sense and perception' Hylas should reply: 'Some material substances (e.g. rocks) are senseless; others (e.g. cats) have senses.' When Philonous asks whether a person perceives one or two sensations when the hand is put near the fire, the answer should be 'none'; sensations are not perceived. The heat of the fire is perceived; but the pain is not. The sense of 'feel' in 'feel the heat of the fire' is quite different from that in 'feel a pain'; only in the former case is 'feel' equivalent to 'perceive'.

Let us grant, for the sake of argument, that my feeling the heat and my feeling the pain are one and the same event. It does not follow that the heat and the pain are the same thing. To take a parallel case, my winning the race may be the same event as my winning the gold medal; it does not follow that a race and a gold medal are one and the same thing.

It would be tedious to follow, line by line, the sleight of hand by which Hylas is tricked into denying the objectivity of the sensation of heat. Parallel fallacies are committed in the arguments about tastes, odours, sounds, and colours. At the conclusion of the first dialogue, Philonous asks how ideas can be like things. How can a visible colour be like a real thing which is in itself invisible? Can anything be like a sensation or idea, but another sensation or idea? Hylas concurs that nothing but an idea can be like an idea, and no idea can exist without the mind; hence he is quite unable to defend the reality of material substances.

Esse est percipi

In the second dialogue, however, Hylas tries to fight back, and presents many defences of the existence of matter; each of them is swiftly despatched. Matter is not perceived, because it has been agreed that only ideas are perceived. Matter, in the common acceptance, is an extended, solid, moveable, unthinking, inactive substance. Such a thing cannot be the cause of our ideas; for what is unthinking cannot be the cause of thought. Should we say that matter is an instrument of the one divine cause? Surely God, who can act merely by willing, has no need of lifeless tools! Or should we say that matter provides the occasion for God to act? But surely the all-wise one has no need of prompting!

'Do you not at length perceive', taunts Philonous, 'that in all these different acceptations of Matter, you have been only supposing you know not what, for no manner of reason, and to no kind of use?' Matter cannot be defended whether it is conceived as object, substratum, cause, instrument, or occasion. It cannot even be brought under the most abstract possible notion of *entity*; for it does not exist in place, it has no manner of existence. Since it corresponds to no notion in the mind, it might just as well be nothing.

Matter was fantasized in order to be the basis for our ideas. But that role, in Berkeley's system, belongs not to matter, but to God. All Christians believe that everything is in the mind of God, in the sense that God knows and comprehends all things. But Berkeley argues for something different. 'Men commonly believe that all things are known or perceived by God, because they believe the being of a God; whereas I, on the other side, immediately and necessarily conclude the being of a God, because all sensible things must be perceived by Him.'

Berkeley offers to prove the existence of God from the bare existence of the sensible world. The world consists only of ideas, and no idea can exist otherwise than in a mind. But sensible things have an existence exterior to my mind, since they are quite independent of it. They must therefore exist in some other mind, while I am not perceiving them. 'And as the same is true with regard to all other finite created spirits, it necessarily follows that there is an omnipresent eternal Mind, which knows and comprehends all things.'

Even if we grant Berkeley his premiss that the sensible world consists only of ideas, there seems to be a flaw in his proof of God's existence. One cannot, without fallacy, pass from the premiss 'There is no finite mind in which everything exists' to the conclusion 'Therefore there is an infinite mind in which everything exists'. (Compare 'There is no nation state of which everyone is a citizen; therefore there is an international state of which everyone is a citizen'.)

Having concluded that everything exists in the mind of God, Berkeley has the task of reinterpreting ordinary language so that our everyday beliefs about the world turn out to be true after all. Statements about material substances are reinterpreted as statements about collections of ideas. 'The real things are those very things I see and feel, and perceive by my senses . . . A piece of sensible bread, for instance, would stay my stomach better than ten thousand times as much of that insensible, unintelligible, real bread you speak of.'

A material substance is a congeries of sensible impressions or ideas perceived by various senses, united into one thing by the mind because of their constant conjunction with each other. Scientific exploration (e.g. by microscopes) and natural laws (e.g. the proportion of gravity to mass) are reinterpreted by Berkeley in accordance with this phenomenalist thesis. What we normally consider to be the difference between appearance and reality is to be explained simply in terms of different degrees of vividness of ideas, and varying scope for volitional control.

Berkeley concludes his exposition by arguing, with varying degrees of success, that his system presents no difficulties for orthodox theology. The thesis that the world consists of ideas in the mind of God does not, he assures us, lead to the conclusion that God suffers pain, or that he is the author of sin, or that he is an inadequate creator who cannot produce anything real outside himself.

Berkeley's system is more counter-intuitive than Locke's in that it denies the reality of matter and all extra-mental existence, and that it makes no room for any causation other than the voluntary agency of finite or infinite spirits. On the other hand, unlike Locke, Berkeley will allow that qualities genuinely belong to objects, and that sense-objects can be genuinely known to exist. If neither system is in the end remotely credible, that is because of the root error common to both, namely the thesis that ideas, and ideas only, are perceived.

BARUCH SPINOZA was described by Bertrand Russell as 'the noblest and most lovable of the great philosophers'.

Spinoza and Monism

The epistemological apparatus of Locke and Berkeley is an adaptation of the Cartesian notion of consciousness. While the British empiricists were working out the consequences of Descartes's epistemology, their continental counterparts were developing the principles of Descartes's metaphysics. The two rationalist metaphysicians *par excellence* were Spinoza and Leibniz, and to them we now turn.

Baruch Spinoza was born into a Spanish-speaking Jewish family living in Amsterdam. He was educated as an orthodox Jew, but he early rejected Jewish theology, and in 1656, at the age of 24, he was expelled from the synagogue. He earned his living polishing lenses for spectacles and telescopes, first at Amsterdam and later at Leiden and the Hague. He never married and lived the life of a solitary thinker, refusing to accept any academic appointments, though he corresponded with a number of savants including the first Secretary of the Royal Society. He died in 1677 of phthisis, due in part to the inhalation of glass-dust, an occupational hazard for a lens-grinder.

Spinoza's first published work—the only one he published under his own name—was a rendering into geometrical form of Descartes's *Principles of Philosophy*. The features of this early work—the influence of Descartes and the concern for geometrical rigour—are to be found in his mature masterpiece, the *Ethics*, which was published posthumously a few months after his death. Between these two there had appeared, anonymously, a theologico-political treatise (*Tractatus Theologico-Politicus*). This argued for a late dating, and a liberal interpretation, of the books of the Old Testament; and presented a political theory which, starting from a pessimistic view of human beings in a state of nature, derived thence the necessity of democratic government, freedom of speech, and religious toleration.

Spinoza's *Ethics* is set out like Euclid's geometry. Each of its five parts begins with a set of definitions and axioms and proceeds to offer formal proofs of numbered propositions, concluding QED. A philosopher, he thought, should proceed in this way in order to make plain his starting assumptions (which should be self-evident truths) and to bring out the logical relationships between the various theses which made up his system. But the elucidation of logical connections is not simply to serve clarity of thought; for Spinoza, the logical connections are what holds the universe together.

The key to Spinoza's philosophy is his monism: that is to say, the idea that there is only one substance, the infinite divine substance which is identical with Nature: *Deus sive Natura*, 'God or Nature'. The identification of God and Nature can be understood in two quite different ways. If one takes Spinoza's message to be that 'God' is just a picturesque way of referring to the ordered system of the natural universe, then he will appear to be an atheist. On the other hand, if one takes him to be saying that when scientists talk of 'Nature' they are really talking all the time about God, then he will appear to be, in Kierkegaard's words, a 'God-intoxicated man'.

The starting-point of Spinoza's monism is Descartes's definition of substance, as 'that which requires nothing but itself in order to exist'. This definition applies literally only to God, since everything else needs to be created by him and could be annihilated by him. But Descartes counted as substances not only God, but also matter and finite minds. Descartes's system of mind plus matter is often called 'dualism'; but it is not clear how many distinct substances he recognized in total. Material objects are often spoken of as if they are simply parts of one single substance, namely matter; but mind does not seem to be as unitary as matter, and each human being seems to have an individual mind which is a distinct substance.

Spinoza took seriously the Cartesian definition of substance, and drew from it the conclusion that there was only one substance, God. Mind and matter were not substances; thought and extension, their defining characteristics, are in fact attributes of God. Because God is infinite, Spinoza argues, he must have an infinite number of attributes; but thought and extension are the only two we know.

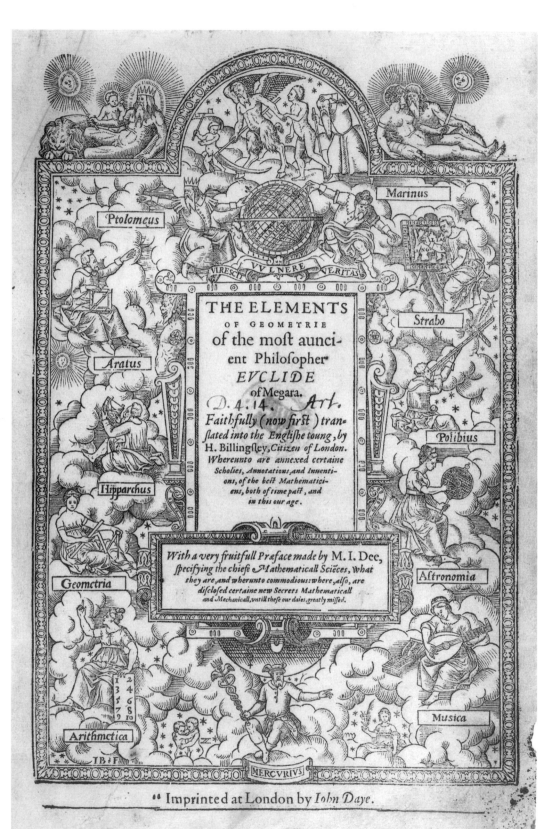

THE ELEMENTS
OF GEOMETRIE
of the most aunci-
ent Philosopher
EVCLIDE
of Megara.
D. 4. 14. Art.
Faithfully (now first) translated into the Englishe toung, by
H. Billingsley, Citizen of London.
Whereunto are annexed certaine
Scholies, Annotations, and Inuenti-
ons, of the best Mathematici-
ens, both of time past, and
in this our age.

With a very fruitfull Præface made by M. I. Dee,
specifying the chiefe Mathematicall Scièces, what
they are, and wherunto commodious: where, also, are
disclosed certaine new Secrets Mathematicall
and Mechanicall, vntill these our daies, greatly missed.

VIRESCIT VVLNERE VERITAS

Ptolomeus

Marinus

Aratus

Strabo

Hipparchus

Polibius

Geometria

Astronomia

Arithmetica

Musica

IB ç F

MERCVRIVS

" Imprinted at London by Iohn Daye.

There are no substances other than God, for if there were they would present limitations on God, and God would not be, as he is, infinite. Individual minds and bodies are not substances, but just modes, or particular configurations, of the two divine attributes of thought and extension.

In traditional theology, all finite substances were dependent on God as their creator and first cause. What Spinoza does is to represent the relationship between God and creatures not in the physical terms of cause and effect, but in the logical terms of subject and predicate. Any apparent statement about a finite substance is in reality a predication about God: adjectives, not nouns, are the proper ways of referring to creatures like us. A scholastic philosopher would have said that God was the cause of extended matter, but was not himself material or extended; in contrast, Spinoza tells us that 'extension is an attribute of God, or God is an extended thing'.

Since 'substance', for Spinoza, has such a profound significance, it is not an obvious assumption that there is such a thing as substance at all. Nor does Spinoza himself take it for granted: the existence of substance is not one of his axioms. Substance is defined at the beginning as 'that which is in itself and is conceived through itself; that is to say, it is that the conception of which does not depend on the conception of another thing from which it must be formed'. Another one of the initial definitions offers a definition of God as an infinite substance. The first propositions of the *Ethics* are devoted to proving that there is at most one substance. We are not told that there is at least one substance until proposition xi where Spinoza offers to prove that 'God, in other words a substance consisting of an infinity of attributes, each of which expresses an eternal and infinite essence, necessarily exists.'

The proof of the existence of substance is Spinoza's version of the ontological argument for the existence of God. The proof goes like this. A substance *A* cannot be brought into existence by some other thing *B*; for if it could, the notion of *B* would be essential to the conception of *A*; and therefore *A* would not satisfy the definition of substance given above. So any substance must be its own cause and contain its own explanation; existence must be part of its essence. Suppose now that God does not exist. In that case his essence does not involve existence, and therefore he is not a substance. But that is absurd, since God is a substance by definition. Therefore, by *reductio ad absurdum*, God exists.

The weakest point in this argument seems to be the claim that if *B* is the cause of *A*, then the concept of *B* must be part of the concept of *A*. This amounts to an unwarranted identification between causal relationships and logical relationships. It is not possible to know what lung cancer is without knowing what a lung is; but is it not possible to know what lung cancer is without knowing what the cause of lung cancer is? The identification of causality and logic is smuggled in through the original, harmless-sounding, definition of substance.

THE WORKS OF EUCLID provided the model according to which Spinoza attempted to set out his philosophical system in geometrical form. The idea was not new: long previously the Oxford philosopher Bradwardine (who died, as Archbishop of Canterbury, in 1349) had set out a treatise on predestination in Euclidian form.

Necessity, Freedom, and Liberation

While Spinoza's proof of God's existence has convinced few, many people share his vision of nature as a single whole, a unified system containing within itself the explanation of all of itself. Many have also agreed with him in thinking that nature operates by necessity, that everything that happens is determined, and that there is no possibility of any sequence of events other than the actual one. 'In nature there is nothing contingent; everything is determined by the necessity of the divine nature to exist and operate in a certain manner.'

Despite the necessity with which nature operates, Spinoza claims that God is free. But this does not mean that God has anything like free choice: a thing is free, says Spinoza, provided that it exists by the mere necessity of its own nature and is determined in its actions by itself alone. Both God and creatures are determined, but God is self-determined while creatures, as modes of God, are determined by God. There are, however, degrees of freedom even for humans. The last two books of the *Ethics* are called 'of human bondage' and 'of human freedom'. We are in bondage to the extent that we are determined by finite outside causes, as we are if we yield to our emotions; and we are free to the extent that we are self-determined, as we are if we exercise the power of the intellect.

Human beings often believe themselves to be making free, undetermined, choices; but this is an illusion due to our ignorance. Because we do not know the causes of our choices, we assume they have none; but the only true liberation possible for us is to make ourselves conscious of the hidden causes. Spinoza offers to lead us to this knowledge and to guide us out of bondage.

Everything, Spinoza teaches, endeavours to persist in its own being; the essence of anything is indeed its drive towards persistence. In human beings this tendency is accompanied by consciousness, and this conscious tendency is called 'desire'. Pleasure and pain are the consciousness of a transition to a higher or lower level of perfection in mind and body. The other emotions are all derived from the fundamental feelings of desire, pleasure, and pain. But we must distinguish between active and passive emotions. Passive emotions, or passions, like fear and anger, are the consequences of the actions of external forces on our body; they are generated by inadequate ideas. Active emotions arise from the mind's understanding of the human condition in the universe. 'An emotion which is a passion ceases to be a passion as soon as we form a clear and distinct idea of it.'

If we are to be liberated, the passive emotions of hope, fear, remorse must be replaced by active emotions such as courage and generosity of spirit. We must give up fear, and especially the fear of death. 'A free man thinks of nothing less than of death; and his wisdom is a meditation not of death but of life.' The key to moral progress is the appreciation of the necessity of all things. We will cease to feel hatred for others when we realize their acts are determined by Nature. Our appreciation of the whole necessary natural scheme of things—'in the light of eternity' (*sub specie aeternitatis*)—is at the same time an intellectual love of God, since God and Nature are one, and the more one understands God the more one loves God. 'He who clearly and distinctly understands himself and his emotions, loves God, and the more he understands himself and his emotions, the more he loves Him.'

Spinoza says that the mind's intellectual love of God is the very same thing as God's love for men: it is, that is to say, the expression of God's self-love through the medium of the attribute of thought. But on the other hand, Spinoza warns that 'he who loves God cannot endeavour that God should love him in return'. Indeed, if you want God to love you in return you want God not to be God.

Clearly, Spinoza rejected the idea of a personal God as conceived by orthodox Jews and Christians. He also regarded as an illusion the religious idea of the immortality of the soul. For Spinoza mind and body are inseparable: indeed he describes the human mind as the idea of the human body. 'Our mind can only be said to endure, and its existence can be given temporal limits, only in so far as it involves the actual existence of the body.' None the less, he says that the mind cannot be totally destroyed with the human body, and that there is a part of it which is eternal; it is eternal in so far as it sees things in the light of eternity.

Spinoza's apparently conflicting statements about the immortality of the soul can perhaps be reconciled if we reflect that for him time was unreal. We think of the past as what cannot be changed, and the future as being open to alternatives. But in Spinoza's deterministic universe, the future is no less fixed than the past. The difference, therefore, between past and future should play no part in the reflections of a wise man. 'In so far as the mind conceives a thing under the dictate of reason, it is affected equally, whether the idea be of a thing present, past, or future'—which is why hope, fear, and remorse are irrational emotions. The once-for-all existence of any given mind as part of the single, infinite, necessary universe is an eternal truth; and in so far as the mind sees things in the light of the eternal truths, the mind reaches throughout the unending, necessary, eternal universe. In that sense any mind is eternal, and can be thought of as having existed before birth as well as after death. But all this is something very different from the personal survival in an afterlife to which popular piety looked forward.

Leibniz and Logic

Gottfried Wilhelm Leibniz was born in 1646, the son of a professor of philosophy at Leipzig University. He started to read metaphysics in early youth, and became familiar with the writings of the scholastics. He studied mathematics at Jena and law at Altdorf, where he was offered, and refused, a professorship at the age of 21. He entered the service of the Archbishop of Mainz, and on a diplomatic mission to Paris met many of the leading thinkers of the day. There in 1676 he invented the infinitesimal calculus, unaware of Newton's earlier, but unpublished, discoveries. On his way back to Germany he visited Spinoza, and studied the *Ethics* in manuscript.

From 1673 until the end of his life Leibniz was a courtier of successive electors of Hanover. He was the librarian of the court library at Wolfenbüttel, and spent many years compiling the history of the House of Brunswick. He founded learned societies and became the first president of the Prussian Academy. He made several vain attempts to reunite the Christian Churches and to set up a European federation. When in 1714 the elector George became King

LEIBNIZ, in a contemporary portrait by Bernhard Francke. He died, a disappointed man, in 1716. His reputation as a philosopher of the first rank was not fully established until the twentieth century.

George I of the United Kingdom, Leibniz was left behind in Hanover; he would have been unwelcome in England because he had quarrelled with Newton over the ownership of the infinitesimal calculus. He died, embittered, in 1716.

Throughout his life Leibniz wrote highly original work on many branches of philosophy, but he published only a few comparatively short treatises. His earliest was the *Discourses on Metaphysics* of 1686, followed in 1695 by the *New System of Nature*. The longest work published in his lifetime was *Essays in Theodicy*, a vindication of divine justice in the face of the evils of the world, dedicated to Queen Charlotte of Prussia. Two of Leibniz's most important short treatises appeared in 1714: the *Monadology* and *The Principles of Nature and of Grace*. A substantial criticism of Locke's empiricism, *New Essays on Human Understanding*, did not appear until nearly fifty years after his death. Much of his most interesting work was not published until the nineteenth and twentieth centuries.

Since Leibniz kept many of his most powerful ideas out of his published work, the correct interpretation of his philosophy continues to be a matter of controversy. He wrote much on logic, metaphysics, ethics, and philosophical theology; it remains unclear how far his significant contributions to these different disciplines are consistent with each other, and which parts of his system are foundation and which are superstructure.

Let us consider first his logic. He distinguishes between truths of reason and truths of fact. Truths of reason are necessarily true and cannot be denied without inconsistency; they are all based on the law of contradiction. Truths of fact, on the other hand, can be denied without contradiction. They are based not on the principle of contradiction, but on a different principle: the principle that whatever is the case has a sufficient reason.

All necessary truths are analytic: 'when a truth is necessary, the reason for it can be found by analysis, that is, by resolving it into simpler ideas and truths until the primary ones are reached'. Contingent propositions, or truths of fact, are, from an ordinary human point of view, synthetic. But, for Leibniz, there is another sense in which they too are analytic. That Alexander conquered Darius is a truth of fact, and human beings can discover it only by empirical investigation. But God,

seeing the individual notion or haecceity of Alexander, sees in it at the same time the foundation and the reason of all the predicates which can be truly attributed to him, as e.g. whether he would conquer Darius and Porus, even to knowing *a priori* (and not by experience) whether he died a natural death or by poison, which we can only know by history.

In 'Alexander conquered Darius' the predicate is in a manner contained in the subject; it must make its appearance in a complete and perfect idea of Alexander. A person of whom that predicate could not be asserted would not be Alexander, but somebody else. Hence, the proposition is in a sense analytic. But the analysis necessary to exhibit this would be an infinite one, which only God could complete. The truth may be called finitely synthetic, but infinitely analytic. And while, from the divine point of view, Alexander's possession of all his properties is necessary—any possible Alexander would possess all those properties—even from God's standpoint the *existence* of Alexander is a contingent matter. God's own existence is the only necessary existence.

The thesis that every predicate, necessary or contingent, past, present, or future, is contained in the notion of the subject is stated by Leibniz in a letter to Arnauld. He draws from it a most important conclusion. 'It follows that every soul is as a world apart, independent of everything else except God; that it is not only immortal and so to speak impassible, but that it keeps in its substance traces of all that happens to it.'

Monadology

A 'world apart' of this kind is what Leibniz later called a 'monad'. A monad is a simple substance, without parts; and in his *Monadology* Leibniz argues for the existence of monads in the following manner. Whatever is complex is made up of what is simple, and what is simple is unextended, for if it were extended it could be further divided. But whatever is material is extended, hence monads must be immaterial, soul-like entities. Whereas for Spinoza there is only one substance, with the attributes of both thought and extension, for Leibniz there are infinitely many substances, with the properties only of mind.

Because monads have no parts, they cannot grow or decay: they can begin only by creation, and end only by annihilation. No other creature, then, can causally affect a monad, 'since it is impossible to displace anything in it or to conceive of the possibility of any internal motion being started, directed, increased or diminished within it, as can occur in compounds, where change among the parts takes place. Monads have no windows, by which anything could come in or go out'. Monads can, however, change; indeed they change con-

'THE IDENTITY OF INDISCERNIBLES' is the title of a principle of Leibniz's philosophy according to which no two distinct objects are totally alike. Here he is shown demonstrating to the ladies of the court that no two leaves resemble each other exactly.

stantly; but they change from within. They have no physical properties to alter so their changes must be changes of mental states: the life of a monad is a series of perceptions.

But does not perception involve causation? When I see a rose, is not my vision caused by the rose? No, replies Leibniz. A monad mirrors the world, not because it is affected by the world, but because God has programmed it to change in synchrony with the world. A good clockmaker can construct two clocks which will keep such perfect time that they forever strike the hours at the same moment. In relation to all his creatures, God is such a clockmaker: he pre-established the harmony of the universe at the beginning of things.

All monads have perception of a rudimentary kind: that is to say, they have an internal state which is a representation of all the other items in the universe. This inner state will change as the environment changes, not because of the environmental change, but because of its own internal drive or 'appetition'; monads are incorporeal automata and are called by Leibniz 'entelechies'.

There is a world of created beings—living things, animals, entelechies and souls—in the least part of matter. Each portion of matter may be conceived as a garden full of plants, and as a pond full of fish. But every branch of each plant, every member of each animal, and every drop of their liquid parts is itself likewise a similar garden or pond.

We are nowadays familiar with the idea of the human body as an assemblage of cells, each living an individual life. The monads which—in Leibniz's system—corresponded to a human body were like cells in having an individual life history, but unlike cells in being immaterial and immortal. While each monad represents the universe, it represents more especially the body with which it is particularly associated. 'Each living body has a dominant entelechy, which in the case of an animal is the soul, but the members of this living body are full of other living things, plants and animals, of which each has in turn its dominant entelechy or soul.' Within the human being the dominant monad is the rational soul. This dominant monad, in comparison with other monads, has clearer perception and more imperious appetition. It has not just perception but 'apperception', that is to say consciousness or reflective knowledge of the inner state which is perception. Its good is the goal, or final cause, not just of its own activity but also of all the other monads which it dominates. This is the reinterpretation, in the Leibnizian system, of the statement that the soul acts upon the body.

Freedom, Possibility, and Evil

Does Leibniz's system leave room for free will? Human beings, like all agents, finite or infinite, need a reason for acting: that is Leibniz's 'principle of sufficient reason'. But in the case of free agents, he maintains, the motives which provide the sufficient reason 'incline without necessitating'. But it is hard to see how he can make room for a special kind of freedom for human beings. In his system no agent of any kind is acted on from outside; all are completely self-determining. But no agent, whether rational or not, can step outside the life

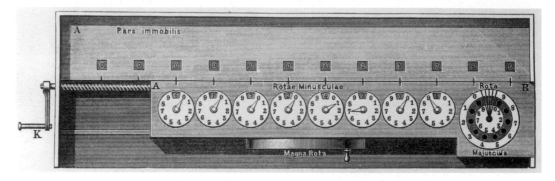

A CALCULATING MACHINE devised by
Leibniz in 1673.

history laid out for it in the pre-established harmony. Hence it seems that the freedom to act upon one's motives is an illusory liberty.

To respond to this objection, Leibniz needs to have recourse to his picture of the relationship between God and the universe. Before deciding to create the world God surveys the infinite number of possible creatures. Among the possible creatures there will be many possible Julius Caesars: and among these there will be one Julius Caesar who crosses the Rubicon and one who does not. Each of these possible Caesars will act for a reason, and neither of them will be necessitated (there is no law of logic saying that the Rubicon will be crossed, or that it will not be crossed). When, therefore, God decides to give existence to the Rubicon-crossing Caesar he is making actual a freely choosing Caesar. Hence, our actual Caesar crossed the Rubicon freely.

But what of God's own choice to give existence to the actual world we live in, in contrast to the myriad other possible worlds he might have created? Was there a reason for that choice, and was it a free choice? Leibniz's answer is that God chose freely to make the best of all possible worlds.

Not all things which are possible in advance can be made actual together: in Leibniz's terms, *A* and *B* may each be possible, but *A* and *B* may not be compossible. Any created world is therefore a system of compossibles, and the best possible world is the system which has the greatest surplus of good over evil. A world in which there is free will which is sometimes sinfully misused is better than a world in which there is neither freedom nor sin. Hence the evil in the world provides no argument against the goodness of God. Because God is good, and necessarily good, he chooses the most perfect world. Yet he acts freely because, although he cannot create anything but the best, he need not have created at all.

It is interesting to compare Leibniz's position here with that of Descartes and Aquinas.

VOLTAIRE's novel *Candide* mercilessly mocked Leibniz's thesis that this is the best of all possible worlds; the novel is now better known than the *Theodicy* itself. Voltaire is here seen dictating to his secretary while dressing, in order to make the best use of his time.

Descartes's God was totally free: even the laws of logic were the result of his arbitrary fiat. Leibniz, like Aquinas before him, maintained that the eternal truths depended not on God's will but on his understanding; where logic was concerned God had no choice. Aquinas's God, though not as free as Descartes's, is less constrained than Leibniz's. For, according to Aquinas, though whatever God does is good, he is never obliged to do what is best. Indeed, for Aquinas, given God's omnipotence, the notion of 'the best of all possible worlds' may be as nonsensical as that of 'the greatest of all possible numbers'.

Leibniz's optimistic theory was memorably mocked by Voltaire in his novel *Candide*, in which the Leibnizian Dr Pangloss responds to a series of miseries and catastrophes with the incantation 'All is for the best in the best of all possible worlds'.

The Leibnizian monadology is a baroque efflorescence of the metaphysical principles which Descartes sought to substitute for the Aristotelian consensus of the Middle Ages. His work marks the high point of continental rationalism; his successors in Germany, especially Wolff, developed a dogmatic scholasticism which was the system in which Immanuel Kant was brought up, and which was to be the target, in his maturity, of his devastating criticism. But before studying Kant, we must turn to the British philosopher who, so he said, woke him out of his dogmatic slumber: David Hume.

Hume

Hume was born in Edinburgh in 1711. He was a precocious philosopher, and his major work *A Treatise of Human Nature* was written in his twenties. In his own words it 'fell dead-born from the press'; unsurprisingly, perhaps, in view of its mannered, meandering, and repetitious style. He rewrote much of its content in two more popular volumes: *An Enquiry Concerning Human Understanding* (1748) and *An Enquiry Concerning the Principles of Morals* (1751). In his lifetime he was better known as a historian than as a philosopher, for between 1754 and 1761 he wrote a history of England in six volumes. In the 1760s he was secretary to the British Embassy in Paris. He was a genial man, who did his best to befriend the difficult philosopher Rousseau, and was described by the economist Adam Smith as having come as near to perfection as any human being possibly could. In his last years he wrote a philosophical attack on natural theology, *Dialogues Concerning Natural Religion*, which was published, three years after his death, in 1776. To the disappointment of James Boswell (who recorded his final illness in detail) he died serenely, having rejected the consolations of religion.

The *Treatise of Human Nature* begins as follows. 'All the perceptions of the human mind resolve themselves into two distinct kinds, which I shall call IMPRESSIONS and IDEAS. The difference betwixt these consists in the degrees of force and liveliness, with which they strike upon the mind.' Impressions include sensations and emotions, ideas are what are involved in thinking and reasoning. The distinction between impressions and ideas is an attempt to remove one ambiguity in the use of 'idea' in Locke and Berkeley. But the criterion of 'vividness' turns out to be difficult to apply. Sometimes in Hume it seems to be equivalent to degree of detail in content, sometimes to manifest effect on action, sometimes to emotional colour-

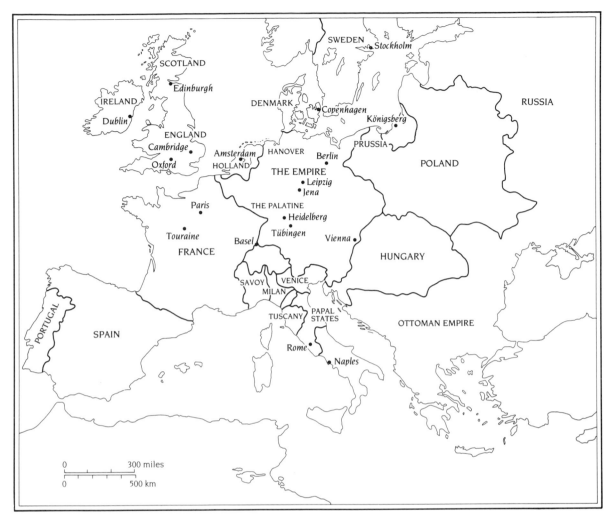

EUROPE IN THE EIGHTEENTH CENTURY.

ing. Such a vague and multiform notion will not serve to make a precise distinction, and by using it Hume makes thought and feeling seem too alike.

Ideas, Hume says, are copies of impressions. Is this a definition or an empirical hypothesis? Sometimes it appears the one and sometimes the other. From time to time, Hume invites the reader to look within himself to verify some philosophical thesis. This pseudo-empirical approach is typical of the British empiricists; but the appearance of scientific psychological enquiry is misleading. Introspection is not experiment, and imagined introspection is at two removes from science.

Whether it is meant as definition or hypothesis, the thesis that ideas exactly resemble impressions is applied only to simple ideas. I can construct a complex idea of the New Jerusalem, without ever having seen any such city. But in the case of simple ideas, Hume says, the rule holds without exception that there is a one–one correspondence between ideas and impressions. It turns out to be no easier to give a consistent account of Humean simplicity

than to give one of Humean vividness. But Hume puts the principle 'no idea without antecedent impression' to vigorous anti-metaphysical use as his system develops.

Hume tells us that there are two ways in which impressions reappear as ideas: there are ideas of memory and ideas of imagination. Ideas of memory are more vivid than ideas of imagination, and memory, unlike imagination, must preserve in its ideas the order in time and space of the original impressions. We may wonder whether these descriptions of memory are meant to provide criteria for distinguishing genuine from delusory memory, or criteria for distinguishing would-be memory, whether accurate or mistaken, from the free play of the imagination. Hume's second criterion might be tried for the second task, but would be unreliable. (My fantasy of myself telling the boss what I really thought of him may be more vivid than any memory of my actual meek acceptance of his rebuke.)

Memory is something much more complicated than Hume makes it appear. There are at least three different kinds of memory. First, there is factual memory: *A* remembers *that p*. Secondly, there is personal memory: *A* remembers that *p* on the basis of his own experience.

Thirdly, there is what we may call perceptual memory: *A* remembers that *p*, recalls and relives it in imagery. Hume's account really fits only the third kind of memory, which is the least fundamental. However vividly we may relive a past event in our imagination, it is only by means of the other kinds of memory that we know what the images mean, and relate them to the dates, places, and persons involved.

'Imagination' covers an even wider variety of different events, capacities, and mistakes. Imagination may be, *inter alia*, misperception ('Is that a knock at the door, or am I only imagining it?'), misremembering ('Did I post the letter, or am I only imagining I did?'), unsupported belief ('I imagine it won't be long before he's sorry he married her'), the entertainment of hypotheses ('Imagine the consequences of a nuclear war between India and Pakistan'), and creative originality ('Blake's imagination was unsurpassed'). Not all these kinds of imagination necessarily involve the kind of mental imagery which Hume takes as the paradigm. And when imagery is involved, its role is quite different from that assigned to it by Hume.

Hume believed that the meaning of the words of our language consisted in their relation to impressions and ideas. It is the flow of impressions and ideas in our minds which makes our utterances not empty sounds, but the expression of thought; and if a word cannot be shown to refer to an impression or to an idea it must be discarded as meaningless.

In fact, the relation between language and images is the other way round. When we think in images it is the thought that confers meaning on the images, and not vice versa. When we talk silently to ourselves, the words we utter in imagination would not have the meaning they do were it not for our intellectual mastery of the language to which they belong. And when we think in visual images as well as in unuttered words, the images merely provide the illustration to a text whose meaning is given by the words which express the thoughts.

Hume on Belief

The difference between remembering and imagining might be thought to be best made out in terms of *belief*. If I take myself to be remembering that *p*, then I believe that *p*; but I can imagine *p*'s being the case without any such belief. As Hume says, we conceive many things which we do not believe. But he found it very difficult, in fact, to fit belief into his general plan of the furniture of the mind. What, for Hume, is the difference between merely having the thought that *p*, and actually believing that *p*?

The difference between believing and conceiving is not a difference of content; if it were, it would involve adding an idea—perhaps the idea of existence. But, Hume says, we have no idea of existence.

'Tis . . . evident, that the idea of existence is nothing different from the idea of any object, and that when after the simple conception of any thing we wou'd conceive it as existent, we in reality make no addition to or alteration on our first idea. Thus when we affirm, that God is existent, we simply form the idea of such a being, as he is represented to us; nor is the existence, which we attribute to him, conceiv'd by a particular idea, which we join to the idea of his other qualities, and can again separate and distinguish from them.

The difference between conception and belief lies not in the idea involved, but in the manner in which we grasp it. Belief must lie in the vividness of the idea, and in its association with some current impression—the impression, whichever it is, which is the ground of our belief. 'Belief is a lively idea produc'd by a relation to a present impression.'

Hume is right that believing and conceiving need not differ in content. As he says, if *A* believes that *p* and *B* does not believe that *p*, they are disagreeing about the same idea. But he is wrong to say that there is no concept of existence. How, if his account were right, could we judge that something does *not* exist? The difficulty is really with the notion of 'idea', which has to do both for concepts (e.g. the concept *God*) and for propositions (e.g. the proposition that Caesar died in his bed, or that God exists).

There are several difficulties in Hume's account of vivacity as a mark of belief. Some of them are internal to his system. We may wonder, for instance, why this feeling attaching to an idea is not an impression, and how to distinguish belief from memory since vivacity is the criterion of each. Other difficulties are not merely internal. The crucial one is that belief need not involve imagery at all (when I sit down, I believe the chair will support me: but no thought about the matter enters my mind). And when imagery is involved in belief, an obsessive imagination (of a spouse's infidelity, for instance) may be livelier than genuine belief.

Hume's account of psychological concepts is flawed because he always concentrates on the private first-person use of psychological verbs, rather than asking how psychological terms are applied publicly by people to each other. Hume prided himself on doing for psychology what Newton had done for physics. He offers a (vacuous) theory of the association of ideas as the counterpart to the theory of gravitation. But his philosophy of mind is so crude and jejune that were it all he had to offer, he would deserve only a very minor place in histories of philosophy. What gives him his importance is his account of causation.

Causation

If we look for the origin of the idea of causation, we find that it cannot be any particular inherent quality of objects; for objects of the most different kinds can be causes and effects. We must look instead for relationships between objects. We find, indeed, that causes and effects must be contiguous to each other, and that causes must be prior to their effects. But this is not enough. 'An object may be contiguous and prior to another, without being consider'd as its cause. There is a NECESSARY CONNEXION to be taken into consideration.' But the nature of this connection is difficult to establish.

Hume denies that whatever begins to exist must have a cause of existence: 'as all distinct ideas are separable from each other, and as the ideas of cause and effect are evidently distinct, 'twill be easy for us to conceive any object to be non-existent this moment, and existent the next, without conjoining to it the distinct idea of a cause or productive principle'. Of course, 'cause' and 'effect' are correlative terms, and every effect must have a cause. But this does not prove that every beginning or modification of being must be preceded by a cause, any more than it follows, because every husband must have a wife, that therefore every man must be married.

If there is no absurdity in conceiving something coming to existence, or undergoing a change, without a cause at all, there is *a fortiori* no absurdity in conceiving of an event occurring without a cause of a particular kind. Why then do we in fact believe that such and such particular causes must necessarily have such particular effects? Knowledge of causes cannot be derived by any reasonings a priori from sensible qualities, whether in the case of unknown, unusual, or intricate objects, or in the familiar standard cases as when one billiard ball moves on collision with another, or when a fire gives off heat. Because many different effects are logically conceivable as arising from a particular cause, only experience leads us to expect the actual one. But on what basis?

What happens is that we observe individuals of one species to have been constantly attended by individuals of another. 'Contiguity and succession are not sufficient to make us pronounce any two objects to be cause and effect, unless we perceive that these two relations are preserved in several instances.' But how does this take us any further? If the causal relationship was not to be detected in a single instance, how can it be detected in repeated instances? Mere repetition can surely not produce the idea of necessary connection.

Repetition certainly produces nothing in the objects. Each causal event is independent of each other such event. 'The communication of motion, which I see result at present from the shock of two billiard-balls, is totally distinct from that which I saw result from such an impulse a twelve-month ago.'

But though the resembling instances do not influence each other, the observation of the resemblance produces a new impression *in the mind*. For, once we have observed a sufficient number of instances of B following A, we feel a determination of the mind to pass from A to B. Here we have the origin of the idea of necessary connection. Necessity is 'nothing but an internal impression of the mind, or a determination to carry our thoughts from one object to another'. The felt expectation of the effect when the cause presents itself, an impression produced by customary conjunction, is the impression from which the idea of necessary connection is derived.

Hume realizes that it appears paradoxical to assert that the necessary connection between cause and effect depends on the inference we draw from the one to the other, rather than the inference depending on the necessary connection. But undeterred by the paradox he insists that necessity is something that exists in the mind, not in objects; and on this basis he offers his celebrated definition of 'cause'—or rather two closely related definitions.

The first is this: a cause is 'an object precedent and contiguous to another and where all the objects resembling the former are placed in a like relation of priority and contiguity to those objects that resemble the latter'. In this definition, nothing is said about necessary connection, and no reference is made to the activity of the mind. Accordingly, Hume offers a second, more philosophical definition. A cause is 'an object precedent and contiguous to another,

THE COLLISION OF BILLIARD BALLS is Hume's paradigm of the relationship of cause and effect. Billiards was a passion of the leisured classes in late eighteenth-century Britain—a passion taken to excess, according to this cartoon by Gillray.

and so united with it in the imagination that the idea of the one determines the mind to form the idea of the other, and the impression of the one to form a more lively idea of the other'.

There are four major elements in Hume's novel analysis of causation. They may be stated as follows.

(1) Neither reason nor experience gives ground for holding that the future will resemble the past.
(2) Cause and effect must be distinct existences, each conceivable without the other.
(3) The causal relation is to be analysed in terms of contiguity, precedence, and constant conjunction.
(4) It is not a necessary truth that every beginning of existence has a cause.

Each of these principles can be separated from the psychological apparatus of impressions and ideas in which Hume's actual account is embedded. Each of them deserves, and has received, intense philosophical scrutiny. Some of them were, as we shall see, subjected to searching criticism by Kant, and others have been modified or rejected by more recent philosophers. But to this day the agenda for the discussion of the causal relationship is the one set by Hume.

Free Will and Determinism

In the second definition of 'cause' quoted above we note that the mind is said to be 'determined' to form one idea by the presence of another idea. We may wonder whether this involves a circularity in the definition: for is not 'determination' synonymous with, or closely connected with, 'causation'?

The objection cannot be rebuffed by saying that Hume is concerned with causation in the world, rather than in the mind. For he applied his constant conjunction theory to moral necessity as well as to natural necessity, to social as well as natural sciences. And the same circularity appears in his definition of the human will as 'the internal impression we feel and are conscious of when we knowingly give rise to any new motion of our body, or new perception of our mind'. Given Hume's official theory, what is 'give rise to' doing in this definition?

Hume regarded human actions as being no more and no less necessary than the operations of any other natural agents. What we do is necessitated by causal links between motive and behaviour. The examples which he gives to prove constant conjunction in such cases are snobbish, provincial, and unconvincing. ('The skin, pores, muscles, and nerves of a day-labourer are different from those of a man of quality: So are his sentiments, actions and manners.') None the less, his arguments against free will have been popular with his admirers.

Our experience of acting out our desires, he argues, will not establish free will. We must distinguish between 'liberty of spontaneity, which is opposed to violence, and the liberty of indifference, which means a negation of necessity and causes'. Experience does exhibit our liberty of spontaneity—we often do what we want to do—but it cannot provide genuine evidence for liberty of indifference, that is to say, the ability to do otherwise than we in fact do. We may imagine we feel a liberty within ourselves, 'but a spectator can commonly infer our actions from our motives and character; and even where he cannot, he concludes in general, that he might, were he perfectly acquainted with every circumstance of our situation and temper, and the most secret springs of our complexion and disposition'.

In fact, neither the fact that we place reliance on the character and actions of others, nor the possibility of making generalizations in the social sciences, really establishes that voluntary actions are necessitated in the same way as natural events. Moreover, given Hume's official philosophy of mind and his official account of causation, there is no room for talking of 'secret springs' of action. Hume's thesis that the will is causally necessitated is inconsistent both with his own definition of the will and with his own theory of causation.

Hume has been much studied and imitated in the present century. His hostility to religion and metaphysics, in particular, has made him many admirers. But his importance in the history of philosophy depends on his analysis of causation, and on the influence which he exercised on the greatest philosopher of the eighteenth century, Immanuel Kant.

Kant's Critical Enterprise

Immanuel Kant (1724–1804) lived all his life in the town of his birth, Königsberg, in what was then the eastern part of Prussia. He was brought up in the Lutheran pietist tradition; he later became liberal in his theological views but was always a man of strict life and regular habit. The citizens of Königsberg, so we are always told, used to set their clocks by him as he passed their windows on his daily walk. After some temporary teaching posts he became Professor of Logic and Metaphysics in his home university in 1770. He never married or held public office, and the history of his life is the history of his ideas.

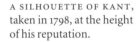

A SILHOUETTE OF KANT, taken in 1798, at the height of his reputation.

As a young man he was more interested in science than philosophy, and when he first began writing philosophy it was of a cautious and conventional kind. It was not until the age of 57 that he produced the work which has given him his deserved reputation as the greatest philosopher of the modern period. His masterpiece, *The Critique of Pure Reason*, appeared in 1781 and then in a substantially revised edition in 1787. It was followed by two other significant works, *The Critique of Practical Reason* (1788) and *The Critique of Judgement* (1790). The account of his philosophy given here is based almost entirely on his first *Critique*.

Kant's aim in that work was to make philosophy, for the first time, truly scientific. Mathematics, he said, had long trodden the sure path of science, since the day when some forgotten mathematician first discovered the role of construction in geometry. Physics became fully scientific only in the time of Bacon and Descartes, when scientists realized the simultaneous necessity for theory to be confirmed by experiment and experiment to be guided by theory. It remained to do the task for metaphysics, the oldest discipline, and one which 'would survive even if all the rest were swallowed up in the abyss of an all-destroying barabarism', but which had not yet reached scientific maturity.

To become scientific, philosophy needs a revolution similar to that by which Copernicus placed the sun, rather than the earth, at the centre of the system of the heavens. Instead of asking how our knowledge can conform to its objects, we must start from the supposition that objects must conform to our knowledge. Only by this method will it be possible to show how it is possible to have knowledge of objects a priori, in advance of experience.

The distinction between a priori and a posteriori is central to Kant's undertaking. A priori knowledge is knowledge which is independent of all experience. All our knowledge indeed begins with experience, but it does not follow that it arises from experience. A priori knowledge may be pure or impure. Our knowledge that every change has a cause is a priori, but is not pure a priori knowledge because it involves a concept derived from experience, namely 'change'. In addition to a priori knowledge there is also empirical knowledge, knowledge derived from experience, which Kant calls 'knowledge a posteriori'.

The marks of a priori knowledge are necessity and universality. The proposition 'Every change has a cause' Kant maintains, against Hume, expresses a judgement which is strictly necessary and strictly universal. 'All bodies are heavy', on the other hand, is simply a generalization to which no exceptions have been observed.

Analytic and Synthetic

In addition to the distinction between a priori and a posteriori judgement, Kant employs a distinction between analytic and synthetic judgements. He introduces the distinction in this way.

In all judgments in which the relation of a subject to the predicate is thought . . . either the predicate B belongs to the subject A, as something which is (covertly) contained in this concept A; or B lies outside the concept A, although it does indeed stand in connection with it. In the one case I entitle the judgment analytic, in the other synthetic.

The distinction thus drawn is not totally clear as it stands. It is clearly meant by Kant to be universally applicable to propositions, yet as he states it it applies only to propositions of subject–predicate form, and not all propositions are structured in this simple way. The notion of 'containing' is metaphorical; and though the distinction is meant to be a logical one, it is made partly in logical and partly in psychological terms. Moreover, it is left uncertain whether there can be a priori falsehoods as well as a priori truths.

In the following century Gottlob Frege took over Kant's distinction and presented it in a clearer form. An analytic proposition, Frege said, is one whose justification depends only on general logical laws and definitions. A synthetic proposition is one whose justification depends on principles of particular sciences. Like Kant, Frege defines an a posteriori proposition as one which depends on particular matters of fact and experience.

Both Kant and Frege frame their definitions in such a way that a judgement cannot be both analytic and a posteriori. But both philosophers leave open the possibility that a proposition may be both synthetic and a priori. In Kant's system, indeed, the realm of the synthetic a priori is extensive and important. All of mathematics, for instance, he regarded as belonging to this realm: arithmetic and geometry were synthetic, since they extended our knowledge widely beyond pure logic, and yet they were a priori, deriving not from experience but from intuition. His position on this matter contrasts with that of many other philosophers: on the one hand it contrasts with that of empiricists, such as John Stuart Mill, who regarded arithmetic as a posteriori, and on the other hand it contrasts with that of Frege and Russell, who, as we shall see in a later chapter, tried to show that arithmetic was analytic.

But it is in relation especially to philosophy that Kant develops the theme of the synthetic a priori. The proper problem of pure reason, Kant says, can be stated in the following terms: How are a priori synthetic judgements possible? Only if this problem can be solved is metaphysics possible. In a sense, the possibility of metaphysics is undeniable, since it actually exists; but it exists only as a natural disposition to ask certain types of question, questions for instance about the universe as a whole. The real question is whether there can possibly be a science of metaphysics.

The task of reason is to decide whether or not we have the capacity to know the objects of metaphysics, so that we can either extend with confidence the realm of pure reason, or set it determinate limits. Reason must be used critically, not dogmatically; that it to say its first task is to understand the nature and limits of its own power. The only possible beginning to a scientific metaphysics must be a 'Critique of Pure Reason'. The study of a priori knowledge, in general, is called by Kant *transcendental* metaphysics. The critique of pure reason is the preparatory part of transcendental metaphysics. It is the architect's plan, which is to set out the elements of which such a philosophy is to be built and the methods to be used in its construction.

'There are two stems of human knowledge,' Kant tells us, 'namely sensibility and understanding, which perhaps spring from a common, but to us unknown, root. Through the former, objects are given to us; through the latter, they are thought.' The operations of sensibility and understanding are interwoven in a remarkable manner. While the constitutions of the sensory organs determine the content of experience, it is the constitution of the understanding which determines its form, that is to say its a priori structure.

The Transcendental Aesthetic

Kant calls the part of his treatise which is devoted to the necessary conditions for human sensibility the 'Transcendental Aesthetic'. Like his seventeenth- and eighteenth-century predecessors, he thinks of sensibility as being in itself a passive power of receiving representations. However, he makes a distinction in experience between matter and form: the matter is what derives directly from sensation, the form is what permits the manifold of appearance to take on order. The matter of sensations would include what makes the difference between a glimpse of blue and a glimpse of green, or the smell of a rose and the smell of a cheese. Kant in the transcendental aesthetic is interested only in the form of sensible intuition, which is a priori.

In human experience any object of sensibility is also an object of thought: whatever is experienced is classified and codified, is brought by the understanding under one or more concepts. The first task of the transcendental aesthetic is to isolate sensibility by taking away from it everything which the understanding thinks through its concepts, so that nothing may be left save empirical intuition. The second is to separate it off, so that nothing is left except pure intuition and its a priori form. 'In the course of this investigation', Kant says, 'it will be found that there are two pure forms of sensible intuition, serving as principles of a priori knowledge, namely, space and time.'

Like his predecessors Kant accepts a distinction between inner and outer senses. Space is the form of outer sense, by which we 'represent to ourselves objects as outside us, and all without exception in space'. Time is the form of inner sense by means of which the mind intuits its own inner states, all ordered in time.

What, then, are space and time? Are they real existences? Are they only determinations or relations of things, yet such as would belong to things even if they were not intuited? Or are space and time such that they belong only to the form of intuition, and therefore to the subjective constitution of our mind, apart from which they could not be ascribed to anything whatsoever?

In answering his questions Kant makes a distinction between a *metaphysical* exposition of an a priori concept, and a *transcendental* exposition. The metaphysical exposition of space and time tells us that space and time are presupposed by, not derived from, experience; that we can imagine space and time without objects, but not objects without space and time; and that there is only a single space and a single time, infinite in each case.

The transcendental exposition of the concepts of space and time sets out to show how it is that we can know truths about space and time which are based on intuition (because they are not analytic), and yet are a priori (because they are prior to any experience). This knowledge

THE RELATION BETWEEN TIME AND CAUSATION was one of the questions at issue between Kant and Hume: is our notion of causation dependent on our notion of time, or is our notion of time dependent on our notion of causation? Painters throughout the ages have preferred to represent the causal effects of time itself, as in this *Triumph of Time* by Andrea Mantegna.

of synthetic a priori truths about space and time is only explicable if there are a priori forms of sensibility.

Space and time are neither absolute nor relative properties of things in themselves. Does this mean that space and time are unreal? Kant's answer is that they are empirically real, but transcendentally ideal. 'If we take away the subject space and time disappear: these as phenomena cannot exist in themselves but only in us.' The nature of things in themselves is unknown to us.

Does this then mean that everything is mere appearance? Not in the ordinary sense. We commonly distinguish in experience between that which holds for all human beings and that which is incidental to a single standpoint: the rainbow in a sunny shower may be called a mere appearance, while the rain is regarded as a thing in itself. In this sense, we may grant that not everything is mere appearance. But this distinction between appearance and reality, Kant says, is merely empirical. When we raise the transcendental question we realize that 'not only are the drops of rain mere appearances, but that even their round shape, nay even the space in which they fall, are nothing in themselves, but merely modifications or fundamental forms of our sensible intuition, and that the transcendental object remains unknown to us'.

This conclusion may seem unpalatable, but it is forced on us if we consider the nature of geometry. Geometry is a splendid achievement of the human intellect: but on what does it rest? It cannot rest on experience, because it is universal and necessary. It cannot rest on mere concepts, because they will not tell you there can be no such thing as a two-sided figure. Therefore it must be a synthetic discipline resting on a priori intuition.

Kant's transcendental aesthetic is one of the least successful parts of his enterprise. At the time he wrote, Euclidean geometry was regarded as the only possible theory of space; shortly afterwards it was shown that there were other consistent non-Euclidean geometries. Moreover, it has come to be seen as a genuine question, to be settled by scientific investigation, whether the fundamental structure of the world we live in is Euclidean or non-Euclidean. But this would be impossible if spatiality was something constructed by the mind in a single, inescapably Euclidean, form.

The discovery of non-Euclidean geometries means that the question 'Is geometry analytic or synthetic?' is not as straightforward as it seems. The response may be that it is a matter of analysis to settle whether a particular set of theorems follows from a particular set of axioms; but that it is a synthetic question whether any given axiom—e.g. the parallel axiom—holds of the world we live in. It may be that Kant is right that such a synthetic proposition can only be known a priori; but if so this needs to be shown by some means other than his argument from geometry.

The question whether arithmetic is synthetic a priori has likewise been transformed, this time by developments in mathematical logic. Once again there is no simple answer to the question; but it has been shown beyond question that Kant's appeal to intuition is quite inadequate as a foundation for arithmetical theory.

It remains a matter of dispute whether the transcendental aesthetic can be reinterpreted in any way which will remain both importantly true and importantly Kantian.

The Analytic of Concepts

In the development of Kant's system the transcendental aesthetic (whose subject-matter is the receptive part of the mind, which is the sensibility) is succeeded by a transcendental logic (whose subject-matter is the creative part of the mind, which is the understanding).

It is the understanding which makes the objects of sensible intuition into objects of thought. Understanding and sense are equal and interdependent. 'Without sensibility no object would be given to us, without understanding no object would be thought. Thoughts without content are empty, intuitions without concepts are blind . . . The understanding can intuit nothing, the senses can think nothing. Only through their union can knowledge arise.'

By 'logic' Kant means the rules by which the understanding operates. Logic may be particular or general. Particular logic is the methodology of particular sciences; general logic 'contains the absolutely necessary rules of thought without which there can be no employment whatsoever of the understanding'. General logic, in its turn, may be either pure or applied. Applied logic is concerned with the empirical, psychological conditions under which the understanding can be exercised. Pure general logic is concerned with the form and not with the content of thought. Pure logic has no interest in the origin of our thoughts; it is independent of psychology and prior to it.

Kant is not himself concerned with expounding or developing formal logic itself. He accepted without criticism the logic of his day (which he wrongly thought was Aristotelian, and which he wrongly thought exhausted the possibilities of the discipline). His transcendental logic is meant to be something different: it is an enquiry into what can be known a priori about the applicability of logic. Transcendental logic is divided into two major enterprises: the analytic and the dialectic. The transcendental analytic sets out the criteria for the valid empirical employment of the understanding; the transcendental dialectic offers a critique of the illusory dogmatic employment of the reason.

Our understanding is employed in the production of concepts and in the grasp of principles. (The distinction between concepts and principles in the understanding may be thought of as parallel to that between words and sentences in language.) The transcendental analytic therefore consists of two parts: the analytic of concepts and the analytic of principles. The major part of the transcendental analytic is devoted to the analytic of concepts, which is also called the deduction of the categories. This deduction is undertaken first metaphysically, and then transcendentally.

What is meant by all this terminology? We may start from the notion of 'category', which Kant took over from Aristotle. Aristotle had attempted to draw up a list of different types of thing which might be predicated of an individual. The list contained ten items: substance, quality, quantity, relation, place, time, posture, action, passion, dress. It would make sense to say of Socrates, for instance, that he was a human being (substance), was five feet nine (quantity), was wise (quality), was older than Plato (relation), lived in Athens (place), was a man of the fifth century BC (time), was sitting (posture), was cutting a piece of cloth (action), was burnt by a fire (passion), and was wearing a cloak (dress). It is hard to know how seriously Aristotle's scheme was meant as an ultimate classification of types of predication. Kant, at all events, rejected the list as hopelessly unsystematic.

In its place, he offers his own metaphysical deduction of the categories. This is based on the relationship between concepts and judgement. A concept is in fact nothing other than a power to make judgements of certain kinds. (To possess the concept *metal*, for instance, is to have the power to make judgements expressible by sentences containing the word 'metal' or its equivalent.) The different possible types of concept are therefore to be determined by setting out the different possible types of judgement. Kant sets out the relationship between the two in the following table.

	Judgements	Categories
Quantity	Universal	Unity
	Particular	Plurality
	Singular	Totality
Quality	Affirmative	Reality
	Negative	Negation
	Infinite	Limitation
Relation	Categorical	Substance
	Hypothetical	Cause
	Disjunctive	Interaction
Modality	Problematic	Possibility
	Assertoric	Existence
	Apodictic	Necessity

The divisions between different kinds of judgement are taken over from contemporary logicians. It was, for instance, a commonplace to distinguish judgements into universal ('Every man is mortal'), particular ('Some men are mortal'), and singular ('Socrates is mortal'). Similarly, logicians classified judgements as affirmative ('The soul is mortal'), negative ('The soul is not mortal'), and infinite ('The soul is non-mortal'). Again, a judgement might be categorical ('There is a perfect justice', to take Kant's example) or hypothetical ('If there is a perfect justice, the obstinately wicked are punished') or disjunctive ('The world exists either through blind chance, or through inner necessity, or through an external cause').

Where Kant is innovating is in claiming to derive from these classifications of judgements a new and fundamental classification of concepts. He does not, however, set out in any convincing detail how to do this, and indeed he leaves us uncertain how to interpret his thesis that a concept is essentially a power of judgement.

Commentators have suggested various analogies for the role which Kant attributed to the categories. Some have suggested that if we compare language to a board-game in which pieces are moved, then the categories are a listing of the ultimate possible moves available (forward, backward, sideways, diagonally, etc.) Alternatively, if we think of language as a tool for coping with the world, we might think of the list of categories as similar to the specification of an all-purpose tool (it must be able to cut, drill, polish, and so on).

Developments in logic since Kant's day have made less natural the classification of judgements on which he based his metaphysical deduction of the categories. A modern elementary logic textbook will contain two elements. It will present the propositional calculus, which formalizes the logical relationships expressed by words such as 'and', 'or', and 'if' which connect propositions to each other; and it will present the predicate calculus, which formalizes the relationships expressed by the quantifiers, such as 'all' and 'some', which occur within propositions. In this context, Kant's division of judgements by quantity, quality, and relation no longer fits neatly, and appears a rather confusing system for their classification.

None the less, we might still ask, in the modern context, whether there are any concepts which are indispensable for the operation of our understanding. We might put the question in a linguistic form: are there are concepts indispensable for a fully fledged language? Any language-users—however alien to us—need to have a concept of negation, and the ability to use quantifiers such as 'all' and 'some'. If they are to be rational language-users they will also need the ability to draw conclusions, which is expressed in the mastery of words like 'if', 'then', and 'therefore'.

The Transcendental Deduction of the Categories

Even if Kant is correct that there must be a nucleus of indispensable categories, it is quite a different question whether our grasp of these categories must be innate. In order to evaluate

THE FIRST EDITION OF KANT'S
CRITIQUE OF PURE REASON.

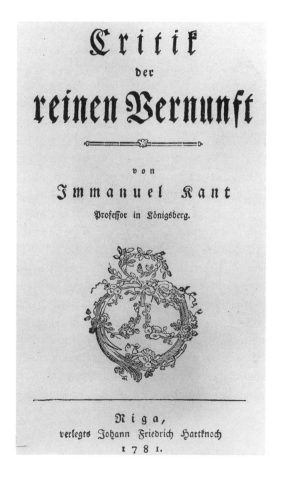

this question, we have to move from the metaphysical deduction to the transcendental deduction. The transcendental deduction of the pure concepts of the understanding stands at the heart of the Kantian philosophy, and to that we now turn.

'Deduction' in Kant's terminology is a quasi-legal term, a metaphor from genealogy and inheritance. A deduction of a concept is a proof that we have a title to use it, that in using it we are acting within our epistemological rights. A deduction of the categories is a proof that we have the right to apply these a priori concepts to objects. A deduction of an a priori concept cannot be a mere empirical explanation of how we come by it: it must be a transcendental enterprise, a proof which shows that the concept is necessary if there is to be any such thing as experience at all.

Consider, for instance, the concept of 'cause', which appears in Kant's list of categories. If it is a priori, then experience cannot be cited as its origin; experience could never establish the necessity and universality of the link binding cause and effect together. No doubt our experience does suggest to us various generalizations. But could there not be a world of experience in which such great chaos reigned that nothing could be identified as cause and effect? The thrust of the transcendental deduction is that without the concepts of the categories, including those of substance and cause, we could not understand—could not conceptualize—even the most fragmentary and disordered experience. Unless we can conceptualize objects whose being is more than mere appearance, we cannot conceptualize intuitions at all.

Three elements are involved in the conceptualization of experience. First, there is the ordering of intuitions in time; secondly, there is the union of intuitions in a single consciousness; and finally, there is the ability of the owner of this consciousness to bring intuitions under concepts. All this, Kant argues, involves the permanent possibility of self-consciousness. 'The manifold representations, which are given in an intuition, would not be one and all *my* representations, if they did not belong to one self-consciousness.'

Self-consciousness involves the necessary ownership of experience. It is not possible to *discover* that something is an item of *my* consciousness. One cannot be, as it were, faced with an item of consciousness, wonder to whom it belongs, and conclude, upon enquiry, that it belongs to none other than oneself. I can, through reflection, become aware of various features of my conscious experience; but I cannot become aware that it is *mine*. The self-conscious discoveries which one can make about one's experience are called by Kant 'apperceptions'. The awareness of one's ownership of experience is not an empirical apperception but a 'transcendental apperception'.

Awareness of experiences as mine is at the same time awareness of experiences as belonging to a single consciousness. But what unites these experiences is not experience itself; my experiences, as Kant says, are 'many-coloured and diverse'. Once again it is the a priori activity of the understanding which is at work, making what Kant calls a 'synthesis' of intuitions, combining them into the unity of a single consciousness.

The way in which the understanding synthesizes intuitions is by linking items as possible elements in a judgement. But a category is simply a scope for judgement; consequently, the manifold in any given intuition necessarily falls under the categories.

The conditions which make possible the self-ascription of experience are the unity and connectedness of a temporal succession of intuitions. But these conditions are the same as the conditions which make it possible for a succession of intuitions to constitute a single objective world. Hence, the possibility of self-consciousness presupposes the possibility of consciousness of extra-mental objects.

Kant goes all the way to meet the empiricist, and then shows him on his own ground that empiricism is not enough. He agrees that for any knowledge of objects—even of oneself as an object—experience is necessary. The original unity of apperception gives me only the concept of myself; for any *knowledge* of myself, intuition is necessary. But empirical knowledge, whether of myself or of anything else, involves judgement; and there cannot be judgement without concepts. There cannot be concepts which are derived from experience without concepts which are presupposed by experience; and therefore knowledge even of appearances, knowledge even of myself, must be subject to the categories.

The source of the objective order of nature is the transcendental self: the self which is shown but not known in the transcendental unity of apperception. Thus we solve the enigma 'how it can be conceivable that nature should have to proceed in accordance with categories which yet are not derived from it, and do not model themselves upon its pattern'.

From the transcendental unity of apperception Kant thus derives the objective nature of the world and shows that there is a difference between reality and appearance. The transcendental unity of apperception is possible only if our experience is experience of a world which is describable by the categories. That is, in essence the transcendental deduction of the categories.

The details of the argument remain obscure. Kant states and restates it, in many different forms; in each statement the chain of reasoning always seems to have some link missing. The reader is left with isolated flashes of insight rather than with an overview of a compelling argument. Kant's transcendental deduction points the direction to the refutation of empiricism, but it does not seem yet to have been really done to death.

The Analytic of Principles

Kant makes a distinction between two powers of the mind: the understanding and the judgement. The understanding is the power to form concepts, the judgement is the power to apply them. The operations of the understanding find expression in individual words, the operations of the judging faculty find expression in whole sentences. Concepts which are a priori are categories; judgements which are a priori are called principles. To every category there corresponds a principle.

A priori judgements, we recall, may be analytic or synthetic. The highest principle of analytic judgements is the principle of non-contradiction: a self-contradictory judgement is void, and the mark of an analytic judgement is that the contradiction of it is self-contradictory. But the principle of non-contradiction will not take us beyond the field of analytic propositions: it is a necessary but not a sufficient condition for the truth of synthetic propositions.

In a synthetic judgement two non-identical concepts are put together. The medium of this synthesis of representations, Kant says, is the imagination uniting them in virtue of the unity of apperception. The highest principle of synthetic judgements can therefore be stated in the following terms: 'every object stands under the necessary conditions of synthetic unity of the manifold of intuition in a possible experience'. It is from this that we derive synthetic a priori judgements by relating these conditions to any possible object of experience.

Kant groups the synthetic principles into four classes. These correspond to the fourfold division of the table of categories. First, there are the axioms of intuition, which correspond to the category of quantity; secondly, the anticipations of perception, which correspond to the category of quality; thirdly, the analogies of experience, corresponding to the category of relation; and finally the postulates of empirical thought, corresponding to the category of modality. Let us follow Kant's explanation of each of these in turn.

Axioms of intuition. The principle of these axioms is that all intuitions are extensive magnitudes: whatever we experience is extended (that is, has parts distinct from other parts) whether in space or time. 'All appearances', Kant says, 'are intuited as aggregates, as complexes of previously given parts.' It is this, according to Kant, which is the foundation of geometrical axioms, such as that between two points only one straight line is possible.

Anticipations of perception. The principle of these is that in all appearances the real that is an object of sensation has intensive magnitude. For instance, if you feel a certain degree of heat, you are aware that you could be feeling something hotter or less hot: what you are feeling is a point on a scale which extends in both directions. Similarly, to see a colour is to see something which is located on a spectrum. The word 'anticipation' is an unfortunate one: it makes it seem as if Kant is saying that whenever you have a feeling, you can know a priori what feeling is going to come next. But of course only experience could show that; as Kant says, 'sensation is just that element which cannot be anticipated'. What is known a priori whenever I have a sensation is simply the logical possibility of similar sensations at other points upon a common scale. 'Projection' might be a better word than 'anticipation' to catch Kant's sense.

Analogies of experience. This section is one of great power and interest: it amounts to a successful refutation of empiricist atomism and Humean scepticism about causation. The principle of the analogies is this: experience is only possible if necessary connections are to be found among our perceptions. There are two main stages to the argument. (1) If I am to have experience at all I must have experience of an objective realm: and this must contain sempiternal substances. (2) If I am to have experience of an objective realm I must have experience of causally ordered interacting substances. In each of the three analogies the argument takes off from reflection on our awareness of time: time considered first as duration, then as succession, and finally as coexistence.

commence li liures du grant Caam qui parole de la grant Ermenie de perfie
tartans et dynde. Et des grans merueille qui p le monde sont.

KANT'S SECOND ANALOGY rests on an insight illustrated by this miniature of Marco Polo leaving Venice for his travels. I watch a ship leaving port: as my eye roams around, I see different bits of houses, and different bits of ships. It is not this experience, but my previous knowledge of the causal properties of the objects I see, that makes me interpret the scene as one of stationary houses and moving ships.

The Three Analogies

The first analogy points out that time itself cannot be perceived. In the experience of a moment, considered simply as an inner event, there is nothing to show when the experience occurs, or whether it occurs before or after any other given momentary experience. Our awareness of time, then, must be a relating of phenomena to some permanent, substantial, substratum. 'In all change of appearances', the principle runs, 'substance is permanent: its quantum in nature is neither increased nor diminished.'

If there is to be such a thing as change (as opposed to mere disconnected sequence) then there must be something which is first one thing and then another. But this permanent element cannot be supplied by our experience, which itself is in constant flux; it must therefore be supplied by something objective, which we may call 'substance'. 'All existence and all change in time have thus to be viewed as simply a mode of the existence of that which remains and persists. In all appearances the permanent is the object itself, that is, substance as phenomenon.'

There are a number of ambiguities in both the argument and the conclusion of the first analogy. 'Substance' sometimes seems to be used as a word whose meaning is already known—perhaps, as in the categories, as something which is expressed always as subject and never as predicate; sometimes it seems to be introduced by definition as the enduring element in change. It is not always clear what type of change is being talked about: does the argument concern the coming to be and passing away of substances, or is it about alteration in the properties of an enduring substance? Consequently, there is doubt about how much is proved by the argument: is the conclusion that there must be some permanent things, or is it that there must be one permanent thing; or is it that there must be an unchanging quantum of substance? It is certainly left unclear why substance should be sempiternal. But even the weakest version of the conclusion—that there must be at least some objective entities with non-momentary duration—is sufficient to refute empiricist atomism.

The second and third analogies launch a more powerful onslaught on the Humean. The second analogy is based on a simple, but profound, observation. If I look at a house, there will be a succession in my experiences: first, perhaps, I look at the roof, then at the upper floors, then at the ground floor, then at the basement. Equally, if I stand still and watch a ship moving down a river I have a succession of different views: first of the ship upstream, then of it further downstream, and so on. What distinguishes between a merely subjective succession of phenomena (the various glimpses of a house) and an objective succession (the motion of the ship downstream)? In the one case, but not the other, the order of perceptions could be reversed: and there is no basis for making the distinction except some necessary causal regularity. 'We never in experience attribute to an object the notion of succession . . . and distinguish it from the subjective succession of apprehension, unless when a rule lies at the foundation.' Hence Hume's idea that we first perceive temporal succession between events, and then go on to regard one as cause and the other as effect, is fundamentally untenable. Matters are the other way round: without relationships between cause and effect we cannot establish objective order in time.

Even if temporal sequence could be established independently of the cause–effect relation, bare temporal succession would be insufficient to account for it. For cause and effect may be simultaneous. A ball, laid on a stuffed cushion, makes a hollow in the cushion as soon as it is laid on it. But the ball is the cause, the hollow the effect; we know this because every such ball makes a dent, but not every such hollow contains a ball. The relation between time and causation is more complicated than Hume dreamt.

In the third analogy Kant takes the third aspect of time, coexistence, and shows that this too is unthinkable without the causal relationship. If *A* and *B* are coexistent in time, then we can turn our regard from *A* to *B* or from *B* to *A* indifferently. But if we suppose that *A* and *B* are.in causal isolation, so that neither can act on anything else, we have no way of telling whether the apparent coexistence is objective or merely a property of our apprehension. Only if our perception of *A* and *B* is a case of *A* and *B*'s acting on us—which is incompatible with their being causally isolated—can we say that our simultaneous perception of them is a perception of simultaneity.

The third analogy is not as convincing as the second, and commentators have suspected that in presenting his triad of analogies Kant was guided not purely by philosophical motives, but by a wish to make his metaphysics of experience parallel to the three great laws of Newton's physics.

The Postulates of Empirical Thought

The most interesting part of the discussion to which Kant gives this title is his refutation of idealism. Kant has in view a twofold target: the problematic idealism of Descartes ('I exist' is the only indubitable empirical assertion), and the dogmatic idealism of Berkeley (an external world is illusory). Common to both of these is the thesis that the inner is better known than the outer, and that outer substances are inferred from inner experiences. The argument goes as follows. I am aware of changing mental states, and thus I am conscious of my existence in time: i.e. as having experiences first at one time and then at another. But perception of change involves, as argued earlier, perception of something permanent. But this something permanent is not myself: the unifying subject of my experience is something of which I am every moment aware but not something of which I have experience. Hence, only if I have outer experience is it possible for me to make judgements about the past.

Kant's Analytic closes with an insistence on the limits of the competence of the understanding. The categories cannot determine their own applicability, the principles cannot establish their own truth. Understanding alone cannot establish that there is any such thing as a substance, or that every change has a cause. All that is established a priori, whether by the transcendental deduction of the categories, or by the exposition of the system of the principles, is that *if experience is to be possible* certain conditions must hold. But whether experience is possible cannot be established in advance: the possibility of experience is shown only by the actual occurrence of experience itself. Concepts must be applied only to objects of possible experience; they may not be applied to things in general and in themselves. Unless we are presented in intuition with an object falling under a concept, the concept is empty and pointless.

Kant observes that philosophers make a distinction between phenomena (appearances) and noumena (objects of thought), and divide the world into a world of the senses and a

THE FIVE SENSES (*above*), sight, hearing, taste, smell, and touch, have fascinated both philosophers and artists. While Descartes and Locke argued for the subjectivity of the deliverances of the senses ('secondary qualities'), artists, such as De Vou in this painting, continued to stress the bodily and behavioural manifestations of sense-perception, to which philosophical consideration would later return.

THE WORLDLY PHILOSOPHER (*left*). The diplomat Constantijn Huygens was also a philosopher and scientist, and one of the first to encourage Descartes in his researches. In this portrait Thomas de Keyser takes the opportunity to depict the typical studio of a seventeenth-century savant.

Omniu̅ q̅ su̅t dedit in de̅s sciaz ua̅z·ę q̅cu̅z su̅t et im̅ı̅n̅sa didici
Phylosophr̅ si qua u̅a dicu̅nt·ęfidei n̅re accom̅oda su̅nt ab eis t̅a
q̅ ab iniu̅stis possesso̅ribꝫ in usum̅ nostrum̅ uindicanda.

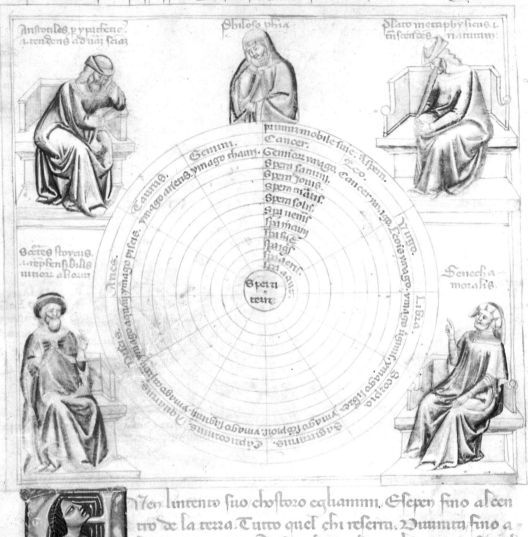

No̅ luntento suo chosto̅ro egliammi. Esepe̅ fino al ce̅n
tro de la terra. Tutto quel chi reserra. Uumtu fino a
la spieru octaua. Aristotel spicchaua. La mente sua ol
tra gliaru insibili. per li sensi munsibili. Cognoue e dechiaro no me̅
che plato. Che contempia da lato. Phylosophra egliaru̅ dui magna
nimi che non fo̅r pusilammi. Reprehese̅ chimulta suo cho̅r so terra.
Scentes oui sa fenu. OSenecha moral po de li i chaua. Cho̅i her cho
stumi e laua. Le menti e netta de certi rixibili. Chosto̅ro fo̅ro re̅
dibili. Di nostra fe̅de et han quei chel bel prato. Cran de scientia
ornato Pchui phylosophra tutti impratcha. Hauen p̅ru̅cinale
e mathematcha.

world of the understanding. His own analytic has shown that there cannot be a world of mere appearances, mere objects of sense which do not fall under any categories or instantiate any rules. But we cannot conclude from this that there is a non-sensible world which is discovered by the understanding alone. Kant accepts that there are noumena in a negative sense: things which are not objects of sensible intuition. But he denies that there are noumena in a positive sense: things which are objects of a non-sensible intuition. The concept of noumenon, rightly understood, is simply a limiting concept, whose function is to set the limits of sensibility. To accept the existence of noumena as extra-sensible objects which can be studied by the use of intellect alone is to enter a world of illusion, whose geography will be studied in the transcendental dialectic.

From Analytic to Dialectic

The Analytic has set out the territory of pure understanding.

This domain is an island, enclosed by nature itself within unalterable limits. It is the land of truth—enchanting name!—surrounded by a wide and stormy ocean, the native home of illusion, where many a fog bank and many a swiftly melting iceberg give the deceptive appearance of farther shores, deluding the adventurous seafarer ever anew with empty hopes, and engaging him in enterprises which he can never abandon and yet is unable to carry to completion.

In the transcendental dialectic Kant aims to set out the logic of illusion and to subject to criticism a priori psychology, cosmology, and theology. He is concerned not with contingent and accidental errors, like optical illusions or logical fallacies, but with something more important and transcendental: the attempt to employ the mind beyond the bounds of experience, which is a 'natural and inevitable' illusion arising from the nature of our faculties.

All our knowledge, Kant says, starts with the senses, proceeds from the senses to the understanding, and ends with reason. Kant's explanation of the difference between understanding and reason is unclear, and perhaps not altogether consistent. But he focuses on three patterns of reasoning, categorical (as in 'All M is P; all S is M; so all S is P'), hypothetical (as in 'If A then B; but A; so B'), and disjunctive (as in 'Either A or B; but not A; so B').

Reason, like understanding, operates through concepts. Having called the pure concepts of understanding, in imitation of Aristotle, 'categories', Kant now calls the concepts of pure reason 'Ideas', in deliberate evocation of Plato. Ideas are necessary concepts of reason to which no object corresponds in sense-experience.

The Ideas of pure reason are arrived at by taking a form of inference, and seeking to absolutize it. We infer conclusions from premises; the conclusions are true if the premises are true. But this seems to be only a conditional truth, since the truth of the premises may be called in question. Reason looks for something unconditioned, a basis which is absolute, that is to say, derived from nothing other than itself. What is absolutely valid is valid unconditionally, in all respects, without restriction.

THE CHALLENGE TO THE COSMOS. The ordered geocentric world of the Middle Ages, as represented here, was challenged by the development of Renaissance scientific philosophy, culminating in the work of Galileo and Descartes. Challenged too was the authority of the past thinkers pictured here.

RATIONALISM AND ROMANTICISM. The critical rationalism of Kant's writing is often illustrated by surprisingly poetic metaphors. His description of the island of insight surrounded by the icy, foggy ocean of illusion recalls the work of the great romantic painter Caspar David Friedrich (1774–1840).

There are three Ideas of pure reason, arrived at by absolutizing the three different patterns of inference. There is the idea of the soul as permanent substantial subject, which arises from the pursuit of the unconditioned in following up the categorical syllogism. There is the idea of the cosmos as the totality of things related as causes and effects, which arises from following up the hypothetical syllogism. Finally, there is the idea of God as the being of all beings, arising from following up the disjunctive syllogism. 'Pure reason thus furnishes the idea for a transcendental doctrine of the soul, for a transcendental science of the world, and finally for a transcendental knowledge of God.'

Three different kinds of dialectical argument lead to the three different ideas. Lines of argument which conclude from subjective experience to the soul as substance are called *paralogisms of pure reason*. The line which goes from the causal relations between empirical objects to the notion of a total cosmos, unconditioned because it contains all conditions, is called *the antinomy of pure reason*. The line which goes from the contingency of the objects of experience to the unconditioned necessity of a being of all beings, namely God, is called *the ideal of pure reason.*

The Paralogisms of Pure Reason

We must make a distinction between empirical and rational psychology. Empirical psychology deals with the soul as the object of inner sense; rational psychology sets out to treat of the soul as the subject of every judgement. Rational psychology, Kant says, 'professes to be a science built upon the single proposition "I think"'. It is based not on the empirical perceptions of the inner sense, but on the mere apperception, with no empirical content. 'I think' is 'the sole text of rational psychology.' 'The I or he or it (the thing) which thinks' is an unknown *X*, the transcendental subject of the thoughts.

Descartes used 'I think' as a generic word to cover all mental states and activities. But when 'I think' is used as the text of rational psychology, thinking is to be taken not as a genus of, but as an accompaniment to, thought. It is the expression of the self-consciousness inseparable from thought. But how do we know that everything which thinks is self-conscious? Answer: Self-consciousness is necessary to think of thinking, and we attribute a priori to things those properties which are conditions of our thinking of them.

Kant lists four paralogisms of pure reason—four fallacies into which we are led by our drive to transcend the limits of merely empirical psychology. In the first paralogism we proceed from the premiss 'Necessarily, the subject of thought is a subject' to the conclusion 'The subject of thought is necessarily a subject'. In the second we pass from 'The ego cannot be divided into parts' to 'The ego is a simple substance'. In the third we move from 'Whenever I am conscious, it is the same I who am conscious' to 'Whenever I am conscious, I am conscious of the same I'. Finally, in the fourth, we argue from the truth of 'I can think of myself apart from every other thing, including my body' to the conclusion 'Apart from every other thing including my body, I can think of myself'.

In each paralogism a harmless analytical proposition is converted into a contentious synthetic a priori proposition. Taken together, the paralogisms add up to the claim that the self is an immaterial, incorruptible, personal, immortal entity.

The Antinomy of Pure Reason

Kant believed that any attempt by reason to form 'cosmical concepts', that is to say, notions of the world as a whole, was bound to lead to irresolvable contradiction. To illustrate the illusory tendencies of pure reason he constructs a set of antinomies. An antinomy is a pair of contrasting arguments which lead to contradictory conclusions (a thesis and an antithesis).

The first antinomy, for instance, has as thesis 'The world has a beginning in time, and is also limited as regards space' and as antithesis 'The world has no beginning, and no limits in space; it is infinite as regards both time and space'.

The two propositions 'The world has a beginning in time' and 'The world has no beginning' have had a long history in the works of philosophers. Aristotle thought the second could be proved. Augustine thought the first could be proved. Aquinas thought neither proposition could be proved. Kant now suggests that both propositions could be proved. That does not mean, of course, that two contradictories are both true; it is intended to show that reason has no right to talk at all about 'the world' as a whole.

In fact, neither of Kant's 'proofs' is watertight. The argument for the thesis depends on the impossibility of completing an infinite series. An infinite series, Kant says, is one that 'can never be completed through successive synthesis'; hence it is impossible for an infinite world-series to have passed away. Mathematicians after Kant offered alternative ways of defining infinity; but even if we accept Kant's definition we can reject his conclusion. It is true that any infinite discrete series must be open at one end: no such series can be 'completed' in the sense of having two termini. But why may it not have an end in one direction, while going on for ever in the other? Elapsed time would then be 'completed' by having a terminus at the present, while reaching forever backward. Kant offers no convincing reason against this proposal.

The impossibility of a world infinite in space is supposed to follow from the impossibility of infinity in time. An infinite world could not be taken in at a single glance; it would have to be viewed bit by bit, and an infinite number of bits would take an infinite time to take in. But why is the believer in spatial infinity committed to the view that it must be possible for someone to count every item in the world? Could one not accept that the world was infinite but unsurveyable?

The argument from the antithesis goes thus. If the world had a beginning, then there was a time when the world did not exist. Any moment of this 'void time' is exactly like any other. Hence there can be no answer to the question 'Why did the world begin when it did?' One can reply that a believer in a temporally finite world does not have to believe in 'void time'. He can agree that it is not possible to locate the beginning of the world from outside (at such-and-such a point in 'void time'), while maintaining that one can locate it from within (so many time-units prior to now).

Kant offers a parallel argument against those who believe in a spatially finite universe. 'If the world is limited in space it must be limited by space; but empty space is nothing.' A parallel response can be made. Kant's argument seems to affect only those who believe in space as an absolute entity, not those who regard the notion of space as an abstract method of referring to spatial relationships between real entities. Altogether, the first antinomy seems ineffective in establishing the impotence of reason.

In all Kant presents four antinomies. The second concerns simplicity and complexity; the third concerns freedom and causality; the fourth concerns necessity and contingency. In each of the antinomies, the antithesis affirms that a certain series continues for ever, the thesis that the same series comes to a full stop. Thus:

> First: the series of items *next to* each other in space and in time comes to an end (thesis) / goes on for ever (antithesis).

Second: the series of items which are *parts of* others comes to an end (thesis) / goes on for ever (antithesis).

Third: the series of items *caused by* another ends in a free, naturally uncaused, event (thesis) / goes on for ever (antithesis).

Fourth: the series of items *contingent upon* another goes on for ever (antithesis) / ends with an absolutely necessary being (thesis).

Each of the underlined relationships is regarded by Kant as a form of *being conditioned* by something else: so that each of these series is a series of conditions. 'The whole antinomy of pure reason rests upon the dialectical argument: if the conditioned is given, the entire series of all its conditions is likewise given; objects of the senses are given as unconditioned: therefore etc.'

Kant thinks that both sides to each antinomy are in error: the thesis is the error of dogmatism, the antithesis the error of empiricism. What the antinomy brings out is the mismatch between the scope of empirical enquiry and the pretensions of the rational ideal. The thesis represents the world as smaller than thought: we can think beyond it. The antithesis always represents the world as larger than thought: we cannot think to the end of it. 'In all cases the cosmical idea is either too large or too small for the empirical regress.' The onus is on us to trim our cosmic idea to fit the empirical enquiry, not the other way round; for the only thing that can give reality to our concepts is possible experience.

It is the idea of the cosmic whole that is the root error common to both the dogmatic thesis and the empiricist antithesis: in each case a task set (e.g. to trace the causal antecedents of an event) is confused with a task completed (e.g. a survey of the totality of causes). The world as a whole could never be given in experience and so 'the world as a whole' is a pseudo-concept. Hence it is not the case that the world is finite and not the case that the world is infinite.

The antinomy provides a proof of transcendental idealism. If the world is a whole existing in itself, it is either finite or infinite. But both alternatives are false (as shown in the proofs of the antithesis and thesis respectively). It is therefore also false that the world (the sum of all appearances) is a whole existing in itself. From this it then follows that appearances in general are nothing outside our representations—which is just what is meant by their transcendental ideality.

The cosmological ideas cannot be taken seriously as genuine concepts. But they have a regulative role. 'The principle of reason is thus properly only a rule, prescribing a regress in the series of conditions of given appearances, and forbidding it to bring the regress to a close by treating anything at which it may arrive as absolutely unconditioned.'

Nature and Freedom

The third antinomy differs from the previous two. In the first two antinomies both the thesis and the antithesis were rejected as false. But when Kant comes to the third antinomy he seeks to show that, properly interpreted, both thesis and antithesis are true. The difference between the antinomies, he says, arises from the fact that the first two deal with empirical homogeneous series (the parts of space and time and matter) whereas the third involves two heterogeneous elements (natural causation and free causation).

The thesis of the third antinomy argues that natural causality is not sufficient to explain the phenomena of the world; in addition to determining causes we must take account of freedom and spontaneity. The antithesis argues that to postulate transcendental freedom is to resign oneself to blind lawlessness, since the intrusion of an undetermined cause would disrupt the whole explanatory system of nature.

Kant's treatment of the third antinomy takes its place among the many attempts which have been made by philosophers to reconcile freedom and determinism. Determinism is the belief that every event has a cause, in the sense of a sufficient antecedent condition. Determinists are sometimes divided into two classes. There are hard determinists, who believe that freedom is incompatible with determinism, and is therefore an illusion; and there are soft determinists, who believe that freedom and determinism are compatible, and can therefore accept that human freedom is genuine. Kant is a soft determinist: he seeks to show that freedom properly understood is compatible with determinism properly understood. An event may be both determined by nature and grounded in freedom.

The human will, for Kant, is sensuous but free: that is to say, it is affected by passion but it is not necessitated by passion. 'There is in man a power of self-determination, independently of any coercion through sensuous impulses.' But the exercise of this power of self-determination has two aspects, sensible (perceptible in experience) and intelligible (graspable only by the intellect). Our free agency is the intelligible cause of sensible effects; and these sensible phenomena are also part of an unbroken series in accordance with unchangeable laws.

The transcendental idea of freedom, and the intelligible character of our action, is brought out by our use of the word 'ought'. We cannot say that anything in nature *ought to be* other than it in fact is. The imperatives which we impose upon our conduct express a necessity which arises not from nature, but from self-determining reason. 'The words *I ought* express a species of necessity, and imply a connection with grounds, which nature does not and cannot present to the mind of man.'

Faced with the difficulty of reconciling divine omniscience with human freedom, theologians have often claimed that there is no problem because humans act in time, whereas God's knowledge is outside time. Faced with the problem of reconciling human freedom with deterministic nature, Kant claims that nature operates in time, whereas the human will, as noumenon rather than phenomenon, is likewise outside time. Thus, the possibility of an active agent which is a sensuous object with both an empirical and intelligible character is made to depend on the thesis that things in themselves are outside time.

Many soft determinists have argued that freedom and determinism are compatible because our actions, while determined, are determined by mental events in our own minds; and an action is free, it is claimed, if it is determined by inner rather than outer causes. Was Kant a believer in psychological determinism of this kind? On the one hand he says 'if we could investigate all the phenomena of human volition to their lowest foundation in the mind, there would be no action which we could not anticipate with certainty and recognize to be absolutely necessary from its preceding conditions'. On the other hand he says that there can be actions which 'have taken place because they were determined, not by empirical causes, but by the act of the will upon grounds of reason'.

It seems that Kant was indeed a psychological determinist, but that his version of compatibilism does not depend on defining free action as action that is psychologically determined. The reconciliation which he proposes does not take place at the level of inner experience. He believed, surely correctly, that causal explanation and explanation by reasons are radically different types of explanation, and that the one is irreducible to the other. But since the reconciliation he offers takes place at the level of the noumenon, the thing in itself, his reconciling project is fatally infected with the obscurity which attends those concepts.

In the fourth antinomy Kant considers arguments for and against the existence of a necessary being. He there leaves open the question whether a necessary being is to be found in the world itself, or outside the world as its cause. It is in the chapter on the ideal of pure reason that he turns to consider the concept of God as the highest reality, a being that is one, simple, all-sufficient, and eternal. The ideal of pure reason is the object of transcendental theology.

Arguments for God's Existence

According to Kant all arguments to establish the existence of God must fall into one of three classes. There are ontological arguments, which take their start from the a priori concept of a supreme being; there are cosmological arguments, which derive from the nature of the empirical world in general; and there are physico-theological proofs, which start from particular natural phenomena. Anselm's argument to the existence of that than which no greater can be conceived is an ontological argument, as is the argument of Descartes in the Fifth Meditation. Aquinas's third way is a version of the cosmological argument, and his fifth way can be regarded as a physico-theological argument. Other proofs offered by Aquinas and other philosophers are less easy to fit into Kant's classification, and it is not clear that it is as watertight as he thought it was.

In Kant's rational theology a very special role is assigned to the ontological argument. He claims that the cosmological argument is only the ontological argument in disguise, and he argues that the physico-theological argument by itself will lead us only to a designer, not to a genuine creator of the universe.

Kant's critique of the ontological argument has been very influential. He begins by asking what is meant by speaking of God as an absolutely necessary being. We have various conceptions of necessity: there is, for instance, the necessary truth of the propositions of logic and of mathematics, which we might call, in a broad sense, logical necessity. There is the physical necessity of causal laws. Is there a such a thing as metaphysical necessity? Can things, as well as propositions, be necessary? Some philosophers have defined a necessary being as one which exists in all possible worlds. If we define God in this way, then surely he exists. Our world is one possible world, otherwise it would not be actual; so if God exists in every possible world, he must exist in ours.

But is it legitimate to build existence—even possible existence—into the definition of something in this way? Kant thinks not. 'There is already a contradiction in introducing the concept of existence—no matter under what title it may be disguised—into the concept of a thing.' The ontological argument seeks to make the statement of God's existence an analytic proposition. If a proposition is analytic, then the predicate is part of the subject and cannot be denied of if; Kant's example is 'A triangle has three angles'. He remarks:

To posit a triangle and yet to reject its three angles is self-contradictory; but there is no contradiction in rejecting the triangle together with its three angles. The same holds true of the concept of an absolutely necessary being. If its existence is rejected, we reject the thing itself with all its predicates; and no question of contradiction can then arise.

But why is Kant so sure that all existential propositions are synthetic? We can argue from concepts to non-existence: it is because we grasp the concepts 'square' and 'circle' that we

THE GREAT ARCHITECT. Kant, when criticizing arguments for the existence of God, had most sympathy for the 'physico-theological argument', or argument from design, 'never to be mentioned without respect'. But he said that it led not to a creator, but to an architect; like Blake's *Ancient of Days*.

know there are no square circles. Why cannot we argue from concepts to existence? If 'There are no unmarried bachelors' is analytic, why not 'There is a necessary being'?

Kant's principal argument is that *being* is not a predicate, but a copula. 'The proposition "God is omnipotent" contains two concepts, each of which has its object—God and omnipotence. The small word "is" adds no new predicate.' If we say 'God is' or 'There is a God', Kant says, 'we attach no new predicate to the concept of God, but only posit the subject in itself with all its predicates.'

The use of 'is' as a copula is in fact very different from its use in existential propositions, but we may agree with Kant that in neither case is it a predicate. Existential propositions do not always 'posit', as Kant implies; someone who says 'If there is a God, sinners will be punished' does not posit God's existence.

An assertion that *A* exists may be used to assign *A* to the realm of fact rather than fiction ('Robin Hood really existed'), to the realm of the concrete rather than the abstract ('Genes really exist'), to the realm of the extant rather than the defunct ('Does the Pharos of Alexandria still exist?'). Whichever of these kinds of existence we are talking about, it is true, as Kant, says, that 'exist' cannot be treated as a straightforward first-order predicate.

In modern logic, existence is expressed by the use of quantifiers. 'God exists' is formulated as 'For some *x*, *x* is God'. This clarifies, but does not settle, the issues surrounding the ontological argument. For the problems about arguing from possibility to actuality return as questions about the domain over which the variable '*x*' is to range: is it to include possible as well as actual objects?

Kant's principal point remains.

By however many predicates we may think a thing—even if we completely determine it—we do not make the least addition to the thing when we further declare that this thing *is*. Otherwise, it would not be exactly the same thing that exists, but something more than we had thought in the concept; and we could not, therefore, say that the exact object of my concept exists.

In other words, whether there is something in reality corresponding to my concept cannot itself be part of my concept. A concept has to be determined prior to being compared to reality, otherwise we would not know *which* concept was being compared and found to correspond, or not correspond, to reality. *That* there is a God cannot be part of what we mean by 'God'; hence 'There is a God' cannot be an analytic proposition, and the ontological argument must fail.

Does this mean that all arguments for the existence of God collapse? Kant thought that the cosmological argument must smuggle in the ontological argument, since it concludes to the existence of a necessary being whose essence implies its existence, which is what he has just shown to be impossible. But many versions of the cosmological argument purport to show the existence of a being which is necessary in some less dubious sense. Without accepting the ontological argument, it may perhaps be possible to produce arguments for the existence of a being which is uncaused, unchanging, and everlasting, in contrast to the caused, variable, and contingent items in the world of experience.

Kant in fact has a criticism of the cosmological argument which is independent of his rebuttal of the ontological argument. He states the argument thus. 'If anything exists, an absolutely necessary being must also exist. Now I, at least, exist. Therefore an absolutely necessary being exists.' This formulation will cover not only Aquinas's third way, but also the argument of Descartes's Third Meditation. The first premiss depends on the argument that a series of contingent causes, however long, can be completed only by a necessary cause. But we are faced with a dilemma if we ask whether the necessary cause is, or is not, part of the chain of causes.

If it is part of the chain, then we can raise in its case, as in the case of the other members of the chain, the question why it exists. But this, Kant says, is a thought that we cannot endure, 'the thought that a being, which we represent to ourselves as supreme amongst all possible beings, should, as it were, say to itself: "I am from eternity to eternity, and outside me there is nothing save what is through my will, *but whence then am I?*" '. On the other hand, if the necessary being is not part of the chain of causation, how can it be its first member and account for the all the other links which end with the existence of myself?

The physico-theological proof is the one which is treated most gently by Kant; it always deserves, he says, to be mentioned with respect. His aim is not to diminish the authority of the argument, but to limit the scope of its conclusion. The proof argues that everywhere in the world we find signs of order, in accordance with a determinate purpose, carried out with great wisdom. This order is alien to the individual things in the world which contribute to make it up; it must therefore have been imposed by one or more sublime wise causes, operating not blindly as nature does, but freely as humans do. Kant waives various difficulties about the analogies which this argument draws between the operation of nature and the artifice of human skill. But he insists that the most the argument can prove is 'an *architect* of the world who is always very much hampered by the adaptability of the material in which he works, not a *creator* of the world to whose idea everything is subject'.

Kantian Morality

The essentials of Kant's moral system are explained with brevity and eloquence in his *Groundwork of the Metaphysics of Morals* (1785). In this work Kant sets out critically the synthetic a priori principles of practical reason, to match his critical exposition of the synthetic a priori principles of theoretical reason.

Kant's starting-point is that the only thing which is good without qualification is a good will. Talents, character, self-control, and fortune can be used to bad ends; even happiness can be corrupting. It is not its achievements which make a good will good; good willing is good in itself alone.

Even if, some special disfavour of destiny, or by the niggardly endowment of stepmotherly nature, this will is entirely lacking in power to carry out its intentions; if by its utmost effort it still accomplishes nothing, and only good will is left . . . ; even then it would still shine like a jewel for its own sake as something which has its full value in itself.

It is not in order to pursue happiness that human beings have been endowed with a will; instinct would have been far more effective for this purpose. Reason was given to us in order to produce a will which was good not as a means to some further end, but good in itself. Good will is the highest good and the condition of all other goods, including happiness.

What, then, makes a will good in itself? To answer this question we must investigate the concept of *duty*. To act from duty is to exhibit good will in the face of difficulty. But we must distinguish between acting in accordance with duty, and acting from the motive of duty. A grocer who is honest from self-interest, or a philanthropist who delights in the contentment of others, may do actions which are in accord with duty. But actions of this kind, however right and amiable, have, according to Kant, no moral worth. Worth of character is shown only when someone does good not from inclination, but from duty: when, for instance, a man who has lost all taste for life and longs for death still does his best to preserve his own life in accordance with the moral law.

Kant's teaching here is directly opposed to that of Aristotle. Aristotle taught that people were not really virtuous as long as their exercise of virtue went against the grain; the really virtuous person thoroughly enjoyed performing acts of virtue. For Kant, on the other hand, it is the painfulness of welldoing that is the real mark of virtue. It is only when it costs us something to do what is right that we can be sure we are acting from the motive of duty. Kant realizes that he has set daunting standards for moral conduct: he is quite prepared to contemplate the possibility that there has never been, in fact, an action performed solely on moral grounds and out of a sense of duty.

What is it, then, to act from duty? To act from duty is to act out of reverence for the moral law; and the way to test whether one is so acting is to seek the maxim, or principle, on which one acts. If I am to act out of reverence for the law, I must never act except in such a way that I can also will that my maxim should become a universal law. This is Kant's famous 'categorical imperative'.

There are two sorts of imperative, hypothetical and categorical. The hypothetical imperative says: If you wish to achieve a certain end, act in such-and-such a way. The categorical imperative says: No matter what end you wish to achieve, act in such-and-such a way. There are many hypothetical imperatives, because there are many different ends which humans may set themselves. There is only one categorical imperative: the imperative of morality. The categorical imperative is the requirement to conform with the pure universality of law. 'There is therefore only a single categorical imperative, and it is this: "Act only on that maxim through which you can at the same time will that it should become a universal law".'

Kant illustrates this with several examples, of which we may mention two. The first is this. Having run out of funds, I may be tempted to borrow money, though I know that I will be unable to repay it. I am acting on the maxim 'Whenever I believe myself short of money, I will borrow money and promise to pay it back, though I know that this will never be done.' I cannot will that everyone should act on this maxim, because if everyone did so the whole institution of promising would collapse. Hence, borrowing money in these circumstances would violate the categorical imperative.

A second example is this. A person who is well provided for, and is asked for help by others suffering hardship, may be tempted to respond 'What does this matter to me? Let every one be as happy as Heaven wills or as he can make himself; I won't harm him, but I won't help him either.' He cannot will this maxim to be universalized, because a situation might arise in which he himself needed love and sympathy from others.

These cases illustrate two different ways in which the categorical imperative applies. In the first case, the maxim cannot be universalized because its universalization involves contradiction (if no one keeps promises, there is no such thing as promising). In the second case, the maxim can be universalized without contradiction, but no one could rationally *will* the situation which would result from its universalization. Kant says the two different cases correspond to two different kinds of duty: strict duties, and meritorious duties.

Not all Kant's examples are convincing. He argues, for instance, that the categorical imperative excludes suicide. But there is no contradiction involved in universal suicide; and someone sufficiently despairing might regard it as a consummation devoutly to be wished.

Kant offers a further formulation of the categorical imperative. 'Act in such a way that you always treat humanity, whether in your own person or in the person of any other, never simply as a means, but always at the same time as an end.' He claims, though he has not convinced many of his readers, that this is equivalent to the earlier imperative, and enables the same practical conclusions to be drawn. It is, in fact, more effective in ruling out suicide. To take one's own life, Kant urges, is to use one's own person as a means of bringing to an end one's discomfort and distress.

As a human being, I am not only an end in myself, I am a member of a kingdom of ends. By 'kingdom', Kant says, is meant 'a systematic union of different rational beings under common laws'. My will, as has been said, is rational in so far as its maxims can be made universal laws. The converse of this is that universal law is law which is made by rational wills like mine. A rational being 'is subject only to laws which are made by himself and yet are universal'. In the kingdom of ends, we are all both legislators and subjects.

Kant concludes the exposition of his moral system with a panegyric on the dignity of virtue. In the kingdom of ends, everything has a price or a dignity. If something has a price, it can be exchanged for something else. What has dignity is unique and unexchangeable; it is beyond price. There are, Kant says, two kinds of price: market price, which is related to the satisfaction of need; and fancy price, which is related to the satisfaction of taste. Morality is above and beyond either kind of price.

'Morality, and humanity so far as it is capable of morality, is the only thing which has dignity. Skill and diligence in work have a market price; wit, lively imagination and humour have a fancy price; but fidelity to promises and kindness based on principle (not on instinct) have an intrinsic worth.' Kant's words echoed throughout the nineteenth century, and still strike a chord today.

4

Continental Philosophy from Fichte to Sartre

ROGER SCRUTON

WHITEHEAD described Western philosophy as 'footnotes to Plato'. With less exaggeration it could be said that German philosophy since the Enlightenment has been footnotes to Kant. Kant's immediate followers could neither think outside the framework of 'transcendental idealism', nor discard the Kantian terminology. And while rejecting or ignoring Kant's greatest insights, they adopted his wilder speculations as established truths. For Reinhold, Beck, Fichte, and Schelling, the achievement of transcendental idealism consisted in the dethroning of the thing-in-itself. And this meant, on their interpretation, that 'objects outside us' are 'constituted' within the mind of a self-conscious subject. Philosophy becomes the study of the 'faculties'—intuition, understanding, reason, imagination, judgement, reflection—through which the self gains possession of its knowledge. The ground of all that exists is the subject of consciousness—unknowable to the understanding, but revealed to practical reason as freedom and will.

But if the self is the source of knowledge, something has been left unexplained. How can a merely subjective entity, beyond the reach of concepts, construct an objective world, and endow it with the order of space, time, and causality? This is the question that motivated the tradition known on the Continent as 'classical German philosophy', but which could be more accurately described as 'romantic German philosophy', not only for its association with romantic literature, but also on account of its manifest preference for lofty visions over valid arguments. The tradition was founded by J. G. Fichte and Friedrich Schelling, and includes, as its greatest representatives, G. W. F. Hegel and Arthur Schopenhauer. Each of those writers erected a vast system of abstract thought on the premiss of the self-conscious subject, and each regarded system-building as the true task of philosophy, since it is for the philosopher to show how the *whole* of things can emerge from this tiny seed of self.

Fichte

Johann Gottlieb Fichte (1762–1814) was the son of a Lusatian ribbon-maker and eldest of a large family. Discovered by a Baron von Miltitz, who adopted him, he was sent in 1780 to the University of Jena and thence to Wittenberg and Leipzig, where he absorbed the prevailing ideas and attitudes of German romanticism, and encountered the critical philosophy of Kant. In 1788 he travelled to Königsberg in order to visit the master, but was received only four years later, after publishing a *Critique of All Revelation*, the success of which (due to the widespread misapprehension that Kant himself was the author) prompted Kant to take an interest in the thinker who was destined to supplant him. Fichte became friendly with Goethe and Schiller, and thanks to their influence was appointed Professor of Philosophy in Jena at the age of 32.

Fichte's lectures were popular, and he published them as the *Grundlage der gesamten Wis-*

FICHTE LECTURING, as sketched by one of his pupils.

THE UNIVERSITY OF BERLIN. In 1810 King Frederick William III of Prussia handed over a royal palace in Berlin to Wilhelm von Humboldt to found a university. Among those who were to teach there were Fichte, Hegel, and Schleiermacher.

senschaftslehre (Foundations of the Science of Knowledge) in 1794. This short but immensely difficult book was later reworked in various versions, one of which, the standard *Wissenschaftslehre*, was published in 1804, others of which appeared posthumously; but it did not lose its rough-hewn and uncouth character. Neither did Fichte: he bridled at opposition and was offensive to colleagues and scathing of his rivals. He lectured in a state of concentrated frenzy that held his students so deeply spellbound that it scarcely mattered whether they understood what he said. He was a republican and a radical, and lost his chair in 1799 when his provocative remarks led not only to charges of atheism, but also to physical attacks on himself and his family. Thanks to influential friends like Goethe, he was able eventually to return to academic life as professor in the University of Berlin; meanwhile, he gained renewed fame as an orator with his *Addresses to the German Nation* (1808), reproaching the Germans for the disunity which had caused them to submit so meekly to the Napoleonic armies. He took an active part in the struggle against Napoleonic rule in 1812–13, and died of typhus contracted while a volunteer medical officer. Regardless of his achievements as a metaphysician, he will always be remembered, for better or worse, as one of the founding fathers of German nationalism.

Fichte wrote that 'the kind of philosophy one adopts depends on the sort of man one is; for a philosophical system is not a lifeless piece of furniture . . . but is animated by the soul of the man who has it'. This is certainly true of his own philosophy, through which a tortured self-obsession acquired sublime metaphysical endorsement, in terms calculated to enlist the sympathy of his Kant-intoxicated readers. In the preface to the *Wissenschaftslehre* Fichte proudly declares that 'my system is nothing other than the Kantian'. Although Kant himself did not agree, he was old and *hors de combat*, and his pedantic disciple Reinhold was unable to resist the demonic upstart who, in the guise of making sense of the Kantian system, inaugurated its overthrow.

There are, Fichte argued, but two possible philosophies: idealism and dogmatism. The idealist looks for the explanation of experience in intelligence, the dogmatist in the 'thing-in-itself'. Although the consistent dogmatist can avoid refutation, his position has been made untenable by Kant, who demonstrated that idealism can explain all that dogmatism explains, while making no assumptions about things beyond the reach of observation. The dispute between the idealist and the dogmatist concerns whether 'the independence of the thing should be sacrificed to that of the self, or, conversely, the independence of the self to that of the thing'. The starting-point of idealist philosophy is therefore the self (*das Ich*): and this, Fichte claimed (with the agreement of other Kantians), was Kant's starting-point too.

Our task is to discover the 'absolutely unconditioned first principle of human knowledge'—i.e. the principle upon which all knowledge can rest, but which itself rests on nothing. Logicians offer us an instance of necessary and indisputable truth, in the law of identity: $A = A$. But even in that law something is presupposed that we have yet to justify, namely the existence of A. This thought enables Fichte to introduce a concept which changed the course of philosophy: the concept expressed by the verb 'to posit' (*setzen*). I can advance to the truth that $A = A$, he argues, once A has been 'posited' as an object of thought. But what justifies me in positing A? There is no answer. Only if we can find something that is posited in the act of thinking itself will we arrive at a self-justifying basis for our claims to knowledge. This thing that is posited 'absolutely' is the I; for when the self is the object of thought, that which is 'posited' is identical with that which 'posits': in the statement that $I = I$ we have therefore reached bedrock. Here is a necessary truth that presupposes nothing. The self-positing of the self is the true ground of the law of identity, and therefore of logic itself.

Kant argued that we cannot understand the world through intuition alone, or through intellect alone: only through the synthesis of intuition and concept do we arrive at knowledge. Hence we know the world as appearance, and never as 'thing-in-itself'. We could know the thing-in-itself only if we could obtain an 'intellectual intuition': something which to us is inconceivable. (To have an intellectual intuition is to know the world as God knows it, with an immediate grasp of its totality, and from no finite point of view.) The concept of an intellectual intuition is, I believe, an insignificant appendage to the Kantian system. But it was received by Kant's immediate followers with rapturous applause as the clue to 'any future metaphysics'. Intellectual intuition became (at least until Hegel denounced it as 'the night in which all cows are black') the Holy Grail of German philosophy: to obtain it would be to reach the perspective of the Creator, the coveted view of the Whole of things.

Fichte therefore described self-knowledge as an 'intuiting' of the self. This, he argued, is the one and only intellectual intuition, and therefore the opening on to all that is really real. To explain the possibility of such an intuition is the first task of philosophy. And here *is* the explanation: the self intuits itself by positing itself. QED.

To this first principle of knowledge, which he calls the principle of identity, Fichte adds a second. The positing of the self is also a positing of the not-self. For what I posit is always an *object* of knowledge, and an object is not a subject; hence that which comes before my intuition in the act of self-knowledge is intuited as not-self. This is the principle of counterpositing (or opposition). From which, in conjunction with the first principle, a third can be derived: namely, that the not-self is divisible in thought and opposed to a 'divisible self'. This third principle (called the grounding principle) is supposedly derived by a 'synthesis' of the other two. It is the ground of transcendental philosophy, which explores the 'division' of the not-self by concepts, whereby the objective order of the world is constituted.

The self is 'determined' or 'limited' by the not-self, which in turn is limited by the self. It is as though self-consciousness were traversed by a movable barrier: whatever lies in the not-self has been transferred there from the self. But since the origin of both self and not-self is the act of self-positing, nothing on either side of the barrier is anything, in the last analysis, but self. In the not-self, however, the self is passive. There is no contradiction in bringing this passive object under such concepts as space, time, and causality, so situating it in the natural order. As subject, on the other hand, the self is active, spontaneously 'positing' the objects of knowledge. The self is therefore free, since the concepts of the natural world (including causality) apply only to that which it posits, and not to the subject which determines them.

All activity in the not-self (including that which we should describe as causation) is transferred there from the self. By exploring this transfer we deduce the 'categories', which are the necessary determinations of the not-self as it is posited by the subject. But transference of activity is also an 'alienation' (*Entfremdung*) of the self in the not-self, and a determination of the self *by* the not-self. This self-determination (*Selbstbestimmung*) is the realization of freedom, since the not-self that determines me is only the self made objective in the act of self-awareness.

Brevity forbids a further examination of Fichte's arguments, which are not so much arguments as impetuous explosions of jargon, in which that fabricated verb 'to posit' kaleidoscopes into a thousand self-reflecting images. Schopenhauer described Fichte as 'the father of *sham philosophy*, of the *underhand* method that by ambiguity in the use of words, incomprehensible talk and sophisms, tries to . . . befool those eager to learn'. This harsh judgement (characteristic of its author) may be deserved; but it does nothing to deny Fichte's enormous influence: an influence which can be seen in the writings of Schopenhauer himself. For what Fichte bequeathed to his successors was not an argument at all, but a drama, the outlines of which may be summarized thus:

Underlying knowledge, yet outside its purview, is the free and self-producing subject. The destiny of the subject is to know itself by 'determining' itself, and thereby to realize its freedom in an objective world. This great adventure is possible only through the *object*, which

F. W. J. VON SCHELLING, fairly or unfairly, is best remembered in the history of philosophy as a conduit of ideas between Fichte and Hegel.

the subject posits, but to which it stands opposed as its negation. The relation between subject and object is dialectical—thesis meets antithesis, whence a synthesis (knowledge) emerges. Every venture outwards is also an alienation of the self, which achieves freedom and self-knowledge only after a long toil of self-sundering. The self emerges at last in possession of the Holy Grail: an intellectual intuition not of itself only, but of the whole world contained in itself as in a crystal ball. The 'process' of self-determination does not occur in time, since time is one of its products: indeed, the order of events in time is the reverse of their order in 'logic'.

That drama, give or take a few details, remains unchanged in Schelling and Hegel, and remnants of it survive through Schopenhauer, Feuerbach, and Marx, right down to Heidegger. What it lacks in cogency it amply supplies in charm, and even today its mesmerizing imagery infects the language and the agenda of continental philosophy.

Schelling and Schiller

Friedrich Wilhelm Joseph von Schelling (1775–1854), who idolized Fichte, was an urbane and cultivated man, son of a scholarly Lutheran pastor, with none of Fichte's rough edges. He taught in various academic posts, and was to end life, duly ennobled, as a Prussian privy councillor and member of the Berlin Academy. His *System of Transcendental Idealism*, published in 1800 when the author was only 25, is indebted to Fichte on every page. Schelling appropriates Fichte's dialectic of subject and object, smartens it up with agreeable prose, and adds the following pregnant suggestion: that transcendental idealism must contain two philosophies, the subjective, dealing with the self and its freedom, and the objective, dealing

FRIEDRICH SCHILLER, here seen in a portrait (*c.* 1790) by Anton Graff, combined creative genius as a poet with philosophical insight as an aesthetician.

with the natural world. These two realms of being have a common source, which is the transcendental subject. The highest task of the new philosophy is that indicated in Kant's *Critique of Judgement* (a work which had been comparatively neglected until Schelling studied it), which is to demonstrate the harmony of nature and intellect, of objective and subjective, of non-conscious and conscious activity. We have an intuition of the unity of these two spheres in the aesthetic experience. Indeed, it is only through the immediate and non-discursive awareness offered by art that we can fully understand the synthesis of Spirit and Nature, and therefore the absolute truth of the world. Art therefore provides us with an immediate and sensuous route to a goal which philosophy can never attain unaided.

In subsequent writings Schelling identified the transcendental subject not as individual self, but as universal spirit (*Geist*), which also expresses itself as Will. 'In the final and highest instance there is no other being than Will. Will is primordial Being, and all predicates apply to it alone...' (*Of Human Freedom*, 1809). Spirit manifests itself in the Other, as well as in the Self, and others have a crucial role to play in my self-realization. In particular, the subject can enjoy true freedom only when aware of the constraints on action, and these constraints are set by all other agents. The journey towards self-knowledge is therefore also a journey towards moral and political order. It is completed, Schelling suggests, through the universal rule of law that Kant had prophesied in *Perpetual Peace*. The final achievement of self-knowledge involves a unification of all that had been formerly understood as diverse. The free being is the one who comprehends reality as the One, the Absolute, or God.

Those ideas, sketchy in Schelling, achieve full elaboration in Hegel, with whom Schelling collaborated in editing the *Critical Journal of Philosophy* while teaching at Jena. Schelling was also noteworthy for his attempt to integrate the philosophy of art into his metaphysics, and to give aesthetics a central place in philosophy as a whole. His lectures on fine art, published in 1807, contain reflections on the meaning of music, painting, and the plastic arts, in which a framework for cultural history was for the first time presented in German. Intellectually, however, Schelling's philosophy of art is far inferior to that of the poet Friedrich Schiller (1759–1805), whose *Letters on the Aesthetic Education of Man*, published in 1794–5, were inspired, like Schelling's lectures, by Kant's third *Critique*. Schiller addresses the question posed by Kant: What is the value of something that can be understood only when viewed as without purpose? The aesthetic experience is entirely 'disinterested', while also involving an evaluation of its object. And how can we evaluate that in which we have no interest?

The answer, according to Schiller, is to distinguish activities valued as means from those valued for their own sakes, as ends. The contrast here can be illustrated through that between work (considered merely as a means) and play. Play is not a means to enjoyment; it is the very thing enjoyed. And it provides the archetype of all activities in which man is at peace with himself: sport, conversation, rambling, art, etc. (Compare the dictum of Mr Jorrocks, that 'all time wot aint spent in huntin' is wasted time'.) Schiller went so far as to exalt play into the paradigm of intrinsic value. With the agreeable and the good, he remarked, man is merely in earnest; but with beauty he *plays*.

From this somewhat paradoxical idea, Schiller developed a theory of aesthetic education, and its place in the formation of the free citizen. Aesthetic education is necessary, he argued, not only for the proper balance of the individual soul, but also for the harmonious development of society. His theory was destined to exert a lasting influence over German romantic philosophy, not the least over Marx, who discovered in Schiller's argument a clue to the distinction between alienated labour and the kind of self-expressive activity in which man is 'restored to himself' and at one with his 'species being' (an expression which came to Marx from Schelling, via Feuerbach).

Hegel

Schelling criticized his own earlier philosophy as the 'negative' philosophy, and devoted his last lectures to a new system, in which his incipient religious feeling received more open expression. But this 'positive philosophy' was overtaken long before its posthumous publication by the writings of his erstwhile friend and collaborator, G. W. F. Hegel (1770–1831). Like all the exponents of German idealism, Hegel was an academic. However, by the time he began writing, idealist systems were two a penny, and you had to wait before acquiring the right to expound one from a university chair. After working as editor, journalist, schoolmaster, and headmaster of a Gymnasium, Hegel finally ascended the Chair of Philosophy in Heidelberg in 1816, moving from there to Berlin two years later. But he had already made a name for himself, first with an essay comparing Fichte and Schelling (1801) and then with the *Phenomenology of Spirit*, published in 1807, and widely received as a work of revolutionary significance. The ideas expounded in the *Phenomenology* were re-expressed and refined in subsequent books and lectures, and eventually summarized in the *Encyclopedia*, which Hegel began at Heidelberg. By this stage Hegel had added philosophies of nature, religion, and history to his system; all were included in the *Encyclopedia*, which did not however, extended to a treatment of art—a subject brilliantly handled in Hegel's *Lectures on Aesthetics*. Hegel died of cholera in 1831, after which those and other lectures were published, greatly adding to his posthumous influence.

The outline of Hegel's system is that sketched by Schelling: the underlying reality is spirit, whose journey towards self-knowledge leads, by dialectical steps, to the Absolute Idea, in which all partial determinations of the intellect are subsumed and transcended. The dialectical journey has two versions: that of subjective spirit (the philosophy of mind) and that of objective spirit (the philosophy of nature). (The two journeys correspond to Fichte's self and not-self.) The journey of subjective spirit is *our* journey, which is a journey outwards into the object and towards the other, a long tale of alienation and self-sundering, through which spirit is at last returned to itself in objective and realized form: in ethical life (the sphere of morality and politics), in art, and in philosophy.

Into this schema Hegel incorporated a critique of the Kantian enterprise, together with a radical theory of the 'dialectic' and a doctrine of 'universal history' (another of Schelling's influential phrases). For all these he is justly famous, as well as for his striking and persuasive account of the human condition, which largely survives the ruin of his dialectical method.

G. W. F. HEGEL was the most influential German philosopher after Kant.

The Kantian philosophy, Hegel argued, had tried to justify our claims to knowledge by showing that our faculties are inherently directed to the truth. But this 'deduction' of our faculties proceeds by means of them, and therefore presupposes precisely what it aims to prove. There can be no non-circular justification of our rational powers: all that philosophy can do is to engage in a continuous critique of knowledge, and so ascend to an ever higher standpoint as the imperfections of each partial cognition are successively overcome. Nevertheless, by this very process, philosophy can reach the perspective (the Absolute Idea) where knowledge, being complete, vindicates itself. This ascent of philosophy towards the Absolute is the dialectic, and it is mirrored in every sphere of human endeavour, since dialectic and reason are one, revealed in the individual striving towards freedom and self-knowledge, in the scientific study of nature, in institutions, religions, art, and history itself.

The principles of the dialectic are set out in Hegel's *Science of Logic*. Hegel did not mean 'logic' in the modern sense, as the theory of inference and argument. He meant the abstract study of the *logos*: word, description, concept, explanation, reasoning. Hence Hegel's *Logic* is an a priori study of the application of concepts. All thought involves the application of a concept, and the first version (or 'moment') of any concept is *abstract*. In trying to grasp reality I necessarily begin by describing it with the most abstract of terms, such as 'thing' or 'object'. I then perceive the inadequacies of this conception, and so acquire a more 'determinate' grasp. But the more determinate concept wars with the abstraction, with which it is in contradiction, since nothing can be both abstract and determinate. ('Every determination is a negation', says Hegel, quoting Spinoza.) Out of this conflict a new concept is born, one which is 'truer' than the first, both in making finer discriminations, and in presenting a more complete picture of reality. At the final point of knowledge, when the dialectical chain has been completed, concept becomes Idea, and the truth of the world stands revealed.

Hegel puts the matter in the following way:

1. First moment: a concept is presented, but it is abstract, 'immediate', and indeterminate. ('Immediate' means stemming *directly* from the process of thought, and without the aid of other, intermediate, conceptions.)
2. Second moment: the abstract concept is mediated by rival conceptions, so as to become 'determinate': i.e. so as to say something specific about its subject-matter.
3. The conflict between the abstract and the determinate conception is resolved by an intellectual 'transcendence' (*Aufhebung*), to a 'truer' (more complete) conception, that embodies both. Thus it is that 'consciousness realizes itself, in that it raises itself from abstract thinking to rationality'.

It is easy to see how concept-application may proceed from abstract to determinate in progressive stages: as when I understand an object first as a thing in space, then as a living thing, then as an animal, and then as a cat. But what is meant by saying that the various stages are reached through *contradiction*? Hegel's thought is roughly this: concepts are by nature universal and therefore abstract. Yet their *application* is always a particularization. However, there is nothing outside concepts which could introduce the element of particularity, for we have no access to a pre-conceptual reality. (That is the underlying assumption of transcendental idealism, in this as in every form.) Concepts must in some way *apply themselves*: they must contain within themselves whatever is necessary to identify the particular instance. Hence the abstract, universal element in every concept must be counterbalanced by a concrete, particularizing element: a vector, if you like, tending *against* abstraction, and therefore against the concept in its abstract form. The clash of the two is what leads to the idea of a concrete reality, which both *is* cat and yet is *not* cat, since it is not identical with the universal.

The concept of being provides an illustration of Hegel's dialectic. As initially conceived, being is entirely abstract; it is 'indeterminate immediacy', as Hegel expresses it. I can understand this idea without the aid of any others (it is 'immediate'), but that is only because it is entirely indeterminate: it applies to everything, and so says nothing in particular about anything. (In Hegel we find the interesting thought that we purchase immediacy at the expense of determinacy, and so certainty at the expense of content. The more certain our knowledge, the less we know.) It follows that, in predicating being, we say nothing about *what* is. To say that there is being is therefore to say nothing. Hegel thinks of this as a contradiction: we have applied not only the concept of being, but also that of nothing or not-being, which was lying concealed, so to speak, within being and eager to wage war against it. Not-being determines or limits being, and compels it to 'pass over' into the next concept in the dialectical chain: that of determinate being, which is the kind of being that genuine particulars have. A table, for instance, exists; but there is a limit to its existence: there are places where it is not, and when we apply the concept table, we divide the world into things that are tables, and things that are not tables. All this is comprehended in the thought that tables have determinate being, in which both being and not-being are contained and transcended. Hegel uses the German word *dasein* to denote this idea. ('*Dasein*' means to exist, but signifies etymologically 'being there'; 'there' captures the determinate element in our idea of existence.)

There then arises a new dialectical opposition, between being and determinate being, which can be resolved, Hegel argues, only through temporal ways of thinking. We give sense to the idea that one and the same thing both is and is not, by postulating its existence at one time, but not at another. Through time we discriminate entities, counting and distinguishing them. Time provides us also with the concept of 'becoming' (the next stage of the dialectic), through which we understand the being of organisms. Organisms are entities in a constant state of becoming, which yet remain the same.

Like Fichte and Schelling, Hegel describes logical relations as though they were *processes*, since for him the 'unfolding' of a concept is also the growth of spirit into self-awareness. However, it is a growth that does not take place in time, since it *produces* time, as one of the forms of sensibility. In the *Phenomenology of Spirit*, the Fichtean drama of the subject is presented in great detail, and there is room here only for a summary of one of its central arguments. Yet it will suffice, I hope, to show the extent to which Hegel transformed the mystagogic rhetoric of his predecessors into genuine argumentation, while retaining the transcendental framework.

The self is first 'posited', according to the original identity canvassed by Fichte: the I = I which, being 'immediate', is also indeterminate and devoid of content. In knowing that I exist, I know next to nothing: for as yet the I, unschooled in contest, is not an object of its own awareness. This indeterminate self is nevertheless a unity: it possesses the 'transcendental unity of apperception', as Kant described it, by virtue of which it is the subject of its own conscious states. Such a unity must, however, be *realized*, as an identity through time. The states of the self *succeed* one another, each tending towards the next and propelled by the activity of the self-positing subject. Hegel speaks of Aristotle's *orexis*, or appetite: the striving through which we seek to possess our world. In the initial stage of consciousness, this is what the self amounts to: the primitive 'I want' of the infant, the contumacious screeching of the fledgling in the nest.

But desire cannot exist without being desire *for* something. Desire posits its object as independent of itself. With this venture towards the object, the 'absolute simplicity' of the self is sundered. In positing the object of desire, however, spirit does not rise to self-consciousness: for it has no conception of itself as *other* than the world of objects, and free in relation to them. It has reached the stage only of animal mentality, which explores the world as an object of appetite, and which, being nothing *for* itself, is without genuine will. At this stage the object of desire is conceived only as a lack (*Mangel*), and desire itself destroys the thing desired.

Self-consciousness awaits the 'moment' of opposition. The world is not merely passively unco-operative with the demands of appetite; it may also actively *resist* them. The world then becomes genuinely *other*: it seems to remove the object of my desire, to compete for it, to seek my abolition as a rival.

The self has now 'met its match', and there follows what Hegel poetically calls the 'life-and-death struggle with the other', in which the self begins to know itself as will, as power, confronted by other wills and other powers. Full self-consciousness is not the immediate result of this: for the struggle arises from appetite, and the self has yet to *find* itself (to determine itself as an object of knowledge). This self-determination (*Selbstbestimmung*) comes only when the subject invests the objects of its world with meaning, distinguishing those things which are valuable from those which are not. The life-and-death struggle does not generate the concept of the self *in its freedom*. On the contrary, the outcome of this struggle is the mastery of one party over the other: the one who prefers life to honour becomes slave to the one who is prepared to sacrifice his life for honour's sake.

This new 'moment' of self-consciousness is the most interesting, and Hegel's account of it was destined to exert a profound influence on nineteenth-century ethical and political philosophy. One of the parties has enslaved the other, and therefore has achieved the power to extort the other's labour. By means of this labour the master can satisfy his appetites without the expenditure of will, and so achieve leisure. With leisure, however, comes the atrophy of the will; the world ceases to be understood as a resistant object, against which the subject must act and in terms of which he must strive to define himself. Leisure collapses into lassitude; the otherness of the world becomes veiled, and the subject—whose self-definition is through the contrast with the world of objects—becomes lost in mystery. It sinks back into inertia, and its newly acquired 'freedom' turns into a kind of drunken hallucination. The self-definition of the master is fatally impaired. He can acquire no sense of the value of what he desires through observing the activities of his slave. For the slave, in his master's eyes, is merely a means; he does not appear to pursue an end of his own. On the contrary, he is absorbed into the undifferentiated mechanism of nature, and endows his petty tasks with no significance that would enable the master to envisage the value of pursuing them.

Now look at things through the eyes of the slave. Although his will is chained, it is not destroyed. He remains active towards the world, even in his submission, and while acting at the behest of a master, he nevertheless bestows his labour on objects, and realizes his identity through them. The result of his labour is seen as *my* work. He makes the world in his own image, even if not for his own use. Hence he differentiates himself from its otherness, and discovers his identity through labour. His self-consciousness grows, and although he is treated as a means, he unavoidably acquires both the sense of an end to his activity, and the will to make that end his own. His inner freedom intensifies in proportion to his master's lassitude, until such a time as he rises up and enslaves the master, only himself to 'go under' in the passivity that attends the state of leisure.

Master and slave each possess a half of freedom: one the scope to exercise it, the other the self-image to see its value. But neither has the whole, and in this toing and froing of power between them each is restless and unfulfilled. The dialectic of their relation awaits its resolution, which occurs only when each treats the other not as means, but as end: which is to say, when each renounces the life-and-death struggle that had enslaved them and respects the reality of the other's will. In doing so each accepts the autonomy of the other, and with it the categorical imperative that commands us to treat the other as an end and not a means. Each man then sees himself as a subject (rather than a mere thing), standing outside nature, bound to a community by reciprocal demands upheld by a common moral law. This law is, in Kant's words, the law of freedom. And at this 'moment' the self has acquired a conception of its active nature: it is autonomous yet law-governed, partaking of a common nature, and pursuing universal values. Self-consciousness has become *universal* self-consciousness.

In this way Hegel offers a kind of proof (or at any rate, a 'legitimizing narrative') of Kant's categorical imperative, from the premiss of the self and its undifferentiated freedom. But, true to the dialectical method, he sees the moral law as itself unstable, subject to yet another *Aufhebung*—this time in the sphere of interpersonal relations. Abstract right, through which individuals accord to each other the space required by freedom, enters into conflict with those bonds of obligation (*Moralität*) which divide us into communities and groups. This conflict can be resolved only in the higher sphere of ethical life (*Sittlichkeit*): the sphere of the *polis*, in which man's earthly existence attains its concrete fulfilment.

Ethical life also has a dialectical structure; for the individual grows in and through it, and enacts in this public sphere the eternal drama of reason. Society begins in relations that are immediate, undifferentiated, and abstract: relations of kinship in which self and other are fused, and obligations stem from obedience and piety. But the spirit strives to realize its potential as individual will, and thereby sunders the family bond: the family members go their separate ways, into the antagonistic sphere of 'civil society', where individuals combine only by agreement, and where contract is the ruling principle. Family and civil society are dialectically opposed: the security and closeness of the one threatens and is threatened by the freedom and coldness of the other. Their dialectical conflict therefore requires a further *Aufhebung*, which is achieved through the state, whose will is law. The state is the 'march of reason in the world', and its institutions constitute the final realization of the Absolute Idea in the ethical sphere.

Marx

In the course of defending the state, Hegel earned the probably unjust rebuke that he was merely defending the Prussian state, and endorsing its dangerous tendency to absolutism. More interesting, however, is the detail of his argument—laid out in *The Philosophy of Right*, first published in 1821, and one of the most subtle and succinct works of political philosophy ever composed. Hegel there mounts an important defence of private property, as an indispensable 'moment' in the realization of human freedom. It was this defence which inspired Karl Marx (1818–83) to 'set Hegel on his feet', by replacing the idealist metaphysics with its materialist negation.

Marx's early philosophy consists in an adroit manipulation of ideas common to the circle of 'Left Hegelians' whose influence he felt during his student years at the University of

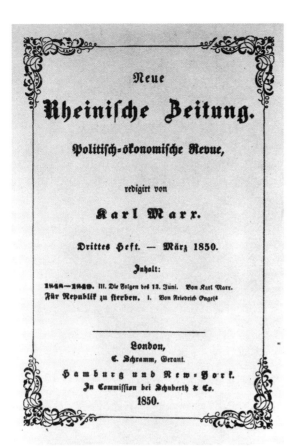

Neue

Rheinische Zeitung.

Politisch-ökonomische Revue,

redigirt von

Karl Marx.

Drittes Heft. — März 1850.

Inhalt:

1848—1849. III. Die Folgen des 13. Juni. Von Karl Marx.
Für Republik zu sterben. I. Von Friedrich Engels

London,
C. Schramm, Gerant.
Hamburg und New-York.
In Commission bei Schuberth & Co.
1850.

THE *NEUE RHEINISCHE ZEITUNG* founded by Marx some years after the banning of the *Rheinische Zeitung* in 1843.

Berlin, and whom he later defended in his vigorous radical newspaper the *Rheinische Zeitung*, suppressed by the authorities in 1843 (an episode which led to Marx's lifelong voluntary exile, first in France and, when he was expelled from there, in Belgium and England). The Left Hegelians, whose leaders were Bruno Bauer (1809–82) and Ludwig Feuerbach (1804–72), contrived to retain many of the leading conceptions of Hegel—and in particular the Fichtean 'drama of the subject'—while rejecting the conservative political vision, and even the idealist metaphysics, which those conceptions had been used to express. The key components of their thinking are two: the dialectic (conceived more as process than as a form of rational argument), and the concept of alienation. Both ideas have their origin in Fichte, but both were now heavily overlayed by Hegelian accretions.

According to the picture bequeathed by Hegel, each mental entity—whether concept, desire, or feeling—exists first in a primitive and 'immediate' form, without self-knowledge, but essentially unified and at home with itself. Its final 'realization' is achieved by a return to this primordial unity, but in a condition of achieved self-knowledge and fulfilled intention. In order to reach this final point, spirit must pass through a long trajectory of separation, sundered from its home, and struggling to affirm itself in a world that it does not control. This state of alienation—the vale of tears—is the realm of becoming, in which consciousness

is separated from its object and also from itself. There are as many forms of alienation as there are varieties of spiritual life, but in each form the fundamental drama is the same: spirit can know itself only if it posits the object of knowledge—only if it invests its world with the idea of the other. In doing this it becomes other to itself, and lives through conflict and disharmony, until finally uniting with the other—as we unite with the object of science when fully understanding it; with the self when overcoming guilt and religious estrangement; with other people when joined in a lawful body politic.

Hegel had justified private property as a necessary realization or objectification (*Entaüsserung*) of the subjective will: part of the subject's attempt to win a place for himself in an objective order, and to claim sovereignty over his world. But objectification, argued Marx, is also alienation (*Entfremdung*), and Hegel's argument is refuted by his own dialectic. No process can be arrested in the moment of alienation, which is essentially 'to be overcome' in a higher unity. Private property, therefore, which sunders man from his 'species being' (*Gattungswesen*) must be transcended, so that man can be 'restored to himself', to live in free community with his fellows. Marx supports this argument (in his *1844 Manuscripts* and elsewhere) with a variety of considerations inspired by Schiller and Feuerbach. Under the regime of private property, he argues, man exists in servitude, an instrument of his own instruments, an object and not a subject, forced to treat himself as an exchangeable commodity in a world where everything, including human life, is a means only, and never an end in itself.

Before he had fully elaborated the argument, Marx underwent a conversion away from Hegelian philosophy towards the empiricist economics of Adam Smith, David Ricardo, and other British writers. He thereafter sought to rewrite his critique of private property and of the system of 'capital' (a term derived from the French utopian socialist Saint-Simon) in the form of a social science. The economic aspect of Marx's theory (the so-called 'labour theory of value') does not concern us, and is in any case now intellectually dead. But the science of history, explored in the mostly unfinished works of his later period, is of perennial interest, not least because of its cataclysmic effect on the events, and the language, of modern politics.

Hegel's theory of history—second in influence only to that of Marx—was based on Schelling's idea of a 'universal history', in which the progress of spirit towards self-discovery is reflected in the epochs of civilized life. (Each 'moment of consciousness' therefore has its parallel in the history of mankind: the moment of master and slave, for example, is also that of the emperor Marcus Aurelius, and the slave Epictetus, who taught him to be free.) Epochs follow one another with the logic of the dialectic, each animated by a spiritual unity (the *Zeitgeist*), and each appearing with the rigorous necessity of a proof in mathematics, moving towards the final 'end of history' when spirit fully knows itself for the first time. (The suggestion that this point in time is marked by the philosophy of Hegel should not be discounted.) According to Hegel, therefore, the prime mover of history is spirit, and the

THE ROUND READING ROOM OF THE BRITISH LIBRARY (*facing*), opened in 1842, where Marx worked on *Das Kapital*.

THE YEAR OF REVOLUTIONS. In 1848 there were risings throughout Europe against the monarchies restored by the Treaty of Paris in 1815. This contemporary lithograph shows the royal cavalry firing on a demonstration in Berlin.

'material' circumstances of mankind, including the mastery over nature and the economic relations that permit it, result from the 'cunning of reason', as it unfolds in dialectical stages.

Marx accepted the view of history as progressing through stages to its final end; but he dismissed Hegel's idealist metaphysics as pseudo-religious mumbo-jumbo. The true motor of history lies in *material* conditions, specifically in the forces of production; and each period of history owes its character to the economic relations (the relations of production) that prevail in it. There are six stages of historical development: primitive communism, slavery, feudalism, capitalism, socialism, and finally full communism, in each of which man's freedom is advanced in proportion to his control over the natural world. Each stage is defined in terms of the prevailing relations of production: those relations between people that are required by the process (itself necessarily social) of producing and distributing economic value. Feudalism, for instance, is the system in which land is controlled by a lord, whose serf is attached to the land, working it in return for a share of the produce. Capitalism is the system in which men sell their labour under a 'wage contract' to those (the capitalists) who control the means of production.

The details of the theory are complex and subtle; but the import is contained in the slogan 'life determines consciousness, not consciousness life' (*The German Ideology*, 1850). The primary significance of the slogan is that law and institutions do not cause social change but are caused by them. They exist because they are functional, relative to the economic relations that produce them. The same is true of 'ideology': this is the system of ideas whereby the ruling class (the class of those who control the means of production) paints a pleasing picture of itself, and endorses its ascendancy as part of the 'natural' order. Laws, institutions, political systems, and religions form the 'superstructure' of society, and exist only so long as the economic 'base'—the system of production relations—retains its stability. However, the forces of production are always developing, and the economic relations that are suitable to them at one level will soon begin to impede them as they grow. With the resulting conflict between forces and relations of production, society enters a period of revolution. The break-up of the economic base brings down the entire superstructure, and for a while there is chaos (*Preface to a Critique of Political Economy*, one of the many works that Marx never finished).

This phantasmagoric history of mankind continues to exert its fascination. And it is not hard to see why. For here, in 'scientific' form, is the old Fichtean drama, usefully endowed with a happy ending. History begins from 'primitive communism'—an 'immediate' unity and harmony—to move outwards through a long self-sundering and alienation as man exploits man and classes 'struggle' for ascendancy. And history returns at last to the original unity, but in the 'higher', self-knowing, and fully 'realized' form of 'full communism'. So great was the grip of the dialectic on Marx's thought that he could not relinquish it, even when sketching a purely 'materialist' theory of social progress. Indeed his followers (notably Plekhanov and Engels) were convinced that the revolutions described and foretold by Marx were brought about by *contradictions*, each being resolved by a kind of *Aufhebung* as society advances towards its goal. They therefore bestowed on Marx's science of history the name by which it has since been known: dialectical materialism.

Schopenhauer

Marx's opposition to Hegel was the expression of a profound and lasting indebtedness, and an act of rebellion against the Father. The opposition of Arthur Schopenhauer (1788–1860) was more a matter of sibling rivalry (they were contemporaneous professors at the University of Berlin, where Hegel drew the larger crowds), although inspired by distaste for the charlatanical side, as Schopenhauer saw it, of Hegel's system-building. Many have seen Schopenhauer as a popularizer, who took over the Kantian framework, and marketed it as a 'philosophy of life'. Others, Schopenhauer among them, have seen his philosophy as the only possible transcendental idealism that would be something more than the *critical* argument of Kant. There is truth in both interpretations. Whatever his standing as a philosopher, however, Schopenhauer deserves to be read as one of the greatest essayists in the German language. To turn to his wise and colourful essays after the groaning paragraphs of his philosophical contemporaries is like opening a window from a smoke-filled room on to the clear air of morning.

Schopenhauer's metaphysical theory is summarized in the title of his major work: *The World as Will and Representation* (1818, expanded edition 1844). Transcendental idealism, he asserts, is the only possible response to the legacy of philosophical argument. It implies that the empirical world exists, for the subject, only as representation: 'every *object*, whatever its origin, is, as *object*, already conditioned by the subject, and thus is essentially only the subject's *representation*'. A representation (*Vorstellung*) is a subjective state that has been 'ordered' according to the primary forms of sensibility and understanding: space, time, and causality. The search for the thing-in-itself behind the representation is futile, so long as we turn our thoughts towards the natural world. Every argument and every experience leads only to the same final point: the system of representations, standing like a veil between subject and thing-in-itself. No scientific investigation can penetrate the veil; and yet it *is* only a veil, Schopenhauer affirms, a tissue of illusions which we can, if we choose, penetrate by another means. He lavishly praises the Hindu writers for perceiving this.

The way to penetrate the veil was stumbled upon by Kant, though he did not see the significance of his own arguments. In self-knowledge I am confronted precisely with that which cannot be known as appearance, since it is the source of all appearance: the transcendental subject. To know this subject as object is precisely not to know it, but to confront once again the veil of representation. But I can know it *as subject*, through the immediate and non-conceptual awareness that I have of the will—in short through practical reason. All this leads Schopenhauer to the following conclusion:

on the path of *objective knowledge*, thus starting from the *representation*, we shall never get beyond the representation, i.e. the phenomenon. We shall therefore remain at the outside of things; we shall never be able to penetrate into their inner nature, and investigate what they are in themselves . . . So far I agree with Kant. But now, as the counterpoise to this truth, I have stressed that other truth that we are not merely the *knowing subject*, but that *we ourselves* are also among those entities we require to know, that *we ourselves are the thing-in-itself*. Consequently, a way *from within* stands open to us to that real inner nature of things to which we cannot penetrate *from without*. It is, so to speak, a subterranean passage, a secret alliance, which, as if by treachery, places us all at once in the fortress that could not be taken from outside.

My essence is will (Kant's 'practical reason'), and my immediate and non-conceptual awareness of myself is awareness of will. But I can know the will, even in my own case, only as phenomenon, since all my knowledge, including inner awareness, is subject to the form of

MASTER AND SLAVE. According to Hegel, each possesses half of freedom: power to exercise it, and insight into its value. As a paradigm of this relationship he took the philosopher emperor Marcus Aurelius (shown here) and the slave philosopher Epictetus who taught him to be free.

Zu Marxens Geburtstag:
Du hattest ja so recht!

Berlin, 5. Mai 1991

time. At the same time (Schopenhauer does not really explain how) the true nature of will as thing-in-itself is revealed to me. I know that will is one and immutable, embodied in the transient will to live of individual creatures, but in itself boundless and eternal.

What, then, is the relation of will to the individual subject? Schopenhauer's answer is framed in terms taken from Leibniz. I am an individual, and identified as such by means of a *principium individuationis* (a principle of individuation). It is only in the world of representation that such a principle can be found: things can be individuated only in space and time, and only when understood in terms of their causal properties. The thing-in-itself, which has neither spatial, nor temporal, nor causal character, is therefore without a principle of identity. In no sense, therefore, am I *identical* with the will. All we can say is that will is *manifest* in me, trapped, as it were, into a condition of individual existence by its restless desire to embody itself in the world of representation. The will in itself is timeless and imperishable. It is the universal substratum from which every individual arises into the world of appearances, only to sink again after a brief and futile struggle for existence.

Will manifests itself among phenomena in two ways: as individual striving, and as Idea. An Idea is something like a complete conception of the will, in so far as this can be grasped in the world of representation. And it is only in the species that the Idea is manifest. In the natural world, therefore, the species is favoured over the individual, since in the species the will to live finds a durable embodiment, whereas the individual, judged in himself, is a passing and dispensable aberration. Schopenhauer expresses the point in one of his many beautiful images:

Just as the spraying drops of the roaring waterfall change with lightning rapidity, while the rainbow which they sustain remains immovably at rest, quite untouched by that restless change, so every Idea, i.e. every *species* of living beings remains entirely untouched by the constant changes of its individuals. But it is the *Idea* or the species in which the will-to-live is really rooted and manifests itself; therefore the will is really concerned only in the continuation of the species.

From this premiss Schopenhauer derives a masterly portrait of nature's indifference to the individual, in terms that anticipate evolutionary biology. His pessimism, which keenly inserts itself into every niche where men seek comfort and consolation, stems partly from his socio-biology. And it is in socio-biological terms that he spells out one of the most impressive theories of sexual love in the philosophical literature. However, Schopenhauer's pessimism has other and more metaphysical roots. According to Schopenhauer individual existence is really a mistake, yet one into which the will to live is constantly tempted by its need to show itself to itself as Idea. The will *falls* into individuality and exists for a while trapped in the world of representation, sundered from the calm ocean of eternity which is its home. Its life as an individual (my life) is really an expiation for original sin, 'the crime of existence itself'.

KARL MARX's philosophical reputation has waxed and waned for non-philosophical reasons. This photograph shows his statue in Berlin decked with flowers on his birthday in 1991. The card on the bouquet reads 'You were *so* right.'

Although intellect is in most things the slave of will, helplessly commenting on processes that it cannot control, it has one gift in its power, which is the gift of renunciation. The intellect can overcome the will's resistance to death, by showing that we have nothing to fear from death and everything to gain. Death cannot extinguish the will, and though what survives death is not the individual but the universal, this should not worry us, since it was the mistake of existing as an individual which caused all our suffering in the first place. In such a way, Schopenhauer justifies suicide: a step that he himself showed no inclination to take.

The will infects all our thoughts and actions. Nevertheless, we can stand back from it, hold it in abeyance, and see things objectively, independently of our transient goals. Then and only then can we be content with the world, having freed ourselves from the restless desire to change it. This detachment from the will comes through art and aesthetic experience. These must therefore be accorded the highest place in man's self-understanding. Indeed, it is

ARTHUR SCHOPENHAUER. This caricature, by Wilhelm Busch, shows the philosopher with his poodle.

through one art in particular, the art of music, that we can comprehend what is otherwise permanently hidden from us, namely, the objective presentation of the will itself (as opposed to its subjective presentation in me). In music I hear not *my* will or *your* will, but the will detached from all individual striving, from all objects of desire and fear, and rendered objective and intelligible. Melodies and modulations present us with a movement that is purely *ideal*, and through which we glimpse the ocean of eternity. That is why, even in the stormiest symphony of Beethoven, we hear only the resolution of contending forces and the achievement of sublime consolation. In music the will plays with itself, like the waves above the ocean's calm.

Schopenhauer's many applications of his philosophy are worked out with imagination and panache, and in his essays he shows a remarkable ability to conjure from his system new, surprising, but always apt and penetrating observations of the human lot. His system was for daily use: not the abstract jargon of Fichte, but a weapon against the 'unscrupulous optimism' by which he saw himself surrounded. He enjoyed his pessimistic conclusions too much to convince the reader that he really believed in them; and his sardonic assaults on popular prejudice reveal a far greater attachment to life than to the renunciation that he advocated. He was certainly arrogant and overbearing in his manner, with a morose streak that led him always to keep a loaded pistol beside him when he slept. But his character was gregarious; he loved wine, women, and song, and lived the normal life of a self-centred academic. He was bitterly distressed by the favourable reception accorded to Hegel. Yet his own philosophy too had a far-ranging influence. Not only did Schopenhauer present the Kantian system in easily digestible form; he made it coincide with the prevailing mood of mid-nineteenth-century Germany, which was one of baffled hope and romantic resignation. By his philosophy of will and renunciation, he gave new forms of life (or at any rate, new forms of death) to Christian culture. Without Schopenhauer there would have been neither Wagner nor Nietzsche as we know them, and it was Nietzsche's final choice of will against renunciation that brought German romantic philosophy to an end.

Nietzsche

'The service which Wagner owes to Schopenhauer is incalculable,' wrote Nietzsche. 'It was the *philosopher of decadence* who allowed the *artist of decadence* to find himself' (*The Case of Wagner* 1888). For Wagner had absorbed from Schopenhauer precisely that which Nietzsche regarded as most poisonous: the life-negating ethic of renunciation. It was because of this that Wagner had 'made music sick'.

Friedrich Wilhelm Nietzsche (1844–1900) shared two features with the majority of his philosophical predecessors: the narrow life of an academic, and an all-engrossing interest in art. Schelling, and to some extent Hegel, had built their systems from an aesthetic idea; Schelling and Schopenhauer had made art into the highest form of knowledge; while behind the pseudo-science of Marx (not an academic, but a perennial student all the same) lie the aesthetic theories of Schelling and Schiller. Only in Nietzsche, however, did philosophy yield first place to art, as the real expression of truth and falsehood. Nietzsche's thought is *criticism*, an extended meditation on the human condition generally, and modernity in particular, in which art is taken not merely as the major symptom but also as the preferred mode of expression. His philosophy is conceived in artistic form, entering the lists alongside the music of Wagner and the poetry of Hölderlin, as a rival contender for the Muses' crown.

The son of a Lutheran pastor, Nietzsche was a lifelong rebel against Christianity, an opponent not only of the gospel morality, but of the personality of Jesus, with whom he never ceased to compare himself (in print, at any rate). Nietzsche's prose—aphoristic, rhythmical, full of images and invocations—is a sustained assault on the citadel of abstract philosophy. Yet it is rich in philosophical suggestions, and offers itself as a bible for the solitary man. (Not, however, for the solitary woman.)

Appointed at the age of 24 to a chair of classical philology at the University of Basel, Nietzsche quickly justified the confidence that had been placed in him, with a revolutionary account of the Greek tragic theatre. *The Birth of Tragedy out of the Spirit of Music* (to give its

NIETZSCHE in uniform as a bombadier in 1868.

full and revealing title) offered a challenge to the view of Greek civilization that had been academic orthodoxy since Winckelman and Goethe. Nietzsche gives for the first time an *anthropologist's* view of the Greeks, arguing that their culture was not the serene and rational affair invoked in Plato's dialogues, but something darker and more atavistic. The life of Greek culture stems from the irrational force personified in Dionysus: the force of the savage dance, which erupts into the life of the city and challenges its fragile order. The spirit of Dionysus, in whose honour the tragedy is performed, is tempered by that of Apollo, god of harmony and discipline. And from the synthesis of the two principles, Dionysian and Apollonian, arises the peculiar muscular beauty of Greek art in all its forms: the beauty of an art in which life is contained but not destroyed, and in which the terrible and the irrational exist side by side with the serene.

The Birth of Tragedy shows the influence of Wagner (whose concept of music-drama it defended) and also of Schopenhauer. Will and representation have become Dionysus and Apollo. But already Nietzsche was on the side of Dionysus. He turned to the Greeks not for their exaltation of the rational principle (he was as antagonistic to Socrates as he was to Jesus), but for their ability to look the gods of darkness in the face, and to preserve in the highest artistic forms the vital spell of savagery. Nietzsche's argument is full of misconceptions about the gods (about Apollo especially), and its speculations about tragedy have been frequently questioned by subsequent scholarship. Nevertheless, he was the first thinker to respond to Greek religion as *religion*, rather than as a set of artistic allegories. What he saw was something that no previous scholar had discerned.

Nietzsche moved a long way from this early work, which he was to condemn as 'smelling of Hegel' (on account of the 'dialectical' opposition between Dionysus and Apollo, transcended in the tragic dance), and as 'affected by the cadaverous perfume of Schopenhauer'. The phrases are typical. Nietzsche's disagreements were never with ideas only, but with *people*: parts of himself which he rejected with a vehemence of self-disgust that betrayed his former love for them. His opponents were enemies who had once been friends, and his attacks on them were assaults on a 'sickness'. To the diseases of nineteenth-century German culture he proposed the remedy of Life. And like most people who make Life into their cause, he wrote far more than he lived.

The aphoristic books which followed—including *Joyful Wisdom* (1882, his main treatise on metaphysics, now absurdly translated as *The Gay Science*) and the brilliant pastiche of Old Testament prophecy *Thus Spake Zarathustra* (1884)—express a vision of life that is at once iconoclastic and full of moral urgency. Philosophy, according to Nietzsche, is not the pursuit of truth: there are no truths, only interpretations, and each system is nothing but the attempt by its creator to interpret reality in his own favour—to bring the world to his side. The real question is whether we should join that side. Is the philosopher inviting us to think in ways that corrupt us, so as to gain power over us and compensate for his inherent weakness? Or is he offering us the tonic that will fortify our 'will to power'?

A philosophy is adopted because it enhances power. But we must distinguish those systems, such as Schopenhauer's, which confer power on the weaker specimens from those, such as Nietzsche's , which unashamedly release what is strongest in us, and enable us to rise to a higher plane. This higher plane is inhabited by the *Übermensch* or Superman, who is both the man of the future, and also the unrealized potential in me (though maybe not in you). Since 'God is dead', I myself must perfect the world; and I do this by *transcending* myself in the Superman. To reach this lofty station I must free myself of the fetters by which the weak impede me. Principal among them is Christianity, with its debilitating distinction between good and evil. Christian morality (and the secular version of it proposed by Kant) condemns self-affirmation as evil, and grants a monopoly of goodness to the meek, the yielding, the pitying—in short, to the slaves. In place of this 'slave morality' Nietzsche recommended (*Beyond Good and Evil*, 1886) a Greek morality, pagan, life-affirming, and rejecting the contrast between good and evil in favour of that between good and bad—meaning good and bad *specimen*.

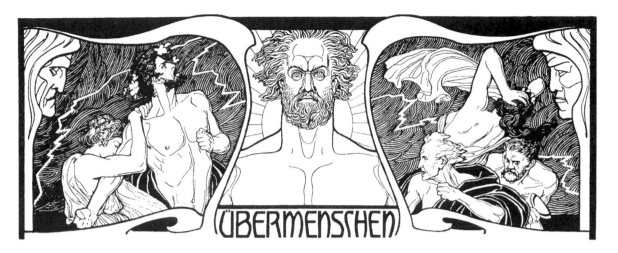

THE SUPERMAN as represented in a book jacket reproduced in the *Berliner Illustrierte Zeitung* in 1903.

The good man, like the good horse or warrior, is the one who is healthy, flourishing, and potent; the bad man is the one who is diseased, enfeebled, impotent. Pride, courage, and the will to power, far from being sinful, are the true virtues, for modern men as much as for the Greeks. To love your neighbour as yourself is fine: but make sure first that you love yourself. To will the maxim of your action as a universal law is also fine: but make sure first that you will your own desire, and will it as law.

To sustain this provocative stance, Nietzsche replaced philosophy by psychology, assessing arguments not for their validity but for the state of mind advanced by them. Once you have seen through all the systems, *only* psychology remains. Nietzsche's ethic is an ethic of suspicion, and his brilliant if one-sided diagnosis of the social order that gave birth to him is also a final revenge against it. In the course of elaborating his diagnosis he made free use of philosophical positions—notably Hume's scepticism about causality and identity, and Kant's demolition of the Cartesian Ego—but he acknowledged, in the end, no master outside his own searing intellect, from whose dominions he banished every trace of a rival deity.

The besetting sin of the world amid which he stood in proud isolation was *ressentiment* (resentment). Nietzsche's use of the French word derives from his affected scorn for the Germans, and from a weird belief that in matters of psychology the French are the real observers. Modern man—that degenerate specimen whom Nietzsche was perhaps first to name—is a creature consumed by resentment towards the power and dignity that he cannot emulate. He suffers from a collective desire, Christianized into unctuous compassion, to replace all distinction by a harmless uniformity, to make everybody equal, to idealize the humble life, and to destroy those who dare to be successful. Nietzsche's hostility to Christianity spilled over, therefore, into an equal hostility towards socialism, positivism, utilitarianism, democracy, and every other nostrum of his age.

Alone on his pinnacle, however, it is possible for the Superman to feel the cold winds of doubt. Was it worth it? Did *I* gain from my self-transcendence, or merely the species in me? Nietzsche offers a kind of consolation in the doctrine of 'eternal recurrence'. The linear and

'THE TRINITY' was the title given by Nietzsche to this photograph, which he posed in 1882, showing Lou Salome on the left and Nietzsche himself on the right.

progressive view of history propagated by the Hegelians is self-deluded nonsense, a transfer of the duty to transcend oneself to the god of history. The truth (or rather, since there are no truths, the best and most life-enhancing interpretation) is that history is cyclical. How I live my present life is how I shall live it eternally. The cycle of becoming is endless, and re-enacts each moment, riding again and again in the groove that here and now I make for it. Live, therefore, so that you can look on yourself eternally with pride: 'to your own self be true', or, in Nietzsche's suprematist version: 'become who you are'.

With such thoughts Nietzsche took leave of his senses. In June 1899, observing a horse that was being cruelly beaten, he flung his arms around the poor creature's neck and, having succumbed to the emotion that he despised above all others, gave up the *Geist*. He survived for eleven years, a silent vegetable, cared for by a sister yet more repulsive than himself.

German philosophy did not end with Nietzsche—far from it. But his belief that he stood apart from the Germans, the prophet of their decline, was not entirely absurd. Although there had been a German precedent for Nietzsche's egotism in the remarkable book *The Self and its Own* (1845) by Max Stirner (1806–56), it was Nietzsche who destroyed the *morality* of idealism, by cancelling the hope for a system that would justify the ways of man to man. His greatest predecessor in this attempt was not Stirner, but Søren Kierkegaard (1813–55), a Danish Christian of strict pietist background who, having been force-fed with Hegel during his time at Copenhagen University, lived his life in rebellion against the idealist system.

Kierkegaard

Kierkegaard is often described as the first existentialist: certainly, he was the first to use the word, though what he would have made of those who later appropriated it is anyone's guess. A melancholy and guilt-ridden Christian, he devoted his considerable literary skills to the defence of faith, conceived as an ultimate and unfounded act of spiritual commitment. Truth, he argued, is truth *for me*, the idea for which I can live and die. And in his *Concluding Unscientific Postscript* (1846) he tried to show that individual existence is the sole ground of all legitimate thinking. I exist as a concrete and freely choosing agent: this alone is certain, and all truth is *subjectivity*. There can be no answer to the riddle of existence—to the question *why* I exist—except in the exercise of choice. And if a choice is to be truly mine it must be criterionless, ungrounded, a pure 'leap of faith' into the unknown. Hence I solve the riddle, and retain my freedom by an unjustified commitment.

This metaphysical position is difficult to recommend to the sceptic: for you can hardly recommend that which is by its nature beyond all justification. The most interesting of Kierkegaard's writings, therefore, consist in skirmishes on the periphery of the black hole into which he promises at every moment to fling himself: in particular the essay *Either/Or: A Fragment of Life* (1843), in which he distinguishes the aesthetic from the ethical way of living, and the explorations of religious pathology—*Fear and Trembling* (1843), *The Concept of Dread* (1844), and *The Sickness unto Death* (1843)—whose grim titles belie the lively poetry contained in them. Like Nietzsche, Kierkegaard was an artist, though one who prided himself on his ability to express points of view that he did not share. And seldom did he write so brilliantly as in the first volume of *Either/Or*, with its justly famous 'Diary of a Seducer' and its penetrating essay on Mozart's *Don Giovanni*, arguing that music alone can capture the 'immediacy' of erotic experience.

The ostensible purpose of the *Either/Or* is to show that it is equally possible to live one's life in obedience to aesthetic ideas, or according to moral duties. There is no *rational* choice between the two alternatives, a fact that illustrates the *ungrounded* nature of all our most significant attitudes. Indeed, it is misleading to talk of choice at all. The aesthete, who pursues every mood, does not choose himself: he falls in love with himself like Narcissus. Even the

KIERKEGAARD, drawn by his cousin Christian Kierkegaard in 1840, at the beginning of his most creative period.

ethical life is unchosen by the one who pursues it, since he receives it as a *command*, which he cannot disobey. The implication seems to be that the religious life is the only life that is truly chosen, because it is the only one in which the irrationality of choice is openly acknowledged and embraced.

In *Fear and Trembling*, therefore, Kierkegaard, drawing on the strange tale of Abraham and Isaac, explores the passage from the ethical to the religious, and the 'suspension of the ethical' whereby Abraham shows himself ready for the 'leap of faith'. In religious faith we confront the mystery of existence—its absurdity. Hence, around the act of faith, gathered as by a magnet, congregate the most extreme and intractable of our feelings: dread, anxiety, despair (the 'sickness unto death'), pressing always towards that indescribable choice in which alone they can be resolved.

Kierkegaard gave a masterly portrait of religious feeling—and particularly of the despair that could turn equally to faith or repudiation. But his contribution to philosophy is questionable, given his reluctance to maintain any stance other than one of comprehensive irony. The reader of Kierkegaard is presented with an array of self-conscious personae, a constantly changing wardrobe of disguises; and if he presses to know what lies behind them, he finds only an enigma, described now as faith, now as truth, now as subjectivity, but unknowable and unsayable under any of its names.

Kierkegaard may have been a Dane; but he has entered history as an honorary German, fighting a battle which would be senseless without German romantic philosophy. What of the rest of continental Europe in the nineteenth century? The brevity of my answer will speak for itself. French philosophy for a long time wandered in the no man's land of speculative

ABRAHAM'S SACRIFICE OF ISAAC (here represented by Ghiberti in the doors of Florence cathedral baptistery) provides the text for Kierkegaard's discussion of the relations between the ethical and the religious dimensions.

sociology, trying vainly to digest the utopian ideas of Saint-Simon, or the cynical anarchism of Proudhon and Babeuf, but eventually colonized by the scientistic religion of Auguste Comte (1798–1857), himself heavily influenced by Saint-Simon. Comte's 'positivism' was a reaction to organized Christianity on the one hand, and modern science on the other: an attempt to produce a system of metaphysics on scientific or 'positive' principles, and so steal a march on the Germans. Comte laid the foundations for modern sociology, and wrote extensively on scientific method, ethics, religion, and the philosophy of mind. Perhaps his most remarkable achievement, however, is the foundation of a positivist Church, a kind of belated offshoot of Robespierre's festival of the supreme being, which had a surprisingly large following in France, and even for a while in England. Little of this extraordinary achievement remains, and Comte's voluminous writings are now seldom consulted by philosophers.

Bergson

More significant was Henri Bergson (1859–1941), whose *Creative Evolution* (1907) and *Matter and Memory* (1896) attempted to integrate the findings of biological science with a theory of consciousness, while retaining some of the scientific optimism of Comte. Before embarking on this venture, however, Bergson wrote an influential *Essai sur les données immédiates de*

HENRI BERGSON wrote imaginatively about time and evolution. Extremely influential in his own day, he is now rather frowned upon by mathematical tense-logicians and evolutionary molecular geneticists.

la conscience (1889), translated as *Time and Free Will*, which had a lasting influence on modern philosophy. In this work Bergson argued that subjective time is quite distinct from objective time. While the physicist observes objects and events in succession, time is presented to consciousness as *duration*—an endlessly flowing process in which one moment grows from another and yields to its successor. The experience of *la durée* is available only inwardly: external observation measures *le temps*. But this inner presentation shows us the true nature of time as process, while the time observed by physics is disaggregated and atomized.

In memory we are granted yet another view of *la durée*: as a process in reverse, and one which is within our control. Memory gives us direct access to the past, and also the power to discover its true order. This true order is an order of meaning, and may be quite distinct from the order of events as recorded by the physicist. The ability to live in and through time, and to order it according to its intrinsic character, is distinctive of consciousness, and one reason for thinking that consciousness is not a physical process at all.

Bergson's observations, recorded with a cheerful tolerance that would have dismayed the Superman, were influential in inspiring Whitehead and the school of 'process philosophers', and in setting the agenda for subsequent attempts, by Husserl, Heidegger, and Merleau-Ponty, to penetrate the inner secret of subjective time. They also left a lasting mark on French literature by giving Proust the idea for his great novel of reminiscence. It is almost certainly true that Bergson is now less read than he should be, largely because he wrote in too lucid and civilized a manner (he was even awarded the Nobel Prize for Literature in 1927). Modern barbarians suspect that he is not really thinking, but merely spinning sentences.

Croce

The same is true of the other great continental philosopher outside the German-language tradition: Benedetto Croce (1866–1952), the founder of modern aesthetics. It is not wholly accurate to place Croce outside the German tradition, since the most important influences on his thought were Kant and Hegel. But he had a directness of style, a freedom from jargon, and a didactic concern for his country and its political future which justify his reputation as a great Italian thinker. From a well-to-do family, Croce lived the life of a gentleman-scholar in Naples, writing about every issue of contemporary concern, while developing his own idealist system. He was a notable defender of liberal ideas in politics, and a distinguished social and literary critic. But he is remembered today for his *Aesthetic* (1902), which decisively changed the philosophy of art.

Croce begins from Kant's distinction between intuition and concept, though interpreted according to his own incipient system. In science and everyday thinking we know the world through concepts, which give a discursive picture of reality, to be assessed for its truth. But concepts are essentially general, and can never capture what is individual and concrete. The concrete particular both is, and is understood through, intuition. In normal experience intuition and concept combine, so that the world is automatically represented in its generality; but in aesthetic experience we hold the two apart, and enjoy an intuition that is free from

concepts, and which therefore displays what is unique and individual. In art such intuitions are expressed, and so achieve objective reality, becoming available not just to the artist but to all who understand his work. But an intuition can be recuperated only by attending to the unique object that embodies it, so as to grasp it as an expression of *that* particular experience. Criticism cannot be founded on rules or discursive theories. The meaning of a work of art is what is expressed by it, and this is always unique to the work, to be understood in terms of the total aesthetic presentation. For similar reasons we could never separate form and content in a work of art, nor should we understand a work in terms of the emotions that it arouses or the thoughts that it inspires: such things are extraneous to the aesthetic experience, which arises only in the intuition contained in the work itself.

We must therefore distinguish expression from representation. Representational works of art—such as figurative paintings, novels, narrative poems—contain a discursive component. They tell a story which might have been told by other means and in other terms. If our interest is merely an interest in this story, then the work becomes a discursive symbol, a means for transmitting information, and hence of merely instrumental (rather than intrinsic) value. When we are interested in expression, however, we are interested in the *unique* experience expressed by *this* work of art. The work is no longer replaceable, nor is it judged as one alternative among others, for conveying information that exists independently. By understanding art as expression we see just why it has the important place in our lives that we accord to it, and just why it is always treated, and must be treated, never as a means only, but always as an end in itself. If representation in art is important, it is because it is a means to expression, a way of presenting the objects of experiences whose uniqueness must be conveyed in another way.

Modern aesthetics grew from the attempt to understand the distinction between representation and expression, though Croce is rarely credited with its first discovery. The neglect into which his luminous writings have fallen is indeed a sad comment on the state of recent philosophy. And to turn from Croce to the last gasps of German romanticism is to recall just how much has been lost, in continental philosophy, since the days when Croce wrote. However, our brief holiday in the sun is over, and we must travel north.

Brentano

Despite his Italian surname, Franz Brentano (1838–1917) was a German-speaking Austrian, whose far-ranging influence is only now being understood. He thought of himself as a psychologist, and began work on a book entitled *Psychology from an Empirical Standpoint*, the first volume of which was published in 1874. A second volume appeared very much later, in 1911, and a third posthumously in 1928. None fulfil the promise made in the book's title, and indeed Brentano came in time to doubt that it is fulfillable. The book consists, in fact, of abstract philosophical reflections on the nature of the mind, which tend to the conclusion that an empirical science of the mental is unlikely to be invented.

Brentano's most important legacy to modern philosophy derived from his search for a defining criterion of 'mental phenomena'. The contents of consciousness are of two kinds: those which represent physical reality, and those which belong to the mental realm itself. These mental 'phenomena' are distinguished, Brentano argued, by their 'direction upon an object' which exists *in* them, but only 'intentionally'. For example, within the experience of fear is contained the 'object' of fear, which need correspond to no reality, but which is nevertheless there, as part of the phenomenon. Each and every mental state is in this way 'directed', and contains a 'mentally inexistent' object which defines its direction. Brentano argued that no physical phenomenon exhibits this peculiar feature, and therefore proposed it as his defining criterion of the mental. Following Edmund Husserl and Brentano (who was himself following a medieval scholastic tradition), the feature is now called 'intentionality' (from the Latin *intendere*, to aim).

Brentano had many distinguished pupils—T. G. Masaryk among them—and was founder of a whole school of Austrian philosophy whose representatives include Alexius Meinong (1853–1920) and Christian Freiherr von Ehrenfels (1859–1932). He taught the founders of empirical psychology, such as Wilhelm Wundt, while many of those who created the thought and culture of modern Vienna attended his lectures, including Sigmund Freud and Robert Musil. For better or worse, however, it is the above-named Edmund Husserl (1859–1938) who is now singled out as his philosophically most important pupil.

Husserl and Dilthey

Husserl was born in Moravia, but spent most of his active life in German universities. He began his intellectual career as a mathematician, composing a *Philosophy of Arithmetic* (volume i, 1891) which, whether or not justly, has been eclipsed by the work of Russell and Frege (who wrote a devastating review of the book). Volume ii of the *Philosophy of Arithmetic* was promised but never published. Husserl turned to logic, and thence to phenomenology. Taking his cue from Brentano, he made intentionality his principal study. It is difficult to know what phenomenology is. The term, invented by the German eighteenth-century mathematician J. H. Lambert to describe the science of appearances, had already been used by Hegel in his account of 'subjective spirit': spirit as it appears to itself. In Husserl it means something similar: the study of what appears to the mind, in the act of self-conscious reflection. But Husserl's two major works of phenomenology—*Ideas* (1913), and *Cartesian Meditations* (1929)—become coy and hyper-subtle at every point where the theory needs explaining, so that commentators are still fiercely divided over what phenomenology really amounts to. It is clear, however, that it is an a priori study, whose results cannot be overthrown by empirical science.

In his earlier writings, Husserl had followed Brentano in analysing mental phenomena into their 'parts' and 'moments' (a moment being a non-detachable feature like intensity). In later writings, however, he came to believe that no study of the mind could proceed until mental phenomena had been separated entirely from residual beliefs about the physical world. To this end we must embark on a 'phenomenological reduction', cancelling or 'bracketing' the reference to external things, so as to confront the pure phenomenon. In studying my fear of spiders, as it inwardly appears, I bracket the reference to spiders, and study only the spider-wards intentionality that points to them. I then bracket the scientific *concept* of spider, using instead the notion of a spider as it appears: threatening, alien, *unheimlich*. Eventually, Husserl thinks, I arrive at what is purely 'given' in consciousness, the phenomenon as it is in itself. The phenomenological reduction now becomes an 'eidetic' reduction or 'ideation', as we plot the limits within which a thing can be imagined to vary without ceasing to be the thing that it is. This process leads at last to an Idea or essence—the 'horizon of potentiality' which is grasped when all contamination of the actual has been thought away.

The process of reduction must be directed even to the thinker himself. As object of my own awareness I am merely an 'empirical self', a component of the contingent world, accidental like everything else. It is only as pure subject that my essential nature is revealed to me. The subject must therefore be understood as such—always as knower and never as known. In short, phenomenology leads us to the transcendental subject, along with the Ideas whereby the world is presented to cognition. The 'transcendental ego', which exists only as subject and never as object, is an active subject: a 'self-constituting ego', in which the objects of awareness are successively brought into being and unified by its organizing power.

Thus, after much groping in the inner darkness, Husserl stumbles at last on the old Fichtean drama: the contest between subject and object. Like his romantic predecessors, he ends by granting ultimate reality to the subject alone. However, because it is always knower and never known, this subject eludes our attempts to describe it. Husserl's transcendental ego becomes, like Kierkegaard's 'subjectivity' or Kant's noumenon, a something about which nothing can be said. At this point Wittgenstein comes to mind, with his famous attack on the possibility of a private language, and his remark that 'a nothing will do as well as a something about which nothing can be said'.

Husserl was aware of the impasse into which he had been driven by his Cartesian meditations, and in his last unfinished work—*Transcendental Phenomenology and the Crisis of the European Sciences*, published posthumously in 1954—he attempted to overcome the subjective emphasis of phenomenology by means of a theory of social reality. The focus shifts from 'I' to 'we', albeit a 'transcendental "we"'. This plural subject is something like the implied community of language-users who together construct the commonsense world in which they are situated. Husserl calls this commonsense world the *Lebenswelt*, or 'life-world': it is a world constituted by our social interaction, and endowed with the 'meanings' that inhabit our communicative acts. We reach the transcendental 'we' by an imaginative self-projection, from the 'here' of first-person awareness to the 'there' of the other. What is given in this process is not the elusive residue of some phenomenological reduction, but the *Lebenswelt* itself.

The concept of the *Lebenswelt* enabled Husserl to revive a project of German romantic

EDMUND HUSSERL, one of the few philosophers who have been equally respected in both the Continental and the analytic tradition.

philosophy which I have so far left unmentioned: the attempt to distinguish the human realm (the realm of meaning) from the realm of science (the realm of explanation). Inspired by Kant's division between understanding and practical reason, the romantic theologian Friedrich Daniel Ernst Schleiermacher (1768–1834) had argued that the interpretation of human actions can never be accomplished by the methods employed in the natural sciences.

FRIEDRICH SCHLEIERMACHER, though primarily a theologian, had considerable philosophical influence throughout Europe. This bust is from a set commissioned by Benjamin Jowett, the reforming Victorian Master of Balliol College, Oxford, of the twelve great thinkers of all time.

The human act must be understood as the act of a free being, motivated by reason, and understood through dialogue. The same is true of texts, which can be interpreted only through an imaginative dialogue with their author. 'Hermeneutics'—the art of interpretation—involves the search for reasons rather than causes, and the attempt to understand a text as an expression of rational activity—the very activity that is manifest in me.

A later Kantian philosopher, Wilhelm Dilthey (1833–1911), extended Schleiermacher's hermeneutical method to the entire human world. Our attitude to other people, he argued, is fundamentally distinct from and even opposed to the scientific attitude. We seek to understand their actions not by explaining them in terms of external causes, but 'from within', by an act of rational self-projection that Dilthey calls *Verstehen*. In understanding human life and action I must find the agent's reasons for what he does. This means conceptualizing the world as he does, seeing the connections and unities that he sees. For example, I understand your fear of speaking in a certain place, once I conceptualize it as you do, as somewhere 'sacred'.

This leads Dilthey to a further and more interesting thought. Our ways of conceptualizing the world in everyday life do not follow the direction laid down by scientific explanation. Rather, they represent the world as 'ready for action'. I see the world under the aspect of my own freedom, and describe and respond to it accordingly. This before me is not a member of the species *Homo sapiens* but a *person*, who looks at me and smiles; that beside him is not a piece of bent organic tissue but a *chair* on which I may sit; this on the wall is not a collection of tinted chemicals but a *picture*, in which the face of a saint appears; and so on. In short, we do not merely enter into dialogue with each other; we are in constant dialogue with the world itself, moulding the world through our descriptions so as to align it with our rational projects. Our categories do not *explain* the world, so much as endow it with *meaning*.

Husserl took this idea a stage further, by suggesting that the pre-scientific vision of the world expresses not merely our identity as rational beings, but our *life*. The world appears to us in the guise of a 'lived environment': a place in which we situate ourselves as acting and suffering organisms. We understand objects as 'friendly' or 'hostile', 'comfortable' or 'uncomfortable', 'useful' or 'useless', and in a thousand ways divide the world according to our interests. Our classifications form no part of the enterprise of scientific explanation, and have an authority that no science could remove. The new task of phenomenology is to awaken us to the *Lebenswelt*, and to vindicate those 'we' thoughts in which the meaning of objects is created and made public.

Dilthey was the first to attempt a systematic distinction between the *Geisteswissenschaften* (humanities) and the natural sciences, suggesting that the first are really extended and transhistorical exercises in *Verstehen*. Husserl recognized, however, that these 'human sciences' had entered a condition of crisis during our century, precisely because natural science had presumptuously invaded their territory, and so prompted people to throw away, as useless remnants of a vanished life-style, the concepts through which the *Lebenswelt* is understood and organized. This crisis is not only intellectual; it is also moral, indeed, a crisis of civilization itself. For the *Lebenswelt* falls apart when not maintained by reflection. The result is a loss of meaning, a moral vacuum, into which we are led whenever we surrender before the false gods of science.

Heidegger

Husserl never completed his investigations into the *Lebenswelt*, nor did he succeed in showing that our pre-scientific concepts have an objective authority that renders them immune from 'disenchantment' at the hands of the scientist. (The term 'disenchantment' was made famous by Husserl's contemporary, the sociologist Max Weber (1864–1920), who was also consciously extending the analysis begun by Dilthey.) However, the legacy of Husserl's later philosophy is enormous: not only a school of phenomenological sociology, founded by his pupil Alfred Schutz (1899–1959), but also the last despairing glimmer of German romantic philosophy, in the writings of another pupil, Martin Heidegger (1889–1976). Like his predecessors in the romantic tradition, Heidegger was an academic, whose most important work, *Being and Time*, was published in 1927, when he was Professor of Philosophy at Marburg. Ostensibly a work of 'phenomenology', the book gives a new interpretation to that elusive word. 'Phenomena', according to Heidegger's reading of the Greek, are 'things that show themselves': phenomenology, therefore, studies the revelation of things in appearance. It is in the context of this study that Heidegger poses what he calls 'the question of being'. This question has 'ontological priority' over all other questions, which is to say, not merely that other questions must wait on it for an answer, but that *we too* depend on that answer. My existence is at stake in the question. And I find the answer only by existing in another way.

Hegel had distinguished two kinds of being: the being-in-itself of objects, and the being-for-itself of the self-conscious subject. To these Heidegger adds a few more, including 'being-in-the-world', 'being-with-others', and 'being-towards-death'. These are not mere features or properties of the things that possess them, but fundamental forms of reality. To pass from one mode of being to the next is as vast and cataclysmic a change as the dialectical *Aufhebung* of the Hegelians, or the revolutionary epoch of Marx.

Heidegger distinguishes *Sein*, mere being, from *Dasein*, which is an 'entity for which being is an issue': in other words, an entity that has not only being but the question of being; in short, the self-conscious subject. *Dasein* must be distinguished from *Existenz*, which is 'the kind of being towards which *Dasein* can comport itself and always does comport itself'. *Dasein* situates itself in time and seeks for the meaning of its existence in time. (*Dasein* has 'historicity'.) The essence of Dasein is its *Existenz*, which would sound like an ontological argument for the existence of the self, were it not the case that *Existenz* is a condition which *Dasein reaches*, and from which it may also fall.

The question of being arises in part from the 'thrown-ness' (*Geworfenheit*) of things, which are dumped in the world without an explanation. I see them in this way, and myself also. Yet there is no 'necessary being' outside the world, no God who will remove the world's contingency. Each of us must come to terms with his own contingency, and find a meaning in contingency itself: only then will the question of being be answered for us. The problem, and the solution to it, are *existential*: they concern our mode of being in the world. It is only by *being* in a certain way that we solve the problem of being. But we then find the meaning of being not in a theory or an argument, but in the fact that being ceases to be an issue for us. The answer to the question of being comes when it ceases to be a question.

Being and Time is a formidably difficult book—unless it is utter nonsense, in which case it is laughably easy. Not being sure how to judge it, and having read no commentator who even begins to make sense of it, I shall content myself with mentioning some of its themes.

First, there is what one might call the 'pure theory of things'. Heidegger adopts from the tradition of Kantian and post-Kantian philosophy the distinction between person and thing (though he does not use that language, perhaps because it would make his observations too readily intelligible). Things, he tells us, are 'ready-to-hand', and 'to-be-used': this is conveyed by the Greek *pragmata*, which he takes to be the word for things, and which derives from the verb *prassein*, to use, or act. Heidegger's theory of readiness-to-hand is phenomenological: it describes how objects appear to us in consciousness, and our posture towards them as self-conscious subjects.

Secondly, there is a theory of persons and personal relations. *Dasein* recognizes others of its kind: its world is full of subjects, who stare from their transcendental nests with intelligent and disconcerting eyes. In response to this, *Dasein* enters that condition which Heidegger

FREIBURG UNIVERSITY in the 1930s, when Martin Heidegger was its Rector. Even those who most admire Heidegger's philosophy blush at his compliance, in office, with Nazi directives.

calls 'being-for-others', in which the awareness of how I seem in the consciousness of others colours and transforms my life. Relations to others can be authentic or inauthentic. They are inauthentic when I use them to conceal the question of being, and so flee from the responsibility for what I am. Inauthenticity comes when I allow others to direct my life: when I surrender to 'them'.

Thirdly, there is a discussion of anxiety—*Angst*—which is the state of being into which I 'fall' when I see that I alone have the *question* of being and the responsibility to answer it. In order to rescue myself from this nameless dread I may throw myself into those inauthentic relations with others which fill the void within me (and so forbid that void to *me*, its proper resident).

The overcoming of anxiety involves an attitude of 'care' (*Sorge*), in which I answer for myself and for the world as it appears to me. This is possible only in the state that Heidegger calls 'being-towards-death', in which I accept my finitude, and death as its boundary.

The religious pulse beneath those ideas is palpable. After a notorious spell as Rector of Freiburg University (during which he had connived at the dismissal of the man to whom he owed everything, including his inspissated jargon, Husserl being of Jewish descent), Heidegger became a recluse, devoting himself to meditative essays on the modern condition. He then gradually emerged from the labyrinth of phenomenology to become a guru. Ceasing to hide behind abstractions, he hid instead in the woods, to the inestimable benefit of his style. His penetrating analysis of the forms of modern life, of the dominance of the modern world by gadgetry, and of our loss of and need for home have been deservedly influential, and an inspiration not only to philosophers, but to critics, poets, and sociologists as well.

Sartre

It was not Heidegger, but the thinker who borrowed his leading ideas, who was to derive from the 'question of being' a morality for modern man, and so create the philosophy, or at least the fad, of existentialism. Jean-Paul Sartre (1905–80) was a writer of protean talents and extraordinary imaginative powers, able to express himself in every literary medium and combining a genuine gift for abstract thought with a lively observation and poetic imagery that make it impossible to convey more than a hint of his impact. A café intellectual in the French tradition, with a never-extinguished desire to *épater le bourgeois* and a constantly redefined commitment to leftist causes, Sartre was a symbol of his age, and one of the creators of post-war France. From government ministers to provincial schoolteachers, from theologians to poets, from doyens of the Gaullist establishment to third-world agitators, all thinking people underwent his influence, and nothing in French culture remained the same after he had burst upon it, guns ablaze. I shall deal only with the philosophical output of his middle years, which coincided with the Second World War, and which culminated in his great work of phenomenological metaphysics, *Being and Nothingness* (1943).

Sartre phrases Heidegger's 'question of being' in a manner that recalls the Thomist tradition of French academic philosophy. Whereas the essence of objects, he argues, precedes

JEAN-PAUL SARTRE, known in academic circles for his existentialism, was known to the wider world for his Marxist-inspired opposition to what he regarded as capitalist and militarist oppression. Here he appears on the extreme right in a pseudo-naïve painting of dissident French intellectuals.

their existence, in our case—the case of the free subject—it is the other way round. 'There is at least one being whose existence comes before his essence, a being which exists before it can be defined by any conception of it. That being is man' (*Existentialism and Humanism*, 1946). What I am is for me to *decide*. And, whether I choose to make this decision or not, I inevitably live in its shadow. Freedom is the fatal flaw in the world of objects, through which the self-defining subject enters the scene. *Being and Nothingness* describes the condition of that subject, and the moral danger that confronts him.

My freedom is my essence: I cannot lose it without ceasing to be. But it is everywhere threatened: I live as a subject among objects, and the danger is that I might 'fall' into that world of objects, and become one with them. In reaction, I may hide from myself, bury myself in some predetermined role, contort myself to fit a costume that is already made for me, so crossing the chasm that divides me from objects only to become an object myself. This happens, according to Sartre, when I adopt a morality, a religion, a social role that has been devised for me by others and which has significance for me only in so far as I am objectified in it. The result is 'bad faith'—the 'inauthenticity' of Heidegger. Thus according to Sartre, 'my Being-for-others is a fall . . . towards objectivity', and 'this fall is an alienation'.

The false simulation of the object by the subject (of the in-itself by the for-itself, to use Sartre's adaptation of the Hegelian language) is to be contrasted to the authentic individual gesture: the free act whereby the individual creates both himself and his world together, by casting the one into the other. Don't ask *how* this is done, since the process cannot be described. (To describe it is to use the concepts of everyday morality, and so to be imprisoned once again by others.) The end-point of the authentic gesture is what matters, and this Sartre describes as commitment. But commitment to what?

There is no answer to that question—or at least no answer that others can make on my behalf. Any adoption of a system of values that is represented as objectively justified and valid beyond my own decision involves an attempt to transfer my freedom to the world of objects and so to lose it. The desire for an objective moral order is therefore inauthentic, a loss of that freedom without which moral order of any kind is inconceivable. As Sartre expresses the point, in *Existentialism and Humanism*: 'I emerge alone and in dread in the face of the unique and first project which constitutes my being: all the barriers, all the railings, collapse, anni-hilated by the consciousness of my liberty; I have not, nor can I have, recourse to any value against the fact that it is I who maintain values in being . . .'.

This paradoxical posture is made more intelligible by Sartre's grim picture of the human reality. Sartre introduces Heidegger's 'being for others' as a description of the state in which I, as a self-conscious being, inevitably find myself. I am at once a free subject in my own eyes and a determined object in the eyes of others. When another self-conscious being looks at me, I know that he searches in me not just for the object but also for the subject. The gaze of a self-conscious creature has a peculiar capacity to penetrate, to create a demand. This is the demand that I, as free subjectivity, reveal myself to him. At the same time my existence as a bodily object creates an opacity, an impenetrable barrier between my free subjectivity and the other who seeks to relate to it. This opacity of the body is the source of the experience of obscenity; and my recognition that my body stands to the other as his does to me is the ori-gin of shame.

Sartre goes on to present an interesting theory of sexual desire. If I desire a woman, this is not simply a matter of lusting to gratify myself on her body. If it were no more than that, then any suitable object, even a doll, would do just as well. My desire would then unite me with the world of objects, as I am united with and dragged under by slime (*le visqueux*, which, for Sartre, is repulsive because it is the image of a *meta*physical, rather than a physical, dissolu-tion). I would then be forced to relinquish the 'for-itself', in order to see myself as a thing. In true desire what I want is the *other*. But the other is real only in his freedom, and is falsified by every attempt to represent him as an object. Hence desire seeks the freedom of the other, in order to appropriate it as its own. The lover, who wishes to possess the body of his beloved only as, and only in so far as, she possesses it herself, is therefore tied by a contradiction. His desire fulfils itself only by compelling the other to identify with her body—to lose the for-itself in the in-itself of flesh. But then what is possessed is precisely not the freedom of the other, but only the husk of freedom—a freedom abjured. In a remarkable passage, Sartre describes sadism and masochism as 'reefs upon which desire may founder'. In sado-masochism one party attempts to force the other to identify with his suffering flesh, so as to possess him in his body in the very act of tormenting him. Again, however, the project comes to nothing: the freedom that is offered is abjured in the very offer. The sadist is reduced by his own action to a distant spectator of another's tragedy, separated from the freedom with which he seeks to unite himself by the obscene veil of tortured flesh.

SARTRE AND FRIEND. In this picture the philosopher is closely followed, as often in his later years, by a representative of the French security forces.

It is useful to recall Hegel's argument about the master and the slave. Personal existence, for Hegel, is achieved only in the condition of mutual recognition; and that in turn requires submission to the moral law, in which the other is no longer regarded as an alien competitor for the possession of my world, but as a sovereign will existing freely within it, the possessor of rights and duties which are the mirror of my own. For Sartre, it seems, we cannot reach that stage of mutuality. The very demand for a radical freedom *excludes* the other from my world, and if he is nevertheless to be found there, it is in the first instance as an enemy. Sartre illustrates this with one of his vivid examples. I am in a park, whose objects organize themselves around me, as I project my purposes towards them. This bench is to be sat upon; that tree is hidden but demands my gaze. (Compare Heidegger's 'readiness-to-hand'.) Suddenly I see another man. At once the park loses its unique distribution according to the principles of my desire, and begins to group itself around *his* purposes too. The bench becomes a bench that he avoids, the tree a tree that he approaches. 'The other is . . . a permanent flight of things towards a goal which . . . escapes me inasmuch as it unfolds about itself its own distance'; the other 'has stolen the world from me'. In short, there is no safety in others, and I am forever alone in my world, cherishing a freedom, and a commitment, which have meaning for no one but me. The dialectic returns me always to the first stage: the life-and-death struggle with the other, from which the postulate of freedom can never release me. This is the real meaning of Sartre's celebrated remark, in the play *Huis Clos*, that 'Hell is other people', namely, that other people are Hell.

This is a fitting place to bring the curtain down on Fichte's drama. The subject's venture towards the object ends at last in a strategic retreat. In his striking phenomenology of nothingness, Sartre tells us that 'not-being lies coiled in the heart of being, like a worm'. What is true of nothingness is true of Sartre's subjective hero: hugging his precious freedom, the self escapes at last from the not-self, into the crevice of not-being from which all this play of shadows once emerged. Better, perhaps, to have told another story.

5

Mill to Wittgenstein

DAVID PEARS and ANTHONY KENNY

The Empiricism of John Stuart Mill

After Kant the history of philosophy took a course in the English-speaking world which was different from that which we have seen on the Continent in the previous chapter. It was the critical rather than the idealist elements in the philosopher's system that had an abiding influence, an influence which continues today in the Anglo-American tradition which is commonly called 'analytic philosophy'. The founding fathers of analytic philosophy were by no means all British: on the contrary, the two most significant figures in the history of the movement, Frege and Wittgenstein, were both German speakers. However, it was in Britain that the thought of these two philosophers was first fully appreciated, and the tradition into which their work was introduced can be traced to the nineteenth-century philosopher John Stuart Mill.

Mill, like his father James Mill and like his father's mentor Jeremy Bentham, devoted much of his attention to moral and political philosophy. His political ideas will be considered elsewhere: in this chapter we are concerned with his contribution to logic and epistemology. Though he did not like to be called an empiricist, Mill could be regarded as a continuator of the tradition of Locke and Hume. He was an admirer of Berkeley, whom he praised for having been the first to put forward the thesis that the externality we attribute to the objects of our senses consists only in the fact that 'our sensations occur in groups, held together by a permanent law'. We think that physical objects persist in existence when they are not perceived: but this belief really amounts to no more than our continuing expectation of further perceptions of the object. Matter is defined by Mill as 'a permanent possibility of sensation'; the external world is 'the world of possible sensations succeeding one another according to laws'.

Mill's philosophy of mind likewise follows the empiricist tradition. 'We have no conception of Mind itself, as distinguished from its conscious manifestations.' However, he admits, there is a difficulty in speaking of mind simply as a series of feelings: how can a series be aware of itself as past and future? 'We are reduced to the alternative of believing that the Mind or Ego is something different from any series of feelings or possibilities of them, or of accepting the paradox that something which *ex hypothesi* is but a series of feelings can be aware of itself.' Any thoroughgoing phenomenalism seems to make it difficult to justify belief in minds other than one's own; but Mill argues that I can know the existence of other minds by supposing that the behaviour of others stands in a relation to sensations which is analogous to the relation in which my behaviour stands to my own sensations. It is difficult to make this argument consistent with Mill's official account either of other bodies or of my own mind.

We can say in summary that Mill's empiricism amounts to this: his analysis of matter is like Berkeley's minus theology, and his analysis of mind is like Hume's minus scepticism about the self. Unlike all previous empiricists, however, Mill had a serious interest in formal logic and in the methodology of the sciences. His *System of Logic* (1843) begins with an analysis of language, and in particular with a theory of naming.

Mill uses the word 'name' very broadly. Not only proper names like 'Socrates' but pronouns like 'this', definite descriptions like 'the king who succeeded William the Conqueror', general terms like 'man' and 'wise', and abstract expressions like 'old age' are all counted as names in his system. Indeed, only words like 'of' and 'or' and 'if' seem *not* to be names in his system. According to Mill, all names denote things: proper names denote the things they are names of, and general terms denote the things they are true of. Thus not only 'Socrates', but also 'man' and 'wise' denote Socrates.

There is a difference, however. For Mill, names are divided into connotative and non-connotative terms. A connotative term 'denotes a subject and implies an attribute'. 'Wise', unlike 'Socrates', is a connotative term: in addition to denoting Socrates (and other wise people), it connotes wisdom. Not only proper names are non-connotative names: 'Wisdom', unlike 'wise', denotes wisdom, and it does not connote anything. When a term is connotative, its meaning is to be identified with what it connotes, not with what it denotes.

For Mill, every proposition is a conjunction of names. This does not commit him to the extreme nominalist view that every sentence is to be interpreted on the model of one joining two proper names, as in 'Tully is Cicero'. A sentence joining two connotative names, like 'All men are mortal', tells us that certain attributes (those, say, of rationality and animality) are always accompanied by the attribute of mortality.

Some propositions, Mill says, are 'merely verbal'; their truth can be derived solely from the meanings of the terms used. Thus, if we know what 'man' and 'rational' mean we can conclude that all men are rational, because rationality is part of the connotation of 'man'. Such propositions, he remarks, correspond to Kant's analytic propositions. But such propositions give no information about things, but only about names. 'All men are mortal', on the other hand, does give real information, because mortality is not part of the connotation of 'man'. From a scientific point of view the most important feature of such a proposition is as a guide to expectation: 'the attributes of man are *evidence of*, are a *mark of*, mortality'.

Inferences, like propositions, can be divided into real and verbal. The inference from 'No great general is a rash man' to 'No rash man is a great general' is not a real inference; premiss and conclusion say the same thing. There is real inference only when we infer to a truth, in the conclusion, which is not contained in the premisses. There is, for instance, a real inference when we infer from particular cases to a general conclusion, as in 'Peter is mortal, James is mortal, John is mortal, therefore all men are mortal'. But such inference is not deductive, but inductive.

Is all deductive reasoning, then, merely verbal? Up to the time of Mill, the syllogism was the paradigm of deductive reasoning. Is syllogistic reasoning real or verbal inference? Mill has this to say:

It must be granted that in every syllogism, considered as an argument to prove the conclusion, there is a *petitio principii*. When we say

> All men are mortal
> Socrates is a man,
> therefore Socrates is mortal;

it is unanswerably urged by the adversaries of the syllogistic theory, that the proposition, Socrates is mortal, is presupposed in the more general assumption, All men are mortal.

We seem to be presented with two alternatives. If the syllogism is deductively valid, then the conclusion must somehow have already been counted in to the first premiss: the mortality of Socrates must have been part of the evidence which justifies us in asserting that all men are mortal. If, on the other hand, the conclusion gives new information—if, for instance, we substitute for 'Socrates' the name of someone not yet dead (Mill used the example 'The Duke of Wellington')—then we find that it is not really being derived from the first premiss. The major premiss, Mill says, is merely a formula for drawing inferences, 'the real logical antecedent or premiss being the particular facts from which the general proposition was collected by induction'.

According to Mill 'all inference is from particulars to particulars'. Inference beginning from particular cases had been named by logicians 'induction'. In some cases, induction appears to provide a general conclusion: from 'Peter is a Jew, James is a Jew, John is a Jew…'. I can, having enumerated all the Apostles, conclude 'All the Apostles are Jews'. But this procedure, which is sometimes called 'perfect induction' does not, according to Mill, really take us from particular to general: the conclusion is merely an abridged notation for the particular facts enunciated in the premisses. Some logicians had maintained that there was another sort of induction, imperfect induction (Mill calls it 'induction by simple enumeration'), which led from particular cases to general laws. But, as stated above, the purported general laws are the formulas by which we make our inferences, not the conclusions which we draw from our inferences. Genuine inductive inference takes us from known particulars to unknown particulars.

If induction cannot be brought within the framework of the syllogism, this does not mean that it operates without any rules of its own. 'What induction is,' Mill says, 'and what conditions render it legitimate, cannot but be deemed the main question of the science of logic.'

Mill sets out five rules, or canons, of experimental enquiry to guide the inductive discovery of causes and effects.

The first propounds the method of agreement: if a phenomenon F appears in the conjunction of the circumstances A, B, and C, and also in the conjunction of the circumstances C, D, and E, then we are to conclude that C, the only common feature, is causally related to F. Similarly—this the second method, that of disagreement—if F occurs in the presence of A, B, and C, but not in the presence of A, B, and D, then we are to conclude that C, the only feature differentiating the two cases, is causally related to F. Mill gives as an illustration of this second canon: 'When a man is shot through the heart, it is by this method we know that it was the gunshot which killed him: for he was in the fulness of life immediately before, all circumstances being the same, except the wound.'

The third of Mill's canons instructs us how we are to combine the two methods of agreement and disagreement. The fourth canon propounds the method of residues. 'Subduct from any phenomenon such part as is known by previous inductions to be the effect of certain antecedents, and the residue of the phenomenon is the effect of the remaining antecedents.' The final method, that of concomitant variation, is applicable in sciences such as astronomy where we have no power to intervene in the processes being studied. The relevant canon states 'Whatever phenomenon varies in any manner whenever another phenomenon varies in some particular manner, is either a cause or an effect of that phenomenon, or is connected with it through some fact of causation.'

Critics have objected that it is unclear whether these canons are methods of discovery or methods of proof. They seem, on the face of it, to be methods of selecting between alternative hypotheses, of deciding, for instance, whether F is caused by A, or by B, or by C. They do not seem to provide either for the origination of hypotheses, or for their definitive confirmation.

Moreover, like all inductive procedures, Mill's methods seem to assume the constancy of general laws. As Mill explicitly says, 'The proposition that the course of Nature is uniform, is the fundamental principle, or general axiom, of Induction.' But what is the status of this principle? Mill sometimes seems to treat it as if it was an empirical generalization. He says, for instance, that it would be rash to assume that the law of causation applies on distant stars. But if this very general principle is the basis of induction, surely it cannot itself be established by induction.

It is not only the law of causation which presents difficulties for Mill's system. So too do the truths of mathematics. Mill did not think—as some other empiricists have done—that mathematical propositions were merely verbal propositions which spelt out the consequences of definitions. The fundamental axioms of arithmetic, and Euclid's axioms of geometry, he maintains, state matters of fact. Accordingly, he has in consistency to conclude that arithmetic and geometry, no less than physics, consist of empirical hypotheses. The hypotheses of mathematics are of very great generality, and have been most handsomely confirmed in our experience; none the less, they remain hypotheses, corrigible in the light of later experience.

In his *Autobiography* Mill described the main purpose of *The System of Logic* as being to give the lie to the notion that truths external to the mind may be known by intuition independent of experience. This notion, he said, is 'the great intellectual support of false doctrines and bad institutions'. And he went on to say 'In attempting to clear up the real nature of the evidence of mathematical and physical truths, the "System of Logic" met the intuition philosophers on ground on which they had previously been deemed unassailable; and gave its own explanation, from experience and association, of that peculiar character of what are called necessary truths, which is adduced as proof that their evidence must come from a deeper source than experience. Whether this has been done effectually, is still *sub judice*.'

In the opinion of most philosophers, the court of history eventually gave a decisive verdict against Mill; and this was due, above all, to the advocacy of Mill's German opponent, Gottlob Frege.

Frege and Mathematical Logic

Frege was the founder of modern logic. As a logician and philosopher of logic he ranks with Aristotle; as a philosopher of mathematics he has had no peer in the history of philosophy. He taught at the University of Jena from 1874 until his retirement in 1918; apart from his intellectual work his life was uneventful and secluded. His productive career can be divided into the following periods: (1) the period of the *Begriffsschrift* (1879), the first presentation of a modern logical system; (2) the *Grundlagen der Arithmetik* (1884), an informal philosophical presentation of the theory that arithmetic is derivable from logic; (3) the development of a system of philosophical logic in the papers 'Funktion und Begriff' (1891) 'Begriff und Gegenstand' (1892), 'Sinn und Bedeutung' (1892); (4) *Grundgesetze der Arithmetik* (1893–1903): the formal construction of arithmetic on the basis of pure logic and set theory; (5) the final period—after a fallow interval following on the discovery of flaws in the *Grundgesetze* system—in which Frege began to write a book on philosophical logic, parts of which were published as articles (*Logische Untersuchungen*, 1919–23). Frege was little known in his lifetime, but had an influence on continental philosophy through Husserl and on analytic philosophy through Russell. His works have been read mainly by other philosophers, but it was his genius that made possible the work of writers who have caught the attention of the general public, such as Wittgenstein and Chomsky. The invention of mathematical logic was one of the major contributions to the developments in many disciplines which resulted in the invention of computers, with all their effects on individuals and society.

Frege's productive career began in 1879 with the publication of a pamphlet with the title 'Begriffsschrift', which we can render into English as 'Concept Script'. The pamphlet marked an epoch in the history of logic, for within some hundred pages it set forth a new calculus which has a permanent place at the heart of modern logic. The concept script which gave the book its title was a new symbolism designed to bring out with clarity logical relationships which were concealed in ordinary language.

For decades now the propositional calculus has been established as the beginning of the curriculum in formal logic. It is the branch of logic that deals with those inferences whose force depends on negation, conjunction, disjunction, etc. applied to sentences as wholes. It systematizes inferences which depend on the meaning of the connectives 'and', 'if', 'or', etc. Frege's *Begriffsschrift* contains the first systematic formulation of the propositional calculus in the axiomatic manner. His symbolism, though elegant, is difficult to print, and is no longer used; but the way in which it is applied is the kernel of modern mathematical logic.

Frege's greatest contribution to logic was his invention of quantification theory: a method of symbolizing and rigorously displaying those inferences that depend for their validity on

WITTGENSTEIN IN NEW YORK, by Eduardo Paolozzi. Throughout his life Wittgenstein was ill at ease with contemporary Western culture. At one time he thought of settling in Russia. Though he had friends in the USA and sometimes visited them, he found American culture very alien—except for cheap movies, which he found mentally cleansing.

I went to New York
to meet Wittgenstein
at the ship. When I
first saw him I was
surprised at his
apparent physical
vigour. He was
striding down the
ramp with a pack
on his back, a
heavy suitcase in one
hand, cane in the
other.

AUGUST 1964

Ceci n'est pas une pipe.

THE WAYS OF PARADOX (*left*). Philosophers give a precise sense to the notion of paradox: it occurs when there is an equally good proof of each of two contradictory propositions. Paradoxes reveal defects in our symbolism, and often reflect a clash between two conventions pointing in different directions. In Magritte's painting *The Treason of Images* the visual and written representations emit contradictory signals.

WHAT CANNOT BE SAID (*below*). Wittgenstein believed that paradox could be avoided if one observed strict rules for meaningfulness, and refrained from making utterances about things which could only be shown, not said. His famous 'Whereof one cannot speak, thereof one must be silent' recalls the advice of Salvador Rosa's sitter 'Keep silent, or utter only what is worth more than silence.'

expressions such as 'all' or 'some'. Using a novel notation for quantification, Frege presented a first-order predicate calculus which laid the basis for all recent developments in logic. He thus formalized the theory of inference in a way more rigorous and more general than the traditional Aristotelian syllogistic which up to the time of Kant had been looked on as the be-all and end-all of logic. After Frege, for the first time, formal logic could handle arguments which involved sentences with multiple quantification, such as 'Nobody knows everybody' and 'Any schoolchild can master any language'.

In the course of his studies in the relationship between logic and arithmetic, Frege worked out also a second-order predicate calculus (in the *Begriffsschrift*) and a version of naïve set theory (in the *Grundgesetze*). He did not develop the branches of logic known as modal logic (that part of logic that deals with necessity, possibility, and kindred notions) or tense logic (the logic of temporal or significantly tensed statements). These branches of logic had been studied in the Middle Ages, and have been studied again in the present century in the light of Frege's innovations; his own predominantly mathematical interests made him comparatively uninterested in those branches of logic which concern inferences about the transient and the changing.

Since Frege's time there have been enormous developments in the areas of logic which he studied. For instance, while he presented axiomatic systems, many non-axiomatic methods of handling propositional and predicate calculus have since been explored. Again, systems of formalized semantics have been developed to match the rigorous formulation which Frege initiated for syntax.

Frege's Philosophy of Logic

Frege not only founded modern logic: he founded the modern philosophical discipline of philosophy of logic, by sharply distinguishing the philosophical treatment of logic from, on the one hand, psychology (with which it had often been confused by philosophers in the empiricist tradition) and, on the other hand, epistemology (with which it was sometimes conflated by philosophers in the Cartesian tradition). In this he was in line with a much older tradition originating with Aristotle's *De interpretatione*. In the *Begriffsschrift* and the *Grundlagen* Frege investigated such notions as *name, sentence, predicate* with a scope and subtlety greater than Aristotle's. One of his most fertile devices was the application of the mathematical notions of *function* and *argument* to the expressions of ordinary language traditionally called 'predicate' and 'subject'. Thus Frege would analyse a sentence such as 'Socrates is wise' by saying that it was the value of the function '. . . is wise' for the argument 'Socrates'; and in the sentence 'Caesar conquered Gaul' the expression '. . . conquered . . .' is a function with not one but two arguments, 'Caesar' and 'Gaul'.

Corresponding to the distinction in language between first-order functions and their arguments, Frege maintained, a systematic distinction must be made between concepts and objects, which are their ontological counterparts. Objects are what proper names stand for: they are of many kinds, ranging from human beings to numbers. Concepts are items which have a fundamental incompleteness, corresponding to the gappiness of a predicate as understood by Frege (i.e. a sentence with one or more proper names removed from it).

Where other philosophers talk ambiguously of the *meaning* of an expression, Frege introduced a distinction between the *reference* of an expression (the object to which it refers, as the planet Venus is the reference of 'the Morning Star') and the *sense* of an expression, which is something quite different. ('The Evening Star' differs in sense from 'the Morning Star' though it too, as astronomers discovered, refers to Venus.)

A highly controversial application of Frege's distinction between sense and reference was his theory that the reference of a sentence was its truth-value: a sentence such as 'Caesar was killed' stood for the True, and 'Caesar died in his bed' for the False. Connected with this were two theses: that in a scientifically respectable language every term must have a reference, and that every sentence must be either true or false. This leads to many difficulties, with which he made only doubtfully successful attempts to cope.

In the articles on philosophy of logic in his final period Frege returned to the relationship between logic and philosophical psychology or philosophy of mind. These writings are not generally regarded as his best work, but they pose in an inchoate way the issues which were discussed with greater attention and insight in the later writings of Wittgenstein, who professed himself a lifelong admirer of 'the great works of Frege'.

Frege's Philosophy of Mathematics

Undoubtedly, Frege's greatest achievement was his work in the philosophy of mathematics. His *Grundlagen* begins with an attack on the ideas of his predecessors and contemporaries (including Kant and Mill) on the nature of numbers and of mathematical truth. The attack

SYMBOLIC LOGIC derives in modern times from the system designed by Frege in 1879. However, his actual symbolism was not taken over by others: though perspicuous once learned, it is clumsy to print. The illustration here corresponds to the build-up of a judgement such as 'If this ostrich is a bird and cannot fly, then it follows that some birds cannot fly'.

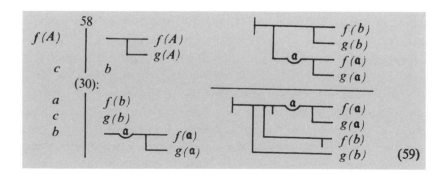

GOTTLOB FREGE,
photographed in 1920, towards
the end of his life, while he was
writing his last essays on
philosophical logic.

was brilliantly successful and no philosopher of mathematics today would defend the views he criticized, though they still surface sometimes in the writings of psychologists and educationalists, so that his arguments still repay study.

Kant had maintained that the truths of mathematics were synthetic a priori and that our knowledge of them depended neither on analysis nor on experience but on intuition. Mill, as we have seen, took a quite opposite view: mathematical truths were a posteriori, empirical generalizations widely applicable and widely confirmed. Frege disagreed with both his predecessors: he maintained that the truths of arithmetic were not synthetic at all, neither a priori nor a posteriori. Unlike geometry—which, he agreed with Kant, rested on a priori intuition—arithmetic was analytic.

As we have seen, Frege had early shown how to present logic in a mathematical manner. But he believed that the relationship between logic and mathematics was much more profound than this. He believed that arithmetic itself could be shown to be a branch or extension of logic in the sense that it involved no special subject-matter of its own and could be formalized without the use of any non-logical notions or axioms. The arithmetical notion of number in Frege's system is replaced by the logical notion of 'class': the cardinal numbers can be defined as classes of classes with the same number of members; thus the number two is the class of pairs, and the number three the class of trios. Despite appearances, this definition is not circular, because we can say what is meant by two classes having the same number of members without making use of the notion of number: thus, for instance, a waiter may know that there are as many knives as there are plates on a table without knowing how many of each there are, if he observes that there is just one knife to the right of each plate. Two classes have the same number of members if they can be mapped one-to-one on to each other. Such classes can be called equivalent classes. We can thus revise the definition of number given above and say that a number is a class of equivalent classes.

A LETTER TO HUSSERL in which Frege sets out his distinction between the sense and the reference of expressions.

THE LAWS OF GEOMETRY, Frege believed, govern our imagination. 'The wildest visions of delirium, the boldest inventions of legend and poetry, where animals speak and stars stand still . . . all these remain, so long as they remain intuitable, still subject to the axioms of geometry'. Escher's drawings show that Frege was mistaken.

To define a particular number *n* we have to pick on a particular class with *n* members and define the number as the class of all classes equivalent to it. Thus, we could define four as the class of all classes which are equivalent to the class of gospel-makers. But such a definition is clearly useless for the logicist programme, because it is no part of logic that there were four and only four evangelists. We need to find, for each number, a class of the appropriate size whose size is guaranteed by logic.

The best way to do this is to start from zero. We can define the number zero in purely logical terms as the class of all classes with the same number of members as the class of objects which are not identical with themselves. As there are no objects which are not identical with themselves, that class has no members. Two classes with the same members are in fact one and the same class, so there is only one class which has no members, the null-class as it is called. Zero is therefore the class whose only member is the null-class.

The fact that there is only one null-class is used in defining the number one: one is defined as the class of classes equivalent to the class of null-classes. Now that zero and one have been defined in purely logical terms, two can be defined as the class of classes with as many members as the class whose members are zero and one, and three as the class of classes with as many members as the class containing zero, one, and two. Frege made use of this procedure to give a general definition of the notion of 'successor of' such that all other numbers (four, which is the successor of three, five, which is the successor of four, and so on *ad infinitum*) can also be defined without using any notions other than logical ones such as identity, class, class-membership, and class-equivalence.

Russell's Paradox and the Theory of Types

Frege's ingenious method of building up the series of natural numbers out of merely logical notions contains, however, a fatal flaw. This was discovered by a brilliant young English philosopher named Bertrand Russell. Russell, grandson of the Prime Minister Lord John Russell, and godson of John Stuart Mill, was at the beginning of a long, varied, and extremely distinguished career. In his later life, and particularly after he inherited an earldom, he was known to a very wide public as a writer and campaigner on various social and political issues. But most of the work which established his reputation among professional philosophers and mathematicians was completed before 1920. In 1903 he was working on a book entitled *The Principles of Mathematics*, and in this work he drew the attention of the British public to Frege's philosophy. Much as he admired Frege's writings, he detected a radical defect in his system, which he pointed out to him just as the second volume of the *Grundgesetze* was in press.

If we are to proceed from number to number in the way Frege proposes we must be able without restriction to form classes of classes, and classes of classes of classes, and so on. Classes must themselves be classifiable; they must be capable of being members of classes. Now can a class be a member of itself? The class of dogs is surely not a dog; but is not the class of classes itself a class, and therefore a member of itself? It seems therefore that there are two

PRINCIPIA MATHEMATICA, by Russell and Whitehead, was an ambitious attempt to derive arithmetic from pure logic. Here is a page on the way to the proof that 1+1=2.

*71·168. $\vdash :. (y) . E ! R'y : (x) . E ! \breve{R}'x : \supset . R \epsilon 1 \to 1$

*71·17. $\vdash :. R \epsilon 1 \to \mathrm{Cls} . \equiv : xRz . yRz . \supset_{x,y,z} . x = y$

This proposition is constantly used in the sequel.

Dem.

$\vdash . \ast 52·4 .$ $\supset \vdash :. \overrightarrow{R}'z \epsilon 1 \cup \iota'\Lambda .$ $\equiv : x, y \epsilon \overrightarrow{R}'z . \supset_{x,y} . x = y :$

$[\ast 32·18]$ $\equiv : xRz . yRz . \supset_{x,y} . x = y :.$

$[\ast 10·11·271 . \ast 11·21] \supset \vdash :. (z) . \overrightarrow{R}'z \epsilon 1 \cup \iota'\Lambda . \equiv : xRz . yRz . \supset_{x,y,z} . x = y$ (1)

$\vdash . (1) . \ast 71·12 .$ $\supset \vdash . \mathrm{Prop}$

*71·171. $\vdash :. R \epsilon \mathrm{Cls} \to 1 . \equiv : xRy . xRz . \supset_{x,y,z} . y = z$

*71·172. $\vdash :. R \epsilon 1 \to 1 . \equiv : xRz . yRz . \supset_{x,y,z} . x = y : xRy . xRz . \supset_{x,y,z} . y = z$

*71·18. $\vdash :. R \epsilon 1 \to \mathrm{Cls} . \equiv :: \exists ! \overleftarrow{R}'x \cap \overleftarrow{R}'y . \supset_{x,y} . x = y$

Dem.

$\vdash . \ast 32·181 . \ast 22·33 . \supset$

$\vdash :. \exists ! \overleftarrow{R}'x \cap \overleftarrow{R}'y . \supset_{x,y} . x = y : \equiv : (\exists z) . xRz . yRz . \supset_{x,y} . x = y :$

$[\ast 10·23]$ $\equiv : xRz . yRz . \supset_{x,y,z} . x = y :$

$[\ast 71·17]$ $\equiv : R \epsilon 1 \to \mathrm{Cls} :. \supset \vdash . \mathrm{Prop}$

*71·181. $\vdash :. R \epsilon \mathrm{Cls} \to 1 . \equiv :: \exists ! \overrightarrow{R}'y \cap \overrightarrow{R}'z . \supset_{y,z} . y = z$

*71·182. $\vdash :: R \epsilon 1 \to 1 . \equiv :. \exists ! \overleftarrow{R}'x \cap \overleftarrow{R}'y . \vee . \exists ! \overrightarrow{R}'x \cap \overrightarrow{R}'y : \supset_{x,y} . x = y$

*71·19. $\vdash : R \epsilon 1 \to \mathrm{Cls} . \equiv . R | \breve{R} = I \upharpoonright \mathrm{D}'R$

Dem.

$\vdash . \ast 34·1 . \ast 31·11 . \supset \vdash . x (R | \breve{R}) y . \equiv . (\exists z) . xRz . yRz$ (1)

$\vdash . \ast 50·1 . \ast 35·101 . \supset \vdash . x (I \upharpoonright \mathrm{D}'R) y . \equiv . x = y . y \epsilon \mathrm{D}'R$ (2)

$\vdash . (1) . (2) . \ast 21·43 . \supset$

$\vdash :: R | \breve{R} = I \upharpoonright \mathrm{D}'R . \equiv :. (\exists z) . xRz . yRz . \equiv_{x,y} : x = y . y \epsilon \mathrm{D}'R :$

$[\ast 33·13 . \ast 10·35]$ $\equiv_{x,y} : (\exists z) . x = y . yRz :$

$[\ast 13·194]$ $\equiv_{x,y} : (\exists z) . x = y . xRz . yRz :$

$[\ast 10·35]$ $\equiv_{x,y} : x = y : (\exists z) . xRz . yRz :.$

$[\ast 4·71]$ $\equiv :. (\exists z) . xRz . yRz . \supset_{x,y} . x = y :.$

$[\ast 10·23]$ $\equiv :. xRz . yRz . \supset_{x,y,z} . x = y :.$

$[\ast 71·17]$ $\equiv :. R \epsilon 1 \to \mathrm{Cls} :: \supset \vdash . \mathrm{Prop}$

*71·191. $\vdash : R \epsilon \mathrm{Cls} \to 1 . \equiv . \breve{R} | R = I \upharpoonright \mathrm{C}'R$

*71·192. $\vdash : R \epsilon 1 \to 1 . \equiv . R | \breve{R} = I \upharpoonright \mathrm{D}'R . \breve{R} | R = I \upharpoonright \mathrm{C}'R$

kinds of classes: there is the class of classes that are members of themselves, and the class of classes that are not members of themselves.

Consider now this second class: is it a member of itself or not? If it is a member of itself, then since it is precisely the class of classes that are *not* members of themselves, it must be not a member of itself. But, if it is not a member of itself, then it qualifies for membership of the class of classes that are not members of themselves, and therefore it is a member of itself. It seems that it must either be a member of itself or not; but whichever alternative we choose we are forced to contradict ourselves.

This discovery is called Russell's Paradox; it shows that there is something vicious in the procedure of forming classes of classes *ad lib.*, and it calls into question Frege's whole logicist programme.

Russell himself was committed to logicism no less than Frege was, and he proceeded, in co-operation with A. N. Whitehead, to develop a logical system, using a notation different from Frege's, in which he set out to derive the whole of arithmetic from a purely logical basis. This work was published in the three monumental volumes of *Principia Mathematica* in 1910–13.

In order to avoid the paradox which he had discovered Russell formulated a Theory of Types. It was wrong to treat classes as randomly classifiable objects. Classes and individuals were of different logical types, and what can be true or false of one cannot be significantly asserted of the other. Similarly, what can meaningfully be said of classes cannot meaningfully be said of classes, and so on through the hierarchy of logical types. If the difference of type between the different levels of the hierarchy is observed, then the paradox will not arise.

But another difficulty arises in place of the paradox. Once we prohibit the formation of classes of classes, how can we define the series of natural numbers? Russell retained the definition of zero as the class whose only member is the null-class, but he now treated one as the class of all classes equivalent to the class whose members are (*a*) the members of the null-class, plus (*b*) any object not a member of that class. Two was treated in turn as the class of all classes equivalent to the class whose members are (*a*) the members of the class used to define one, plus (*b*) any object not a member of that defining class. In this way the numbers can be defined one after the other, and each number is a class of classes of individuals. But the natural-number series can be continued thus *ad infinitum* only if there is an infinite number of objects in the universe; for if there are only n individuals, then there will be no classes with $n+1$ members, and so no cardinal number $n+1$. Russell accepted this and therefore added to his axioms an axiom of infinity, i.e. the hypothesis that the number of objects in the universe is not finite. This hypothesis may be, as Russell thought it was, highly probable; but on the face of it it is far from being a logical truth; and the need to postulate it is therefore a sullying of the purity of the original programme of deriving arithmetic from logic alone.

Linguistic Analysis

Hand in hand with Russell's attempt to establish arithmetic on a logical basis went a desire to set out non-mathematical language in a logically perspicuous form. It was this that made Russell, along with Frege, one of the founders of the analytical tradition in philosophy. Logical or linguistic analysis was originally regarded as a technique of substituting a logically clear form of words for another form of words which was in some way logically misleading. It made its first significant appearance on the scene of British philosophy in Russell's article 'On Denoting' in *Mind*, 1905. At that time Russell and G. E. Moore were leading a realist reaction against the neo-Hegelian idealism of F. H. Bradley and his associates, until then the predominant strain in English philosophy. This reaction at first took the form of an exaggerated realism which had great affinities with the views of Alexius Meinong, an Austrian philosopher who had studied under Brentano at Vienna. In their Meinongian period, Moore and Russell believed that in order to save the objectivity of concept and judgement it was necessary to believe in a world of Platonic ideas and of subsistent propositions. Moore argued that a concept was 'neither a mental fact, nor any part of a mental fact'; it was something eternal, immutable, existing independently of our thinking. And Russell wrote in 1903 'Numbers, the Homeric gods, relations, chimeras and four-dimensional space all have being, for if they were not entities of a kind, we could make no propositions about them. Thus being is a general attribute of everything, and to mention anything is to show that it is.'

The common sense on which Moore and Russell were later to pride themselves did not rest easily with the conclusion that there was a shadow-world of chimeras and quasi-Platonic numbers and classes. Yet, if to mention anything is to show that it is, how were they to avoid the conclusion? Perhaps, they came to think, there are cases where we only *seem* to mention things, without really doing so. Perhaps there are some expressions which merely appear to be names of entities, but in fact are not names at all. This was the theory which Russell first worked out in 'On Denoting'.

In this article he discusses what he calls 'denoting phrases'—a class of phrases which he did not define, but illustrated by examples, such as 'every man', 'a man', 'some men', 'all men', 'the present King of England', 'the present King of France', 'the centre of mass of the solar system at a certain moment'. Russell selects for specially detailed treatment phrases beginning with 'the'—phrases which he would later call 'definite descriptions'. He regard these as 'by far the most interesting and difficult of denoting phrases'.

Denoting phrases, Russell maintains, never have any meaning in themselves; only the propositions in whose verbal expression they occur have a meaning. For Russell there is a big difference between a sentence such as 'James II was deposed' (containing the name 'James II') and a sentence such as 'The brother of Charles II was deposed'. An expression such as 'the brother of Charles II' is what Russell calls a 'denoting phrase'. Such a phrase, Russell tells us, has no meaning in isolation; but the sentence 'The brother of Charles II was deposed' has a meaning none the less. It asserts three things:

(1) that some individual was brother to Charles II,
(2) that only this individual was brother to Charles II,
(3) that this individual was deposed.

G. E. MOORE (1873–1958) was one of the leaders of the reaction against Idealism in Britain in the first years of the twentieth century. His work *Principia Ethica* was for a time very influential, and particularly excited the Bloomsbury Group. More enduring philosophically were his papers on the relationship between scepticism and common sense.

Or, more formally:

For some x, (1) *x* was brother to Charles II,
and (2) for all *y*, if *y* was brother to Charles II, $y = x$,
and (3) *x* was deposed.

The first element of this formulation says that at least one individual was a brother of Charles II, the second that at most one individual was a brother of Charles II, so that between them they say that exactly one individual was brother to Charles II. The third element goes on to say that that unique individual was deposed.

Cumbersome as it is, this is the only translation of the sentence, according to Russell, which enables one to avoid philosophical puzzles which arise on any other theory of the meaning of denoting phrases. Such a translation enables us to analyse all propositions in which denoting phrases occur into forms in which no such phrases occur. This is very important, for it enables us to avoid the Meinongian conclusion that the present King of France must somehow have being because there is an expression 'the present King of France' which refers to him. In Russell's rewritten sentences no such expressions occur, and so there is no need to postulate any dubious entity for such expressions to refer to.

Whole sentences which contain such empty denoting expressions, however, are not meaningless, but false. Consider the following two sentences:

(1) The sovereign of the United Kingdom is male.
(2) The sovereign of the United States is male.

Neither of these sentences is true, but the reason differs in the two cases. The first sentence is not true, but plain false, because the sovereign of the United Kingdom is female; the second fails to be true because the USA has no sovereign. On Russell's view the second sentence is not just untrue but positively false; and consequently its negation 'It is not the case that the sovereign of the USA is male' is true. Sentences containing empty definite descriptions differ sharply in Russell's system from sentences containing empty names, i.e. apparent names which name no objects. For Russell a would-be sentence such as 'Slawkenburgius was a genius' is not really a sentence at all, and therefore neither true nor false, since there was never anyone of whom 'Slawkenburgius' was the proper name.

Why did Russell want to ensure that sentences containing vacuous definite descriptions should count as false? He was, like Frege, interested in constructing a precise and scientific language for purposes of logic and mathematics. Both Frege and Russell regarded it as essential that such a language should contain only expressions which had a definite sense, by which they meant that all sentences in which the expressions could occur should have a truth-value.

This requirement drove Russell in the direction of a philosophy which he came to call 'Logical Atomism'. He believed that once logic had been cast into a perspicuous form it would reveal the structure of the world. Logic contained individual variables and propositional functions: corresponding to these the world contained particulars and universals. In logic complex propositions were built up out of simple propositions as truth-functions of the simpler propositions (that is to say, their truth or falsity could be determined solely from the truth or falsity of the constituent propositions). Similarly, in the world there would be independent atomic facts corresponding to the simple propositions. Atomic facts consisted either in the possession by a particular of a characteristic, or else in a relation between two or more particulars.

The task of philosophical analysis was to lay bare the structure of language, and thereby of the world. Here Russell's theory of descriptions was of service. He began to apply it not only to round squares and to Platonic entities, but also to many things which common sense would regard as perfectly real, such as Julius Caesar, tables, and chairs. The basis of this further application was Russell's distinction between knowledge by acquaintance and knowledge by description. In 1911 he wrote 'Every proposition which we can understand must be composed wholly of constituents with which we are acquainted'. Acquaintance was immediate mental presentation: we could be acquainted with universals, or with our current sense-data; we could not be acquainted with Queen Victoria or our own past sense-data.

BERTRAND RUSSELL's best work in pure philosophy was done in his thirties and forties. But he lived to be ninety-eight and he was best known to the general public in his old age (as pictured here). In 1950 he won the Nobel Prize for Literature, and in the 1950s and 1960s he campaigned for nuclear disarmament.

In the sentence 'Caesar crossed the Rubicon', uttered in England now, we have a proposition in which there are apparently no constituents with which we are acquainted. How then can we understand the sentence? To solve this problem Russell analyses the names 'Caesar' and 'Rubicon' as definite descriptions. The descriptions, spelt out in full, no doubt include reference to the names, but not to the objects they named. The sentence is exhibited as being about general characteristics and relations, and the names with which we become acquainted as we pronounce them.

For Russell, then, ordinary proper names were in fact disguised descriptions. A fully analysed sentence would contain only logically proper names (words referring to particulars with which we are acquainted) and universals (words referring to characters and particulars). It is not altogether clear what count as logically proper names. Sometimes Russell seems to countenance only demonstratives such as 'this' and 'that'. An atomic proposition, therefore, would be something like '(this) red' or '(this) beside (that)'.

Russell presented his logical atomism at a famous set of lectures in 1918. He explained that many of his ideas were due to his former pupil, the Austrian philosopher Ludwig Wittgenstein. Wittgenstein, originally an engineer, had studied with Russell before the Great War, in which he had served as a volunteer in the Austrian army, first on the Eastern and then on the Italian Front. He had continued his logical studies and as a prisoner of war in Monte Cassino had completed a manuscript, *Logisch-Philosophische Abhandlung*, which he dispatched to Russell. This was published in 1922 with an English translation under the title *Tractatus Logico-Philosophicus*, with an introduction by Russell, and was, among other things, the definitive statement of Logical Atomism.

Wittgenstein's Tractatus

Wittgenstein was arguably the greatest philosopher of this century, and his influence has been strong and extensive, especially in Britain and North America. It is, therefore, surprising that the interpretation of many of his leading ideas should remain controversial. But it is not entirely inexplicable. A profound thinker can often be understood at different levels. If, like Wittgenstein in his later writings, he works in a tentative, piecemeal way instead of offering dogmatic theories, it is natural that commentators should be struck by different aspects of his thought and that each should be disposed to heighten the importance of what he himself has seen. However, it is not impossible to give a balanced account of the general character of his philosophy and its place in the history of ideas, provided that there is no claim to completeness or finality.

Wittgenstein is a philosopher's philosopher and his writings can hardly be understood by anyone without previous acquaintance with the work of his predecessors and contemporaries. His first book, the *Tractatus Logico-Philosophicus*, is a critique of language designed to reveal the essential structure of the thought which is expressed in language and to discover, through that structure, the limits of thought. Kant's aim in the *Critique of Pure Reason* had been similar, but the medium investigated by Wittgenstein, language rather than anything in

LUDWIG WITTGENSTEIN had two separate philosophical careers, one before and during the First World War, and the second beginning in the 1930s. This photograph of 1905 shows him while still an engineering student, before studying philosophy at Cambridge with Russell.

the mind, gave his critique advantages: it was a concrete medium and the critique could be based on recent advances in logic and semantics.

The *Tractatus* starts from the ideas of Frege and Russell which we have been considering. Frege held that the sense of any sentence must be definite: that is, before a sentence is used, it must be settled which possible situations would make it come out true and which would make it come out false. Russell held that the sense of any sentence can be understood only by someone who is acquainted with the objects designated by the names that occur in it. Wittgenstein took over these two theses, developed them in his own way, and made two deductions from them. First, he argued that the essential character of every sentence is pictorial, and, second, that every sentence can be analysed into elementary sentences in which the names designate simple objects (objects with no internal structures). He then applied these results to the theories of other philosophers and claimed that many of them did not conform to the requirements of sense, and therefore did not express genuine thoughts.

A strong conclusion like this one needs strong arguments. Perhaps the weakest link in Wittgenstein's reasoning is the theory of simple objects. This certainly came from Russell, but, characteristically, Wittgenstein had made the idea very much his own. He was not concerned with Russellian acquaintance or with his empirical claim that we discover that there are certain words whose meanings can be learned only by direct confrontation with the things designated by them (compare Hume's theory of simple impressions). What interested Wittgenstein was the requirement that the sense of a sentence be derived either from the objects designated by the names occurring in it, or, if it were analysable, from the objects designated by the names in its analysis. It seemed to him that an analysis driven by this requirement must terminate with simple objects. For if it terminated with complex objects, the sense of the original sentence would depend on the truth that those complex objects had whatever structure they did have. But, he assumed, a sentence (with a sense) must be either true or false, with no third alternative. So he concluded that, if the sense of the original sentence did depend on a truth about the structure of a complex object, it would not have a definite sense, and the only way to give it a definite sense would be to continue its analysis until it did reach simple objects.

Wittgenstein gave up philosophy after the publication of the *Tractatus*, and when he took it up again in 1929, this extreme version of Logical Atomism was the first thing that he repudiated. It had possessed a twofold importance in his early system. First, it was the unavoidable consequence of his assumption that any sentence must be either true or false, or, to put this in another way, that anything required for the truth of a sentence must be included in what it actually says and not left in the background as a presupposition. When he gave up this assumption, he was free to treat many things as parts of the background against which sentences possess their senses, and that was the origin of his later holistic idea that they have their senses only within a language-game playable only under certain conditions (a form of life).

The Logical Atomism which he abandoned in 1929 had a second important feature. A sentence was elementary by the criterion of the *Tractatus* if and only if it was logically independent of any other sentence belonging to the same level of analysis. It followed that sentences ascribing colours to objects were not elementary, and an incompatibility between two such sentences would be attributed to the internal structure of the colours, which would then have to be analysed. The abandonment of this programme was another important move towards holism: he had come to think that the grouping of predicates in ranges of incompatible alternatives was a feature of descriptive language which could not be eliminated, and that any attempt to give the meaning of a predicate separately, outside its group, was bound to fail.

The theory that sentences are essentially pictorial (the picture theory), which is the other main claim made in the *Tractatus*, was designed to make good a deficiency in Russell's semantics. Russell had tried to explain our understanding of the senses of sentences by appealing to extensional acquaintance with the objects designated by the names that occurred in them: in other words, he believed that all that was needed was that those objects should have been presented to us and not that they should have been presented to us as objects of certain types. Now Wittgenstein was not concerned with Russell's epistemology at this point, but, rather, with his underlying assumption, that the sense of a sentence could be derived from the objects named in it without the mediation of any categorization. It is true that Russell introduced his Theory of Types at a later stage to deal with this problem, but

5

4·43 Das Zeichen, welches durch die Zuordnung jener Abzeichen und der Wahrheitsmöglichkeiten entsteht, ist ein Satzzeichen.

4·431 Also ist z.B.

p	q	
F	F	W
W	F	W
F	W	
W	W	W

ein Satzzeichen

4·432 Der Deutlichkeit halber schreiben wir dieses Zeichen um so:

p	q	
F	F	W
W	F	W
F	W	F
W	W	W

Die nach §4·43 auf diese Weise gebauten Satzzeichen nennen wir Satzzeichen der ersten Art.

4·44 Ist die Reihenfolge der Wahrheitsmöglichkeiten im Schema durch eine Combinationsregel ein für allemal festgesetzt dann ist die letzte Kolonne allein schon ein Ausdruck der Wahrheitsbedingungen.

4·441 Schreiben wir diese Kolonne als Reihe hin so wird das Zeichen in 4·432 zu: „(WWFW)(p,q)" oder „(W,W W)(p,q)"

3·02 Der Gedanke enthält die Möglichkeit der Sachlage, die er denkt. Was denkbar ist, ist auch möglich.

3·111 Es ist eine Projection der Möglichkeit einer Sachlage.

3·14 Im Satzzeichen entsprechen den Gegenständen der Wirklichkeit die einfachen Zeichen.

3·15 Das Satzzeichen besteht darin, daß sich die einfachen Zeichen in ihm auf bestimmte Art und Weise zu einander verhalten.

7

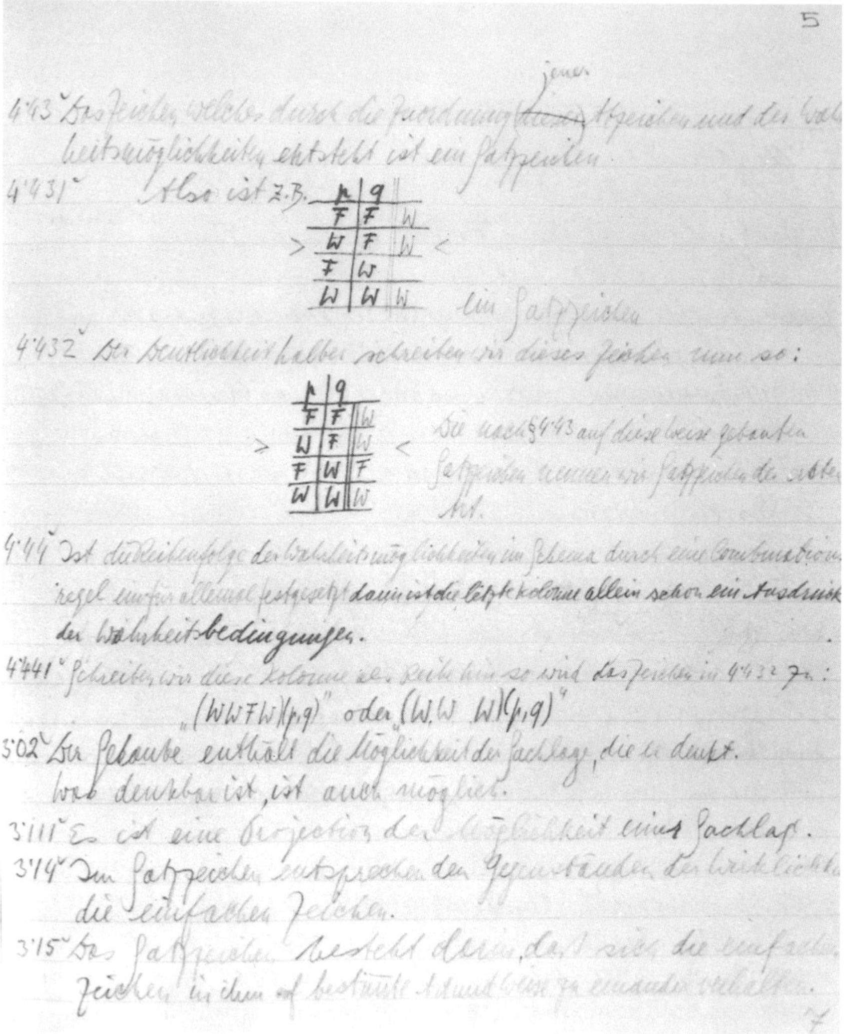

THE PICTURE THEORY OF THE PROPOSITION was expounded in this early manuscript of the *Tractatus*. This illustration shows the use of truth-tables, an innovation of Wittgenstein's which became standard in logic.

Wittgenstein thought that it was an explanation of the wrong kind and that, anyway, it came too late. The right explanation would bring in types at the point where sense first makes its appearance and it would not list them or classify them.

The claim of the Picture Theory to be the right explanation starts from the way in which an array of coloured points on a surface—e.g. land and sea on the surface of the earth—can be mapped on to a piece of paper and the message can be immediately understood. It is true that in this case the immediate intelligibility is partly the result of the homogeneity of object and medium, especially if the colour-code is identity. It is also true that the sense of the map, or of any part of it, will depend on the method of projection, which need not be orthogonal. However, the immediacy of understanding is still very striking in this case. Now the case of language is much less straightforward, but the difference is arguably only one of degree and not of kind. It is only that the correlation of names with objects is much less systematic than a map projection, but once it has been grasped, there is the same immediate intelligibility of any new sentence in which the names have been put together in a way that reflects the possibilities open to the named objects.

This is the way in which the Picture Theory tries to make good the deficiency in Russell's semantics. If Russell had retorted that his Theory of Types had already dealt with the point, Wittgenstein's reply would have been that in that case Russellian acquaintance was not really extensional after all; and that anyway the typology of objects was not something that could be expressed in a theory, because the language in which the theory was expressed would raise the same problem over again. Typology is something which could only be shown.

Here we have the central point of the Picture Theory: anything that we can say in words or pictures will depend on other things which cannot be said but only shown, and so cannot be taught by precept but only by example. This important doctrine was to be developed in a new way in Wittgenstein's later writings after the other element in the Picture Theory, its uncritical treatment of the relation between name and object, had been superseded. But before that development is described, something needs to be said about the use that he made of the Picture Theory and Logical Atomism in his early system.

The essential nature of language and its atomic foundations are dealt with early in the *Tractatus* and Wittgenstein then proceeds to use his results to fix the limits of language. It is already noticeable that the Logical Atomism, which was soon to be superseded, gets far less attention than the Picture Theory. Evidently, the questions how individual sentences acquire their senses and how they can then be combined to form sentences of greater complexity were more important than the question how far analysis has to go in the opposite direction in order to reach elementary sentences. The later history of the use of these ideas by the philosophers of the Vienna Circle confirms this assessment.

Wittgenstein's answer to the question about the combinability of sentences was that the only method of constructing complex sentences out of simpler ones was truth-functional: that is, the truth or falsity of any complex sentence must depend entirely on the truth or falsity of the simpler sentences out of which it was constructed (The Thesis of Extensionality). To put the point in another way, elementary sentences are the bricks with which we construct everything that we can meaningfully say.

This theory of language encountered many difficulties. It was, for example, unclear how a report of a belief could be analysed truth-functionally. However, the theory seemed to be confirmed by its success in explaining logical truths. According to Wittgenstein, they were tautologies, the limiting case of truth-functional combination, where the senses of the component sentences cancelled out, leaving no claim on reality, like the number zero in mathematics.

If any claim on reality had to conform to the strict conditions of meaningfulness laid down in the *Tractatus*, much of our discourse would be beyond the pale. The philosophers of the Vienna Circle drew that conclusion and adopted Wittgenstein's early system as a model for Logical Positivism. However, the *Tractatus* is a work with many different facets and it was not intended to eliminate value judgements or expressions of religious belief. True, the theory of language was a theory of factual language, but other kinds of discourse were not rejected, provided that they played a role (which would, of course, be a different kind of role) in our lives. So he gave factual or scientific language the central place without adopting scientism. What he rejected was the assimilation of the softer periphery to the hard centre, and especially the kind of metaphysics which masqueraded as a super-science.

The Vienna Circle

The ideas of the *Tractatus* were put to anti-metaphysical use during the 1930s by the Logical Positivist philosophers of the Vienna Circle. This group, which grew up round Moritz Schlick after his appointment as Professor of the Philosophy of Science in Vienna in 1922, consisted of philosophers, mathematicians, and scientists; among its members were Friedrich Waismann, Rudolf Carnap, and Otto Neurath. In 1929, after a congress in Prague, the circle issued a manifesto enshrining an anti-metaphysical programme of philosophy, the *Wissenschaftliche Weltauffassung der Wiener Kreis*. This echoed, in part, the positivism of Mach, who had campaigned against metaphysics as an outdated precursor of science. The ideas of the circle were publicized in the journal *Erkenntnis*, founded in 1930 and edited by Carnap in conjunction with Hans Reichenbach of Berlin. The circle was broken up in 1939 as a result of political pressure, after Schlick had been killed by an insane student.

The Positivists were particularly attracted by the idea that necessary truths are necessary only because they are tautologies and tell us nothing about the world. In the past, logical and mathematical propositions had presented serious difficulties for empiricism. An empiricist is committed to saying that no general proposition concerning a matter of fact can be known universally to be valid. How then is he to deal with the truths of logic and mathematics? Few were willing to follow Mill in denying the necessity of such propositions. It was much more attractive to accept that they are necessary but not factual. This enabled the positivists to reconcile thoroughgoing empiricism with the necessity of mathematical truths, and left them free to devote themselves to the attack on metaphysics.

The great weapon in this attack was the Verification Principle. This, in its original form, ruled that the meaning of a proposition was the mode of its verification. Such a view of meaning enabled one to rule out of court as meaningless all statements which could neither be verified nor falsified by experience. Faced with a dispute about the nature of the Absolute, or the purpose of the universe, or Kantian things-in-themselves, the Positivist need only say to the warring metaphysicians: 'What possible experience could settle the issue between you?' If the opposing schools are in agreement about the empirical facts and possibilities, they can give no answer and their conflicting statements are shown up as meaningless.

Almost as soon as the principle was stated disputes broke out about its status and its formulation. Was the principle itself a tautology, or was it verifiable by experience? If not, it seemed to stand self-condemned as meaningless. Further if stated in its strong form (any proposition, to be significant, must be capable of being conclusively verified) it seemed to rule out not only metaphysics, but also scientific generalizations. Some Positivists adapted

MORITZ SCHLICK (1882–1936) was the most influential member of the Vienna Circle of logical positivists until his untimely death at the hands of a disappointed student.

Karl Popper's suggestion that the criterion of significance for a scientific proposition was not verifiability but falsifiability. Thus general propositions would be significant because they were conclusively falsifiable. But how, on this view, were existential propositions significant? Short of an exhaustive tour of the universe, no experience could conclusively falsify such a proposition. So the principle was reformulated in a 'weak' form which laid down that a proposition was significant if there were some observations which would be *relevant* to its truth or falsity. And it was allowed that there were many significant propositions which, while 'verifiable in principle', could not be verified in practice. Even thus qualified, it was not easy to apply the Verification Principle to matters of history; and any further modifications of the principle ran the risk of making it so wide as to admit metaphysical statements.

Despite these difficulties, the Positivists pressed on with their philosophical programme. Philosophy was not a body of doctrine, but an activity of clarification. Only science was qualified to search for truth; philosophy's task was to analyse and clarify the concepts which figure in scientific use of language, thus shielding the scientist from the danger of lapsing into metaphysics. Philosophy was identical with logic, and the statements of philosophers were concealed tautologies.

In clarifying the language of science, the philosopher must show how all empirical statements were built up truth-functionally from elementary or 'protocol' statements. One would understand a complex empirical statement if and only if one could see how it was built up from protocol statements. These, as Carnap explained in *Der logische Aufbau der Welt* (1928), were to be direct records of experience. In knowing which experiences would make one accept or reject any particular protocol one would, in virtue of the Verification Principle, understand what it meant. The words occurring in non-protocol statements derived their meaning from the possibility of the translation of such statements into protocol statements; and the words occurring in protocol statements derived their meaning from the possibility of an ostensive definition—of a gesture which would point (literally or metaphorically) to the feature of experience to which the word referred.

A difficulty here presents itself. What protocol statements record seems to be something which is private to each individual. If meaning depends on verifiability, and verification is by mental states which I alone experience, how can I ever understand anyone else's meaning? Schlick tried to answer this by making a distinction between form and content. The content of my experience—what I enjoy or live through when I look at something green—is private and incommunicable. But the form, the structural relationship, between my private experience and other people's private experience is something public and communicable. I cannot know whether, when I see a tree or a sunset, other people have the same experiences as I do; for all I know, when they look at a tree they see the colour which I see when I look at a sunset. But as long as we both agree to call a tree green and a sunset red—as long, that is, as the form or structure of our experience patterns is similar—we are able to communicate with each other and construct the language of science.

Schlick's response to the threat of solipsism was not found satisfactory by his Positivist colleagues Neurath and Carnap; but the solutions which they proposed were in their turn found equally unconvincing by others. The problem received its most insightful treatment in the later work of Wittgenstein, who had at one time had close links with the Vienna Circle, but who, as the 1930s wore on, distanced himself more and more from Logical Positivism.

The Later Wittgenstein

Something has already been said about the change in Wittgenstein's philosophy which set in when he took up his problems again after a long interval in the 1920s. The excessive demands of Logical Atomism were dropped and a more holistic view of language, which had been latent in the *Tractatus*, began to emerge. The sense of a sentence was now seen to depend on its place in a group of sentences: it was one move among many alternative moves in a language-game which presupposed the conditions that made it possible for us to engage in it.

There was far more tolerance of the idiosyncrasies of these language-games and even those which were classifiable as factual were not forced into a single mould. In short, language was no longer treated in the abstract, sublime manner of the *Tractatus*, but presented realistically in its place in human life with its many functions illustrated by homely examples.

The forcefulness and precision of Wittgenstein's later writings explain the kind of popularity that they have won among people with no philosophical training. But he is still a philosopher's philosopher, and even when the immediate points that he is making can be understood without any knowledge of the philosophical theories under attack, reading him in this way would only be skimming his thought. Or rather, it would be like trying to appreciate the movements of a fencer on a film from which his adversary's image had been obliterated.

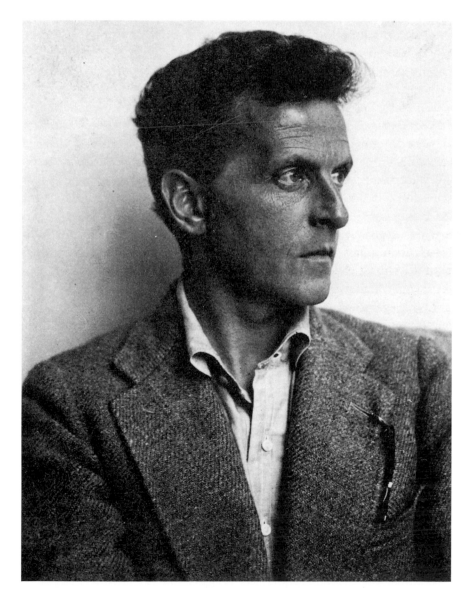

WITTGENSTEIN IN CAMBRIDGE. The portrait photograph taken of Wittgenstein when he took up his fellowship at Trinity in 1930 after returning to philosophy.

Meaning and mind are inseparable and when language is put back in its place in human life, the philosophy of language immediately links up with the philosophy of mind. Is it something in our minds that gives our words their meanings? If so, then since each of us speaks from a different mind, it is not easy to see how we succeed in communicating with one another. Success would be even harder to achieve if what we talked about were also within the mind of each speaker. But that is what traditional theories of perception ask us to believe. Can they really be right? These questions were Wittgenstein's main preoccupations in the second period of his work.

It would be an exaggeration to describe this as a completely new point of departure. For though the philosophy of mind is recessive in the *Tractatus*, there is an assessment of solipsism. This exceptional passage is important in two different connections. First, we can see Wittgenstein actually dealing with a deeply rooted metaphysical theory. Second, it is the opening chapter of the polemic that he continued later in *Philosophical Investigations* against the traditional assumption that philosophy can establish order and certainty within the mind before venturing forth into the physical world.

Solipsism may originate in reflection on oneself as subject or in reflection on the subject's immediate objects of awareness. In the *Tractatus* Wittgenstein confines himself to the first of these two approaches. The solipsist is presented as someone impressed by the indubitable fact that his life is lived from a single point of view and by the apparent fact that everything in it, including his own body, might have been different except the point of view itself. So he detaches his mental world from the physical world in which it is somehow nested, and he claims that the only things that exist belong to his mental world. Wittgenstein objects that this claim lacks sense but concedes the uniqueness of the solipsist's standpoint which his claim was intended to express.

The claim lacks sense, according to Wittgenstein, because the solipsist uses the word 'I' to refer to himself not as an embodied person but as a detached ego, identifiable only through the objects presented to it (him). The trouble is that those objects in their turn are identified only as the objects presented to that ego. This is obviously circular and so the solipsist's claim lacks sense. Evidently, his ego needs to be identified by its attachment to a particular body. But though that would give his claim a sense (as a factual claim), it would also make it obviously false. Therefore, some other way of doing justice to his original insight has to be found.

This treatment of solipsism is an early example of the therapeutic attitude to metaphysics which is explicit in Wittgenstein's later writings. It is never sufficient to reject a metaphysical claim, and it is always necessary to identify the conceptual forces behind it, and to do justice to them by tracing them back to their origin in familiar features of our use of the word 'I'. However, this task was not completed in the *Tractatus* and it proved to be a difficult one. For the view from the first person combines a powerful tendency to self-aggrandizement with unbreakable reticence about the point on which it is based. The analysis of this paradox and its dissolution are spread through the work that he did between 1929 and 1936.

Meanwhile, the other aspect of solipsism began to claim his attention. If the identification of the subject is taken for granted in this metaphysical theory, so too is the identification of the objects of its immediate awareness. But how does the solipsist think that he can identify the category of his sensations or their specific properties? Categories and properties always need criteria of identity and Wittgenstein challenged the traditional assumption that they would be available in the solipsist's private world. He argued that all such criteria are, and must be, dependent on links with the physical world, and he completed his case with a diagnosis of the origin of the traditional view: *it treats sensations like objects.* For it assumes that the properties of sensations have criteria of identity which do not depend on the physical world just as the properties of physical objects have criteria of identity which do not depend on any third world.

His critique of this aspect of solipsism culminates in the Private Language Argument of *Philosophical Investigations.* This controversial argument is concerned with the properties of sensations and it is only part of a larger movement of thought. Much of the disagreement about its interpretation has been the result of taking it out of its context. It does not stand alone and it is a further development, rather than a criticism, of his early ideas about solipsism.

The Private Language Argument

The Private Language Argument starts from the fact that speaking a language is an acquired skill. This entails the need for a criterion of success which can be used not only to settle disputes about the correct application of the vocabulary, but also, more importantly, to enable a learner to judge his own progress. The criterion cannot merely be his *impression* that he is now using a word for a sensation-property correctly, because his aim is success and not something which might only be the illusion of success. The criterion, therefore, must be an independent one, not based on anything confined to his mind, but on some link between his sensations and the physical world.

Commentators have differed about the nature of the link required by Wittgenstein, and some have taken it to involve not only physical objects, but also other people's verbal reactions to them. This is certainly the link used by a learner in a family, and it is one that must be used if sensation-language is to serve as a means of communication between people. However, though Wittgenstein puts heavy emphasis on its importance, he does not rule out the possibility that a human child brought up from birth by wolves would be able to set up a language for his own use based only on the links between his sensations and physical objects.

The Private Language Argument puts language back in its place in human life. It insists on the need for criteria of correct application which are based on links between sensations and the physical world, and this need is met by connections which were part of the natural history of our species before the advent of language. For example, among us, as among other social animals, pain is connected with a characteristic cry, and when we use the word 'pain' instead of that cry, we are relying on a natural connection which does most of the work of ensuring that we are using it correctly. So the acquisition of this skill is not a purely intellectual achievement. Similarly, the conviction that someone else is in pain is not founded on an

GILBERT RYLE (1900–76) became Waynflete Professor of Metaphysical Philosophy in 1945 and was for many years the most influential philosopher in Oxford. His book *The Concept of Mind* was a brilliant sustained attack on the Cartesian 'myth of the ghost in the machine'.

argument from analogy with one's own case, but on a natural sympathy which antedates language. This reversal of the accepted order of things can be generalized to many other cases: for example, the correlation of a point in one's visual field with a point in physical space is not an intellectual achievement but something established as a motor-habit very early in one's life.

Wittgenstein's aim is to destroy the intellectualism on which his adversaries' position was based. They worked within the Cartesian tradition, and so they assumed that the foundations of empirical knowledge and of the language used to express it can be laid by the intellect alone, and laid successfully, however restricted the resources available to it. If Wittgenstein is right, this assumption is indefensible. When the mind turns its back on the physical world, it obviously loses more than half the material on which its skills were exercised. What is not so obvious is that it also loses all the skills that were originally based on a network of connections involving the body, its place in the physical world, and its needs.

At this point a reminder is needed. Wittgenstein always drew a firm line between philosophy and science and held that while science investigates the world, philosophy is a purely conceptual investigation. That raised a question which had been raised earlier by the critical philosophy of Kant. What exactly is the status of a philosophical critique of our modes of thought? If the critique works through language, as it does in Wittgenstein's hands, there must be something which differentiates it from a scientific investigation of language. According to the *Tractatus*, the difference is that philosophy deals with things that can be shown but not said. This is hardly a perspicuous explanation, but it does have the clear implication that philosophical results are not contingent or factual. They present the a priori features of our schematization of the world rather than the world itself. But why would that not be merely a scientific investigation of our intellectual apparatus, instead of the material to which it is applied?

In his later writings Wittgenstein disclaims any interest in the causes which led us to adopt one conceptual scheme rather than another, and focuses on our life within the frame of our adopted scheme, and, in particular, on our inveterate tendency to overstep its limits without realizing that we are doing so. We might, therefore, expect his later philosophy to be differentiated from science by its therapeutic purpose. But though this would preserve a firm line between the two disciplines across much of the ground covered in *Philosophical Investigations*, it seems to leave the premises of the Private Language Argument hanging somewhere between a conceptual and an anthropological investigation.

The argument was primarily concerned with sensations, but its conclusions, that inner things stand in need of outer criteria, was evidently generalizable. For a similar need exists for beliefs, desires, thoughts, and intentions, and almost anything else that could be categorized as mental. On first reading, the argument often strikes people as uncompromisingly behaviouristic, a denial of their inner lives. But that was not Wittgenstein's intention. A sensation is 'not a something, but not a nothing either'. He saw himself as a philosopher steering a new course between uncompromising behaviourism and uncompromising introspectionism.

The middle way has important implications for the concept of knowledge. Wittgenstein argued that when someone is learning the application of a word in the sensation-vocabulary, he can make mistakes; but that when he has mastered it, he can no longer make mistakes. So in sensation-language sincerity entails truth, but this short cut to success is available only after the vocabulary has been mastered through its links with the physical world, where no such short cut to success is available.

It is not clear whether he generalized this account of sensation-language to a case in which someone describes an unfamiliar sensation, but he certainly thought that it held good for cases in which a familiar sensation is expressed. In all cases of the latter kind he argued that a claim to knowledge is inappropriate, because such a claim would presuppose the possibility of mistake. So even his adversaries' reason for halting scepticism with the claim 'At least I know when I am in pain' was undermined.

He returned to the problem of knowledge late in his life, reiterating his axiom that knowledge presupposes the possibility of error and offering a holistic objection to general scepticism: some statements about the world achieve immunity from mistake not because they are more thoroughly confirmed than others, but because they provide the background against which other statements can be questioned and confirmed or rejected.

The philosophy of mind took the centre of the stage at the beginning of the second period of Wittgenstein's work. It had not been entirely absent from the *Tractatus*—witness the early treatment of solipsism—but it had not made any contribution to the theory of meaning, which, therefore, remained inhumanly abstract. So it is worth enquiring what happened to the Picture Theory at the beginning of the second period, and what were the new contributions which led to its supersession.

Meaning and Rule-Following

What the *Tractatus* had neglected was the continued identity of a language through time. A sentence was a picture composed of words naming objects. But what kept the words attached to the same objects and so preserved the sense of the sentence? The answer was, of course, 'Their use'. But what kept that constant? On that point the *Tractatus* was silent.

Now in the tradition there had never seemed to be any problem about what counted as constancy of meaning and it was assumed that the only problem was its preservation. When Wittgenstein took up this topic, he exploded that assumption. The Realists' claim, that a property-word was used with the same meaning so long as it remained attached to the same property, was a piece of empty metaphysics. No doubt we all feel constrained to call the same things blue, but someone who projected the feeling on to the property without giving the property a criterion of identity independent of its effect on us would be substituting shadow for substance.

That type of Realism had not been part of the *Tractatus*. The book did defend a deeper Realism, according to which the fundamental laws of logic are imposed on any language by the structure of the world (a view which he later rejected); but it did not even pose the question which might have led others to a Realist theory of universals. On that point the *Tractatus* was not Nominalist but pre-theoretical.

Wittgenstein's criticism of the assumption that it is unproblematical what counts as constancy of meaning starts from a point which had been made in the *Tractatus*, but left with its further implications unexamined. The point of departure was the most important part of the doctrine of showing: the sense of a sentence might be given by a translation, but at the end of any sequence of translations there would always be something which could not be specified in informative language, namely, the application of the words in the final translation to things. That could only be shown by the actual practice of applying those words to things.

Wittgenstein emphasizes the point in the lectures in which he explained the leading ideas of the *Tractatus* to a Cambridge audience in the early 1930s. Its implication soon became

BERTRAND RUSSELL

Comes Russell tertius, O.M. huius Collegii socius,
philosophiae praesertim mathematicae scriptor
et interpres inclaruit. Idem, amentiam hominum
diu indignatus, senex iuuenili impetu paci inter
gentes seruandae totus incubuit donec tandem
multis adfectus honoribus et per orbem terrarum
obseruatus anno aetatis suae XCVIII, salutis MCMLXX,
e laboribus conquieuit.

LVDOVICVS WITTGENSTEIN

HVIVS COLLEGII SOCIVS
IN ACADEMIA PHILOSOPHIAE PER VIII ANNOS PROFESSOR
PHILOSOPHANDI NOVAM VIAM MVLTIS MONSTRAVIT
RATIONEM EX VINCVLIS ORATIONIS VINDICANDAM ESSE
RERVM NATVRAM SIC MAGIS MAGISQVE PERNOSCI
SENSIT ATQVE EXEMPLIS DOCEBAT
VERVM ADSEQVENDO SINGVLARI INTEGRITATE DEDITVS
OBIIT A.D. MCMLI AETATIS SVAE LXIII

GEORGE EDWARD MOORE O.M.

collegii socius et philosophiae professor qui
studiis graecis et latinis adulescens imbutus mox
philosophiae ita se dedidit ut acumine mentis hanc
disciplinam paene renovaverit. vir modestia comitate
lepore insignis, omnium reverentiam amorem sodalium
unice adeptus, anno aetatis quinto et octogesimo
mortem obiit A.D. IX kal. Nov. A.S. MCMLVIII

clear: there really is a problem about what counts as constancy of meaning. We may say, if we like, that someone who follows a rule continues to use a word in the same way. But the rule's specification of the correct application of the word must rely on more words, themselves governed by further rules, and so it may seem that we are never really tied down to a definite procedure. Yet when we call those hyacinths blue, we all know that we are not improvising. The implications of the doctrine of showing reached further than he had realized when he was working on the *Tractatus*.

In *Philosophical Investigations* the elusiveness of the concept of correct use is presented in a *reductio ad absurdum* of its denial. It is, of course, not an elusiveness which results from ordinary ambiguity and so can be eliminated by further instructions, but an unavoidable general feature of all words, however precisely they are defined. It affects any point of transition from language to the world, because at any such point incompletely specified practice makes its contribution to what counts as the correct use of the word. The *reductio* is directed against a philosopher who tries to formulate a self-sufficient rule which will pin down the correct use of a word without allowing for the contribution made by the actual practice of speakers of the language. It would immediately be apparent that he had not really provided us with any way of distinguishing obedience to the rule from disobedience. For his verbal formulation of correct use of the word would always leave open the possibility that an application that he had wanted to rule out as incorrect was, after all, correct.

In this account of rule-following there is, of course, no suggestion that people are likely to exploit the opportunities available at the point of transition from language to the world and to continue sequences of applications of words in bizarre ways. On the contrary, we all find the accepted continuations so natural that our learning of the meaning of a new word often runs ahead of the lesson. Wittgenstein is making a deep conceptual point which leaves the phenomena on the surface undisturbed. His point is that there is only one legitimate way of answering the question 'What counts as continuing to apply a word in the same way?' and that is to describe the practice of applying it in its place in our lives.

This strikes many people as a sceptical point, because it gives them less than they expect. They would be content with the Platonic answer, that a word is applied in the same way so long as it is applied to things that instantiate the same universal. But according to Wittgenstein, the comparison, which casts an unfavourable light on his own answer, is illegitimate. Platonic universals are merely an empty projection and that kind of metaphysics only offers us a picture, which is just another part of the problem rather than its solution.

At this point his position is often misunderstood. When he rejects Platonism as an empty answer to the question 'What counts as continuing to apply a word in the same way?' he is not even conceding that it is a failed answer of the right sort. For, according to him, any answer which selects a single thing as the criterion of identity of use is the wrong kind of answer. So behind the obvious fault of Platonism, its adherence to a metaphysic of shadows, there is a second fault: it assumes that the criterion of identity of use must be a single thing.

It ought not to be so easy to miss the point that Wittgenstein does not offer any single thing as the criterion of identity of use. He explicitly treats the life of a language as something sustained by many different connections, all, fortunately, able to work together, and he repeatedly reminds us that his task is not to explain this network but only to describe it. His philosophy would never have been misunderstood if it had not been so complex and so new. Confronted by his labyrinthine investigations, people find the search for a single key irresistible, and unable to appreciate the novelty of his philosophy, they find the key in some theory which can be pitted against traditional theories.

That said, it must be admitted that there is one feature of his account of identity of use which encourages misunderstanding. His aim is to give a full description of the actual practice of applying words to things and to exhibit all the ramifying connections which keep meaning constant without singling out any one of them as *the* criterion. However, although he rejects the choice between Realism and Nominalism, he does give pride of place to things which would be cited by Nominalists in support of their theory. So though he professes neutrality, his descriptions of practice have a recognizable tendency. For example, he often points out the importance of the fact that even a short sequence of applications of a word is usually one which we all find it natural to continue in the same way. Then, even more frequently, he makes a second point with the same tendency: training and standardization massively reinforce our natural inclinations.

The result is that his account of rule-following looks very like Hume's account of causal inferences: the ultimate reason why we infer effect from cause with such conviction is that certain associations of ideas come naturally to us and these associations are then reinforced by reflection on the rules for judging causes and effects. But this suggests the question 'Why treat these dispositions as ultimate?' After all, they must have evolved in response to our environment. For example, the basic properties of the things around us that we have singled out and recorded in language must be connected, directly or indirectly, with our physical needs. Hume's answer to the question is that he treats the association of ideas as ultimate simply because he does not know how to push the enquiry any further.

Similar questions can be asked about the point at which Wittgenstein halts his enquiry, human nature and training. However, his answer would be different, because he does not share Hume's view that philosophy and science are both parts of a single, seamless enquiry. He would point out that he is not offering a theory: it is not even his task to select a single criterion of identity of use, still less to explain why we have adopted the ramifying criteria that he has been describing. But in that case why does he give such prominence to the kind of factor that would be cited by a Nominalist? Why treat human nature and training as 'bedrock'? Why not say more about the forces that shaped our lives and caused us to find certain continuations of sequences natural and to do everything possible to reinforce these tendencies of training?

His answer would be that to go beyond the point where he stops would be to blur the clear line between philosophy and science. But the discussion of his Private Language Arguments developed above ended by questioning the clarity and firmness of that line. Now in that case it was suggested that what distinguishes philosophical anthropology from scientific anthropology might be its therapeutic purpose, but it was pointed out that this would not cover the premises of the Private Language Argument. In the case of rule-following another doubt might be raised about this suggestion. Are not the *reasons* why we feel that certain classes have a natural structure an important component of the forces that drive us in the direction of Platonic Realism? If so, philosophy practised as therapy ought to include them.

In *Philosophical Investigations* Wittgenstein remarks that it would be possible to develop a philosophy of mathematics along the same general lines as his philosophy of language. This enterprise is undertaken in *Remarks on the Foundations of Mathematics*, but it has made fewer converts. That may be only because it is more difficult. Certainly, his treatment of mathematics is more tentative, its precise import more uncertain, and it does not have the unity and finish of his treatment of language.

The difficulty is not that the rejection of Realism is less plausible in the philosophy of mathematics than in the philosophy of language. In both cases alike he describes our practice and his aim is to discover which features of it create the illusion that we can appeal to independently specifiable rails on which it runs. If this way of dealing with the metaphysics of reduplication is viable anywhere, it ought to be viable everywhere. The difficulty comes at an earlier point in his philosophy of mathematics: the accuracy of his description of our practice is questionable in this case.

The point at which his description might be challenged is not his account of the structure of a sequence of numbers generated by a rule. There really is an analogy between such a structure and the structure of a sequence of applications of a descriptive word. The difficulty lies in his account of the systematic character of mathematics. His idea that a proof fixed the meaning of its premises is directly opposed to the assumption made by any mathematician that he starts from premises which already have a fixed meaning and moves forwards to an already entailed conclusion. If this is an illusion, it is not a philosophical illusion, but part of a mathematician's basic description of what he is doing. We might try to reconcile this description with Wittgenstein's description by suggesting that the latter only means that a proof closes a road which, anyway, nobody was inclined to take (like an explicit ruling against a bizarre application of a descriptive word). But that interpretation seems to be excluded by Wittgenstein's insistence that proofs fix new meanings.

Finally, it is worth noting that a similar problem arises in the philosophy of logic. So the contrast is not between a plausible philosophy of language and a questionable philosophy of mathematics, but between a plausible philosophy of non-logical language and a questionable philosophy of logic and mathematics.

6

Political Philosophy

ANTHONY QUINTON

Introduction

Political Philosophy   The phrase 'political philosophy' is often used as if it had very much the same meaning as 'political theory' or 'political thought'. What can be said definitely about all three of them is that they do not mean the same as 'political science'. That is a firmly empirical or factual study of the structure and workings of political institutions—the state and its familiar parts: legislative, executive, judiciary, civil service, and so forth—and, in our more sociological age, of the political behaviour of individuals and social groups. Political science has almost as long a history as political philosophy. There is not much of it in Plato, but it is a large, perhaps the largest, element in Aristotle's *Politics*, which was based on a study of over a hundred Greek city-states.

'Political theory' is a bit less inclusive than 'political thought'. The advocacy of any substantial policy, provided that it is thoroughly reasoned for, is a piece of political thought: Gladstone's policy of Home Rule for Ireland, for example, or de Gaulle's project for the revival of France after the Second World War. But these are not political theories, as the phrase is ordinarily understood. They are insufficiently systematic and general for that: too much enclosed in a particular time and place. Nationalism, however, of which they are both instances, is a political theory.

The distinction between political theory and political philosophy is fine, to the point, indeed, of being barely discernible. The sequence of large-scale and systematic doctrines to be considered later makes up a well-established tradition. Within it three main components can be picked out: statements of fact about politics, society, and human nature; advocacy or recommendation of political goals and of institutional means to them; and, finally, reasonings of a conceptual kind about the essential nature, to use an old-fashioned term, of the state, the rights of citizens which it exists to protect, and their duty to obey it.

Under the influence of a widespread conception of philosophy as an exclusively analytic or conceptual undertaking, concerned, in an ideologically neutral spirit, with the ideas that figure centrally in various kinds of discourse, it has been supposed that only the third of these three components is political philosophy strictly so called. That involves an excessive degree of idealization. Few, if any, of the great works making up the tradition are predominantly, let alone wholly, composed of philosophy in this restricted sense.

The reason for that is that the vocabulary of political discourse consists of political terms, terms, that is to say, which refer to the products of the purposes of intelligent beings, human or, perhaps, divine. The state is not simply a natural object like a mountain or a rainbow. It was created by human beings (or conceivably God) with a certain end or ends in view. It is, crudely, *for* something, for example to protect people from the harm that other people might be disposed to do them. The nineteenth-century idealist T. H. Green reflected that fact when he said, with some rhetorical exaggeration, that tsarist Russia was not a state. It was in the same spirit that Matthew Arnold declared that Dryden and Pope were classics of our prose. Political terms are essentially disputable or controversial.

The conclusion implied is that there is no great advantage to be gained from distinguishing political philosophy, defined in terms of the analytic ideal, from political theory. But both are distinct from political thought that is neither general nor systematic. One narrowly philosophical feature common to both is that their reasonings are presented as coercive and not merely persuasive, are aimed to prove and not merely to convince or convert.

The Unity of the Tradition   Those who consider the views of the great philosophers of the past are subject to a common, and not unreasonable, reproach: that they treat them as contemporaries, as concerned with just the same problems as those who discuss them and as attaching the same meaning to the terms they share with their successors as the latter do. R. G. Collingwood, arguing for the thesis that there are no eternal problems in philosophy, shrewdly based his argument on the huge differences between the kinds of state on which the philosophers of different epochs were reflecting. 'Plato's *Republic*', he plausibly said, 'is an attempt at a theory of one thing, Hobbes's *Leviathan* is an attempt at a theory of something else.'

Some objects of philosophical study are much more historically mutable than others. At one extreme are the mind, language, and knowledge, which are presumably much what they were at the outset of Western philosophy two and a half thousand years ago. At the other extreme are art, religion, history, science, and, above all, politics, with morality lodged somewhere between the two extremes. It follows that philosophy, when it treats the more historically sensitive institutions, must take account of the intervening changes. But it does not follow that the views of philosophers of different periods are simply incommensurable. Substantial change is compatible not only with continuity but also with an element of persisting identity.

The history of Western political philosophy, since the beginning of serious reflection on the subject with Plato, can be divided into five main segments, between which there will naturally be a measure of overlap. First, there is the world of the Greek city-state and of the Italian city-state that developed into the Roman republic. Secondly, there is the period of the

L est dit deuant
quantes et qlles
sont les differen
ces du prmcey

Texte, serien de ces chofes est
residu et demoure teneft pas mois
bon de confiderer de ce auectques les
chofes deffufdictes et de mettre de

ARISTOTLE'S *POLITICS* was
influential throughout the Middle
Ages in ways which he could never
have foreseen. An illustration (*above*)
to a fifteenth-century manuscript of
his text shows an insurrection of
artisans.

THE EMPEROR JUSTINIAN (seen
here, *left*, in a mosaic from Ravenna),
crowned in 527, was the most
renowned legislator in history. He
compiled and reformed all previous
imperial enactments and
harmonized the work of all previous
legal commentators. His codification
set up the canon of Roman Law
which was influential for centuries in
political philosophy.

MACHIAVELLI'S WRITING-DESK reflects the chilling austerity of his famous treatise *The Prince*.

quasi-oriental despotism of Alexander and his successors, of the Roman emperors from Augustus to the fall of Rome, and of the Byzantine Empire in the east until it fell to the Turks in 1453. Thirdly, there is the period of the barbarian kingdoms, which flourished in the former dominions of the western Roman Empire, and of the feudal monarchies into which they developed, many of them loosely associated in the Holy Roman Empire. Fourthly, there is the epoch of centralizing monarchies, inaugurated in Britain by Henry VII, if not by Edward IV before him, and culminating in the absolutism of Louis XIV. Finally, there is the modern state, in which hereditary monarchies are displaced or marginalized by the supremacy of more or less representative institutions. This began with the Hanoverian 'crowned republic' of Britain after 1714, was fully fledged with American independence in 1776, and was fitfully dominant in France between 1789 and the installation of the Third Republic in 1870. Representative government, republican in fact if not in form, is now the usual arrangement in the three Western continents (Europe, North America, and Australasia) and in India and Israel. It is also insecurely and intermittently established in Latin America. Sections of this chapter will be devoted to political theories of the city-state, the feudal state, and the dynastic state. The three final sections, covering the last three centuries, will be concerned with the modern state. The quasi-oriental despotisms of the Roman and Byzantine Empires generated little political philosophy. The Romans were unoriginal at the level of theory, although great developers of law. Byzantine culture was backward-looking and dominated by theology.

In all its historic variations the state has sought to discharge two connected functions: the maintenance of order within its domain by the promulgation and enforcement of law and the defence of the nation against external enemies. Social change has added other functions: the incorporation or regulation of towns, control of the currency, the support and regulation of trade, poor relief, and the maintenance of a state religion or management of relations with an independent and supranational church. In the last 200 years, the old concern with poor relief has expanded into a broad array of social activities in the provision of welfare, education, and medical treatment. But the protective function has remained primary and has persisted as an identical core within the variety of the state's operations. Plato's city-state and Hobbes's nation-state were not the same thing, but they were things of the same kind as the states we have today.

There is a further discontinuity to be considered, that between the pre-Christian civilizations of Greece and Rome (before the conversion of the emperor Constantine) and the civilization of Christendom. To make this distinction is to follow to some extent the view of large-scale theorists of history, in particular Spengler and Toynbee. But it is not to follow them all the way. It is certainly not to follow Spengler in his idea that the classical and Western civilizations are totally distinct from and closed to each other.

The decline and fall of the Roman Empire has reasonably been taken to be the greatest event in history and so an appropriate topic for the greatest of historical writers. But it did not involve a complete break. The barbarian kings who took over the Roman domains in the west for the most part imitated and preserved what they could of Roman culture and institutions. Christianity was established as the official religion of the Roman Empire a century

·PAX· ·FORTITVDO· ·PRVDENTIA·

THE THEORY OF THE STATE has varied through the ages, but two functions have remained essential: to provide order within a community, and security from its enemies. Ambrogio Lorenzetti's frescos in the Palazzo Pubblico in Siena, *The Effects of Good and Evil Government*, express medieval expectations of the state's role.

before that empire fell in the west. At that time the formal theology of the church was being elaborated by the Fathers on the basis of Greek philosophy, particularly that of Plato, as filtered through Plotinus. After 1200 and the recovery of the whole range of Aristotle's works, theology took on a comprehensively Aristotelian form. The thinkers of the Renaissance saw themselves as the revivers of classical, especially Platonic, learning. Classical themes were constantly adverted to in the Enlightenment. Since Latin and, from the Renaissance onwards, Greek were the main ingredients of higher or serious education from the fall of Rome until the middle of the nineteenth century, that is not surprising. So, despite the very large changes, political, social, and cultural, that took place after the fall of the Roman Empire in the west, there was still a large measure of continuity between the two civilizations.

The Problems of Political Philosophy   Political philosophy used to be described as a study of the 'essential nature' of the state. That was understood, not so much as an account of what the state universally is under all its various historical manifestations, but as a matter of determining what the state ideally ought to be—what, in all its historical forms, it could be seen as striving to become. Plato presented his *Republic* as an enquiry into the nature of justice. It turned out, however, to be the delineation of an ideal state or, at least, to be an answer to the question: what sort of people should rule and how should they be prepared for the task? Aristotle's *Politics* is explicitly engaged with the topic of the state's essential nature, although, as it turned out, the utopian project is very marginal to his discussion of the forms of states and their strengths and weaknesses.

In the sixteenth and seventeenth centuries the emphasis was not so much on what a state ideally ought to be as on what an institution had to be in order to be a state at all. The idea of sovereignty was propounded to explain the difference between the state and other institutions seeking to regulate human activity. The absolutist demand implicit in this doctrine called forth an insistence on the conditions a state must satisfy if its claims on its citizens are to be legitimate. The duty to obey it was taken to be conditional on its respect for their rights, their 'natural' rights, prior to the state's own positive law. That put at the centre of political philosophy the problem of the basis of political obligation, the conditions under which alone an individual person has a duty to obey the state. Interest began to focus on proclaimed natural rights—to liberty, property, and equality of various kinds: under the law, of participation in government, of wealth and income—seen at least as tests for the adequacy or excellence of government, if not as strict conditions of political obligation. Political obligation is a primary issue for those whose only political choice is between obedience and disobedience. As the range of available political activity has enlarged, these particular political values become relevant to people's new possibilities of choice, whether only as voters, or also as members of political parties and expressers of opinion.

Nothing is to be gained from laying down a more definite and specific list of problems before the detail of particular bodies of political philosophy has been described. Enough has been given to circumscribe the field to be considered as that in which the state, and the purposes it must or should pursue, and the manner in which it pursues them, are examined and critically evaluated by rational argument.

Greece and Rome

The City-State The Greek world of the fifth and sixth centuries BC, in which Western thinking about politics in general terms began, was composed of 150 or more city-states. Athens, the largest, had a population of about a quarter of a million; most of the rest were much smaller. They were usually on or near the sea, the valleys behind them isolated from their neighbours by mountains. These geographic facts explain the political disunity of Greece, despite its proud awareness of a common culture. By going to sea, first for food, then for trade, Greeks became aware of moral practices and political institutions radically different from their own.

WHO IS FIT TO RULE? Since the time of Plato, some philosophers have considered the description of the just ruler the key task of political philosophy. The theme is allegorized in this painting by De Poorter (1635) representing Merit assuming Temporal Power.

These circumstances encouraged, but can hardly explain, the extraordinary intellectual explosion of the Greek golden age which contained the first and still unsurpassed examples of tragedy, philosophy, abstract mathematics, history, democratic government, and, of course, political theory. Early tribal kingdoms gave way, in the period of colonization from the eighth to the sixth centuries BC, to tyrannies, charismatic rule based on broad popular consent. Colonies were established to the east in Asia Minor and to the west in Sicily and southern Italy to relieve over-population. Athens acquired its democratic constitution in 507 BC from the tyrant Cleisthenes.

The Athenian democracy, which united the Greeks against Persian invasion at Marathon in 490 BC and Salamis in 480 BC and which was finally defeated, but not destroyed, by the rigid military autocracy of Sparta in 404 BC at the end of the Peloponnesian War, was direct, not representative. All adult males who were neither resident foreigners nor slaves were members of the Assembly, from which a ruling Council was chosen by lot. That was an exceptional arrangement. Most city-states were aristocratic oligarchies or more or less popular tyrannies. But everywhere, because of the smallness of the sovereign political units, politics was a face-to-face business in which everyone was involved. Class conflict between well-off landowners and poorer craftsmen, sailors, and small traders was pervasive. There were, therefore, both the motive and the opportunity for thought about the fundamentals of politics.

Greek philosophy, in the form of reasoned speculation about the nature of the universe as a whole, began in the colonies of Asia Minor. It turned inwards to the study of man and society with the work of the Sophists from the middle of the fifth century, some thirty years after the defeat of Persia and twenty years before the outbreak of the main conflict between Athens and Sparta in 431 BC. The Sophists were primarily teachers of rhetoric, of the essential oratorical skills required for participation in democratic politics. Plato's teacher, Socrates, was one of them in his methods and interests, but was opposed to their scepticism, their emphasis on argumentative success rather than on the discovery of truth. Socrates was put to death in 399 BC by the restored democracy, perhaps because he had had among his pupils the gifted traitor Alcibiades and the ruthless oligarch Critias, who had just been overthrown. Two of Plato's uncles were among the oligarchs and he was of aristocratic birth. The ideal state of his *Republic* is an intellectual aristocracy in which philosophers are put at the head of a society like Sparta. Plato had strong personal reasons for his dislike of democracy.

The battle of Chaeronea in 338 BC, nine years after Plato's death and sixteen years before Aristotle's, brought to an end the political significance of the Greek city-states. All were absorbed into the comparatively barbarous empire of Macedon, soon to be inherited by Aristotle's pupil Alexander the Great and turned by him into a vast, if short-lived, world-empire. Greece remained incorporated in one of the three parts into which it dissolved until that fell to Rome. Rome began as a city-state, but within fifty years of Chaeronea it had established its power over central and southern Italy, and in 202 BC it emerged victorious from a series of wars with its north African rival, Carthage. Rome was a republic controlled by an aristocratic and exclusive senate; none the less, its constitution contained elements of popular representation. Its large and rapid conquests led to a long-drawn-out civil war and the establishment of the empire by Augustus after the battle of Actium in 31 BC. His descendants ruled until the death of Nero and were followed, after a period of disturbance, by four abler emperors, from Trajan to Marcus Aurelius, in a century in which the empire reached its greatest extent and enjoyed its greatest peace and prosperity. After that a long period of polit-ical instability, economic decline, and barbarian pressure continued until the final collapse of the western empire in 476 AD.

In this period of massive empires, largely dominated by generals, philosophy retreated from the public realm into private life, confining itself mainly to personal morality and the attainment of peace of mind. Although unprecedentedly skilled in law and administration, Roman civilization was derivative in political thought. Its collapse was the occasion for Augustine's *City of God*, the first major attempt to deal with political topics from a Christian point of view. This introduced a period of 1200 years during which political thinking was embedded in religion and preoccupied with the problem of the relations between church and state. Hitherto religion in the West had been civic rather than transcendental, whether as the organized public rituals of the Greek cities and the Roman republic or as the cult of a deified emperor, as in the empires of Alexander and Augustus.

Plato   Three of Plato's dialogues are concerned with politics: the *Republic* first and fore-most, but also the *Statesman* and the *Laws*. The *Republic* goes far beyond politics, not simply into the connected fields of education and the social aspects of literature and art, but also into metaphysics and the theory of knowledge. Its chief political ingredients are its delin-eation of an ideal state and its account of the various forms in which actual states fail to attain this ideal. Plato's theory of knowledge is brought in to support the view that only the few who have true knowledge should rule. The whole discussion begins with a series of arguments about the nature of justice, directed against the moral scepticism of the Sophists.

Justice is treated in the first two books as a property of individuals and their actions rather than of political systems. Naïvely superficial conceptions—that it is repaying what one owes or that it is helping friends and harming enemies—are dispatched in a trivial and quibbling fashion. The more serious challenge of Thrasymachus, who maintains that justice is the interest of the stronger, is also none too satisfyingly handled. He is disingenuously manœu-vred into asserting that justice does not pay, which is an answer, not to the question what is justice, but to the question whether justice is worth pursuing. In the *Gorgias* a sceptical posi-tion opposite to that of Thrasymachus is criticized, the fairly Nietzschean idea that justice is a conspiracy of the weak to keep down the strong. In the *Republic* that line of thought is pre-sented in a milder and eminently sensible form by Glaucon, who holds that it is an agreement by which all abstain from injury to others for the sake of self-protection (the central princi-ple of the political theory of Hobbes). Against this Plato's mouthpiece, Socrates, makes the point that self-protection supplies no motive for abstention from evil-doing that is going to escape detection.

After these ethical preliminaries explicitly political issues are raised, when Socrates says that justice is more clearly perceptible in a large-scale instance, the state, than on the small scale of the individual soul. He goes on to assert that a state is just and well ordered to the extent that its citizens are assigned to the positions for which their capacities best fit them: those who are most rational and have real knowledge to the task of ruling it, those conspicuous for energy and spiritedness to that of its defence and the maintenance of order, and the large remainder, who act on impulse and from unreflective appetite, to the production of the goods that are needed by all. Plato infers that a parallel hierarchy of reason, 'spirit', and desire is what constitutes justice or proper order in the individual soul.

Plato gives much attention to the manner of life and educational preparation of his ruling class of 'guardians'. They are to be chosen partly by heredity (assisted by eugenic arrangements in mating) and also by selection on the basis of merit. They are to have no personal property but to live in communal barracks, so as to prevent corruption. They are to have no family life: spouses are to be communal and the guardians are to be kept ignorant of the identity of their children, so as to inspire public spirit and prevent favouritism. On its negative side, their education is to shield them from metaphysically and morally deficient forms of art, music, and literature. Homer, with his unedifying stories of the bad conduct of the gods, is ruled out. Positively aspiring guardians are to be led by way of mathematics to the highest, most abstractly rarefied level of knowledge (the assumption being that it is a course few will prove qualified to follow). In its concern with the eternal and unchanging, whose nature and relations are apprehended in a purely intellectual way, mathematics is an essential preparation for philosophy, above all for knowledge of the good.

The conviction that the objects of knowledge, and, above all, the good, are abstract and timeless is the first politically relevant thesis of Plato's theory of knowledge. The second is that we needs must love the highest when we see it, or, more accurately, needs must pursue the good when we know what it is. Virtue is knowledge, as the usual formula puts it. No doubt in some sense we always do what, at the time and however irrationally or short-sightedly, we take to be somehow the best thing to do. His second thesis is, at any rate, more plausible than his first, that knowledge of the good generally and the knowledge needed by a good ruler is like pure mathematics only more so.

In books 8 and 9 of the *Republic* Plato considers the varieties of unideal states, presenting them as an unhistorical sequence of progressive degenerations from his speculative ideal of government by the wisest men (or even the wisest man). The ideal society gives way—something Plato finds it hard to explain—to 'timocracy', the rule of soldiers, governed by knightly honour. That gives way, in its turn, to oligarchy, in which the rich replace the honourable. Oligarchy succumbs to democracy and democracy, finally, is displaced by tyranny, the worst of all forms of government.

Concern with the actual forms of government reappears in the two later political dialogues, the *Statesman* and the *Laws*. Here Plato sets out the classification of forms of government into rule by one, rule by the few, or rule by the many. He identifies a good and a bad variety of each: monarchy and tyranny, aristocracy and oligarchy, constitutional democracy and lawless democracy. The main topic of the *Statesman* is whether the state should be run in accordance with a fixed law (an idea altogether absent from the *Republic*) or by the insight of the truly wise. By this stage in his career, disillusioned by his wholly fruitless utopia-building efforts on behalf of the tyrants of Syracuse, Plato concedes that the discretionary ideal is unrealizable and, therefore, that law is essential to a well-ordered state.

In the *Laws* this watering-down of the proposals of the *Republic* is carried out in detail. Many of the themes of the earlier dialogue recur, such as the equality of women and the need for controlled and organized education. In conformity with the replacement of individual wisdom by impersonal law is the concession of marriage (under a measure of public control) and of property to the rulers (also within limitations). The second-best state that Plato prescribes in face of the weakness of human nature seeks harmony by allowing some constitutional role to all citizens and not just a small intellectual élite. Social order is to be secured not by the subjection of the foolish to the wise but by a balance of forces. These principles of the inescapability of law and the need for a balance of classes were to be the main elements of Aristotle's *Politics*.

For all its impracticality and indifference to the real needs of rulers, Plato's *Republic* has been persistently revered: it was admired, for example, by Rousseau and by liberals prepared to divert their attention from the more totalitarian aspects of the project. It inspired the creation of the examination-selected civil service of the final, not inglorious, century of the British Empire and it remains the most seductive presentation of intellectual élitism, attractive to academics for the elevated, if laborious and ascetic, place it accords them in the social scheme of things.

Aristotle   Aristotle prepared himself for writing his somewhat miscellaneous *Politics* by studying the constitutions, the arrangements for allocating public office, of some 150 Greek city-states. Although he died, aged 62, sixteen years after the Macedonians' incorporation of the Greek city-states into their empire, he insisted that a true state must be small enough for its citizens to know one another. In its details, therefore, the *Politics* is a retrospective anachronism. Aristotle's pupil Alexander the Great, although he spread Greek civilization into Asia far from its birthplace, was the deified ruler of the largest empire the world had yet seen.

Aristotle begins with his famous remark that man is by nature a 'political animal'. That does not mean that all men are naturally politicians but that only in a politically organized society can human beings realize their natural potentialities of excellence. The lesser groupings of family and tribal village, merely economic and productive associations, are not enough. The biologically based conception of a thing's nature as that in which it achieves its highest development has worn less well than his idea that the good life for mankind can be secured only within a state. It did not justify the form of slavery that prevailed in his age: Greek slaves were captives in war and their descendants, not people who had failed examinations. Despite his view that the state is necessary for civilization, Aristotle did not believe, as Plato did, that political activity is the highest form of life. That form he took to be contemplation, the pursuit of knowledge for its own sake, a professorial ideal more appropriate

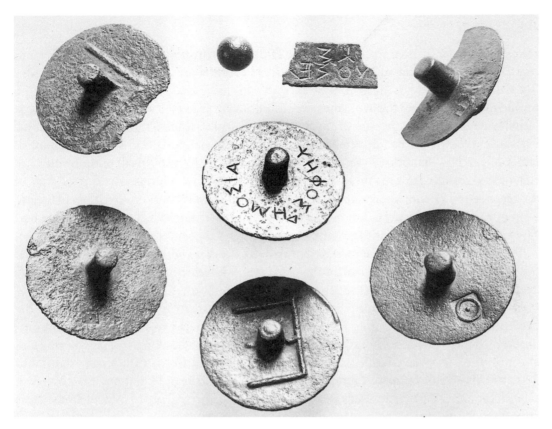

THE ORIGIN OF DEMOCRACY is commonly traced to the reforms of Cleisthenes in Athens in 508 BC. The bronze wheels illustrated here are public ballots used there in the fifth or fourth century BC.

to Plato, who maintained, nevertheless, that it was only a training for public service as a ruler. Statecraft is a practical, not a speculative, science.

In politics as elsewhere Aristotle's views tend to be more or less commonsensical dilutions of Plato's theoretical extravagances. Just as he derives his arguments against Plato's theory of forms from Plato's own *Parmenides*, so his critique of the *Republic* has much in common with Plato's *Laws*. He holds that there is no guarantee that the ideally informed and virtuous philosopher-kings Plato calls for can be found: self-interested passions are impossible to extirpate. The best practicable state is one based on law, which he describes as 'passionless reason'. Plato's conception of an ideal ruling class is incompatible with actual human nature. If it was put into effect it would install rule by the miserable, who would have miserable subjects.

A citizen, for Aristotle, is someone with a constitutional right to office and a constitution is a set of rules for the allocation of offices. Citizenship requires leisure and the ability and opportunity to think, so that manual workers (as well as slaves, of course) cannot aspire to it. The three main possible forms of constitution—rule by one, few, or many—can be right, aiming public-spiritedly at the common good, or perverted, pursuing the self-interest of the rulers. Monarchy, aristocracy, and 'polity' (a kind of constitutional, limited democracy) are right; tyranny, oligarchy, and lawless democracy (in other words, mob rule) are perverted.

Aristotle is, like Plato, much concerned with education as a political issue and with the problem of stability and the avoidance of revolution. For him education, and moral education in particular, is not the imparting of theoretical expertise but a training in good habits. City-states owe their instability to the endemic conflict of rich and poor, striving to establish either oligarchy—plutocracy might be a better word—or the free-for-all of mob rule. The rule of law can serve to keep these colliding partialities within bounds. The special skills of the few need to be supplemented by the consent of the many since—as Aristotle may have been one of the first to say in a political sense—the wearer knows where the shoe pinches. Thus if the former should rule the latter should be able to vote.

The middle books of the *Politics* (4, 5, and 6) are taken up with the factual details of the political life of the city-state. Since the main cause of revolution is class conflict, a stable state needs a middle class to bridge the gap between rich and poor. Allocation of some power to the citizenry at large will reduce the danger of sedition. Aristotle generally argues that the best constitution for a state must depend to some extent on its size, its style of economy, its physical character. One fairly casual observation early in the book was to have a profound effect on the European Middle Ages. Although property is, in Aristotle's view, natural to mankind, its extent should be limited by need and it should be used, not made the object of accumulation. In particular, usury is an improper and unnatural use of money. In the same economically primitive spirit Aristotle insisted that a state should be self-sufficient and should rely as little as possible on trade; he forgot the fact that it was trade in wine and olive oil that had enabled the cities of Greece to support a large number of citizens who had risen above mere subsistence, making possible an unprecedented level of culture.

Stoics and Epicureans   The absorption of the Greek city-states into the empire of Alexander the Great and then into the troubled, purely Macedonian, kingdom of the Antigonids brought to an end the Greek political experiment, some two centuries in length, of direct participation in government by a large part of the people ruled by it. It had provided raw material, in the form of rapid political change, for fundamental thinking, freed from customary assumptions and accelerated by the wholly new circumstance of widespread alphabetic literacy. Writing, no longer an esoteric mystery confined to religion, or a practical device used for financial records, made possible the thorough study of treatises containing sustained argument.

Greek civilization persisted throughout most of the states into which Alexander's empire was divided. It was Hellenistic rather than Greek, since it was influenced by the oriental cultures, notably of Egypt and Persia, in which its Greek-dominated cities were implanted. The greatest of these was Alexandria, the centre of the original thought of the age, principally specialized study in mathematics and natural science. The predominance of government by military emperors—usually remote, sometimes deified—completely transformed the character of political thought and action. Philosophy largely gave up politics and retreated into concern for the individual soul, its happiness and salvation. In its Greek form it remained secular, but oriental religion, mystical or superstitious, increasingly overshadowed it.

The philosophical doctrines of the Hellenistic period took as their primary topic the wise management of life in a disordered world, the achievement of peace of mind in circumstances where ordinary well-being was constantly at risk. The Epicureans recommended a life of temperate withdrawal from public life. The Cynics rejected all the conventional goods of civilization—family, property, government—in the first of those outbreaks of primitivism that recur throughout history, by way of medieval millenarianism up to Rousseau and Tolstoy. The Stoics held invulnerability by fate to be best assured by the extinction of desire.

There is little political philosophy in Epicurus or in the great poem of Lucretius on which we rely for much of our knowledge of Epicurus' opinions. The wise man lives so as to avoid harm, a more reliably achievable end than positive pleasure. The state is a human contrivance, in which men agree not to harm others so long as others abstain from harming them. It is not, as with Plato and Aristotle, an indispensable agency of human self-development or perfection. Both in its materialistic rejection of transcendental religion and of the idea of immortality, dispelling fear of the gods and of eternal punishment, and in its strictly instrumental conception of the state as a protective convenience, Epicureanism anticipated Hobbes, although focusing on fear of injury rather than on fear of death as Hobbes did. The idea of contract as the source of political authority had already been suggested in Plato's *Republic*, but had there been brushed aside without serious consideration. It was to dominate political thought from the end of the sixteenth until the middle of the eighteenth century.

The Cynics' passionate dismissal of conventional worldly goods modulated into the more unemotionally disdainful attitude to them of the Stoics. The self-sufficient wise man of the Cynics is isolated from other men. The Stoics, looking behind the distinctions between men which the Cynics had repudiated, concentrated on the common humanity which united them. Seeing all human beings as endowed with reason, they took them, on that account, to be, in a fundamentally important respect, equal. They arrived at a cosmopolitan conception of an ideal community of all people, a potential world-state of which everyone is a citizen. Taking the world as a whole, nature in the most straightforward sense, to be a rationally harmonious order, governed by a rational God, they went on to conceive mankind, by analogy, as answerable to a law of nature, a universally applicable set of rules of rational conduct. This speculative notion, in which an objective morality is detached from custom and from positive religion, had a vivifying influence on Roman law. As the Roman Empire came to incorporate more and more of the world, its law had to accommodate the legal systems of other communities. The way had been prepared by the idea of the law of nations (*jus gentium*), a kind of common residue of the laws of different communities, set up to deal with legal interactions between Romans and non-Romans. This practical makeshift was endowed with a more authoritative status by being embedded in the Stoic conception of a law of nature binding on all men; it provided a legal completion to the practice of making the subjects of conquered states Roman citizens.

Zeno, the founder of Stoicism, was on good terms with Antigonus II of Macedonia (like Epicurus, Zeno founded his school around 300 BC, twenty years or so after the death of Alexander) and one of his followers taught Antigonus' son. But it was not until the Roman period that Stoicism became politically influential, first in solving a problem about law for the vastly increased reach of Roman power and then as something like the official philosophy of the Roman Empire. The last notable Stoic, after all, was the emperor Marcus Aurelius, who died in AD 180, half a millennium after the school's foundation. Epicureanism faded away at about the same time, having had no direct political influence.

Cicero and Seneca   The Romans, great in warfare, administration, and law, were not original thinkers. Their most notable philosopher, Cicero, killed in 43 BC on the orders of Octavian (soon to be Augustus) in the civil war that replaced a republic by an empire, was an eclectic who, perhaps over-modestly, described his own philosophical productions as merely compilations. We have, at any rate, to rely on him for much of what we know or believe about post-Aristotelian thought. The intellectual authority with which he was generally accredited in his own age was strengthened by his public fame and his literary gifts. He was a prominent conservative defender of the senatorial and essentially aristocratic republic, active in politics and the courts, who wrote copiously on a wide variety of subjects in a Latin prose that was the main intellectual diet of European schoolboys from the Renaissance to the beginning of this century. The republic he idealized had already disintegrated in all but form. In his immediate political loyalties he was as out of touch with his age as Plato or Aristotle.

On the basis of a somewhat whimsical interpretation of the course of Roman history he arrived at the conclusion that the Roman republic, as a mixed state, approximated to the ideal: monarchical in its consuls, aristocratic in its senate, democratic in its assemblies (and democratic, he could have added, in the institution of the tribunate, which, put to revolutionary use by the Gracchi, inaugurated the civil war of which he was a victim). More significant was his theory of natural law, of the priority of morality to politics (and not, as with Plato and Aristotle, their near identity). This has been a recurrent (and, for long periods of time, dominant) ingredient of Western political thought ever since, wherever legal systems of Roman origin have prevailed and wherever the church has been unified and therefore powerful enough to limit the activities of the state. It is alive today in the notion of the rights of man or 'human rights'.

Stoicism had begun as a doctrine of private individual wisdom, a prescription for detached serenity. But with Panaetius of Rhodes, around the end of the second century BC, at the moment when Rome, having overwhelmed Carthage in the third century and Macedonia in the second, had become master of the whole Mediterranean world, it became more public-spirited and outgoing. In Panaetius' doctrine the service of the state recovered something of the position that it had had in Plato and Aristotle. All men are fundamentally equal, whatever their differences of ability, wealth, and social position, in having rationality in common with the universal reason of God. This providential God prescribes a universal law of nature to men, knowledge of which they possess innately. The positive law of states emerges

MARCUS TULLIUS CICERO was the greatest philosophical prose writer of classical Rome. He was active in politics in the last days of the Republic, and as Consul in 63 BC suppressed a revolutionary conspiracy. When Julius Caesar came to power he withdrew from political life and devoted himself to writing on philosophy and rhetoric. After Caesar's death he was murdered at the orders of Caesar's adopted son Octavian. The illustration shows a second-century copy of an original portrait bust carved shortly after his death.

from custom, in which the law of nature is obscurely embedded. Brought to consciousness it can be seen as a criterion for the adequacy and authority of positive law. Where in Plato reason is the monopoly of an intellectual élite, in Cicero it is present in all men. This equalizing feature should be recognized by law. The true authority of a state depends on its adherence to objective justice. Rulers are said to owe their authority to some elusive endorsement by the people, even if no explicit democratic machinery is envisaged to give that endorsement a concrete form.

This was not, as it might at first seem, merely pious rationalization of the brutal realities of power. Roman law, as authoritatively codified by Justinian nearly 500 years after Cicero's death, made much more humane provision for such oppressed groups as women, children, slaves, and criminals than had the harsh laws of the old Roman republic. The idea of a natural law as somehow overriding the state's own positive law was an underlying assumption of the Roman lawyers whose work culminated in Justinian's codification.

Cicero's revival of the idea of politics as man's highest vocation could hardly flourish in the

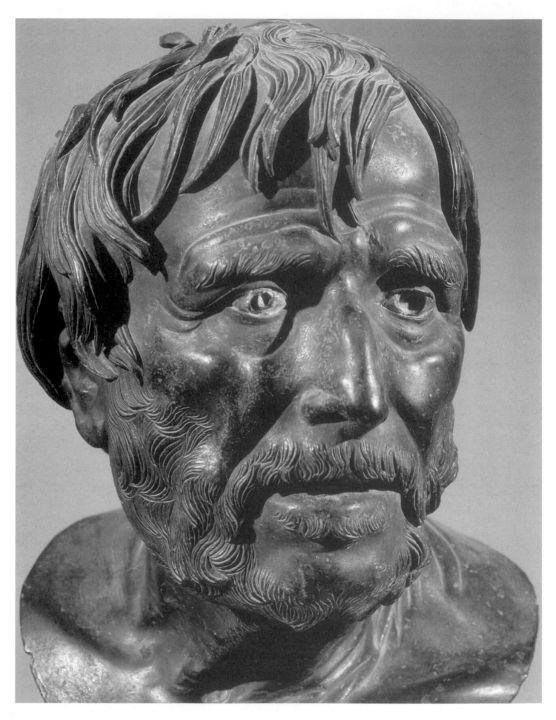

LUCIUS ANNAEUS SENECA was a courtier of the emperor Claudius who, after a period in disgrace, was made tutor to the future emperor Nero. When Nero came to the throne, Seneca became his chief adviser, and persuaded him, for a few years, to govern well. But Nero became impatient of restraint and corrupted by power, and Seneca retired into philosophical exile and was finally forced to commit suicide. This is a second-century Roman copy of a Greek original bust, found in Herculaneum; its authenticity as a portrait is contested.

period of Augustus' grotesquely cruel and despotic successors. Seneca was tutor to Nero, the worst of them, and was compelled by him to commit suicide. He too was a Stoic, but a much less hopeful one than Cicero, a century earlier. With the accession of Trajan, about thirty years after Seneca cut open his veins, a century of good, secure, and comparatively peaceful government began, to last until rule by barbarian generals and their armies prevailed after Marcus Aurelius. Seneca understandably repudiated the idea that the wise man will take no part in politics, since it is both dangerous and morally degrading. He detached altogether from politics the objective, eternal morality which Cicero had tried to bring into relation with the actual political practice of the state as the test and foundation of positive law.

Seneca did not take that to imply complete withdrawal from the public realm. He emphasized, in a way no philosopher had done before, the central position in morality of an active concern for the relief of suffering in others. Greek ethical theory understood virtue in a self-regarding way, as personal excellence rather than beneficent activity. Looking at the world around him, and perhaps into himself, he was sharply aware of what Kant was to call 'the radical evil in human nature'. He conveyed that idea through the myth of a golden age in which all had lived in harmonious contentment. The fall of man came about, in his view, because of the lust of appropriation. The state and the institution of property, therefore, are devices set up to control the evil in man, as 'remedies for sin'. The state should be obeyed, but it has nothing much to do with the pursuit of perfection, which, although social in his conception, is non-political.

Cicero's doctrine of natural law gradually permeated the legal thinking of the Roman Empire. By the time the process had culminated in Justinian's code the barbarians had already destroyed the Roman Empire in the west. But Roman law survived in Byzantium and reappeared in the west in the eleventh and twelfth centuries. The idea of natural law was incorporated in the political thinking of the High Middle Ages. Seneca's melancholy detachment of beneficent morality from sin-curbing politics was more immediately prophetic. It corresponded with the political attitude of early Christianity, which saw the state as part of the burden of fallen mankind, something to be passively put up with, while moral perfection was to be pursued by private benevolence, as well, of course, as by faith, ascetic practices, and ritual observances.

The City of God   Christianity derived an intense and demanding monotheism from pre-Christian Judaism. St Paul rejected Judaic exclusiveness, seeking to convert all men to Christianity and dropping the obstructive formalities of circumcision and the dietary laws. The early kings of Israel had been subjected to vehement moral criticism by the prophets, an anticipation of medieval conflicts between church and state (beginning with the bold practice of St Ambrose in the fourth century). Subsequently, Judaea was, for a time, a theocracy, ruled by high priests; the Romans installed direct rule by procurators soon after the death of King Herod, around the time of Christ's birth. The Jews had expected the Messiah soon to establish his kingdom on earth, compensating for their historic sufferings. But their persistent misfortunes invigorated what had been a fairly tenuous belief in the soul's survival of death into a fully fledged doctrine of another world. This was central to Christianity, which abandoned all ambitions for worldly power of any but a spiritual kind.

As the leaders of a small body of radical outsiders, Christ and St Paul propounded a political doctrine of passive obedience to the state, expressed in Christ's 'render unto Caesar the things that are Caesar's' and Paul's 'the powers that be are ordained of God'. That political submissiveness had one crucial limitation. Christians could not worship emperors who claimed to be divine. To the Roman authorities that amounted to treason and led to savage persecution, which was, of course, not ultimately effective. The body of Christian believers grew greatly in number, particularly among soldiers, whose profession naturally made the idea of another world appealing, and also in organizational strength. In making Christianity the official religion of the empire, Constantine recognized the extent of its hold on his subjects.

In Byzantium, where imperial power persisted with much of its original vigour, the church, while glorified and enriched, fell firmly under the control of the imperial authority which had established it. The emperor appointed its leading officers. In the disintegrating west the Christian community spread across a range of competing powers. Most of the barbarian kings were converted. They, like the later emperors, were never strong enough to dominate the church for long. St Ambrose, by threatening the emperor Theodosius with excommunication for a massacre in Thessalonica, obtained his submission. But Ambrose claimed only spiritual authority over the secular power. That is already a long way from the retiring submissiveness of Christ and St Paul, but it is further still from theocracy proper. These older notions were not to come into their own until the Protestant Reformation: passive obedience with Luther, theocracy with Calvin.

St Augustine wrote his *City of God* in the first quarter of the fifth century, in the first instance as an answer to the claim—still part of Gibbon's diagnosis in the eighteenth century—that the fall of Rome to Alaric in 410 was the fault of Christianity. An elaborate distinction is drawn in it between the city of God and the city of the world, whose respective emblems are Jerusalem and Babylon. Augustine is explicit that these are not, on the one hand, church as opposed to state, or, on the other, heaven as opposed to earth. Some of what states do merits divine approval; some of what Christians do—although not the infallible church—does not. By way of the church, carrying out its spiritual tasks in the world of teaching the faith and guiding conduct, the city of God is present on earth. If states protect the church and act justly, they too are to that extent part of it. But if the church is, as spiritual, above the state, it is not to do the state's work, only to protest and apply purely religious sanctions if the state acts wrongly.

After Augustine's time the strength and unity of the church steadily increased, while states became ever weaker, more unstable, more fragmented. The church's advantages compensated for its lack of military power, its spiritual armoury was more enduringly potent than the ordinary weapons at the disposal of the state. The church's conviction that the true destiny of man is not of this world allowed it to confine itself to the aspects of human life which bear on salvation: holding the right beliefs, performing the required religious exercises, act-

ing rightly by loving one's neighbour. It regarded the state's management of affairs as outside its competence as long as these spiritual requirements were respected. Like other divided jurisdictions this arrangement led to continuous boundary disputes, but the demarcation of largely independent spheres of influence for church and state survived, despite such interruptions as the Great Schism from 1378 to 1415, until the Reformation of the sixteenth century.

The Middle Ages

From Barbarian Kingdoms to Feudal Society   The final collapse of the western Roman Empire in 476 did not lead at once to fundamental social and political disintegration. Rome's western possessions were divided in sizeable portions among a set of Germanic tribes: Vandals in north Africa, Visigoths in Spain, Ostrogoths in Italy, and Franks in Gaul. They were already largely Christianized and by no means merely destructive in their attitude to Roman civilization. They preserved much of it in the substantial kingdoms they set up. But the ambition of Justinian, only briefly and partly realized, to re-create the Roman Empire in its previous glory, led, in its collapse, to more violent incursions, such as that of the Lombards in Italy, and to a general increase in political disorder and fragmentation after his death in 565. From the beginning of the seventh century his reconquests were steadily nibbled away by fresh invaders. The later reunification of much of western Europe by Charlemagne, celebrated by his coronation as Holy Roman Emperor by the Pope in 800, soon came to pieces.

Feudalism was the device by which a measure of cohesion was introduced into the fragments into which the centralized Roman polity had dissolved. Lesser lords, masters of economically self-sufficient manors, with their own courts and modest armed forces, were the vassals of greater lords, with widespread holdings, to whom they gave armed support and, increasingly, money. The greater lords were, in their turn, vassals of kings, who were much like them only on a larger scale. If vassalage may have started by grants from kings to lords, there was equally movement in the other direction, with lesser lords putting themselves under the protection of greater ones. Eminence and land had been secured by military prowess in the first instance, but they were preserved by custom and law and passed on by inheritance rather than seizure.

In time, as services gave way to money rents and direct taxation, monarchs of geographically defined and culturally coherent regions, such as England, France, and Spain, gradually began to reduce their nobles to the status of subjects, even if very rich and powerful ones, and local jurisdictions began to be absorbed in the kings' courts. This was evident in England by the time of Edward IV; in France, where there was also an inheritance of Norman centralization to draw on, with the cautious and fortunate Louis XI; and in Spain with Ferdinand and Isabella. By the sixteenth century the nation-state had emerged, after a thousand years of variegated political improvisations, during which sovereign states had had only a marginal and fitful existence.

Because of the destructive indifference of the West's barbarian invaders and the devotional and philistine obsession of the church with religion, culture and learning were obscure and repressed for a long time. Between Boethius, who died at the hands of the Ostrogothic king Theodoric in 525, a century after the death of Augustine, and Anselm, the first great truly medieval philosopher, some six hundred years later, there was only one philosopher of note. John Scottus Eriugena, the ninth-century Neoplatonist, emigrated from the isolated cultural sanctuary of Ireland, soon to be overwhelmed by the Northmen, to the court of the Frankish king Charles the Bald. He had nothing to say of the smallest relevance to politics.

I HAROLD:SACRAMENTVM:FECIT:✧ HIC HAROLD:D
VVILLELMO DVCI:✧

THE SOCIAL STRUCTURE OF FEUDALISM depended on the personal engagement of a vassal to his lord. When William the Conqueror invaded England his principal justification was based not on grounds of inheritance, or nationalism, but on the oath of allegiance which, he claimed, Harold had previously sworn to him, as here shown in the Bayeux Tapestry.

During the Dark Ages from the fifth to the eleventh century there was no one much to think about politics in abstract or general terms and there was no audience to be addressed. The mental equipment of Dark Age rulers was a compound of Germanic memories of the war band and some colourful mementoes of the Roman imperial past, the most notable of them being Charlemagne's inauguration of the Holy Roman Empire. After his brief imperial episode it came to life again in the mid-tenth century and, until the end of the Hohenstaufen dynasty in the thirteenth, it could plausibly represent itself as the supreme political authority of western Christendom. From then it was, in effect, the elective headship of the German nation.

The central topic of medieval political thought is the proper relation between church and state. Both acknowledged a universal head. But while the Pope steadily became stronger as head of a centralized church, the emperor's supposedly universal state steadily contracted and weakened. In practical terms the conflict between church and state came to a head in the late eleventh century with Gregory VII's condemnation of the lay appointment of bishops as simony and his excommunication of Henry IV, the emperor, for committing that sin. The emperor had to submit himself to the Pope at Canossa, since the Pope, by absolving the emperor's vassals from their allegiance to him, undermined his imperial power. In the tenth century the papacy had been corrupt and degraded. But the Cluniac reform movement, which began at that time, had restored and empowered it by the middle of the eleventh century.

Church and State   Europe enjoyed a new stability and prosperity in the post-millennial eleventh century. Outside invaders had largely been repelled or absorbed, orderly government was generally established, and new agricultural technology together with the revival of trade increased population and wealth. Conflict between the refined and much strengthened papacy and the imperial power was the occasion for renewed political thinking. The prevailing assumption was that church and state are universal institutions, each under a single head: Pope and emperor. Each had its proper field of action: the spiritual government of men as possessors of immortal souls and the temporal government of men going about their affairs on earth. Collision between the two was inevitable, principally because the actions of lay rulers often incurred the moral censure of the church and also because the church had come to be a great property-owner, whose leading figures were feudal magnates.

Neither party supported the extreme positions: of theocracy, that the state is nothing more than the church active in temporal matters, or of Erastianism, which takes the church to be a department of state, as, in effect, it was in the Byzantine Empire. Government was a divine, not an ecclesiastical, institution; the church, likewise, was a divine, not a political one. Sacred and imperial power were seen as distinct. Arguments in defence of the independence of the state largely relied on custom. Supporters of the supremacy of the church harked back to precedent: to the creation of the Jewish kingdom under Saul by the prophet Samuel, and to the papal coronation (and so, by inference, authorization) of Charlemagne. They also appealed to a couple of late Dark Age forgeries, the false decretals, which sought to preserve the freedom of bishops from secular interference, and the Donation of Constantine, which held imperial authority to be a matter of papal concession since Constantine, on becoming Christian, was held to have surrendered his power to the Pope, who returned it to him only conditionally.

The Germanic conception of kingship, imported by the barbarian rulers of the former Roman Empire, took it to be hereditary and divinely instituted, but also limited by the customary law of the community. The question of what was to be done if a king broke this law invited the allocation of a power of moral censure to the most obvious moral authority: the church. Defenders of the immunity of the state from church interference could appeal to the early Christian doctrine of passive obedience and could argue that the papal centralization of the church was an innovating encroachment. To admit the moral authority of the church is not to ascribe supreme authority to the Pope.

To censure a monarch is one thing. To excommunicate him is another, for it absolves all his subjects of their duty to obey him. In general, supporters of the papacy argued that there is a right of resistance to a monarch who, by misconduct and breach of fundamental laws, goes back on his coronation oath. A more extreme position was adopted by John of Salisbury, who, in his *Policraticus* of 1159, defended tyrannicide as a right and even, in extreme circumstances, as a duty. He lived at a time of general intellectual awakening, first in the new

MANEGOLD OF LAUTENBACH was the leading exponent of the papalist political theories on which Pope Gregory VII relied in his investiture conflict with the emperor Henry IV. This shows Manegold presenting his works to the Archbishop of Salzburg, a leader of the papalist party within the empire.

THE HOLY ROMAN EMPERORS claimed authority in two different, and inconsistent ways: first, as the successors of the emperors of the classical *imperium* which preceded the papacy; second, as the successors of Charlemagne, who was crowned in 800 by Pope Leo III.

monastic schools and then in the universities that developed from and alongside them. His book was the first substantial work of political thought since Augustine's *City of God* more than seven hundred years earlier. His mode of thought is traditional, invoking Cicero, Roman law, and the Fathers. The recovery of Aristotle, which was to dominate the thinking of the late Middle Ages, was only just beginning and he owed nothing to it. However, there are two ways in which John of Salisbury is like Aristotle: his treatise is comparatively unsystematic and it ignores the chief political realities of its own age. He wrote as if the Roman Empire still existed and ignored feudalism, just as Aristotle had ignored the decrepitude of the city-state in an epoch of world-empire.

There were three main collisions between church and state in the High Middle Ages, that is to say, between the late eleventh and late fourteenth centuries. Each provoked an outburst of serious political thinking. The first was caused by Pope Gregory VII's prohibition in 1075 of the lay investiture of bishops and his excommunication of the emperor Henry IV in the following year, an event which led to the emperor's submission to the Pope at Canossa. Manegold of Lautenbach in the late eleventh century and John of Salisbury in the mid-twelfth stand out as supporters of the papacy, arguing for its authority to condemn evil rulers as tyrants. Manegold described tyranny as a breach of the fundamental agreement between a ruler and his subjects. That was an idea implicitly subversive of the supremacy of the church, since it based the ruler's authority not on church endorsement but on popular consent. The second collision, which ran from 1296 to 1303, was between Pope Boniface VIII and King Philip the Fair of France over the taxation of ecclesiastical property. Boniface's very large claims for papal supremacy were followed by complete defeat in practical political terms. Shortly before this second collision the most representative and influential body of medieval political thought was produced by Thomas Aquinas in a series of works, some unfinished at the time of his death in 1274. Aristotle's *Politics* had been translated into Latin in 1260 and Aquinas was the first medieval thinker to incorporate his political ideas in a Christian framework.

Boniface's claims for church supremacy were set out theoretically by Aegidius Colonna (also known as Giles of Rome), a follower of Aquinas, in 1302, and this was rapidly followed by a defence of the opposite position by John of Paris. Ten years after that, Dante's *Monarchia* put forward an anachronistic compromise proposal affirming the co-ordinate authority of church and state. Ten years later still, an attempt by the Pope to interfere in the election of the emperor, following a period of civil war in Germany, led to the third of the collisions, inspiring the even more unmitigatedly secular political doctrines of Marsiglio of Padua and William of Ockham. They raised the question, which had not been much considered before, of the Pope's claim to supremacy *within* the church. With the Great Schism of 1378, the start of a long period of competition between different claimants to the office, a widespread movement of thought supported the idea that only a general Council of the church, by implication representative of all Christians, had ultimate ecclesiastical authority. Anticipations of later Protestant resistance to the claims of Rome had by then been expressed by Wyclif and John Hus.

Aquinas   Much of medieval political thinking rested only marginally on abstract philosophical foundations. A great part of its reasoning invoked precedent, scriptural, patristic, historical, and legal—such matters as the relations of the kings of Israel to the prophets, the attitudes of Christ and St Paul to the powers that be, Augustine's Senecan view of the state as a remedy for sin, the long success of the Roman Empire interpreted as a sign of divine endorsement, and Ulpian's dictum that what the ruler decrees is law. To that extent it is more part of the history of political controversy than of political philosophy. But with Aquinas, inspired by the seemingly timeless and unprecedentedly comprehensive work of Aristotle, an attempt is made to set political principles on a universally rational foundation.

Although moderately papalist in his sympathies, Aquinas accords a substantive and inde-

BONIFACE VIII's claims of papal supremacy went beyond any made by his predecessors or successors. Here he is seen on his tomb, sculptured by Arnolfo di Cambio.

pendent authority to the state. Man is naturally social, in that he cannot achieve the perfection of which he is capable, which comprises happiness as well as virtue, unless he is a member of a community, and government, Aquinas holds, is necessary to a community. Goodness is a unity, the common good, and should be pursued by something unitary, a monarch, an earthly analogue of the universal monarch, God. The state is not, therefore, a result of man's fall and loss of innocence; it is part of the divinely instituted nature of things, prior to man's exercise of his freedom. So too is inequality, of which political subjection is a species. Slavery and the institution of property, on the other hand, are the consequences of human weakness. So, while disagreeing with Aristotle about slavery, which Aristotle saw as 'natural' for some, he accepts Aristotle's argument for property that each man looks best after what is his own. He maintains that the relief of poverty is a duty of the state as well as the individual and, in the same spirit, says that a starving man is no thief if he takes what he needs. He forbids usury as the selling of something that does not exist.

Since the state is natural, in Aquinas' sense of being a part of God's purposes for man, it is independent of the church and the church should not interfere with the exercise of temporal power. But that is conditional on the ruler's not being a tyrant, which Aquinas rather loosely explains as being unworthy to rule or as having acquired power by violence or as using it against the common good. A tyrant, he says, is more guilty of sedition than someone who overthrows him. The church or spiritual power is supreme in all matters connected with man's ultimate end, the next world. Exactly what these are is an obvious topic for disagreement.

The most carefully worked-out part of Aquinas' political philosophy is his account of the varieties of law. They are four in number. First, there is God's eternal law, the general system of order God has imposed on the universe at large. Secondly, there is divine law, what God has revealed to man by way of the scriptures. Thirdly, there is natural law, universally applicable rules of conduct, evident to reason at all times and places. Finally, there is human law, which consists of specific rules either deduced from natural law or applied, in accordance with natural law, to particular circumstances. Not all of these conform very well to Aquinas's celebrated definition of law as 'an ordinance of reason for the common good, made by him who has the care of the community, and promulgated'. Rationality is the speciality of natural law, promulgation is that of human law. Aquinas does not so much combine reason and will in theory of law, as conjoin them in neighbouring parts of it.

It is a bit ungracious to mention briefly Aquinas' objectionable, but no doubt fairly representative, thoughts about Jews. Because they killed Christ they are condemned to servitude. They should be moderately oppressed by making them wear distinctive costume and by removing the gains from usury on which they ordinarily subsist, since it is a kind of theft. There is some tension between this licence to oppress and Aquinas's view that the Christian faith should be preached and not imposed by force.

His follower Aegidius Colonna is much more emphatic about the supremacy of the spiritual power. Both property and political authority are, in his view, forms of mastery or *dominium*, and that is only legitimate if it is endorsed by the church. The spiritual is intrin-

sically higher than the temporal and should rule it; the two are related as the soul is to the body. The Pope, the spiritual sovereign, must therefore have *plenitudo potestatis*, absolute authority to establish and control the temporal power whenever (and Aegidius thinks that will be very often) its use involves mortal sin. Only the Pope, the vicar of Christ, has, because of his direct relation to God, a divine right to rule.

At the moment when this extreme version of ecclesiastical and, specifically, papal absolutism was being put forward, the papacy itself was falling under the power of the new national monarchy of France. Boniface VIII, the pope whom Aegidius was defending and who claimed that belief in the supremacy of the Pope is a condition of salvation, died in 1303. Six years later, under a French pope, Clement V, the papacy was transferred to Avignon and French control. There was a pope at Avignon until early in the fifteenth century and, with the Great Schism of 1378, one at Rome as well. The luxury and corruption of Popes and many other leading figures in the church excited vehement criticism among the Franciscan order of friars, of which William of Ockham was a member. The papacy was eventually re-established at Rome. It has remained a predominantly Italian institution ever since and has never regained the commanding position in public affairs it had between its eleventh-century revival and its Babylonian captivity in Avignon.

Antipapalism: Dante, Marsiglio, and Ockham   John of Paris was the contemporary and counterpart of Aegidius, supplying intellectual support for King Philip of France as Aegidius did for Pope Boniface. In an interesting recognition of the political realities of his time, he, in effect, abandons the idea of a universal empire. Faith, he argues, is one and so must be taught and conserved by a single church. But human circumstances on earth are various and can be best taken advantage of by different means in different places. Kingdoms are self-sufficient communities. But that does not imply that the church should control the state. Secular government is older than the Christian revelation, which adds new responsibilities to the state—namely the preservation of conditions in which the church can flourish—but does not supersede it. On the issue of the church's right to property, which was the point of conflict between Boniface and Philip, he held that the property of the church is communal, so that the Pope is its steward, not its owner. There is no natural right involved, so the king may justifiably tax it. As well as circumscribing the spiritual power, John seeks to reduce the Pope's standing within it: he is an administrative convenience, not an absolute monarch, and he is subordinate to the general Council of the church, an idea that was to preoccupy fifteenth-century political thought.

A less practical and businesslike version of antipapalism was put forward about ten years later by Dante in his *Monarchia*. In its assumption that the empire is the primary political institution it is a backward-looking work. Its place in the history of political thought is a tribute to Dante's supreme literary distinction and to the elegance of its presentation rather than to the force and relevance of its reasonings. Dante draws on all the recognized sources: Aristotle, Jewish and Roman history, the Bible, civil and canon law. Ostensibly he is even-handed between church and state, resurrecting the notion of the fifth-century Pope Gelasius that God had two swords, one of which he conferred on each of them. A universal monarch is indispensable for the peace of the world, the prime condition of its well-being. Its authority comes directly from God, not from the vicar of God. The Romans were right to accept the original Roman Empire, whose long success establishes its providential nature, an argument that questionably assumes, amongst other things, a real continuity between the Roman Empire proper and its fading, Holy Roman descendant. Dante argues, quaintly, that Christ's submission to Pilate, his acceptance of Roman punishment, amounts to an endorsement of its right to execute him. That is hard to square with Christ's 'Father, forgive them, for they know not what they do'. He denies that the church derives any authority from the Donation of Constantine (not proved a forgery until 1440) on the ground that the emperor had no right to confer on the Pope a sovereignty he had received from the people.

The attempt of the papacy between 1323 and 1347 to interfere in the election of the emperor, who was by then, at most, the ruler of Germany and Italy, had been preceded in 1321 by a papal declaration that the Franciscan doctrine of evangelical poverty was heretical. Opposition to the Pope now developed on two fronts, directed against his encroachment in temporal matters outside his domain of spiritual authority, on the one hand, and against his autocratic rule of the church itself, on the other.

The most impressively systematic assault on papal authority outside and inside the church was the *Defensor pacis* of Marsiglio of Padua in 1324. Marsiglio, like Dante before him and Machiavelli nearly two centuries later, was particularly concerned with the disastrous political effect of papal machinations on the political life of Italy, above all on the growing city-states of northern Italy. National monarchies were emerging in France and England, a process delayed, but in the end intensified, by the Hundred Years War. In the German and Italian domains of the empire unification was held up until the nineteenth century. But Marsiglio's doctrine is of general, not merely local, application. He has little to say about the empire.

In a crucial departure from Aquinas's fourfold classification of laws, Marsiglio acknowledges only two: divine law, the moral and religious content of revelation, and human law, the positive legislation of states. He sees government, in Aristotle's way, as natural to man. Law is its basis, the purpose of law being the negative one of preventing conflict rather than the more dignified one of assisting human perfection. True law involves coercive sanctions, so divine law, without earthly sanctions, is really a metaphor. The government as legislator is identified with the people or their representatives, who are conceived as the 'stronger part' (*valentior pars*) of the community, the most highly qualified. The legislator he sees as distinct from the executive. If the executive does not rest on consent—it should ideally be elective—it is tyranny and so illegitimate. Here are intimations of the ideas of the separation of powers and of popular government.

Marsiglio is particularly keen to apply these principles to the church. The priesthood is simply an addition to the social ingredients of the community; neither it nor the Pope is identical with the church itself, which is the whole body of Christian believers. The true institutional expression of the Christian community is a general Council. By analogy with his political legislator, a Council, he believed, should be numerically representative. The Pope, who is the church's executive, is essentially an administrative convenience. The task of the church is to preach and instruct, to concern itself with other-worldly matters, not to rule.

There are anticipations in these ideas of Luther's conception of the 'priesthood of all believers' and of the later Protestant conception of the voluntary character of religious association. Not surprisingly, Marsiglio was condemned by the church, but his doctrines do not seem to have had much immediate influence. His thesis that the ultimate authority within the church is a general Council was to be the leading issue of political controversy in the fifteenth century. But his Erastian view of the church as more or less a department of state took longer to be seriously considered. He was ahead of his time in his uninhibited secularism.

His general position has much in common with that of William of Ockham, although Ockham's religious faith is less questionable and although they disputed with each other. Like Marsiglio, Ockham had a negative conception of the state, in his case as an instrument for the penalization of wrongdoers. Since he fled from papal wrath to the emperor, Lewis of

DANTE IN POLITICS inclined to the imperialist rather than the papalist position. Here he appears in an allegorical sixteenth-century portrait in the National Gallery at Washington.

Bavaria, in Munich, he understandably emphasizes the idea of the emperor as supreme political authority. Men have a natural right to select their rulers, which they exercise, in the imperial case, by way of the electors. The Pope has nothing to do with the authority of the emperor or other temporal rulers.

Ockham's main purpose is to resist papal absolutism and aggression, particularly the Pope's condemnation of the doctrine of evangelical poverty, upheld by the Franciscan order, to which Ockham belonged. Priests require the use of some property in order to sustain life,

THE EMPEROR CONSTANTINE, according to a medieval belief here represented in a fresco of 1246 from San Silvestro, conveyed the sovereignty of Rome to the Popes in the person of Pope Silvester I. The 'Donation of Constantine', the document alleged in support of this belief, was proved a forgery by the fifteenth-century humanist Lorenzo Valla.

but the right to use is not the same as ownership. He regarded the recent acts of the papacy, both in the temporal domain and within the church, as unacceptable absolutist innovations, bringing with them the corruption of the papal office and of the church, to the extent that the Pope dominates it. Like Marsiglio, but with a less radically secular intent, he wants the Pope to be limited and controlled by a general Council, representing the will of the Christian community at large.

The End of the Middle Ages   Old-fashioned history books used to date the end of the Middle Ages in 1453, with the fall of Constantinople to the Turks (and, incidentally, the end of the Hundred Years War). However, Petrarch, the first recognizable Renaissance man, died in 1374. The transition from the one historical phase to the other can reasonably be placed in the period from the mid-fourteenth century to the end of the fifteenth, by which time aspects of the thought and culture of the Renaissance had even reached England. Apart from Wyclif there were no notable political thinkers, indeed no notable thinkers of any kind, in England in this period, at least as compared with the remarkable host of productive thinkers between

Grosseteste at the start of the thirteenth century and the death of Ockham in 1347. Continental Europe was less infertile but produced no one of major importance until Machiavelli early in the sixteenth century.

The most oppressive issue for political thinking in the earlier part of this period was the scandal of there being two, and for a time three, Popes. That state of affairs undermined an institution already the object of strong criticism, and to meet it the church turned to the critics' remedy: a general Council, or, to be precise, a sequence of them. The Council of Constance, sitting from 1414 to 1418, brought about the reunification of the papacy, leaving it weaker than it had been before. The Council as an institution was eventually repressed by the papacy: none was held between Trent in 1545 and Vatican I in 1869.

John Wyclif addressed the problem of reforming a corrupt church with an elusive doctrine of *dominium* or lordship. It held that rights to property and to political power were conditional to claimants' being in a state of grace, something connected to, but apparently not

THE COUNCIL OF CONSTANCE (1414–18) brought to an end the Great Schism. This illustration from a fifteenth-century chronicle of the council shows the electors leaving the conclave after electing Pope Nicholas V.

identical with, their being among the elect, predestined for eternal bliss. He used this idea to resist papal claims against the royal power (which, for a time, gave him some standing in official circles) and to support the idea of the disendowment of the church. When he proceeded, on abstractly metaphysical grounds, to deny transubstantiation, he went too far and was banished to a country living. To his Augustinian frame of mind the true church is the whole body of Christians, past, present, and future, or those within it who make up the predestinate elect, and the difference between that and the visible church was profound and obvious. Wyclif died in his bed, but his follower, John Hus, was burnt in Prague in 1415. Wyclif's ideas had an affinity, in their radical unworldliness, with the contemporary current of revolutionary populism, exemplified by the Peasants' Revolt of 1381.

John Gerson, who died in 1429, was also an opponent of papal absolutism, but he did not follow Marsiglio in thinking that the church should be ruled by the body of Christians in general. The ecclesiastical hierarchy, which should constitute the Council, should rule it, and the Pope should be their agent rather than a divinely authorized autocrat. Gerson went to apply this broadly constitutionalist view to the state, arguing that a mixed state, one in which monarch, nobles, and property-owners are harmoniously balanced, is the best form of government and that France approximated to it, a notion favoured by other French thinkers, for example Bodin and Montesquieu.

Constitutionalism is also to be found in the thought of Nicholas of Cusa. Starting from a more or less mystical theory of the universe as a divinely organized harmony, he conceived both church and state as partial harmonies within the whole. In both, authority should rest on consent; it is through the people in general that the will of God expresses itself. But Cusa was sufficiently a man of his time to understand a people's consent as mediated through the leading figures who serve to represent it. Late in his life, when he had become a cardinal, he retreated from his original enthusiasm for the rule of the church by general Councils.

The Early Modern World

The Dynastic State   The end of the Middle Ages was marked by four major innovations in thought and action: the Renaissance, the Reformation, the discoveries which led to the expansion of Europe into the rest of the world, and the establishment of centralized national monarchies aspiring to absolute power. The last of these was the most politically important. But in the realm of theory its effect was more negative than positive. It mainly fostered theories circumscribing the authority of monarchs, claiming that it derived not from God, but from the people, usually by some form of contract. The two great exceptions to this rule—the theories of Bodin and Hobbes—in fact indirectly support it. For all his emphasis on the unrestricted nature of sovereignty, Bodin hedges it in a number of ways. Hobbes, in a brilliant *tour de force*, uses the contractual machinery of the age to justify an almost absolutely powerful sovereign.

A learned historian of medieval political theory has said that it is chiefly concerned with authority as *descending* from God to rulers, but by the end of the Middle Ages innovating thinkers like Marsiglio were intimating that authority *ascended* from the people to their rulers. The theory best tailored to absolutism, that of the divine right of kings, did not appear until the seventeenth century with James I of England, Sir Robert Filmer (the object of Locke's criticism), and Bossuet, the eloquent but fairly fatuous apologist for Louis XIV.

The three new, post-feudal monarchies of western Europe emerged in the late fifteenth century: England in 1485 with the installation of Henry VII, the first Tudor king; France in 1453 with the end of the Hundred Years War; Spain in 1469 with the marriage of Ferdinand and Isabella. Germany remained divided into a multitude of princely states, and the Empire (apart from the curious interlude of Charles V) dwindled into insignificance. In Italy a group of prosperous city-states in the north (Milan, Florence, Venice) were separated from backward Naples in the south by the central Italian possessions of the Pope. The political task of the new monarchs was to centralize administration and law and subdue the feudal lords who obstructed it. For this they needed standing armies and revenue from taxes with which to pay for them. New weapons, notably cannon, helped to nullify the castles of the nobility. The right of the French king to impose a tax for his army in 1439 was a crucial acquisition.

The Renaissance had no obvious expression in political thinking apart from the lonely and peculiar figures of Machiavelli and More. Until Hobbes in the mid-seventeenth century political writers argued scholastically, for the most part with massive citations of scripture. The Reformation carried the disruption of a unitary Christendom to a much greater extent than the late medieval vicissitudes of the papacy. Protestants (and some Jesuits) had to address the problem of the citizen's duty to obey a heretical ruler, which proved to be the chief stimulus to the contract theory. The Counter-Reformation provoked in the Catholic church led to its moral, but not doctrinal, reform and re-established the authority of the Pope over what was left of the universal church. The discovery and exploitation of the Americas, shifting the economic centre of the trade of the west from the Mediterranean to the Atlantic, was soon to shift the balance of strength further to the west in Europe. For political theory its only service was to provide images of the state of nature.

Machiavelli Machiavelli's place in the history of political theory has been unreasonably inflated by a number of factors: his literary brilliance; the shocking effect at first glance of his fairly banal advice to an ambitious prince; the extremely marked discontinuity between his way of going about his project and the traditional procedure, in which large abstractions are supported by copious quotation of authorities; even the down-to-earth modesty of his aims, in *The Prince*, at any rate.

That book tells a prince how to secure and retain power, by seeming to be virtuous while not being so, by distributing favours himself and leaving the dirty work of punishment to subordinates, by abstaining from the property and women of his subjects, by inflicting injuries as rapidly as possible, by supporting weak allies rather than great ones, by inspiring fear rather than love, and so on and so forth. All this is set out in an impressively unapologetic way and argued for by reference to the history of Rome and of recent Italy. Because of its uncompromising abstention from the respectable pieties *The Prince* has thrown many readers into a confused frenzy of interpretation. Is it really a satire? Is its real point the closing passage in which the prince to whom it is dedicated is implored to save Italy from its invaders?

What is true is that it is not the whole of what Machiavelli has to say about politics. It is confined to a specific issue: that of the best way, as indicated by a discriminating study of history, of seizing and hanging on to effective power in a state. In his *Discourses* Machiavelli tackles the larger question of the long-term health and stability of a state, the effective preservation of what *The Prince* shows how to achieve in the first place. Here the more elevated aspects of the Renaissance appear in Machiavelli's high regard for the morals and religion of pagan antiquity. In his account of the civic virtue which a well-ordered state requires of its citizens he rejects Christian humility and other-worldliness for the more assertive virtues of courage and resolution. From men endowed with these qualities a powerful and reliable citizen army can be formed. Here, as in *The Prince*, Machiavelli expresses his intense distaste for mercenaries, the military jackals preying on the corpse of Italy. But he is not opposed to warfare. A state must, in his view, expand or decay; growth is the law of political life. That is inconsistent with his idealization of the city-state in the *Discourses*, a serious anachronism in an age dominated by large, national monarchies.

The narrowly practical character of Machiavelli's purposes, even in the less monocular *Discourses*, gives him a somewhat dwarf-like appearance in a procession of major political theorists. He is not concerned with justification but effectiveness. Not only is his style of reasoning purely secular; he treats morality and religion simply as means to political ends. In true Renaissance style he takes real virtue to be *virtù*—excellence, power, self-assertion. Yet he has a good word for the security-loving masses who are the natural allies of a true prince, unlike self-aggrandizing noblemen. The procedures he made explicit continued to be the general practice of rulers, although by making them public he may have warned people about what was going on. On the eve of a great religious convulsion (Machiavelli was writing his books at the time Luther stuck his theses to the church door at Wittenberg) any influence he could have had on thought was inevitably delayed.

In 1516, a year before Luther posted his theses, Thomas More's *Utopia*, at once more charming and more inscrutable than Machiavelli's writings, was published. It gave its name to a kind of political fantasy whose first example could be said, a little unkindly, to be Plato's *Republic*. Agreeing with Rousseau that the source of all social ills is property, More proposes a commonwealth in which all is held in common, in which people work, agriculturally, but not commercially, for six hours a day, and in which religious variety is tolerated. That combines uncomfortably with More's own career as a cruel and violent persecutor of heretics.

The Reformation: Luther, Calvin, and the Monarchomachs   Luther, seeking to reform long-standing abuses of the church, the corruption and luxury of its leading figures, produced a

HENRI IV, the first Bourbon King of France, on his deathbed. A Protestant convert to Catholicism, he decreed religious toleration in the Edict of Nantes, but himself fell victim to a bigoted tyrannicide in 1610.

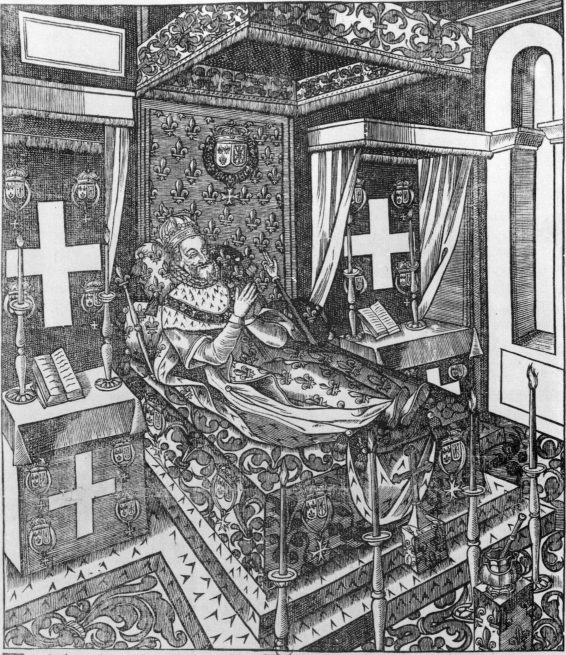

Le plus grand Roy qui fut pour la gloire des armes
Et des vertus, surpris d'vn iniuste trespas,
Comble nos cœurs d'ennuis, noye nos yeux de larmes:
Mais nos cris & nos vœux ne le r'animent pas.
    La France restablie, augmentee, & regie
Par son Sceptre innocent : parfaisoit son bon-heur
Si l'execrable coup d'vne lame rougie
En son sang, n'eut tourné nostre ioye en douleur.

Le Ciel tient son Esprit assis au rang des Anges,
Sainct Denis a son corps au Sepulchre des Roys,
O Empire tu n'as que les seules louanges,
Et les faits de celuy que tant tu desirois.
    Les siecles ja passez & les suiuants encore,
N'ont veu & ne verront vn Prince tant parfaict,
Dans les trois parts du monde & au lict de l'Aurore
Son redoutable nom vn beau chemin sest faict.

division of Christendom almost by accident. What he aimed at was to make religion more inward, private, and spiritual. It was in keeping with this withdrawal from the world that he should have been an unswerving defender of the political doctrine of early Christianity, that all men should unquestioningly obey the rulers set over them. Circumstances made it easy for him to maintain that position. The rulers of the north German states in which his followers were mainly found were themselves Protestants.

Calvin was, in principle, equally committed to passive obedience. In fact, he and his followers moved away from it. His Protestantism was much more active and outward than Luther's. The state, although distinct from the church, which was to be aristocratically ruled by an assembly of elders, had as its first duty, higher than that of securing peace and good order, the protection of piety and religion and the giving of support to the church as an active censor of morals. In his own Geneva he presided over a theocracy. He died in 1564, before the situation of his followers in France and Scotland, under Catholic rulers, became precarious. A hundred years of religious wars now began: first in France in the last three decades of the sixteenth century, ending with the localized toleration of the Calvinist Huguenots brought about by the Edict of Nantes in 1598; then in Germany with the Thirty Years War of 1618 to 1648; finally, on a more modest scale, and perhaps only marginally religious, the English Civil War of 1642 to 1645.

The problems of the Calvinist minorities in France and Scotland led to the revival of the old medieval notion of a right to resist or even kill tyrants in the works of a group of anti-monarchist thinkers (the 'monarchomachs'). The most important of these is the *Vindiciae contra tyrannos* of 1579, of doubtful authorship, written in France some seven years after the St Bartholomew's Day massacre. It is held there that a king may be disobeyed if he breaks God's law and may be resisted if, by heresy or oppression, he breaks the alleged original contract between God on the one hand and king and people on the other. This elusive, and indeed flimsy, conception was based on the original covenant in the Old Testament between God and his chosen people, Israel. More important is a second contract between king and people. The people cannot be conceived to enter into this unless for a purpose, so that while for the king it sets up an absolute obligation, that which it imposes on the people is only conditional. The author goes on, expressing the prevailing dread of Anabaptist and peasant uprisings, that resistance to tyrants is not to be carried out by individuals but by established lesser authorities: magistrates and assemblies.

A similar view was advanced by George Buchanan, tutor to the future king James I, in and for Scotland. The idea that all authority stems from the people and that royal power is conditional was also taken up by Catholic, particularly Jesuit, thinkers. Mariana held that since the people confer authority on the king they may get rid of him, if necessary by tyrannicide. In a Machiavellian spirit he argued that war (and therefore standing armies) are inevitable, and gave practical advice of a none too edifying kind, such as that warfare conveniently diverts public attention from internal causes of discontent. In Mariana the notion of a state of nature as a social order preceding the institution of government is clearly present. Suarez was less challenging, although still anxious to keep the power of monarchs within bounds, for the sake of the autonomy of the church. In a compromising spirit he attributes the law of nature both to God's will and to right reason, distinguishing it from the law of nations, that customary law which prescribes slavery and private property, as the more fundamental law does not.

Sovereignty, Contract, and Natural Law   From the beginning of the seventeenth century onwards, the more or less secular ideas relied upon by thinkers whose interests were more religious than strictly political to limit the authority of monarchs were taken up and used for primarily political purposes. Before that a broadly secular theory had been elaborated by Bodin for the opposite purpose, to extrude religion from politics, rather than the state from religion. Bodin was the most impressive thinker of the *politiques*, who were repelled by the warfare to which religious difference had led. He himself was a Catholic, but not a crusading one. He was learned in the law and in history, a penetrating, if untidy, thinker. He is principally remembered for his doctrine that what defines a state is the presence within it of a sovereign, a source of law who is not himself bound by law. Sovereignty is indivisible and inalienable. That is not entirely the smuggling-in of a political preference under the disguise of a definition. It is natural to suppose that a plurality of ultimate authorities is a recipe for chaos. But perhaps the advantages of a stable, orderly state can be secured without a single supreme power.

As it turns out, Bodin's sovereign is not all that absolute. Since he was first created by families, the most natural of associations, property, which is incident to families, is not at his unlimited disposal; indeed Bodin thought taxation requires consent by the taxed. He is clear that society, a product of the social instinct, is distinct from the state, which is a creature of force. He opposed slavery as being neither natural nor useful and as being no more universal than the practice of human sacrifice. But the sovereign is, in his view, further limited by the *leges imperii*, the ancient customs of the community. He has, however, no human superior. In Bodin's doctrine an analytical concept, useful for identifying the ultimate source of positive law, is combined with advocacy of strong government.

The German jurist Johannes Althusius gives a more commanding place to the notion of contract than anyone before him. Like the author of the *Vindiciae*, he distinguishes two contracts, his being a contract of association and a contract with an authority. The first creates the group out of individuals or lesser groups; the second is of the group created with an authority they bring into being. All associations, not merely the state, are contractual in nature. Since the state is an association of associations it is not for individuals but for their representatives, leading figures in those associations, to bring pressure to bear on the 'chief magistrate'. With recent Dutch history in mind, he claims that secession from an association is a right of the parties contracting to form it. Althusius' odd federalist kind of contract theory is peculiar to him. It is plainly a device for limiting the pretensions of kings while not giving free rein to the political passions of dissident individuals.

Much more influential than Althusius was Grotius, generally reckoned to be the first major theorist of international law. Natural law is rational, in the sense of being evident to reason as necessary if man's social needs are to be met. Prominent articles require the keeping of promises and respect for property. Natural law is universal and unchanging; its criterion is universal acceptance. Grotius too distinguishes society, as the outcome of social instinct, from government, created by a contract to which men are impelled by self-interest. His assumptions implied more popular sovereignty than he was prepared to admit. For him the sovereign is not constrained by the interests or judgement of the people. He may be disobeyed, but not resisted.

The law of nations is, as usual, a different thing from the law of nature. It governs the relations between states and is determined by what has been customarily consented to (as a matter of profession, perhaps, rather than performance). Grotius considers the notion of a just war and concludes that it is principally one which is waged for self-defence or the defence of property. It must involve violation of the law of nature and not just the law of nations. He concludes that preventive war is not just.

In these thinkers there is to be found the first development, free from religious entanglements, of the battery of conceptions in which the classical political theory of Hobbes and Locke is articulated. Hobbes used the ideas of contract and natural law to put forward a defence of absolute sovereignty much more comprehensive than Bodin's and only just falling short, by the logical necessity of his contractarian case, of unrestricted absolutism. Locke, perhaps the most influential political thinker yet, used them, more straightforwardly but less consistently than Hobbes, for the purpose for which they were designed: the limitation of government.

Thomas Hobbes John of Salisbury, William of Ockham, and Wyclif were Englishmen but their views had little application to the strictly political life of England, either because, in the case of John and Ockham, their perspective was European, or because, in the case of Ockham and Wyclif, their prime concern was ecclesiastical—the confinement of papal power to the spiritual domain for Ockham and the reformation of a corrupted, luxurious church for Wyclif. English thought about the principles of English politics in the Middle Ages was largely practical and descriptive, as in the writings of Bracton in the mid-thirteenth century and of Fortescue in the late fifteenth. From their and comparable reflections on the laws of England emerged the idea of the common law, based on custom and precedent and serving as an explicit, and not merely pragmatic, limit to the power of the king. Even the statute law which was added to it had to be endorsed by parliament before it received royal authorization. In the early seventeenth century it was the instrument by which the pugnacious judge Edward Coke, Francis Bacon's chief enemy, resisted the absolutist pretensions of James I.

Adventurous political thinking was dangerous under the irascible despotism of Henry VIII in the first half of the sixteenth century and in the two short, ecclesiastically oppressive reigns that followed. Under Elizabeth, in the second half of the century, Calvinism revived in England, aiming to make the church of England Protestant, as well as national. Richard Hooker's *Laws of Ecclesiastical Polity* was, as a whole, a defence of the Elizabethan church settlement against the Puritans and their Bible-worship, but it was also a work of political

Clarior è tenebris

IMMOTA TRIUMPHANS

Beatam et Æternam gloria

Coeli Specto

Asperam at Levem.

Gratia

IN VERBO TUO SPES MEA

Christi Tracto

SCIT SUB PONDERE VIRTUS

Splendidam at Gravem

Vanitas

Mundi Calco

Guil: Marshall Sculpsit

THE DOCTRINE OF THE DIVINE RIGHT OF KINGS, upheld by supporters of the Stuart monarchs, did not save Charles I from the scaffold; but the book *Eikon Basilike*, based on his writings and published at the time of his death, went through thirty-five editions within a year and consecrated his execution as a martyrdom.

theory, especially because Hooker saw church and state as the same community, looked at from different points of view. Hooker argued for a more or less Thomist account of natural law, distinguishing it, as the Puritans did not, from God's law as given to men, not through reason, but by way of biblical revelation. He rejected both the passive obedience which the Tudor monarchs saw as their due and the theory of divine right. For him the king is under the law and is a product of human consent and contrivance, not of divine institution. A good example of the judiciousness with which Locke credited Hooker is the latter's thesis that natural law is comparatively indeterminate and needs to be intelligently and variously applied in different circumstances. The implicit constitutionalism of medieval English legal theorists becomes explicit doctrine in his commonsensically reasonable dealings with Puritan and royal extremists.

In the years leading up to the English Civil War of 1642–7 resistance to royal encroachments—denial of customary rights, ruling without parliament—led to the bandying-about of a phrase with an important future: 'life, liberty, and property'. The original Presbyterian leaders of the rebellion were not democrats; their main interest was getting rid of the bishops. But the Independents, or Congregationalists, of the army, of whom Cromwell was the

THE FRONTISPIECE OF HOBBES'S *LEVIATHAN*, which presents state absolutism as the only alternative to a state of nature which would be a war of every man against every man, and in which life would be 'solitary, poor, nasty, brutish, and short'.

chief, although their first concern was the freedom of any voluntary association of Christians to form a church, were much inclined to the democratic doctrine of the Levellers, which ascribed rights to individuals, not just to the people as an organized community. They favoured universal suffrage and regularly re-elected parliaments, which were, however, to have no authority over property and religion. Other, smaller, and rapidly repressed, groups, such as the Diggers, went further, supporting equality or community of property.

Two years after the execution of Charles I a book was published that has a good claim to being the greatest work of political philosophy ever written: the *Leviathan* of Thomas Hobbes. Apart from the rough-hewn magnificence of its prose and the electrifying clarity and rigour of its argumentation, it is an amazing *tour de force*, applying all the intellectual apparatus of the state of nature, the law of nature, and contract, which resolute limiters of state power like Althusius and Grotius had elaborated, for a purpose exactly opposite to theirs, that of magnifying state power to the utmost.

Hobbes saw the Civil War and the violent extinction of the monarchy as an unmitigated disaster. He attributed it to the unlimited exercise of private judgement in matters of religion endorsed and practised by anti-episcopal Protestants. His immediate practical aim in politics was to turn the church into a department of state, with its scriptures to be authoritatively interpreted by the sovereign and not at the whim of excited fanatics.

His official starting-point is a comprehensively materialistic metaphysical system for which all that exists is matter in motion (including, apparently, God). This is connected to Hobbes's politics by a congruously materialistic philosophy of mind, which takes mental events to be 'small motions in the head', physical modifications of the brain. More directly to the purpose is his account of human motivation. We feel as pleasant what is conducive to vitality, as pain what is not, and these experiences cause desire and aversion, incipient movement towards or away from the pleasing or painful thing. This is interesting in itself and can be seen as a support for his political doctrines, an issue that has been elaborately debated by commentators. It is not, as he admitted himself (and revealed by publishing *Leviathan* on its own), essential to them. A more significant background assumption is Hobbes's theory of knowledge, a kind of geometrical empiricism, which derives all ideas from sensation, but attributes our power of seeing relations between them to 'reckoning', the humblest imaginable variety of rational insight.

It is enough for Hobbes's political purposes that men are predominantly animated by a self-interested desire for power and self-preservation, something he thinks we can see perfectly well without benefit of his metaphysics. In a state of nature, where there is no common sovereign to prevent them, this leads to dire consequences. Every man seeks power over others, to subject them to his will and to take their goods. So universal fear prevails, exacerbated by men's rudimentary equality in being mortally vulnerable to each other, by their competitive love of glory at the expense of others, and by the insatiability of appetite which distinguishes them from animals.

In the state of nature everyone has a natural right to whatever he can get and keep. But, since the state of nature is a state of war, that is likely to be very little. The first law of nature, evident to the reason of all, is: seek peace, the elemental security of life. Men being as they are, the only way of achieving peace is for them to agree with each other in giving up all their natural claims, apart from that to life itself, to a sovereign, whose form and particular identity they also agree to remit to the choice of the majority. That one should 'keep covenants made' is a further law of nature. But 'covenants without the sword are but breath'; to be effective they must be enforced by sanctions. So the initial contract which creates civil society must at the same time install the sovereign power without which it will not hold together. Hobbes observes that his description of his rule *seek peace, even if it can be secured only by transferring all your natural rights or liberties, apart from that to life, to a sovereign* is not really a law. It is not the command of one with authority, as whatever is literally a law must be, but a 'theorem of reason', a rational maxim of prudence.

The parties to Hobbes's contract are the warring individuals. The sovereign is not one of them for the excellent reason that he does not exist as such until the contract is made. But Hobbes uses this truism rhetorically to exalt the power of the sovereign. The formation of a state 'by institution', a contract between free, natural individuals, is not the only legitimate possibility. There is also 'commonwealth by acquisition' where the conquered acknowledge the authority of their conqueror out of a rational fear of the consequences of not doing so.

Hobbes's sovereign is the creator of law (apart from the metaphorical 'law of nature'). All property is held by his permission. He governs the church, prescribes its organization, and determines the interpretation of its scriptures. All other authority is derivative from him. Liberty, in its political sense, is simply the silence of the law, those fields of action which the sovereign, in his wisdom, has not considered it necessary to control. It looks as if Hobbes has brought off the paradoxical feat of basing the absolute subjection of individuals to the state on their own rational consent. That is, of course, impossible. He admits that the sovereign is not entitled to order a citizen to kill himself, since security of life is the whole purpose of his submission; even to the extent of allowing citizens to refuse dangerous military service. It is far from clear how the Hobbesian subject is to enforce these claims of right. A more substantial concession is that if a sovereign fails to provide adequate protection for his subjects they are released from their obligation to obey him. Hobbes's own behaviour in returning to England from exile with the royalists in France and making his peace with the parliamentary authorities in 1651, the year of *Leviathan*'s publication is in strict accordance with that principle.

There are many aspects of Hobbes's great construction which are open to criticism, which is made all the easier by its clarity and boldness. A very fundamental one, seldom stressed except by implication, is that his theory turns on an equivocation with the word *life*. The life that is the, so to speak, collective object of a man's desires, that which he calls good, is vitality in a broad sense, enhanced life, self-realization or self-fulfilment. The life for the sake of which the rational Hobbesian individual sacrifices so much is *mere* life, vitality in the minimal sense, i.e. being alive and not dead. Plainly, mere life is a presupposition of enhanced life. But it may not be worth much on its own, in much the same way as salt, although essential to a healthy diet, is not a complete dietary regime on its own.

Hobbes combined a devotion to the new scientific rationalism (whose greatest emblem was Galileo), something subversive, dangerous, and revolutionary, with an acute fear of anarchy, heightened by the political turbulence of mid-seventeenth-century England. The influence of his rationalism prevailed over that of his fear. The social and political doctrine of Bentham and James Mill, combining rigorous argument with very selective observation, is the residuary legatee of Hobbes's.

Although *Leviathan* might be held still to apply pretty well to the circumstances of post-colonial Africa and eastern Europe, a few years after its publication generally peaceful conditions came to prevail in Britain and western Europe. In 1660 Charles II resumed his hereditary throne without significant bloodshed and 29 years later his brother was deposed in a comparably painless way. The Peace of Westphalia ended the Thirty Years War in Germany in 1648. Peace was made between France and Spain in 1659. In 1661 the 23-year-old Louis XIV took over absolute power in France, which soon attained its highest point of political domination in Europe (from which it steadily declined later in his reign) and, more enduringly, its cultural supremacy. Louis XIV's practice was cast into doctrinal, but hardly theoretical, form, in the dignified prose of Bossuet, for the most part laboriously reinterpreting biblical texts about kingship in an absolutist fashion. Absolute monarchy, he maintained, is the oldest and most natural form of government. It is analogous to the rule of the father in a family and to that of God in the universe at large. He does not deny that the sovereign has duties, but they are duties to God, not to his subjects, and it is up to God to require their performance. Oppressed subjects may only pray.

Outside France religious tolerance was everywhere growing. Within France, the revocation in 1685 of the Edict of Nantes, which had given limited rights to Protestants, was a disastrous movement in the opposite direction. But in Germany Protestantism in the north and west cohabited exhaustedly with Catholicism in the south and east. In England dissenters and Catholics had to endure civil disabilities but were increasingly left alone in the practice of their religion. In Holland a much more comprehensive tolerance prevailed. There Spinoza derived arguments for toleration from premises closely similar to those of Hobbes. All human action is motivated by a fundamental impulse to self-preservation and self-enhancement, which makes them naturally enemies. A society with a sovereign who, like Hobbes's, determines what is just, is to be preferred to a warlike state of nature. Spinoza held that a state guided by reason is more powerful and independent and that an irrational tyrant would undermine his own power, so his conception of citizenship is less abject than Hobbes's. The order it provides makes possible the subjection of men's unreflective passions to reason, which is what, for Spinoza, constitutes genuine liberty. A ruler, he contends, cannot control thought and should control its expression only when not to do so would endanger the security of the state, a fairly overwhelming qualification. He differs from Hobbes in preferring aristocracy to monarchy but agrees with him that sovereign states are in a state of nature with respect to each other.

A classical synthesis of the lines of thought which had used the ideas of contract and natural law to supply a wholly secular justification of government was worked out by Pufendorf,

who was born in 1632 as were Spinoza and Locke, but who published his chief work in 1672, nearly two decades before Locke's *Treatises on Government*. The law of nature, he says, can be discerned in the state of nature by natural reason and it is Grotius' ethical law rather than Hobbes's self-interestedly prudential one. Since property is essential for any form of human life it is prior to government. What makes government necessary is the irrationality of the mass of mankind, expressing itself in social conflict. Following Althusius and, to some extent, anticipating Locke, he distinguishes two contracts, one forming civil society by an agreement to set up a sovereign by majority choice, the other between the sovereign the majority chooses and the community that chooses him. The sovereign is limited, therefore, not just by the law of nature, which is absolute and unalterable, but also by the requirement of pursuing the common welfare which he is conceived to have undertaken by the second contract. The task of deciding when a sovereign has not carried out his side of the bargain is rather unhelpfully remitted to the judgement of 'sane men', a faint echo of those representative assemblies of the *Vindiciae* a hundred years earlier.

The political theory of Milton, developed in writings between the execution of Charles I in 1649 and the final collapse of the Commonwealth in 1660, is much less timidly and marginally liberal than anything that had gone before. Men are naturally free and have a natural right of self-preservation. They agree to choose kings and magistrates but such agreements are not binding in perpetuity, failing some major offence by the holders of power, and can be given up by agreement—a parallel, perhaps, to Milton's attitude to divorce. In a neat *argumentum ad hominem* against divine-right theorists he asks: if the choice of a king is an act of God should not his removal be seen as one as well? He argues for religious tolerance and a free press on the ground that freedom is necessary for the exercise of the reason which is the distinctive mark and real dignity of man. But he is no democrat. The best form of government is parliamentary oligarchy, elected by property-holders.

An interesting variant on this theme of rule by the propertied is to be found in the *Oceana* of James Harrington, also published in the interregnum in 1656. Harrington criticized Hobbes for his failure to recognize that military force is dependent on economic power: armies have to be fed. If government is to be stable it must reflect in its form the distribution of property (which, for Harrington, meant landed property) prevailing in the community. Pure monarchy requires for stability that the king should own most of the land; 'mixed monarchy' that the king and a few great nobles should; 'commonwealth', or a republic, that property should be widely distributed. The distributive effects of the Wars of the Roses and the dissolution of the monasteries meant that England was ripe for a republic. An agrarian law, setting an upper limit for holdings and forbidding primogeniture, would assist this broad distribution. There is an element of Milton's Platonic élitism in his proposal that the government should consist of a senate to think up laws, a more popular council to judge its schemes, and a magistracy to enforce them.

As Charles II's reign came towards its end the prospect of his obstinately Catholic brother's succession precipitated a crisis. The attempt to exclude him by the party of Locke's patron, Shaftesbury, led to the publication, some forty years after its composition and thirty after its author's death, of the *Patriarcha* of Robert Filmer. This defended the divine right of kings against the notion of popular or parliamentary control of the crown by unconvincing argumentation based on God's gift of royal authority to Adam and its inheritance from him by subsequent monarchs. Much more cogent was his criticism of the concept of rule by the people. The people is not an institution; without a supreme legislative authority there is no government. Filmer was himself laboriously criticized by Algernon Sidney (executed in 1683) in his posthumously published *Discourses*. The republicanism that Sidney shared with Milton and Harrington aroused the anger of Cromwell and was to be submerged in the literal wording of subsequent English political theory, although it was to become the prevailing English political practice from the accession of George I in 1714 until, at least, the Reform Bill of 1832.

The Eighteenth Century

The Enlightenment State   Eighteenth-century Europe was the epoch of the enlightened despot. He was the ideal of various characteristic theorists, such as Voltaire and the Bolingbroke of *The Patriot King*. There were several more or less close approximations to the ideal in practice. The closest was Joseph II, emperor in Austria from 1765 to 1790, who carried out

JOSEPH II, reforming Austrian emperor from 1765 to 1790, is shown in the uniform of the Imperial Dragoons in this portrait by Joseph Hickel.

a vast and fitfully successful array of reforms, abolishing serfdom, torture, and capital punishment among other things, all in a blissfully high-handed way. Catherine the Great, empress of Russia from 1762 to 1796, patroness of Diderot, came as near to enlightened rule as the barbaric condition of Russia allowed. Frederick the Great, king of Prussia from 1748 to 1786, patron of Voltaire, was more enlightened in theory than in practice, writing a morally disapproving critique of Machiavellianism when young. The reign of Louis XV in France was more enlightened in practice than in theory. The *ancien régime* remained formally in being during its sixty years' span from 1715 to 1774 but there was enough liberty of thought and expression for the extraordinary intellectual efflorescence of the French Enlightenment. Even backward and priest-ridden Spain had a beneficent and reforming king in Charles III, who ruled from 1759 to 1788 and expelled the Jesuits. The last enlightened despot was, perhaps, Napoleon, with the possible exception of Alexander I of Russia, at least until he succumbed to mystical Christianity.

Matters were very different in Britain. In 1689 William III was called in by parliament to replace the deposed, Catholic James II, the parliamentary basis of his title to the throne being emphatically declared and his powers hedged in by a Bill of Rights. With the death of William's wife's sister Anne in 1714 the problem of the Protestant succession could no longer be fudged by putting the deposed James's Protestant daughters on the throne. The Hanoverian kings now installed were, with the exception of George III, of limited capacity and bad character. The first two spoke no or little English and were more interested in Hanover than in Britain. Anne was the last British monarch to veto a bill passed by parliament. The Whigs, a party dominated by the greater landowners, who were much involved in the country's growing trade, were dominant until the death of George II in 1760. His grandson George III for a while attempted to rule rather than reign, but this attempt collapsed with the loss of the American colonies. The king's final abandonment of direct involvement in politics, with the Prime Ministership of William Pitt in 1784, was timely in view of the recurrent insanity which struck him a few years later. Monarchs legally dependent on parliament for their position abetted by their own weaknesses of character and intellect the process by which they became largely ornamental. The result was that Britain became, in the phrase of H. G. Wells, a crowned republic, in which the effective constitution was gently concealed under a thin layer of monarchical decoration. Until the middle of the century and the defeat, in 1745, of the second Jacobite rising, there was some danger of a return of the Stuarts, committed to the Catholic religion and the divine right of kings. The personal charm of Charles Edward Stuart could not compensate for totally inadequate support. The British were soon reconciled to the unattractive dynasty which has occupied the throne ever since.

Locke and Hume   Locke, in giving theoretical expression to the principles underlying the Glorious Revolution of 1688–9, inspiring the political thought of the French Enlightenment (although not that of the Jacobins of the French Revolution) and in providing the intellectual bone-structure of the American Declaration of Independence, must be acknowledged to be the most influential of political thinkers, above even Plato, Aristotle, Hobbes, Rousseau, and Marx. His *Treatises of Government* were published in 1690, immediately after the accession of William and Mary, and some features of them were highly apposite to the local political concerns of the moment. But it is clear that the main outlines of Locke's political doctrine had been worked out at least ten years earlier.

He begins, unpromisingly, with a first book wholly devoted, like Algernon Sidney's much longer work, to the far from difficult task of demolishing the arguments of Filmer. Their attention to this apparently unworthy object was due to the fact that it was the only serious defence of the monarchical position available. Locke annihilates Filmer's positive doctrine at great length and with comfortable ease. What reason have we to suppose that God gave Adam *royal* authority, or that any king ruling now inherits his position from Adam? He naturally does not raise the question of what reason we have to suppose there ever was any such person as Adam.

The second *Treatise* begins with an account of the state of nature, of the social life of mankind without government. He reasonably assumes, with Aristotle, that men are essentially social beings and also that they are rational; rational enough, at least, to acknowledge the law of nature, which prescribes that men should not interfere with each other's life, liberty, and property. In conformity with his far from empirical account of moral truths as being susceptible of demonstration, like the truths of mathematics, he takes the law of nature to be universal in application and evident to reason. In the state of nature men have the right to resist infringements of the natural rights the law of nature ascribes to them. But this is, as he puts it, inconvenient. They may be too weak to protect their rights or, from partiality, judge wrongly that a right has been infringed. Injustice and conflict will be the result. A few bad men can turn the state of nature into a state of war. So men agree to give up their natural right to exercise 'the executive power of the law of nature', declaring, applying, and enforcing it, to a common superior; they concur in a common intention to put themselves under whatever specific form of government the majority may choose.

The formation of this common intention creates what Locke calls a community. Its fulfilment is not a second contract between government and community but the acceptance of a trust by the former to protect the untransferred rights of the latter. Such a trust can be broken either by tyranny, where the government invades the retained natural rights of the citizens, or usurpation, in which one part of the government takes over the functions of another (as in the case of the Stuart kings failing to call parliament and ruling without it). If a government is dissolved or forfeits its authority the citizens do not lapse into the state of nature again, but revert to a community, a group with a common intention to have a government to protect their rights. The contract, unlike the trust, is irrevocable. Locke argues that his account of the dissolution of government is not an incitement to constant rebellion. Men need a lot of provocation to rebel and will not do so unless enough of them agree about it to make success likely.

Locke believed that the contract was a historical event. Since government everywhere precedes the keeping of records there can be no documentary evidence for its occurrence. Men born within existing states, however, are held to have obliged themselves to obey by *tacit* consent, which need amount to no more than 'barely travelling on the highway', but is more widely conceived as accepting the benefits of citizenship, such as the inheritance of property. Locke allows for the legitimacy of slavery, at any rate as imposed on captives in a just war. More interesting and less retrograde is his account of how the right of property is acquired. One owns whatever unowned thing one has 'mixed one's labour' with, imparted value to by picking it or hunting it or tilling it and so forth. Two limitations are put on the amount it is legitimate to amass: one must not take more than one can use and there must be enough and as good left over for others. The force of the first condition is removed by Locke's view that since money does not spoil and has value only by human convention it follows that men have implicitly agreed to its unlimited accumulation.

Locke distinguishes the legislature from the executive, seeing the former as supreme but not permanently in session. The legislature's supremacy follows from the fact that it is the most direct expression of the community, the ultimate, if ordinarily dormant, sovereign. There is a problem about reconciling the government's need for revenue from taxation with the natural rights of property-owners, which is weakly dealt with by saying that all taxation must be sanctioned by the legislature. Locke is not very specific about the nature of the liberty it is the business of the government to protect. It seems clear that an important part of it was religious liberty, the topic of his writings on toleration. Despite his general deference to Hooker he does not share Hooker's view that there must be a single, comprehensive church for the whole community. In the spirit of the Independents or Congregationalists (Cromwell's sect), he defines a church as a voluntary association, one whose other-worldly purposes detach it from the state. The toleration he calls for has its limits: Catholics are excluded as subjects of a foreign monarch, the Pope; atheists because they have no motive for keeping promises.

Little reference is explicitly made to Hobbes in Locke's second *Treatise* but he is everywhere present behind the scenes, above all in the general structure of his theory, which Locke takes over in its entirety while filling it with wholly opposite content. The states of nature and war, the contract, and the distinction between rights retained and transferred are there in both, but with very different import. Locke's state of nature is not always and inevitably a state of war; it is, rather, liable to degenerate into one. In his contract only one right is given up, where in Hobbes's only one is retained, the right to preserve one's life. Both distinguish church and state: Hobbes by making church a department of state, Locke by seeing it as an aspect of private life. For all their differences, however, both are entirely secular and, in the end, both are exponents of popular sovereignty, although neither is anything like a democrat.

Locke's political writings became something like the sacred text of eighteenth-century Whiggism. They inspired little new thinking in Britain, where there was not much political theory of interest for nearly a hundred years, during which the Lockean message was being influentially and interestingly developed in France. Only two other eighteenth-century thinkers in Britain require mention: a brief one for the voluminous Bolingbroke, a little more for Hume, the earliest and most forceful critic of the Lockean apparatus of natural rights and contract from within Locke's own system of secular, empiricist assumptions.

Bolingbroke has suffered from his bad reputation. He combined remarkable gifts with equally remarkable defects of character; his political career, after brilliant early success, ended in total and long-drawn-out failure. He was deplored by Dr Johnson and Burke for his deistic assault on Christianity, but was deeply admired by his contemporaries Swift, Pope, Voltaire, and (for whatever this may be worth) Lord Chesterfield. In practical politics he was the most penetrating opponent of the moneyed interest, led by his chief enemy, Walpole, which he saw as undermining the 'ancient constitution' and its traditional liberties, protected by a balance of power, through subjecting the legislature to the bribe-wielding executive. This was supported on a theoretical level by a critique of Locke's individualism and his abstractly rationalistic conception of natural law and rights. He saw subordination as natural to mankind in all stages of development, existing before civil society in the family and persisting continuously into it. Following Locke's empiricism in his writings on religion, he rejected Locke's quasi-mathematical conception of morality and the law of nature, taking a consistently empirical view of them as respectively directed to and enjoining the pursuit of the general happiness. Like Hume and unlike Bentham, he used his utilitarianism for conservative rather than reforming purposes.

Hume is a less copious and much more formidable critic of the contract and natural-law apparatus. He wrote a number of political essays—sketching an 'ideal commonwealth' on Harringtonian lines and arguing that, up to a point, 'politics may be reduced to a science'. His main theoretical contribution is to be found in the few pages of his essay *Of the Original Contract*, which signalled, if it did not exactly inaugurate, a major new departure in the background assumptions of political theorists. He allows that the very first states might have been created by a contractual agreement between the comparatively few people involved. But that has no bearing on current political relationships. These cannot be attributed to tacit consent. Most people have no idea that they are giving such consent, nor could mere presence within the boundaries of a state add up to it, since for most people there is no real choice but to stay where they are. The governments which exist in the world today mainly originated in conquest or usurpation, but that does not deprive them of legitimacy. Obedience to them arises from custom and habit, not from any kind of promise.

Hume's crucial argument against the contract theory is that if allegiance is based on fidelity or promise-keeping the question arises: why should one keep promises? The answer is that it is to the advantage of the community at large that one should do so. But exactly the same answer can be given to the question: why obey the government? Since both allegiance and fidelity are directly justifiable by reference to the general interest it is an 'unnecessary circuit' to base the former on the latter. Both, along with respect for property, which he curiously identifies with justice, are what he calls elsewhere artificial virtues, courses of action which will have an advantageous result only if they are generally followed. He contrasts them with benevolence which still does good if not part of a general convention and to which we have a natural inclination in our instinctive sympathy with others, a mild passion which diminishes with distance. A small residue of the contract way of thinking is still present in his acknowledgement that there is an element of convention involved in the effective maintenance of the general rules of artificial virtue.

Hume, even more than Locke, seems to confine government to the protection, or, as he puts it, the stabilization, of property, ignoring the more urgent requirement of bodily security. Society is possible, he believes, without government, and exists and has existed without it. It begins with the family and enables us to combine our strength with that of others, to reap the benefits of the division of labour and of mutual aid. It is property, he thinks, as Rousseau was to do later, that necessitates government. Bolingbroke had said that the state was the result not so much of a contract as of a bargain and Hume develops the point: allegiance is a matter of enlightened self-interest. Hobbes had, in a way, done the same, but the

LORD BOLINGBROKE, Tory chief minister to Queen Anne, fell out of favour after her death, and devoted himself to political theory and journalism, in opposition to the Whig ministries of Robert Walpole.

self-interest on which his sovereign depends was too terrified to be acceptable. Hume was not exactly a utilitarian. He used our expectation of utility to explain our moral reactions rather than using utility itself as the criterion of their justification. But since he was inclined to see the customary as the reasonable, there is not all that great a gap between the two. By way of Helvétius and Beccaria the utilitarianism to which he approximated led on to the full-blooded doctrine of Bentham and the philosophical radicals.

Eighteenth-Century France: Montesquieu and the Philosophes   The effect of the importation of Locke's doctrines into France was much like that of alcohol on an empty stomach. In Britain his principles served to endorse a largely conservative revolution against absolutist innovation, protecting parliament, the common law, and the established church from the danger of Catholic despotism. In France Catholic despotism had been long installed and there were no serious institutional barriers to its prerogative. Louis XV was in practice more liberal, or at any rate easy-going, than his grandfather, and criticism of the established order in church and state was possible within limits, although at times risky. Voltaire was Locke's most ardent and effective exponent in France. But his prime concern was the church as the suppressor of intellectual freedom and thus of the progress to which that freedom could be expected to lead.

Locke's prestige was enhanced by his association with Newton, who seemed to have completed the work of natural science with his all-encompassing and universal system. Britain's success in worldly terms, its defeat of France in the War of the Spanish Succession and again in the Seven Years War in the middle of the century, which led to its absorption of most of France's possessions in India and North America, showed that a comparatively small liberal state could overpower a large despotic one.

Montesquieu is the most impressive of French eighteenth-century political theorists but is distinct from the main body of the *philosophes*. His *Spirit of the Laws* of 1748 is for the most part a rambling attempt at a sociology of politics, arguing that if states are to be stable, as in fact they generally are, they should be attuned to a broad array of circumstances: the prevailing climate, terrain, occupations, and national character of the lands and peoples they rule. He distinguishes three main kinds of state and associates with each an appropriate size, climate, and governing principle. Despotism suits large states, with hot climates, and rests on fear. What he calls mixed monarchy (Britain is an example) is appropriate to states of middle size, with temperate climates, and rests on honour. A republic is fitting for small states with cold climates and rests on civic virtue. This way of thinking is implicitly critical of the kind of universalistic rationalism which supposes that there is a single law of nature for all mankind (not that Montesquieu denies this, but it plays little part in his thought) and a universal human nature, something which even the sceptical Hume took for granted. Montesquieu's enlargement of the scope of political thinking was not much more influential than the roughly contemporary and more brilliant historical system of Vico, with his cyclical account of the succession of ages of gods, heroes, and men and his conception of the connectedness of all the aspects of a people's culture: its language, literature, religion, and politics. Vico's anticipation of the history-mindedness of the nineteenth century culminated in the vast, fascinating contraption of Spengler's historical system. Sociology, as now understood, owes less to Montesquieu and Vico than to the more solid ideas of Adam Ferguson, embodied in his *Essay on Civil Society*.

Montesquieu combined his detached, relativistic survey of what was available to him of the whole political experience of mankind with an enthusiasm for liberty of an altogether more committed sort. His definition of liberty is unimpressive: it is, he says, the ability to act as the law permits. At the same time he acknowledges that existing law is in need of rational reform. At any rate, liberty, understood as something the British have and the French do not, is attributed to an institutional arrangement: the separation of powers. The long battle between parliament and crown from the reign of Elizabeth to the arrival of the Hanoverians lent colour to this reading of British constitutional practice. Montesquieu learnt it from Bolingbroke (who saw it as threatened by Walpole's programme of corrupting parliament) and handed it on to Blackstone. Accurate or not, it played an essential part in the work of the framers of the American Constitution. The historic experience of independent America confirms Montesquieu's doctrine. It is worth mentioning, as a postscript, his effective condemnation of slavery. Against justifications like Locke's he argues that conquerors have no right to kill prisoners of war and also that no one has a right to sell themselves.

Politically the most considerable of the *philosophes* proper was Helvétius, who combined an abstractly rationalistic account of human nature, generalizing Locke's doctrine that the human mind is at birth a blank slate, acquiring its entire character from environmental influences by which it is completely malleable, with a rejection of Locke's rationalistic ethics in favour of a clear and explicit utilitarianism. Morality is not innate; it must proceed from education. The educational problem is to harmonize what men take to be in their interest with the general interest, which is the proper criterion of morality. Helvétius, like his disciple Bentham, saw that liberty was not necessarily prescribed by considerations of general utility. Nor did he even consider that utility implied democracy, as Bentham eventually came to believe. In general the *philosophes* were liberals, but not democrats. They wanted intellectual and religious freedom so that an enlightened élite could apply reason to assist progress and the general happiness. But they had no taste for the idea of rule by the masses. That was Rousseau's principal innovation.

Rousseau Rousseau's main work on political theory is called *The Social Contract*, but the contract plays no significant part in it, nor do natural rights and the law of nature, although the state of nature is constantly adverted to. Rousseau was almost certifiably paranoid, a hopelessly unsociable human being—for most of his life, in fact, in a state of nature with respect to the rest of mankind, an ignoble savage.

Before his main work he wrote three discourses. That on the arts and sciences declared that they had corrupted innocent, primitive man by the introduction of needless luxuries and the stimulation of artificial wants. Civilization had enslaved mankind. In that on inequality natural man is more fully described. He is a pre-moral, but none the less innocent, being, independent of others and so neither harming nor harmed by them. He is not primarily rational but moved to action by his feelings, particularly self-interest and pity for others. Crime and conflict are brought into the world by appropriation and that leads to the institution of oppressive government. In the discourse on political economy his famous notion of the general will makes its first appearance, the central and dominating conception of his political thought.

In *The Social Contract* the general will is offered as the solution to the problem of how men can subject themselves to government while remaining as free as they were before. The general will is brought into existence by men giving up all their powers (he does not talk, like Locke, of rights) to the community and then receiving them back in a more elevated, moralized form. The general will, essentially directed toward the common good, is always right, although what appears to be the general will, that which is agreed upon by all or by the majority, may be deceived. The general will is not identical with the will of all. On the other hand, the will of the majority can be an indication of it, if certain conditions are complied with.

JEAN-JACQUES ROUSSEAU in this contemporary etching draws the viewer's attention to his opera *Le Devin du village. The Social Contract* lies, apparently unregarded, on the ground.

Most important is the requirement that the general will, the sovereign community, should concern itself only with wholly general matters. Particular applications of the laws promulgated by the general will are the business of the 'prince', in other words the government, which is the agent of the sovereign community and quite distinct from it. The sovereignty of the general will is inalienable, so that it cannot be found in the decisions of representative bodies, which, like all other partial associations, will develop a pseudo-general will of their own, directed towards their special interests. That entails that there cannot be an independent church; there must be a civic religion with minimal, more or less deistic, doctrines. It also entails in practice that for a state to have an operative general will it must be small enough for all to participate actively and directly in law-making. Commentators have seen this entirely consistent view as reflecting Rousseau's loyalty to his home town, the city-state of Geneva.

The citizen of a united community exchanges his natural liberty for something better, moral liberty. The general will expresses the real will of the citizens who combine to form it. In recognizing it they achieve a kind of moral maturity. The problem of how innocent, pre-moral men turn into moral beings is dealt with by a mythical device, the legislator who supplies the initial laws compliance with which socializes and moralizes the citizens subject to them. The existence of such a *deus ex machina* might seem an extraordinary stroke of luck, hardly to be relied on in the normal course of events. Later theorists sympathetic to Rousseau's idea of the state as expressive of the real will of its citizens interpreted it as the historic social experience of the community, a process of moral development over a long time, rather than as the magical, instantaneous act of a semi-divine lawgiver.

Rousseau remarks at one point that democracy is unrealistic, too good for imperfect mankind. He may mean that the government should not be democratic in form because the community as a whole could not both confine itself to the common good in its legislative, general will-realizing work and carry out the implied particular applications of the laws it makes. He certainly subjects the prince to powerful democratic constraints: the sovereign people are to be assembled at regular and fairly frequent intervals to consider whether the constitution needs to be reformed and whether the office-holders under it should be confirmed or replaced. The second of these provisions, at any rate, seems to conflict with the requirement that the general will should confine itself only to general objects. Office-holders are particular people.

A more substantial difficulty is that the only community whose common interest can plausibly be identified with what is morally correct is the whole human race (perhaps the whole sentient creation). In the context of mankind as a whole, one of Rousseau's small populist states is no more than a partial association. To circumvent this obstacle he would have to require that the common will of a small state is only morally right if it is quite independent of all other states, a none too realistic proposal.

The subsequent political history of the civilized world has led to the accusation against Rousseau that he was the inventor of totalitarianism. Certainly he holds that it is necessary for people to give up *all* their powers if the general will is to be brought into being. He allows for no reserved set of individual rights, immune from the state's interference. At least his totalitarianism is democratic; although, in saying that the decision of a well-informed and public-spirited majority is a reliable indication of the general will, he supplies no protection against the tyranny of the majority that was to exercise John Stuart Mill. The elusiveness of the general will at least leaves it open to inspired leaders, with an apparatus of dedicated parties, instruments of terror, and managed plebiscites, to claim that they are its authoritative expounders. Rousseau drew the conclusion that citizens who are unaware of what their real will is may be properly compelled to act in accordance with it—may be forced to be free, in the famous phrase. To act in accordance with one's real will is to obey oneself. That is Rousseau's solution to his original problem. It allows for compulsion of unenlightened backsliders; but not by an inspired leader, at any rate.

If Rousseau's parental relation to totalitarianism is fairly remote, there is no doubt that he is the most influential and explicit proponent of democracy. It was in that light that he was regarded by his Jacobin admirers in the French Revolution, even if they soon perverted his message into dictatorial terror. At a slightly greater remove he contributed to the idea of nationalism. The social groups from which a general will can most effectively emerge will be genuine cultural communities and not casual dynastic accumulations of mutually unsympathetic people. But he does not draw that conclusion explicitly. Along with democracy it was to be the leading theme of the political life of Europe in the following epoch.

Paine and Godwin   Thomas Paine was the most influential of late eighteenth-century English radicals, expressing a point of view that had been largely submerged since the restoration of the Stuart monarchy in 1660, after a lively efflorescence in the Civil War period. Paine, and many others, were stimulated into thought and action by the American and French Revolutions. Paine, a close associate of Jefferson, was an actively involved supporter of the former and, until it declined into Jacobin excess, of the latter. His *Rights of Man* is more a controversial pamphlet than a work of theory: generalities are overwhelmed by detailed debate about current issues. But the force and clarity of its prose secured it a wide readership.

The first, and less interesting, part was mainly a reply to Burke's *Reflections on the French Revolution*, and called forth Burke's *Appeal from the New to the Old Whigs* in reply. It presents essentially Lockean doctrines in a combative way. Society, which is produced by our wants and is a blessing, is firmly distinguished from government, produced by our wickedness and a necessary evil. There are natural rights—to intellectual and practical freedom, the right of seeking one's own happiness, provided the natural rights of others are not infringed, and also to security and protection. The latter are handed over to government and so become civil rights. Government should not be based on superstition or force but on 'the common interest of society and the common rights of man'. Paine's failure to distinguish common interest and common rights, the main topic of disagreement between the political thinkers of his age, reveals the limits of his theoretical capacity. Only a republic will consistently pursue the common interest, and in practice it will have to be representatively democratic. He thinks it is essential that it should have a real, that is to say written, constitution like that of the United States. Against Burke's hymns to the glory of the British Constitution, Paine contends that there is no British Constitution, only a collection of political habits. In general Paine is anxious to minimize the scope of government activity. But the interesting final chapter of the second part of *The Rights of Man*, on ways and means, emphasizing the general happiness to the exclusion of the protection of rights as the end of government, sketches an elaborate and prophetic scheme of social welfare. After attacks on restraint of trade, the financial privileges of corporations and landed proprietors, and the national debt, Paine proposes to replace poor rates with child allowances and old-age pensions, festooning this part of his book with masses of imaginative statistics. The putting of something like his proposals into effect has decreased neither the scope of government nor the burden of taxation.

William Godwin, Shelley's father-in-law, a much more intellectually substantial theorist, carried hostility to government to its utmost conceivable limits. He combined consistent

TOM PAINE supported the cause of American independence in the 1770s and the French Revolution in the 1790s; but he was imprisoned by Robespierre after opposing the execution of Louis XVI and later emigrated permanently to the United States.

utilitarianism with the optimistic assumption that men can be rationally persuaded, or trained, to pursue justice, by which he means the general happiness. Ideally there should be no government at all and people should be led to act rightly by rational persuasion. He is as much concerned to encourage virtue, the disposition to act justly, as to ensure that justice is done, assuming that virtue is the most reliable producer of just acts. Although a determinist, he insists that people should run their own lives independently, for no very obvious utilitarian reason. He is hostile not only to government, but to all practices and institutions which limit individual autonomy, such as promises, including those involved in marriage, and all forms of co-operation, including orchestras. His argument against promises is characteristic of his sublime indifference to the practical. Either what I have promised to do is, when the time comes, in the general interest or it is not. If it is, the promise is superfluous, I ought to do what I have promised to do anyway; if it is not, I should not keep the promise. In the same spirit, if I can save only one person from perishing in a fire, I should save an important person rather than a relation who would contribute less to the general well-being.

Government is required to repress crime and repel invaders. The former task can be discharged at the parish level. Although Godwin could hardly have predicted the Mafia, that seems an over-hopeful arrangement. Inequality of property (of the degree that prevails, at any rate) is unjust. Property should be redistributed to those whose possession of it will yield most in the way of public benefit. As a thoroughgoing utilitarian he acknowledges no natural right to property, or to anything else. All forms of government are objectionable and even universal consent does not necessarily lead to justice.

Godwin is as unqualified a believer in the malleability of human nature as Helvétius. Men are perfectible, by which he means indefinitely improvable. Sin and crime are due to error and ignorance and are curable by rational persuasion. Godwin is as hostile to violent revolution as a means for bringing about the reforms he considers necessary as he is to the forms of compulsion he wants to displace. He is perhaps the most exquisitely theoretical of political thinkers. All his extraordinary conclusions are scrupulously argued for with the utmost clarity of exposition, like the comparably amazing theses of the metaphysics of McTaggart. Beside Godwin Bentham looks like a hard-bitten realist. It is not surprising that Godwin, after a short period of fame, disappeared into obscurity, while Bentham became the leader, at a respectful, theoretical distance, of the greatest reforming movement of the nineteenth century. *Political Justice* was published in 1793, the year of the Terror in France, which withered sympathy for the Revolution in Britain and for those, like Godwin, who were supposed, in his case questionably, to endorse it.

Burke   Burke is at the opposite extreme from Godwin; not just in specific opinions but in mode of expression. All his important political writings are reactions to immediately current events; the greatest of them, his *Reflections on the Revolution in France*, to the greatest event of his time. And that was particularly directed to some bold observations of the moral philosopher Richard Price, who had asserted that we choose our governors, and that we can cashier them for misgovernment and frame a government for ourselves. Everywhere Burke's doctrine is embedded in polemic, in the preoccupations of an active political career. This fact has led to a good deal of discordant interpretation. But there is a measure of convergence about his leading principles.

The first of these, viewed on its negative side, is a hostility to large political change and particularly to violent change of the sort most lavishly exemplified by the French Revolution. The other, positive, side of this principle is his respect for tradition, for the customary and habitual, for the elaborate accumulation of the political wisdom of many men over many generations, incorporated in an inherited body of institutions and practices. Burke does not maintain that there should be no change whatever. But political, and especially constitutional, change should always be in response to some change in non-political circumstances. As he puts it, 'a state without the means of some change is without the means of its conservation'. But change should be continuous and gradual. Prescription, which he intends in its legal sense as 'uninterrupted use or possession from time immemorial', is the best title to government, as it is to property.

His second principle is that the knowledge required for sound political judgement is not purely, or even predominantly, rational. It is rather a kind of prudence, acquired by protracted practical experience of public affairs, and not to be excogitated, like geometry, at a desk or in an armchair. The radical political thinkers who were enthusiasts for the French Revolution, with their deductive systems of abstract natural laws and natural rights, proclaimed as universally valid, he regarded as ignorant, although possibly sincere, charlatans who really had no understanding of what they were so enthusiastically talking about. Furthermore, political wisdom is not primarily an individual possession. It is collective, the result, embodied in traditional customs and institutions, of a long and massive sequence of specific decisions by politically capable people. He did not suppose political wisdom to be literally hereditary, but thought it most likely to be found among those who had grown up in a ruling-class environment, amid informed discussion of public affairs. Burke's rejection of abstract theory is the basis for his traditionalism.

Thirdly, underlying his second principle is a theory of the nature of society and of the relations of human beings to the societies of which they are members. A society is not a merely casual and contingent assemblage of human beings who happen to be in much the same place at the same time. The members of a society are made what they are, in all but the barest physical terms, by the society they belong to. It is to their society that they owe their culture and essential humanity: it endows them with moral capacity and convictions, its language constitutes the indispensable vehicle of their thinking, it helps determine their tastes, their habits of feeling, and their primary loyalties. It is no mere external association—not, as he puts it, 'nothing better than a partnership agreement in a trade of pepper or coffee, calico or tobacco or some such other low concern'. It is, rather, constitutive of the social identity of man, who is an essentially social being.

This is the first clear expression of something faintly intimated in Rousseau's idea that an individual develops a real will, becomes moralized through his membership of society, the notion, that is to say, that society is an organism. The elaborate interrelatedness of its parts

EDMUND BURKE is seen in this portrait by Thomas Hickey in company with the Whig Charles James Fox. Despite the great difference between their theoretical positions, the two were often allies in opposing British oppression whether in America, India, or Ireland.

means that it cannot readily be taken to pieces and reassembled. From that fact follows the necessity of only small and gradual change. Society's complex nature makes it difficult to understand; we cannot securely predict the results of even modest interventions and must always be ready to withdraw them.

Burke's conviction that people are made what they are by the historically evolved communities of which they are members and that their true rights are those to which time has accustomed them underlines the contrast, which some have mistakenly seen as an inconsistency, between his attitude to the American Revolution—and also to the problems of British rule of Ireland and India—and his absolutely opposed attitude to the French Revolution. In the cases of America, Ireland, and India he was concerned to defend the traditional customs and rights of the societies involved. In that of France he was roused to passionate condemnation of the thoughts and deeds of the political equivalents of amateur brain-surgeons. Burke, despite the tumultuous and polemical nature of his writing, brought into the open, in a way that had never really been done before, the central principles of conservatism. For all the detail in which their expression was immersed they were clear enough to Wordsworth, writing in an 1832 revision of *The Prelude*:

> While he forewarns, denounces, launches forth,
> Against all systems built on abstract rights,
> Keen ridicule; the majesty proclaims
> Of Institutes and Laws hallowed by time;
> Declares the vital power of social ties
> Endeared by Custom; and with high disdain,
> Exploding upstart Theory, insists
> Upon the allegiance to which men are born . . .

The Nineteenth Century

The Constitutional State   At the end of the eighteenth century the enlightened, and unenlightened, despotisms of Europe were still almost wholly agricultural. Only in comparatively undespotic Britain had industry established itself, increasing wealth and trade, concentrating ever-expanding population into large cities. By the end of the century industry had come to dominate the economic life of all western Europe and North America. Of the three politically backward empires of eastern Europe, Germany had become a leading industrial power, while industry was developing in parts of the Austrian Empire and had at least a foothold in Russia.

Of the two classes created by industrialization and rendered politically conscious by it, the business class made itself felt in the first half of the century, the industrial proletariat in the second. After a period of stagnant immobility in the first post-Napoleonic decades, pressure built up for some constitutional concession of power to the middle class. In Britain the response was a series of bills widening the franchise, in France a series of upheavals which settled down into comparative stability with the Third Republic after the German defeat of the Second Empire in 1870. A constitution was the topic of protracted convulsions in Spain.

In 1848, the Year of Revolutions, liberal constitutionalism inspired eruptions all over Europe. Their main result was the eclipse of liberalism by nationalism, which was successful in bringing about a united Italy in 1861 and a united Germany in 1870, but failed in Poland and among the national minorities which made up the greater part of the Austrian Empire.

The other new class, the proletariat, was catered for at the level of theory by various forms of socialism—some idealist and utopian, Marx's materialist and, allegedly, scientific. At the level of practice governments sought to meet the needs of the urban poor with welfare legislation of various kinds and by slowly giving way to workers' demands for the legalization of trade unions. Industry came to require a more educated work-force, as did the new, more sophisticatedly equipped armies. So national systems of education for all were slowly installed.

The two phases of nineteenth-century political thought and practice were influenced by two large movements of thought contemporary with them. Romanticism was favourable to the idea of nationality, conceived as an emotional unity, not an abstract set of individuals. The doctrine of evolution, in the latter part of the century, exerted its influence everywhere in the life of the mind. Marx dedicated *Das Kapital* to Darwin, and the materialist conception of history presents it as an evolutionary process. Equally fierce theorists on the other side, such as Herbert Spencer, took evolutionary theory to underwrite encouragement of competition to the utmost so as to weed out the weak and incapable.

The population of Britain increased more than threefold between 1800 and 1900, despite much emigration. The political problem of an epoch, unprecedentedly preserved from warfare for most of its duration, was how to provide for the needs of these new urban populations, not the least of those being the need for some participation in the processes of government. A rapidly changing mass society had taken the place of the stable, agricultural community that had prevailed since the Neolithic age.

German Romantic Idealism   Romanticism rejected the Newtonian picture of the world, which had become incorporated in common sense, as a vast mechanical system made up of distinct, persisting objects whose changes are in accordance with mathematically formulable laws, in favour of a conception of nature as an organic, continuous process, apprehended by a kind of poetic intuition. Man is not a prudent, calculating creature, using scientific knowledge to maximize his satisfactions, but a creative spirit, driven by a chaos of passions. Society is not a scientifically rational arrangement to prevent conflict between men at the least cost to their individual satisfactions.

For literary, non-philosophical romantics intuition and feeling were enough to undermine scientific reason. A romantic philosophy had to find a more argumentative way of arriving at its conclusions. This was achieved by transforming a crucial distinction in the philosophy of Kant, who was not a romantic, although influenced by Rousseau in his ethics, but a man of the Enlightenment. Kant held that understanding, what I have called scientific reason, produces our common-sense and scientific conception of the world by applying forms (the ideas of space and time, the concepts of substance and cause) to the formless chaos of sensations presented to us in experience. The attempt to apply these formal notions beyond the range of experience—to the world as a whole, to the infinite, to what lies altogether beyond experience—is fruitless and leads to metaphysical illusion. The use of the intellect for this purpose he confusingly described as reason, pure and simple. I shall call it metaphysical reason.

His successors, most notably Fichte and Hegel, reversed his valuation of scientific and metaphysical reason. The former they saw as abstract, yielding a practically useful caricature of reality. Metaphysical reason was a higher faculty, but still an argumentative one, operating with its own 'dialectical' logic, in which everything short of reality as a whole, the Absolute, provokes its own contradictory, which, doing the same in its turn, yields a reconciling synthesis of the first two. For the romantic idealists reality is not only an organic unity, it is also spiritual in character. Kant, wondering about the origin of the chaos of sensations, the passively received raw material of knowledge, attributed it to noumena or things-in-themselves. By claiming to know that there are such things, that they are plural, and that they cause our sensations, Kant contradicted his own basic thesis about the inapplicability of the forms of experience to what lies altogether beyond it. His idealist successors maintained that nature is a product of mind. Fichte said that the primary datum, the Ego, 'posits' the non-Ego in order to have something to exercise its will on. Hegel said that the Idea (his version of the Kantian system of forms) 'resolves to let its moment of particularity go forth freely out of itself as nature', a proposition it is not necessary to discuss further here.

Kant is not important as a political theorist. He presents the appearance of a high-minded liberal, fudging his ideas so as not to provoke the wrath of the oafish Prussian monarchy under which he lived, which had warned him sharply for his writings about religion. He sees the contract as converting free and equal men from a mere collection into a people, endowed with a common, general will. Combining Rousseau with Montesquieu, he calls for the separation of the legislature, the embodiment of the people's will, from the executive. A state is essentially a republic, whatever the form of its executive, provided that the legislature expresses the general will. Well-disposed to the French Revolution, he nevertheless prudently denied the existence of a right of revolution. Of more interest is his account of man's 'unsocial sociability', his persisting disposition to compete with and try to dominate others, despite his essentially social nature. It is the nerve of progress but must be kept within bounds by law. Ultimately, for the sake of perpetual peace, nations, by leaguing together, must accept analogous restraints. Hegel, as will be seen, took exactly the opposite view.

Fichte made explicit the idea that outside society man is 'abstract', not fully human, which was present in Rousseau. Association is a necessary condition of true freedom. The creation of the general will is more important than security and the protection of property. Two special tasks are imposed on the state. The first, and more bizarre, is to ensure balance between social classes by economic planning and, in particular, by forbidding private trade with other countries. The other is to educate the people, so that, in the end, government is no longer necessary; this is an anticipation, from an odd quarter, of Marx's withering-away of the state. In his later years Fichte elaborated a high-minded form of German nationalism (in 1807 Germany, divided and defeated, was too feeble for this to be anything but high-minded). Germany, he held, was particularly qualified to conduct a mission of cultural and moral regeneration to the world. He was thus the fairly innocent begetter of the most virulent form of European nationalism.

Hegel   Hegel's political theory is a part of his theory of 'objective mind', in effect his general social philosophy. Social ethics, as he calls it, is represented as emerging logically, and perhaps historically, from 'abstract right' and its contradictory, 'subjective morality', which is the kind of rigorous conscientiousness proclaimed as the essence of true morality by Kant. Right and subjective morality have their place in the scheme of things, but each is incomplete: right is external, concerned with outward compliance; subjective morality is internal, preoccupied with purity of motive. The two are 'synthesized' or brought together and reconciled in dialectical fashion by 'social ethics'.

Three great social institutions are paraded before us. First is the family, the most immediate of human groups—perhaps a way of saying that it is biologically inescapable and that it is the group in which individuality is most immersed, where self-interest proper is only fitfully distinct from the interest of the group. Families, however, inevitably disintegrate when the children grow up. Emancipated from it and conscious of their individuality, they enter into voluntary relationships with others for the pursuit of ends in which they have a common interest. This is civil society, an essentially economic form of organization, in which division of labour prevails and where self-interest is prudently pursued with the aid of scientific reason. It bears a certain resemblance to early nineteenth-century Britain, the world's first industrial society and at that point the world's greatest trading nation, as it would be for some time to come.

The family is held to be universal, since individuality is only latent in it. Civil society, on the other hand, is particular, with its self-conscious members keeping each other at arm's length as they collaborate economically with each other. What synthesizes the two is the state. This has some resemblance to the Prussia of Hegel's time, but it is too much of an idealization for him to be regarded, as he often is, as its slavish apologist. In the state man finds his real will 'actualized'; that is to say, by subjecting his own interests to those of the state he obtains true freedom. Since a constitution must reflect the *Volksgeist*, the spirit of the people, which changes and which varies from one *Volk* to another, it must vary with its spiritual circumstances. Hegel, however, expresses a preference for constitutional monarchy: monarchy because there must be a symbol of the unity of the state; with a constitution, providing for corporate representation, to ensure, cautiously, that the real, general will of the community is made effective.

An interesting peculiarity of Hegel's political doctrine is his theory of the universal class. This the class of bureaucrats and magistrates, a subdued early nineteenth-century version of Plato's élite. It is the particularly rational part of the community, according to Hegel, as compared with the other, agricultural and business classes, and must participate in legislation along with them.

The state, for Hegel, is one of the culminating points in the development of spirit, which in one sense is reality as a whole, in another its conscious representation in finite individuals. It is the form in which man as a social being reaches the highest level of rationality and freedom. Its service is his fullest public realization. Beyond it, however, in Hegel's hierarchy lies Absolute mind or spirit, the domain of art, religion, and philosophy. Compliance with the duties of citizenship, then, does not, in Hegel's view, exhaust man's spiritual vocation. The extremely frequent resolution of states to interfere with all three aspects of Absolute mind is not considered or provided for.

Hegel firmly identified the state with the kind of linguistically and culturally homogenous nation-state that prevailed in most of western Europe—Germany being a painful exception—in his time. It has seemed to most readers of Hegel that it would be required by his overriding preference for the whole over its parts that he should argue for the rational necessity of a world-state. On the contrary, he maintains that war is beneficial to states as heightening their unity and national self-consciousness. Where a treatment of an ultimate world-state might have been expected we find an account of world history, in which Oriental, Greek and Roman, and Germanic periods follow one another, according freedom respectively to one, few, or all.

The philosophy of Hegel fell out of fashion in Germany soon after his death in 1831. But after some decades of hibernation it was enthusiastically thawed out in Britain, notably by T. H. Green and F. H. Bradley in Oxford. Green modified the full rigour of the Hegelian doctrine in a liberal direction. He rejected natural rights: there can be no rights that are not socially (which does not mean legally) recognized. The end of the state is the self-realization of its citizens, but, since moral self-realization must be autonomous, the state should aim not to moralize directly, but to create favourable conditions for moral improvement. Bradley, attacking the abstract individual and seeing man's highest moral task as the fulfilment of the duties of his station, was more ferocious and less melioristic.

Post-Revolutionary Conservatism The ideas of Burke, the first major theoretic assailant of the principles of the French Revolution, were widely taken up, in Europe as well as Britain, in the years after the fall of Napoleon, the military dictator, who realized Burke's prediction of the Revolution's ultimate outcome. De Bonald, in a lucid, deductive style most unlike Burke's rhetorical tumult, argued that there must be a single ultimate authority, and that it had better be a hereditary monarch. He needs the assistance of a nobility, with inherited wealth sufficient to inoculate them against corruption. The fundamental law of a state must rest on custom; it cannot be planned in advance and explicitly set out in a written constitution.

Hostility to the idea of a rationally planned, written constitution is prominent in the thinking of Joseph de Maistre, most formidable of French reactionaries. States are natural growths, not artificial constructions. Political wisdom is derived from experience and an intuitive understanding of national character. A society is not a random assemblage of individuals. Individualism and democracy can lead only to chaos. De Maistre's strong medicine

is an infallible Pope (where he was ahead of his time) and an absolute monarch. It is a commonplace of the history of political philosophy that the export of Locke's doctrines to France had explosive results because the ideal they proposed was so much more remote from the French than from the British *status quo*. Much the same is true of Burke. What he wanted to defend already existed, even if threatened by radicalism. What the French conservatives wanted to restore had been long ago and very comprehensively swept away.

Coleridge, the most gifted and influential British conservative of the early nineteenth century, began as a disciple of Godwin. Visiting Germany in the very last years of the eighteenth century he became entranced by Kant and the romantic idealists Fichte and Schelling, applying their distinction between mere understanding and the higher faculty of reason in his literary distinction of fancy and imagination. He acknowledged Burke as his master in politics, but his attempt in his main political work, *The Constitution of Church and State*, to elicit the rational Idea, which is dormantly present in the actual state of things and which should or will emerge from it, is metaphysical in a way Burke would deplore. What is presented is a cosmetic redescription of the main working parts of the historic British Constitution in unfamiliar, poetically archaic terms. The barons in the Lords and the franklins (the county members) in the Commons represent the permanent or landed interest; the burgesses (or borough members) represent the commercial and industrial or progressive interest.

The most substantial part of Coleridge's pursuit of the Idea is his account of the church. (His book was initially provoked by what he saw as the danger of Catholic emancipation.) He saw it as, or hoped it might become, an educational rather than a devotional or sacerdotal institution. The Idea of the national church ascribes to it the task of civilizing the community, which includes, but goes well beyond, the familiar responsibility for moral improvement. Preparation for eternal life falls into the background. This Fichtean note, without Fichte's ardent nationalism, inaugurated the pronounced Victorian concern with the defence and encouragement of culture, most evident in Matthew Arnold, but also clearly present in Newman. Another conservative theme, first expressed, perhaps, in Bolingbroke's denunciations of the moneyed interest, but with much broader application in Coleridge, is hostility to industrialism, both as replacing a traditional form of life with urban squalor and distress and as fostering a base, calculating, crudely pragmatic style of thought.

Coleridge's influence was large. He converted John Stuart Mill from the bleakly mechanical Benthamism in which he was brought up to larger conceptions of the true nature of human happiness and fulfilment. He inspired the Christian socialist movement to involve the church in the social problems of the age. His influence on Newman and Matthew Arnold has already been mentioned. His critique of urban industrialism and the debasing kind of work to which it condemned those caught up in it was continued by Ruskin and William Morris. As a social, rather than a strictly political, thinker, Coleridge inspired much of reflective British thought in the Victorian age.

The Utilitarians   The Utilitarians or Philosophical Radicals had Bentham for their loquacious inspirer, James Mill as their hard-headed administrator, and his son John Stuart Mill as their culminating and most civilized exemplar. They supplied a firm and definite intellectual backbone to the reforming impulses, encouraged by the increasing power and wealth of the industrial and commercial middle class, which came to the surface again after the fall of Napoleon and the disappearance of the threat of France. James Mill, indeed, had established himself as Bentham's associate seven years before the battle of Waterloo.

Bentham had already been active as a writer for more than thirty years. His main interest had been in legal, penal, and, increasingly, constitutional reform. In his *Fragment on Government* of 1776 he had attacked the authoritative glorification of the laws of England in the *Commentaries* of Blackstone. These had been preceded by some preliminary political theorizing of a much more vapid kind than the strictly legal matter which it introduced. Bentham had an enjoyably destructive task in demolishing its uneasy combination of the old social-contract and natural-rights doctrine, its reverence for the wisdom of our ancestors as embodied in the common law, and the principle, supposedly embodied in the constitution, of mixed government and the separation of powers.

The contract had never happened and could not bind later generations anyway. Natural rights are nonsense (and natural and imprescriptible rights are 'nonsense on stilts'), a theme he returned to in his *Anarchical Fallacies*, an assault on the Declaration of the Rights of Man of the French Revolutionaries. The only rights are legal rights, set up by the commands of a sovereign and backed by penal sanctions against those who infringe them. If law is to be definite, as it should be if it is to be effective, it must have a single, identifiable source, to whom the citizens are in a condition of habitual obedience. The common law is an irrational muddle, serving the interests of lawyers, not that of the community. It should be replaced by a codified system of law, drawn up in accordance with the principle of utility, requiring the prohibition of actions only in the interests of the greatest happiness of the greatest number. This formula, derived from Hume and Helvétius, was combined with a theory of punishment like Beccaria's, which, seeing punishment as an evil in itself, required it to be justified by its yielding a larger amount of public benefit.

To start with, Bentham was not any kind of democrat. A man of the eighteenth century, he saw his role as that of the enlightener of despots. Since they proved incapable of being enlightened, he was converted by James Mill to democracy, to parliamentary reform which comprised universal suffrage, the secret ballot, and annual parliaments. James Mill's argument was based on the account of human motivation attached to the utilitarian principle: that all action arises from the pursuit of pleasure (widely construed) and the avoidance of pain. It follows from this that the members of any restricted governing class will use sovereign power to serve their own interests at the expense of their subjects. The only group that is automatically going to pursue the general interest is the generality, the public at large. That did not lead James Mill to propose votes for women. Their interests, he maintained, were adequately cared for by their husbands, or, if they were unmarried, their fathers.

Bentham held, consistently with his Hobbesian command theory of law, that there could be no right of resistance to government, but contended that government was limited by the possibility of disobedience or rebellion by those whose customs, wishes, and interests were sufficiently trampled on. He favoured strong government, but conceived it in a narrow, traditional way as simply a source and enforcer of law. He did not envisage it as redistributing property or providing welfare for the old, the young, the sick, and the poor. John Stuart Mill memorably departed from the Benthamite orthodoxy in which he had been brought up in a number of fundamental respects.

The most important of these was his enlargement and watering-down of the official utilitarian conception of pleasure and happiness. He ascribed this modification to the influence of Coleridge, a necessary corrective to the crudities of his mentors, and Coleridge's voice is present in his account of the principle of utility as making the criterion of value service to 'the permanent interests of man as a progressive being'. His touchstone was the active improvement of human nature, not the passive satisfaction of a community of consumers. Esteeming autonomous self-direction over mere enjoyment, he concluded that the largest possible measure of individual liberty is required for it to flourish. A further consideration is that the progress of mankind depends on human variety, even eccentricity. He laid down, therefore, that society has no right to limit the freedom of its individual members except for what he calls 'self-protection', by which he means protection against harm to others. That would presumably forbid people to grow or manufacture hard drugs, but permit them to take them. The vagueness of this principle is a more serious defect in the doctrine of *On Liberty* than the avoidable inconsistency about higher and lower pleasures.

In the end Mill favoured democracy and, perhaps, like de Tocqueville, thought it was inevitably going to prevail. They shared the fear that it would lead to the 'tyranny of the majority', the domination and exploitation of the gifted by the mediocre mass of mankind. In his *Representative Government* Mill argued for a system of proportional representation so as to counteract this tendency of democratic government, and also proposed plural voting to give more weight to the opinions of the educated. He supported democracy less as a device for seeing that the general interest is pursued than as an educative instrument, making men more active, tolerant, and public-spirited, as they need to be to some extent in the first place

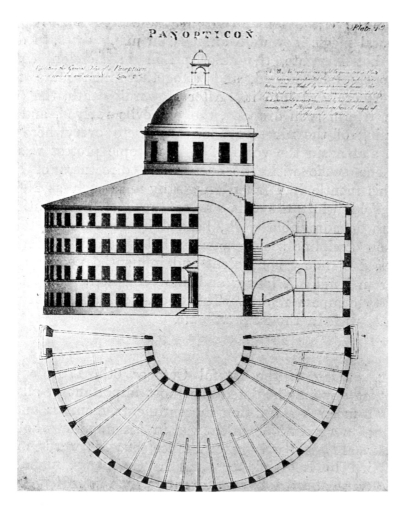

THE PANOPTICON, a scientifically designed high-security prison, was one of the more striking products of Jeremy Bentham's fertile reforming imagination.

MARY WOLLSTONECRAFT, wife of William Godwin, and mother of Mary Shelley, wrote one of the founding tracts of feminism, the *Vindication of the Rights of Woman*.

to be entrusted with the vote. In the same spirit, he thought education should be compulsory, but, out of distaste for bureaucracy, that it should not be controlled by the state.

Godwin's wife, Mary Wollstonecraft, had published her *Vindication of the Rights of Women* in 1792 at the height of the revolutionary tumult. It was a confused but eloquent call for the education of women, alongside men in coeducational schools, so as to fit them to be the companions, not the slaves or playthings, of men. Three-quarters of a century later, John Stuart Mill took up the subject again, with his usual lucidity, in his *On the Subjection of Women*. Mary Wollstonecraft had only alluded to the admission of women to the suffrage in a single, rather parenthetical sentence. Mill did not think it necessary to be so cautious. His main specific problem was the legal subordination of women, above all in the matter of their husbands' control over their property, but he also sought the admission of women to occupations hitherto closed them by law or custom, and argued that they should be given the vote. Of particular force is his scornful refutation of the prejudice that women are dependent by nature. They are compelled into dependence by men. What is the value of such an appeal to nature anyway?

Politics and Science: Saint-Simon, Comte, Spencer   In the sixth and last book of his *System of Logic* Mill, at that time much under the influence of Comte, had addressed himself to 'the logic of the moral sciences'. The obstinate backwardness of the social sciences as compared with their counterparts in the field of non-human nature had been a persisting and irksome hindrance to the programme of the Enlightenment. Rational knowledge of man and society was needed for social progress, but where was it to be found? Drawing heavily on Comte, but with large infusions of his own cautiousness, Mill maintained that such a science is possible, but can be only slowly and tentatively approximated to. What one billiard ball will do to another when it hits it depends on few factors: the shape, weight, hardness, and smooth surface of the balls, their position on impact, and the speed at which the first is moving. Things are very different in the human and social domain. The enormously greater complexity of human agents, and the consequentially much greater variety of circumstances determining their reactions, rule out a comparable rigour and certainty in the sciences of society.

Hitherto the demand for reason in political life had been either for the criticism of institutions by self-evident principles of political right, conceived on the analogy of geometry, or for the commonsensical tracing of the commonsensically pleasant or painful consequences to which they lead. In the nineteenth century the idea of applying science to politics emerged in various forms. For Saint-Simon, applied technological science was the indispensable motor of progress. It appeared to follow that the management of the new, progressive, industrial societies should be in the hands of scientists and the leaders of industry. The Baconian idea of science as important most of all for the services it could give to the 'relief of man's estate' was the object of his more or less religious veneration. His inclusion in the tradition of socialism is due to his insistence that society must endeavour to improve the physical and moral condition of its poorest members. For this purpose he argued that there is no right to inherited wealth. In the interests of peace he proposed a European parliament and imagined, as Comte and Spencer were to do later, that industrialism and militarism were essentially exclusive of each other.

Much of what he believed reappears in the voluminous writings of Auguste Comte, who was for a time his secretary. His famous law of the three stages enlarges on Saint-Simon's military–industrial contrast. The first, theological, age is military; the last, scientific, age is industrial; the intervening, metaphysical, age is one of transition. Believing in the possibility of a real, physics-like science of society, Comte goes beyond Saint-Simon's technology, which will merely solve the problem of poverty. Comte's social science, grasping the laws of social cohesion in its statics and of social change in its dynamics, will transform man's capacity to improve society and himself. The Saint-Simonian conclusion is drawn that government must be by an élite, expert in Comtian science. Although social change and progress is governed by law, it is not all that strict: men can influence the rate of change, even if not its direction. Comte follows Saint-Simon also in holding that, since science has undermined traditional Christianity, a new religion (of 'fraternal love' in Saint-Simon's case, of humanity in Comte's) must discharge its valuable, moralizing functions in its place. Comte was, like Hegel and Marx, a pre-Darwinian evolutionist, even if the evolutionary process they per-

HERBERT SPENCER applied evolutionary ideas—even before Darwin's *Origin of Species*—to moral, social, and political issues.

ceived was not biological and did not operate by natural selection. Comte died two years before Darwin's *Origin of Species* came out. By that time Herbert Spencer had already published a great deal, but he lived long enough to derive some reflected, and largely unearned, glory from Darwin's work.

Spencer, like Comte, saw himself as an originator of sociology, a serious, theoretical science of society. Everything in the world, he thought, passes from incoherent homogeneity to coherent heterogeneity, from the condition of the sea, that is to say, to that of a well-arranged general store. On the level of society this reveals itself in the form of an increase of individuality as men move from the military to the industrial form of social organization. He argues strenuously that increasing individuality—the human variety of differentiation—gives survival power; perhaps largely for that reason, he approves of this increase. Surprisingly, the more individual people become, the less need they have for government. Conscious compulsory co-operation will give way, as industrialization proceeds, to unconscious, spontaneous co-operation. Spencer saw government as in its nature destructive of individuality, and in its mid-nineteenth-century ameliorative form, with factory legislation, poor relief, compulsory state education, as desperately so, calculated to reduce men from autonomy to infantilism—an idea present, less ferociously expressed, in the work of John Stuart Mill. For Spencer society should be arranged so as to weed out its feebler members, not by positive eugenics but by unrestricted *laissez-faire*. He was not an enthusiast for democracy, saying that the divine right of parliaments was no improvement on the divine right of kings. Elimination of the weak may have some evolutionary sanction, but the adaptiveness of individuality is less obvious. Spencer does not seem to have drawn any lessons from the extraordinary evolutionary success of the social insects, among whom individuality is completely smothered by public spirit.

Marx and Socialism   The idea that there is some kind of absolute right to property has proved very tenacious in the history of Western political thought. Locke had to reconcile it with the state's need for tax revenue by requiring a special consent to the latter. At the point where traditionalist defences of economic inequality were losing their hold, the newly developed science of political economy supplied it with a new, more rational justification: it was seen as necessary to motivate entrepreneurs in making innovations.

There had been various fantasies of common ownership in the distant past, including the arrangements for the ruling class in Plato's *Republic* and in the *Utopia* of Thomas More. But the industrial revolution drew attention to the problem of the poverty of the masses. Saint-Simon's doctrine of a society rationally planned by experts implied interference with the irrational distribution of property, an implication his followers drew. Fourier, much more wildly, envisaged modest-sized co-operative communities, 'phalanxes', in which people worked at whatever they liked, for the love of the thing and of each other. Robert Owen, in Britain, more tamely, inspired model co-operative communities, which did not discredit the idea underlying them, even if they ended in nothing.

Two main directions in socialist thinking were evident by the middle of the nineteenth century: an idealistic, utopian one in Owen and Fourier, emphasizing the redemptive effect of free co-operation instead of competition, and an autocratic, centralizing one which envisaged no large immediate change in the industrial mode of life, only the vesting of property in the community at large and the more or less equal redistribution of its product. Proudhon, a utopian, was the most passionate critic of the institution of private property; Marx the most intellectually impressive of the centralizers and, of course, the most influential socialist of any kind. The idealists were not theorists: they simply protested morally against the social consequences of industrialism and proposed, in more or less colourful detail, imaginary social orders from which the evils of industrialism were absent. Their failure to explain how the move was to be made from the actual to the ideal was their chief weakness in Marx's opinion, one which he perhaps overcorrected by arguing that his ideal was bound to come about through historical necessity, without giving any definite account of what his ideal was, except in negative terms.

The official foundation of Marxist doctrine is the general metaphysics of dialectical materialism. Since it is no more than an ornamental façade to the essentials of Marxism it need not be considered here. It was of little interest to Marx, who handed it over to the care of his less gifted associate Engels. What is important, in itself and for politics, is Marx's historical materialism or materialist conception of history. This is, first of all, an account of the determination by the economic basis of society of its non-economic 'superstructure': its legal and political institutions and its ideas and beliefs. The state, as the pre-eminent legal and political institution, is, it follows, simply an instrument with which the ruling class preserves and enhances its power and wealth. Eventually, after the revolution has eliminated property and class division, it will 'wither away'.

The economic basis of society consists of 'forces of production'—natural resources, labour, and technology—and 'relations of production'—the way in which these forces are controlled and organized, for most of human history in conflicting social classes. 'All history', Marx and Engels wrote, 'is the history of class struggle.' The second aspect of historical materialism is a theory of change as the outcome of collision arising within the economic basis between new forces of production and ossified relations of production with which they are incongruous. No clear account is given of the causes of change in the forces of production. Advances in technology would seem to be crucial, since they underlie population increase and the exploitation of new natural resources, such as oil.

Most of Marx's attention is focused on the capitalist socio-economic system. The emergence of mechanically powered industry led to the displacement of the feudal nobility by the bourgeoisie as the ruling class, and other such by-products as the Protestant ethics of work. But by the late nineteenth century capitalism had reached, in Marx's view, a condition of terminal crisis. By the exploitation of the proletariat it had built up a great accumulation of industrial equipment available for the service of human beings rather than their degradation. The competitive struggle between firms was concentrating capital in ever fewer hands. An ever-diminishing bourgeoisie was thus confronted by an ever-increasing proletariat, which was becoming more and more conscious of its own strength. In industrially advanced

KARL MARX, AFTER THE PROSCRIPTION OF HIS JOURNAL, is represented here as the mythical Prometheus, devoured by an eagle as a divine punishment for teaching human beings the use of fire. At his feet the cities of the Rhineland petition for the repeal of the ban on the *Rheinische Zeitung*.

societies the time was now ripe for the proletariat, in inevitably violent revolution, to eliminate or absorb the bourgeoisie and so to bring the division of mankind into classes to an end. There would be a short transition period: 'the dictatorship of the proletariat'. After that there would be no further need for government. Co-operation would replace competition.

Marx's account of the workings and destiny of capitalism was supported by two economic theories: the labour theory of value and the theory of surplus value. The first, derived from Ricardo, states that the value of commodities is proportionate to the amount of labour involved in their production. That is true only in exceptional circumstances, but this does not really matter for Marx since he interprets the theory as holding that the value of commodities is wholly attributable to the labour, and by that he means manual labour, involved in their production. The suggested implication is that the fruits of production are wholly due, in justice, to the manual workers who produce it. The theory of surplus value points out, quite correctly, that only a part of these fruits are actually given to the proletariat. Marx contends that the proletarian share of industrial revenue is subsistence wages, the minimum required to enable proletarians to continue at work. The large residue is appropriated by capitalists, a massive and systematic exploitation. What is ostensibly neutral economic science is saturated in Marx with moral condemnation. His simple, politically practical message is that the wealth of the rich is rightly due to the poor who actually created it and that the time is ripe for the tables to be turned.

There is plainly much truth in Marx's historical materialism, although not the comprehensive truth he ascribed to it. Economic considerations have significant effects on politics and beliefs; but so do such factors as religion and nationality. History is made up of the struggles of creeds and peoples as well as of classes. Much of what he calls surplus value is a reward for work: management, professional skill, entrepreneurial risk-taking. In his own lifetime the incomes of industrial workers were steadily rising above subsistence level, as they have continued to do ever since. The monopolistic concentration of capital which he correctly observed did not reduce the capitalist class, which was much enlarged by the diffusion of share ownership, directly and through insurance and pension funds. Furthermore he failed to recognize the significance of the great increase of those he called *petit-bourgeois*, the managerial and administrative class. They, far from sharing the class interests of the proletariat, came to supplant the old-fashioned entrepreneurial bourgeoisie, to a great extent in the industrially advanced capitalist nations and completely in the Soviet Union, the part of the world ostensibly governed in accordance with Marx's prescriptions.

Marx's own political activism, as a tireless propagandist for social revolution and as creator and leader of a major political movement, is sometimes thought to be incompatible with his determinist claim that revolution is inevitable. But he could well regard his own political activity and that of the adherents he inspired as an indispensable, if causally determined, part of the system of events he was predicting. At a common-sense level he urged his followers to 'ease the birth pangs' of the new social order which was inevitably coming into existence. Although the revolutionary outcome is strictly determined, the form and speed of its happening is not.

A major tactical issue led to dissension among his followers. The orthodox position was that socialists should not seek parliamentary representation or support reformist welfare legislation. To do so would enfeeble their revolutionary resolve. The palliation of the proletariat's misery would simply postpone any substantial improvement in their condition. Kautsky, leader of the movement after the death of Marx and Engels, took that line at first, but eventually concluded that the revolution did not have to be violent. Eduard Bernstein, the first 'revisionist', went much further. He rejected the theory of surplus value and denied that the workers were becoming more miserable and that the capitalists were becoming less numerous. His 'evolutionary socialism' was the operating doctrine of the Social Democratic party in the German parliament, whatever its orthodox professions. In 1914, in a final repudiation of Marx, it supported the war. In Russia, having no constitutional means of expression, social democracy remained revolutionary and conspiratorial. Its Bolshevik part repudiated Marx's thesis that revolution could succeed only where the full development of bourgeois industrialization had made conditions ripe for it. In 1917 the Bolsheviks proved they were right so far as the seizure of power was concerned. But that power was used to install not socialism but a new kind of despotism.

The Twentieth Century

The Collectivist State   Everywhere in the twentieth century the state has increased its power and scope. Industrial advance required universal education which only the state could provide effectively. The traditional agencies of church and family, undermined respectively by science and by geographical and social mobility, surrendered to the state the provision of social welfare: support for the old, the poor, and the ill. The proportion of the national income spent by the state steadily approximated to half. Socially necessary industries like mines and railways, strategically important but often unprofitable, were nationalized. More and more of the working population became employees of the state.

The totalitarian state was the extreme development of this tendency. In it every aspect of society was brought under the state's control: economy, education, the media of communication, culture in all its manifestations—high and popular, intellectual and imaginative—even religion, whose traditional form was supplanted by worship of the state or its leader. The Soviet Union was the purest instance of totalitarianism; this was an outcome of the comprehensiveness of the collapse of the tsarist regime (and the feebleness of autonomous institutions in Russia). In Nazi Germany the penetration of society by the state and the party that controlled it was less complete. Private property was not much disturbed, the Christian religion was spurned but not outlawed. But state terrorism and mass murder played as large a part in Germany as in the Soviet Union. Mussolini's Italy and Franco's Spain were diluted versions of totalitarianism, in part because of the persistence in them of church and family.

In the liberal-democratic nations (the USA, Britain, France, and the small, largely Protestant countries of north-western Europe) the institution of private property survived throughout the century, although attenuated by taxation and nationalization, while freedom of expression and conduct even increased as social constraints on thought and behaviour weakened. But in social organization these countries became increasingly statist and centralized. After 1945 Germany and its explicitly totalitarian allies had liberal democratic regimes imposed on them by their conquerors by force of arms, with a measure of success. The Soviet Union finally collapsed from a combination of internal pressures (economic, nationalistic, and others) whose relative importance is not yet clear, as well as from a failure of will in its ruling circles, whose members had long ceased to believe in the official ideology. But the victory of the West was a victory of societies that were themselves, if not totalitarian, at any rate highly collectivized. The colonies they liberated after 1945 failed, with the signal exception of India, to adopt liberal democracy and its underlying individualism. In much of sub-Saharan Africa tribal despotisms emerged. In many countries of the Islamic world fierce, authoritarian nationalism was combined with some commitment to the unity and triumph of the Islamic religion. China persisted in quasi-Marxist totalitarianism.

In this century the social structure of the advanced countries has undergone an important change. Nineteenth-century societies were of the same pyramidal shape, in class terms, as most had been before them. At the top was a small élite—of nobles or of great capitalists and merchants. Below them was a larger group of lesser property-owners. Below them, again, was the great mass of the population: agricultural and industrial workers. Modern societies are pear-shaped, with a sizeable ruling élite, a large mass of skilled, even professionalized, people in the middle, and an underclass at the bottom. The members of the central mass own houses and cars, are investors, if only by way of insurance and pension funds, take holidays abroad, eat out. The traditional confrontation between rich and poor has lost its revolutionary potential. Too many have too much to lose from revolution. But in this process Marx's forces of production can be seen to be operating. Modern production needs many skilled workers but little brute labour. What the implications of this may be for legal and political institutions and for ideas and beliefs remains to be seen. The degradation of culture, both high and popular, in the post-war epoch is a discouraging feature. The glories of early twentieth-century modernism, whose members were deeply involved with the tradition against which they were reacting, have given way to expressive triviality in painting and music. Lower down there are the pornographies of sex and violence.

Lenin and Soviet Communism   Marxism made its way into Russia, to compete with other radical doctrines in the oppressive environment of tsarist autocracy, with the translation in 1863 of *The Communist Manifesto* by Bakunin, Marx's anarchist rival and fellow revolutionary. Just before the end of the century a social democratic party was founded there, with Plekhanov as its leading figure. It soon came to be dominated by Lenin. The Russian party soon divided over the question of the proper rate of revolutionary change. Should the birth-pangs of the new order be accelerated by a political Caesarean or should economic factors be allowed to take their predicted course? With Russia still in the earliest phase of the process of industrialization it seemed that revolution must be postponed until that process had fully matured. Lenin, fully aware of the risk of failure, chose immediate revolution and carried it out successfully in the autumn of 1917. Lenin's opportunistic practice of hastening the dialectical unfolding of history was the first of his three major innovations.

The second was his theory of the party. The proletariat on its own, he held, could generate only a trade-unionist ideology. A small disciplined élite of doctrinally expert middle-class intellectuals, working largely in secret, was necessary to bring about a revolution, perhaps anywhere, certainly in Russia. Given the oppressiveness of the imperial government radical politics in Russia had to be conspiratorial. This, as Plekhanov saw, was not a propitious recipe for the withering-away of the state; it would lead inevitably to dictatorship *over* the proletariat. The party as Lenin conceived it could not allow divisions of opinion within itself or, once it had seized power, within the community at large. The need for extravagantly ruthless means in Russia ensured that the ends which they were meant to serve receded ever fur-

AUTOCRATIC IN POWER, LENIN liked to be portrayed as a simple worker or intellectual, as in this photograph of him playing chess in a rural setting.

ther from view. Lenin's doctrine of the vanguard party was a major departure from orthodoxy since it implied that ideas are essential for revolutionary change, ideas of whose agents no economic explanation was even hinted at.

Lenin's third original contribution was a therapeutic addition to Marxist orthodoxy rather than a departure from it. The advanced nations were evidently not getting nearer and nearer to revolutionary crisis. The bourgeoisie there was not shrivelling, the proletariat was not increasingly miserable. Lenin explained this by the fact that the great capitalist societies had seized colonies, thus acquiring cheap raw materials, new markets for their products, and, generally, an outlet for excess capital. Imperialism served to postpone revolution by exporting exploitation.

The wild chance Lenin took in 1917 was made more acceptable by the assumption that other countries, particularly Germany, the birthplace of Marxism, would rise in revolt. But tumult there, and in Hungary, was rapidly suppressed. The closing injunction of *The Communist Manifesto*—'Workers of the world, unite'—remained a dogmatic principle of Soviet Marxism for some time after Lenin's death. Its most passionate exponent was Trotsky with his doctrine of permanent revolution. By the end of the 1920s, when Stalin had secured absolute power and Trotsky was in exile, the former's more realistic doctrine of socialism in one country came to prevail. With the German invasion in 1941 Stalin appealed to elemental patriotic sentiment to nerve the defenders of the Soviet system to their grim and protracted task. By that time most sincere Marxists had been purged—shot or sent to the Gulag—and a despotism run by a nervous élite of careerists was all that was left of the original emancipatory dream.

Outside Russia after the revolution socialism became increasingly revisionist and evolutionary, except among the servile Communist parties of the West, which pursued the interests of the Soviet Union by propaganda, agitation, and espionage. Altogether anti-revolutionary were the British Fabian socialists, who believed in the gradual penetration of ruling circles, especially the civil service, by those convinced that public ownership was more efficient than capitalism. Bernard Shaw, who later came to admire the dictators of the 1930s, and H. G. Wells, who favoured rule by a scientific élite, were the most conspicuous, but not the most typical, of the Fabians. There were Christian socialists, simply concerned to alleviate the sufferings of the poor, and Guild Socialists, who believed in the creative regeneration of work and of rule by producers rather than consumers. But there were no important theorists in the English-speaking world. The intellectual vigour of socialism lived on only in the 'Western Marxists' of Germany and Italy, who will be considered later.

The Precursors of Fascism   Fascism combines aggressive nationalism with passionate opposition to democracy, calling for rule by an inspired leader and an inspired élite. The chief remote source of its nationalism is Fichte, of its heroic élitism Carlyle. More oblique encouragement is derived from Nietzsche, mainly through misunderstanding, since, for all his detestation of the masses, he was neither a nationalist nor an anti-Semite. His élite heroes or supermen are conceived in cultural, not political, terms. Another intellectual current favourable to Fascism is the irrationalism provoked by the extravagances of Hegel. In Schopenhauer that reaction took the form of passive withdrawal from a cruelly indifferent universe. In Kierkegaard it inspired intense inward religiosity. Neither of these philosophers had anything to say about, or any discernible interest in, politics. But, in undermining the pretensions of Hegel's dialectical musings to be a product of reason, they, and Nietzsche, enthroned deeply felt intuition as the supreme faculty of the mind.

At the level of political theory this irrationalist tendency made itself most obtrusively present in the thought of Georges Sorel (1847–1922). He was an adherent of the philosophy of the politically mild Bergson, who had systematically elevated intuition over intellect as a means of grasping reality. Sorel believed that only man-made mechanisms are causally deterministic, the rest of nature being a chaos or muddle. Mankind can achieve only some patches of order in the enveloping sea of randomness and entropy by means of heroic activity, inspired by myth. A myth is not simply a stirring falsehood, but the vision of a possibility in the unpredictable future. With many others he saw the ruling bourgeoisie of *fin-de-siècle* Europe as decadent and corrupted by trivial pleasure. Together with Marx, but in a very different spirit, he saw the industrial working class as the most promising reservoir of heroic vitality, to be galvanized into violent action by the myth of the general strike. Gen-

STALIN, EVEN MORE RUTHLESS THAN LENIN, was represented in propaganda pictures as a benign father of his people. Here he presents a bouquet to the wife of a factory manager.

erally, he supported an ethic of active producers against the reigning ethic of passive consumers. Capitalism, now devoid of creative energy, should be replaced by associations of active producers—a highly coloured foretaste of the position of the Guild Socialists. Sorel endorsed violence, not in an exclusively physical sense, as a sign of spiritual health and vitality. This feverish body of ideas led him into unstable alliances with Marxism, the enraged French royalists, and, finally, Lenin, who was not flattered. Mussolini acknowledged a debt to him. He was not a nationalist or a racist, but Fascism drew on his admiration of heroic activity and violence, his conception of struggle as an end in itself, and his contempt for the idea of progress and of the kind of calculating rationality that was supposed to ensure it.

The great Italian economist Vilfredo Pareto (1848–1923) arrived at somewhat similar conclusions from a very different starting-point. His social theory purported to be rigorously scientific. Democracy, above all the economic democracy of socialism, is impossible. All societies are run by élites who make manipulative use of the confused, 'non-logical' desires and beliefs of the masses to pursue their aims. Ideologies are rationalizations of deeper, unacknowledged impulses. Élites inevitably decay and are replaced by others; the élites 'circulate' and history is cyclical in form. Two main types of élite are distinguished: one of adventurous, speculative foxes, the other of fierce, possessive lions. Convinced, like Sorel, of the degeneracy of his age—of which the corrupt parliamentary government of recently united Italy supplied a compelling instance—he deplored the obstruction of economic initiative by high taxation and acquiescence in the demands of trade unions. Pareto resembles Marx in extracting a fervent ideology from what is presented as an objective scientific account of society and its history. Rule by an élite is inevitable (the iron law of oligarchy); therefore it ought to prevail. Pareto's élite is closer to that of Plato, its superiority resting on higher intellectual qualifications, than to that of the fascists, for whom militancy of will and a readiness for violence are primary. The riff-raff who sustained Hitler and Mussolini in power would have been as distasteful to him as Lenin's vanguard of conspiratorial doctrinaires or Stalin's petrified and slavish court.

Oswald Spengler (1880–1936) is another thinker who was led by his sense of the degeneracy of his own age to reject the liberal-democratic politics and belief in progress that had been inherited from the Enlightenment. His main idea is that history is not a single, beneficently progressive linear sequence but is composed of the life-cycles of a number of self-sufficient cultures—Chinese, Indian, Classical, Magian (i.e. Arabian), Western, and so on—each of which goes through phases of vigorous, barbaric youth, productive maturity, ripe, cultivated decline, and final collapse. This vision, or 'morphology', of history is arrived at by a kind of aesthetic contemplation of the known facts, supplemented by a good deal of guesswork and fudging. It is, all the same, an arresting picture, full of particular insights. It puts the widespread sense of the deterioration of the Western world in a large and persuasive historical context. In the final, moribund stage of each major society culture declines into mere civilization. The population, deserting the countryside for vast cities, comes to form a rootless proletariat which is manipulated by demagogues in the interests of a plutocracy. Heroic virtue is replaced by sensualism. Art becomes corrupted and esoteric. Religious faith is undermined by scepticism. It is not a wholly uncompelling account of our present condition. Decline cannot be wholly averted, in Spengler's view, but it can be delayed, or at any rate confronted with heroic fortitude. By him too an élite is summoned to the historic tasks of preventing a revolution by the masses within the West and the overwhelming of the West by the races of the rest of the world.

Fascism and Nazism   Fascism is, in one sense, an inclusive kind of which Italian Fascism and German Nazism are species. There is little more than pathological interest in the literature in which its doctrines were expounded at length, although there are many works of distinction explaining the background of previous German thought from which it arose. Hitler's *Mein Kampf*, as the title makes clear, is an autobiography, filled with panegyric of Germany and coarse anti-Semitic invective. Fascism is not a theory but a faith, to be set out in a creed rather than a treatise. The main elements are clear enough. First, the nation is supreme. Its power and well-being take absolute precedence over the wants and needs of the individuals who compose it. Their highest duty and greatest fulfilment is to serve it and, if necessary, die for it. It is also superior to other nations (a thesis which it is hard to universalize) and must always be ready to dominate or repel them by force of arms. A healthy nation is always mobilized for war. Secondly, an effective nation must have a unity of will, incarnated in an inspired leader, backed by a devoted élite. No dissent from the party's beliefs and decisions is to be permitted. It should control all aspects of social life.

Fascism's relation to capitalism and private property is a little complicated. Mussolini began his political career as a socialist and abandoned socialism only because of his ardent support for Italy's entrance into the First World War. His Italian version of Fascism involved the idea of the corporate state, in which the state controls productive organizations and eliminates class struggle by imposing harmony on capitalists and workers. The rather feeble condition of capitalist enterprise in Italy meant that this arrangement did more for capitalists than for workers. The full title of Hitler's Nazi party was the National Socialist German Workers' Party. But he was subsidized and supported in his advance to power by industrialists, and they benefited from his destruction of the trade-union movement without suffering the imposition of corporate arrangements in the Italian manner. So in both countries property-owners gained more than workers. But all benefited from full employment and from the soothing of deep-seated resentment and frustration brought about by a revival of national self-confidence and self-esteem.

A further element added to Fascism by Hitler, and integral to his conception of it, was racism, in particular anti-Semitism. The German idea of the nation, the *Volk*, was not so much cultural or historical as racial. The Italians took it up half-heartedly after the formation of the Axis. Jews were more numerous and important in Germany than in Italy and Hitler's intense anti-Semitism had a large reserve of similar, if less hyperbolic, sentiment to draw on in his subjects. The Jews bore the terrible brunt of Hitler's theories but his racism was not confined to them. Other 'Nordic' nations—those inhabiting the Protestant northwest of Europe—he regarded as fellow human beings and even potential allies. Latins were objects of suspicion and disdain; non-white nations were objects of contempt. A pseudo-Darwinian conception of history as a struggle for existence and primacy between races rather than classes lay behind Nazi racism.

In Hitler's system of beliefs we find many elements combined and hideously magnified: Fichte's idea of the special national mission of Germany; Nietzsche's idea of the superman, who casts aside Christian humility and philanthropy for an ethic of heroic self-affirmation; Sorel's notion of readiness for violence as an index of spiritual health; widespread repudiation of rationality and objective truth in favour of intuition: and finally the idea of struggle as an end in itself. Resentment at Germany's failure, after reunification in 1871, to take its place beside the imperial nations of western Europe was exacerbated into despair by defeat in 1918, the Treaty of Versailles, and subsequent economic crisis and massive unemployment in the 1930s. Other Fascisms were less monstrous than Germany's. Most had collapsed by the end of the Second World War in 1945. The main survivor, the Fascism of Franco's Spain, quietly petered out, giving way to the restoration of the monarchy and the successful reintroduction of parliamentary democracy. After 1945 the only major instance of aggressive, élitist nationalism was Stalin's Soviet Union, which even took over the anti-Semitism of Hitler's Germany.

Western Marxism   The exigencies of dictatorial rule by a small, inexperienced party over the complete social chaos of Russia after the end of the civil war left little room for the development of theory. The only notable figure, Bukharin, produced an official textbook, which Stalin pillaged for his own even more undistinguished writings. After obliterating Bukharin politically in 1929, Stalin had him shot on the usual fraudulent charges in 1938. Bukharin's position was scientistic: it took Marxism to be an objectively true, predictively reliable natural science of society. He affirmed explicitly that, 'in the last resort', technological change is the driving force of history.

In western Europe, where revolution, in defiance of Marx's prophesies, had neither come about nor shown any signs of being about to do so, a radical reinterpretation of Marx, in a sense opposite to that of Bukharin, was begun by György Lukács (1885–1971). He started from an assertion of the essentially Hegelian character of Marx's doctrine. Hegel had described the dialectical passage of the 'Idea', or unconscious Spirit, through its opposite, Nature, replaced in its turn by Mind, or Spirit conscious of itself. Lukács saw this as an allegorical mystification of the Marxian sequence: labour, the capitalist order in which it is 'alienated', and the communist future in which it will reappropriate its alienated self. Labour is alienated under capitalism since it does not control how it is used nor enjoy the fruits of its use. By way of 'false consciousness' it treats its own activity and products as substantially external to it ('reification'). The correction of this error will enable the proletariat, the class of those who labour, to recover, through revolution, what has been alienated from them.

This Hegelian, spiritualized version of Marxism was not just a disaffected intellectual speculation. Ten years after Lukács published his account of the matter the discovery of Marx's early 'economic and philosophical manuscripts' revealed that the young Marx had held pretty much the views Lukács ascribed to him, before moving on to a more naturalistic, straightforwardly economic point of view. For the young Marx, alienation, a spiritual complaint, was of more concern than exploitation, an economic disadvantage. But because of his deviation from the doctrine of the official, later Marx, Lukács, in the first of a long series of cringing compliances, was compelled by the party to recant.

Two implications of his Hegelianization of Marx became widespread among independent-minded Western Marxists for the ensuing half-century. Their development, especially by the 'critical theorists' of the Frankfurt school, notably Herbert Marcuse, served as the operating myth of the New Left in the upsurge of radical protest in the 1960s. The first of them was a categorical rejection of the determinism affirmed by the later Marx and, even more comprehensively, by Engels. In effect this was to deny that economic factors are historically fundamental and to make ideas, in particular the liberated class-consciousness of the proletariat, the crucial agency of revolution. Lukács held that this proletarian consciousness is not explicit. It is, rather, imputed to the proletariat by the revolutionary vanguard. That idea was entirely congruous with Lenin's brilliantly opportunistic seizure of power, and with what followed it. But that did not protect it from condemnation.

The second implication was an abandonment of the assumption that true knowledge of the world is authoritatively provided by applying the methods of natural science. Philosophical reflection on the totality of nature and history, which is always relative and incomplete, must replace analytic study of isolated fragments of the whole. It followed that Lenin's naïvely representationalist picture theory of knowledge must be discarded. What that view takes to be real, above all in the world of social institutions, is only appearance, that which is essentially labour being misconceived as the objective necessities of economic life. The idea that what revolution removes is not so much exploitation as alienation amounts to a rejection of industrialism itself rather than of its prevailing capitalist form. A liberating revolution must transform the entire culture, not merely its economic arrangements. It must transform man himself, not just the distribution of goods. That at least helped to account for the enslaved condition of the masses under Soviet communism. It is also in accordance with the economic utopianism of the early Marx, who seemed to think that after the revolution there need be no more division of labour.

In Italy Antonio Gramsci (1891–1937), influenced by the more or less Hegelian Croce, also rejected determinism and Lenin's theory of knowledge. He was an early and persistent critic of the tendency of the party, overwhelmingly realized by Stalin, to become a purely manipulative, bureaucratic piece of political machinery. Such a degeneration, he maintained, could be avoided only by workers' councils, involving the mass of the proletariat in their activities. These were much the same as the soviets, influential in the first, primitively democratic phase of Lenin's rule but swiftly neutralized once power had been seized. For Gramsci there is no scientific socialism to be applied by an authoritative party élite whose special possession it is. A prerequisite of successful revolution is working-class 'hegemony', the acquisition by the masses of a conscious working-class culture and conception of society and its history.

Liberal and Conservative Anti-Socialism   The exponents of evolutionary or democratic socialism in the century and a half since Marx and Engels published *The Communist Manifesto* in 1848 have been productive, but not of major intellectual significance. Some, admittedly, such as Bernard Shaw and Bertrand Russell, have achieved the highest distinction in other fields. Tawney, Cole, and the fellow-travelling Laski in Britain stand out as small eminences on a level plain. George Orwell was more than that but, like William Morris, was an imaginative writer, not a theorist. Other countries have even less to offer. There were distinguished socialist leaders in France, such as Jaurès and Blum, but no notable socialist theorists. It was as if the huge, tangled growth of Marxism, orthodox or heretical, casting its thick metaphysical shadow around it, had stunted the development of its more pacific and ethical rival.

Nevertheless, as mentioned earlier, the advanced nations of the West were becoming more collectivist, indeed more socialistic, in the enlargement of the scope of the operations of their governments. In the field of distribution they brought about large equalizing reallocations of income by welfare provision which was financed by graduated taxation of income and inheritance. In that of production they brought industries into public ownership, thus removing them from the disciplines of the market. Even if the only socialist theory that called for serious consideration was Marxism, there was widespread socialist practice to be examined. There have been two major theoretical assaults on collectivism in the last half-century; one, that of Hayek, broadly liberal, the other, that of Oakeshott, broadly conservative. Their doctrines are not just restatements in an up-to-date idiom of the central ideas of Mill on the one hand and Burke on the other. Each embodies a substantial and original philosophical component, strongly opposed to the calculating rationalism of Mill and the Utilitarians, although drawing on ideas from Adam Smith and Burke.

Epilogue

At its most inclusive, political philosophy is reasoned discussion of the nature of the state, of its actual or justifying purposes. In its first great incarnation in Plato it took the form of an imaginative elaboration of a utopian political ideal. Aristotle, more terrestrially, dealt with the political actualities of his time, making reasoned comparisons of the merits and defects of different kinds of state. In the Middle Ages a new direction was given to the subject by concentrating attention on the legitimacy rather than the possible excellences of the state. In one way or another that remained the prevailing style of what has been called classical political theory, culminating in Hobbes and Locke. They enquired into the basis of political obligation, bringing it down from the heaven of medieval political philosophy to the earth of a social contract and, in the end, utility. Despite the title of his chief political work, Rousseau was not concerned with the social contract. He tried to short-circuit the problem of political obligation by undermining its starting-point: the supposed necessity of political obedience. In his view the citizens of a true democracy obey only themselves, or, more precisely, their better selves.

Under autocratic governments the political options open to individuals are limited. They can obey or disobey or revolt. In such circumstances the obligation to obey the state is inevitably the main problem for political thought. But as the influence of citizens on government grows it is appropriate for them to consider what they would wish governments to do, what moral, or collectively prudential, or just individually advantageous ends they would like it to pursue. The main line of battle here has been drawn between the partisans of liberty and the partisans of equality, which sometimes appropriates the name of justice. Security and prosperity have been left in the background, as if taken for granted. Security remains the first, because most plausibly defining, purpose of the state. Recent events, inside and outside the disintegrating Soviet empire, have cast doubt on the assumption that the direct pursuit of prosperity is something to be carried on by the state at all.

Afterword

ANTHONY KENNY

WHEN this Illustrated History was planned, an editorial decision was taken that the work of living authors should not form part of the narrative. The decision has had some odd consequences. Nothing is said in the text, for instance, about Sir Karl Popper or about Friedrich von Hayek, both of whom were alive at the time this planning decision was taken. Each of these authors has been highly influential—the one especially in epistemology and philosophy of science, the other in moral and political philosophy—during the lifetime of others who have taken their place in this history. Both of them will undoubtedly occupy a significant place in histories published after their deaths. However, a boundary has to be drawn, any boundary leaves some anomalies, and in a history the line between life and death is the least arbitrary and the least invidious boundary line to draw.

In this concluding note, without discussing the work of individuals, I will merely indicate the general lines of philosophical development during recent decades. About the year 1960 the world of Western philosophy could be mapped, without too crude a degree of oversimplification, by means of a simple diagram. You could represent the overall position by

EXISTENTIALISM	ANALYTIC PHILOSOPHY
MARXISM	SCHOLASTICISM

PHILOSOPHICAL SCHOOLS OF THE 1950S can be diagramatically represented in the quadrants of this square.

taking a square and dividing it into four quadrants. In the top left-hand corner, place the existentialism then in vogue in the western part of continental Europe; in the top right-hand corner, place the analytical tradition dominant in English-speaking countries on both sides of the Atlantic. In the bottom left-hand corner place Marxism, then the official philosophy of eastern Europe and China; in the bottom right-hand corner place the Scholastic philosophy which was taught throughout the world in the seminaries and universities of the Roman Catholic Church.

The location of these quadrants in the square represents the features in which these philosophies resembled and differed from each other. The philosophies in the upper part of the diagram shared with each other a concern for the intellectual and moral autonomy of the individual: philosophy was not a set of authoritative doctrines but a method of thinking (analysis) or a style of life (existentialism). The philosophies in the lower part were both historically linked to institutions whose primary purpose is non-philosophical, and shared a conviction that the most important philosophical truths have been settled once for all so that they can only be expounded, and never seriously called into question. The philosophies on the right-hand side of the diagram resembled each other in their interest in the examination of purely theoretical minutiae and in their close ties with systems of formal logic. Those on the left-hand side prided themselves on their practical commitment to the basic realities of human experience, work, power, love, and death; neither contributed significantly to the development of the mathematical aspects of logic.

In the 1960s these philosophical blocks began to crumble, fissure, and shift. The second Vatican Council, inaugurated in 1962, led to a period of liberalization within the Roman Catholic Church; in the course of this, neo-Scholasticism lost much of it canonical status in the Church's institutions of higher education, and by the next decade the staff of a seminary was likely to be as well versed in existentialism as in Thomism. But simultaneously, classical existentialism was losing its power where once it had held sway: Heidegger's influence went into severe decline, and Sartre himself, in the latter part of his life, was more interested in Marxism than in the themes of his earlier battles against essentialism.

Whereas in the 1950s and early 1960s the English Channel had marked an almost impenetrable barrier between Anglo-American philosophy and Continental philosophy, by the 1970s many cross-cultural links had begun to thrive. Germany, Italy, and (after the death of Franco) Spain became hospitable to analytical methods in philosophy, while philosophical ideas engendered in France found great favour in Britain and the USA, though more commonly in departments of literature than in departments of philosophy.

In Germany, for instance, at the end of the 1960s, in some of the main universities the dominant influences were analytic philosophy (which had able evangelists among some of the most sophisticated faculty members) and Marxist philosophy (which had vocal exponents among some of the most energetic student leaders). The surviving school of thought closest to German existentialism was the hermeneutic school, which made the nature of understanding its central topic of study; the nature of understanding in general, the understanding of works of literature more specifically, and the understanding of works of philosophers in various traditions in particular.

The hermeneutic school in Germany operated in an eirenic manner, taking the unavoidably fluent and flexible activity of interpreting a text as a general model for the understanding of human activities and institutions of different kinds. In France thinkers of a more combative spirit seized on the idea that all the world's a text and made it the battle-cry of an iconoclastic crusade.

The crusade was waged in the name of structuralism. Structuralism, as a method, invites us to make the assumption, with regard to a particular structure, that the interrelationship between its elements is more important than any relationship between an individual element and any item exterior to the structure. Structuralism, as a theory of a particular field of study, is the thesis that the structuralist method is the key to the understanding of that field. Thus, in respect of language, it is the thesis that if we wish to understand meaning, we must study the interrelationships between signifying elements within a language, rather than look for a relationship between any signifier and what it signifies.

Post-structuralism carried structuralist theses to extreme, indeed self-refuting, positions. If we are to understand a text, we must rigorously exclude all extra-textual elements. This means not only abandoning the search for any external reality represented by the text, but also ceasing to look on it as the expression of the thought of any extra-textual author. It is the reader who plays the major part in the production of meaning; but since each reader interprets every text differently, no definitive meaning ever emerges, and hence each text undermines its own claim to be meaningful.

There have been various forms or factions in French post-structuralism. Each school has shone briefly with magnetic brilliance, attracting a voluble throng of devotees before burning out as a rival version began to glow more enticingly. All of these groups have claimed descent from distinguished exponents of linguistic theory such as Saussure and Jakobson, and in that sense their members can be classed as linguistic philosophers. But they are at the opposite pole from the style of philosophy which has long regarded itself as linguistic philosophy *par excellence*, the Anglo-American analytic tradition.

Analytic philosophy, too, has altered greatly since the simple squaring-off of the 1960s. The most obvious changes have been a decline in self-confidence, and a change in centre of gravity. In 1960 Oxford was the unquestioned centre of the analytical movement, and philosophers came from the United States to sit at the feet of Oxford philosophers. Analytic practitioners prided themselves on being the heirs of two philosophers of undoubted genius, Russell and Wittgenstein. They saw their task as being to exploit this happy endowment and share it with the rest of the philosophical world. In the years since the 1960s the leadership of the analytic movement has moved definitively across the Atlantic, though no single American university has inherited the dominant role once enjoyed by Oxford. The tradition of Russell and Wittgenstein no longer commands universal respect; but no newer genius has emerged to succeed to an equal uncontested esteem. No one has succeeded in redefining the nature of philosophy, as they redefined it by placing the study of language in the centre of philosophy, and convincing their adherents that the task of philosophy was to study the language we use to express our thoughts, and to make those thoughts clear by tidying up the confusions in the language in which we express them.

ANGLO-AMERICAN AND CONTINENTAL PHILOSOPHY were brought together in this conference of 1976 in Christ Church, Oxford, to which leading philosophers were invited from Britain, the USA, and Germany. The presiding figure in the middle of the front row is Gilbert Ryle.

Consequently, Anglo-American philosophy no longer presents even the appearance of a unified school. The tradition continues to be linguistic, in the sense that there is no lack of philosophers offering theories of language. But the theories of language currently most fashionable are very far removed from the philosophy of language presented by philosophers such as Frege and Wittgenstein, and for that reason they are bitterly criticized by those who strive to preserve the insights of the founding fathers of the analytic tradition.

Both Frege and Wittgenstein made a sharp distinction between philosophy and psychology. For Frege, logic, which was at the heart of philosophy, was an a priori science very different from an empirical science like psychology; for Wittgenstein, philosophy differed from psychology because it was not any kind of science at all, whether empirical or a priori. The Oxford philosophers of the 1950s followed Wittgenstein in this; and their psychological colleagues, interested at that time much more in animal behaviour than in human language, were happy to agree that a deep chasm separated the two disciplines.

By contrast, American philosophers, since they took up the torch of the analytic tradition, have tended to see philosophy as a scientific discipline with rigorous special techniques of its own, rather than as an informal quest for understanding rooted in reflection on the un-schooled activities of the ordinary person. Philosophy of mind, in particular, is now often seen as having as its task the construction of a model of mind such as a student of artificial intelligence might aim to create. Great hopes are held out of a new joint discipline called cognitive science, which will combine the conceptual skills of the philosopher, the model-making ability of the artificial-intelligence expert, and the empirical findings of the experi-mental psychologist. These hopes have been spread backwards across the Atlantic to Britain and to Oxford itself.

This development, though it has been promoted by philosophers trained in the analytic tradition, in fact reverses the linguistic turn which gave that tradition its defining character-istic. From Frege's first denunciation of psychologism in logic, through the writings of the earlier and later Wittgenstein, up to the Oxford philosophy of ordinary language and its reception into the United States, it was accepted by all that the way to understand thought was to reflect on language. It was common ground that thoughts could only be identified and individuated through their expression in language, and that there was no such thing as a structure of thought which was accessible independently of the structure of language. The aspirations of the cognitive scientists run clean contrary to this fundamental principle of the philosophy of linguistic analysis. The hope of the new discipline is to explain language by relating it to mental structures which can already in principle, and in future in practice, be investigated quite independently of any linguistic expression.

Simultaneous with this dramatic change in the direction of Anglo-American philosophy of language, there has been a similarly striking development within analytic moral and political philosophy. In the heyday of the analytical movement it was popular to believe that there was a sharp distinction between ethics and morals. Morals consisted of first-order questions about how one should behave, questions such as whether lies were ever permiss-ible, or whether it was justified to bomb cities in order to shorten a war. Such questions and their answers belonged to the first-order discipline of morals. It was not quite clear whose job it was to answer such questions, but any Oxford philosopher of the 1950s would have told you that it was certainly not the philosopher's. The philosopher did something quite different, which was called ethics; that was a second-order study of the concepts which we used in asking and answering the first-order questions, and the philosopher's relation to the moral-ist was no closer than that of the garage mechanic's to the driver of the car.

All this, too, changed between the 1950s and the 1980s. In English-speaking countries it is now regarded as quite proper for philosophers to use their own professional expertise in making specific proposals for reform in public affairs, or specific denunciations of policies and administrations. Philosophers have interested themselves greatly in first-order ques-tions about the rights of women or the wrongs of nuclear war in ways which used to be re-garded as more the province of the politician or the cleric than the professional philosopher.

Analytic philosophy, therefore, is no longer, if it ever was, a homogeneous unity. The very conception of philosophy has become looser and more open at the edges. This has a further consequence, which is most relevant to the present work: philosophy in the English-speaking world has changed its attitude to its own history. In eras of crusading self-confidence, such as marked the heyday of ordinary-language philosophy, the history of philosophy tends to be neglected. A revolutionary era does not waste time dissecting minutiae which preoccupied the *ancien régime*; it proclaims the newly discovered truth which was at best ignorantly worshipped by its predecessors. The indentation and fragmentation of the analytical monolith has led to a revived interest in the history of philosophy. A particularly striking example of this is the recent renaissance of medieval studies: medieval philosophy, once a handmaid or nursemaid to theology taught only in seminaries, is now taught expertly in secular universities as a significant element of the philosophical heritage. Astonishingly, even the ontological argument for the existence of God, regarded in the 1950s as the most exploded weapon in the philosophical armoury, has been fitted out with sophisticated modern accessory devices and redeployed to effect on the contemporary battlefield of philosophical theology.

We can return, for the last time, to our initial diagram to follow briefly the recent course of Marxist philosophy. In the 1950s Marxism, like Scholasticism, owed its place in academic institutions to organizations whose primary agenda were not philosophical; and, like Scholasticism, it was vulnerable to non-academic changes in those organizations. But for Marxism, unlike scholasticism, the decade of the 1960s was an era of expansion, and many philosophers in the West adopted Marxist approaches, though their interests tended to focus on the works of the younger Marx rather than on *Das Kapital*. At the same time, disillusion with the corrupt and despotic nature of Marxist regimes made students of philosophy in Eastern bloc countries cynical about the value of the official philosophy which underlay them. In the 1970s, paradoxically, Marxism in the East was universally taught and almost universally disbelieved, while Marxism in the West was taught, as a minority subject indeed, but to an audience of passionate believers. Now, of course, as a result of the dissolution of the Soviet Empire, and the liberation of the Soviet satellites, the institutional support for Marxist philosophy in eastern Europe has almost totally collapsed. That philosophy must depend for its survival on the efforts of its devotees in the universities of the West.

Great philosophical ideas can permeate every aspect of human thought and endeavour; but they take a long time to do so, and an even longer time is necessary for their influence to be evaluated as sound or unhealthy. The philosophies of the latter half of the twentieth century are too close for us to make a definitive judgement about them all, even if some can already be seen to be ephemeral.

Any reader who has persevered through the pages of this book will have been struck by the fact that even the greatest philosophers of the past propounded doctrines which we can see—through hindsight of the other great philosophers who stand between them and ourselves—to be profoundly mistaken. This should be taken not as reflecting on the genius of our great predecessors, but as an indication of the extreme difficulty of the discipline. The ambition of philosophy is to achieve truth of a kind which transcends what is merely local and temporal; but not even the greatest of philosophers have come near to achieving that goal in any comprehensive manner. There is a constant temptation to minimize the difficulty of philosophy by redefining the subject in such a way that its goal seems more attainable. But we philosophers must resist this temptation; we should combine unashamed pride in the loftiness of our goal with undeluded modesty about the poverty of our achievement.

This thought has been well expressed by the American philosopher Thomas Nagel, in his brilliant synopsis of philosophy, *The View from Nowhere*. 'Even those', he writes, 'who regard philosophy as real and important know that they are at a particular and, we may hope, early stage of its development, limited by their own primitive intellectual capacities, and relying on the partial insights of a few great figures of the past. As we judge their results to be mistaken in fundamental ways, so we must assume that even the best efforts of our own time will come to seem blind eventually.'

CHRONOLOGICAL TABLE

Many of the dates given, particularly in earlier centuries, are conjectural or approximate.

BC

776	First Olympian games	
753	Foundation of Rome	
550	Death of Zoroaster	
538	Return of Jews from Babylon	
530		Pythagoras active
515	Second Temple of Jerusalem	
509	Roman Republic begins	
505		Heraclitus active
500		Birth of Anaxagoras
490	Battle of Marathon	
484		Birth of Empedocles
483	Death of the Buddha	
481		Birth of Protagoras
479	Death of Confucius	
469		Birth of Socrates
458	Aeschylus' *Oresteia*	
447	Building of the Parthenon	
431	Peloponnesian War	
430		Birth of Plato
429	Sophocles' *Oedipus Rex*	
428		Death of Anaxagoras
424		Death of Empedocles
423	Aristophanes' *Clouds*	
404	Peloponnesian War ends	
399		Death of Socrates
387	Rome captured by Gauls	
386		Plato founds the Academy
384		Birth of Aristotle
357		Death of Democritus
356	Alexander the Great born	
347		Death of Plato
335		Aristotle founds the Lyceum
331	Foundation of Alexandria	
323	Death of Alexander	Death of Diogenes
322		Death of Aristotle
310		Pyrrhon of Elis active
307		Epicurus founds school
300	Great Wall of China begun	Euclid's *Elements*
295		Zeno of Citium active

285		Death of Crates
275	Septuagint Bible	
271		Death of Epicurus
254	Punic Wars begin	
265	Judas Maccabeus active	
240		Archimedes active
207		Death of Chrysippus
146	Destruction of Carthage	
106		Birth of Cicero
100	Birth of Julius Caesar	
98		Birth of Lucretius
86	Sulla sacks Athens	
85		Andronicus edits Aristotle
55	Caesar in Britain	Lucretius dies
44	Murder of Caesar	
43		Murder of Cicero
30	Antony and Cleopatra die	
27	Augustus becomes emperor	
19	Vergil's *Aeneid*	
4	Death of Herod the Great	

AD

14	Death of Augustus	
30	Crucifixion of Jesus	
39		Philo the Jew in Rome
43	Romans invade Britain	
64	Fire of Rome under Nero	
65		Suicide of Seneca
67	Martyrdom of St Paul	
70	Temple of Jerusalem sacked	
79	Eruption of Vesuvius	
89		Epictetus active
117	Trajan's column	
140		Ptolemy active
161	Marcus Aurelius emperor	
162		Galen comes to Rome
180		Marcus Aurelius' *Meditations*
185		Clement of Alexandria active
200		Alexander of Aphrodisias active
		Sextus Empiricus active
230	Origen active	
240		Plotinus active
280		Porphyry active
293	Diocletian organizes Empire	
325	Council of Nicaea	
354		Birth of Augustine
378	Battle of Adrianople	
386		Conversion of Augustine

396		Augustine becomes bishop
401		Augustine's *Confessions*
410	Sack of Rome by Visigoths	
419		Augustine's *On the Trinity*
426		Augustine's *City of God*
430		Death of Augustine
431	Council of Ephesus	
432	St Patrick in Ireland	
440	Leo I becomes Pope	
451	Attila the Hun defeated	
	Council of Chalcedon	
476	End of Roman Empire in West	
486	Clovis founds Frankish Kingdom	
510		Boethius consul in Rome
523		Boethius' *Consolation of Philosophy*
525		Execution of Boethius
534	Justinian's *Code* of laws	
570	Birth of Muhammad	
590	Gregory I becomes Pope	
610	Westminster Abbey founded	
623		Isidore's *Etymologies*
632	Death of Muhammad	
637	Caliph Omar in Jerusalem	
711	Muslims invade Spain	
731	Bede's *Ecclesiastical History*	
732	Muslims defeated at Tours	
770	Arabic numerals introduced	
800	Charlemagne crowned in Rome	
843	Carolingian Empire divided	
850		Eriugena at Carolingian Court
877		Death of Eriugena
910	Abbey of Cluny founded	
980		Birth of Avicenna
1010	Birth of Lanfranc	
1054	Schism between East and West	
1066	Battle of Hastings	Anselm's *Proslogion*
1079		Birth of Abelard
1086	Domesday Book	
1096	First Crusade	
1108		Anselm on God and free will
1109		Death of Anselm
1116		Abelard teaches at Paris
1126		Birth of Averroes
1140	Gratian's *Decretum*	
1158		*Sentences* of Peter Lombard
1159		John of Salisbury's *Policraticus*
1170	Murder of Becket	
1187	Saladin takes Jerusalem	

1198		Death of Averroes
1200		Charter of Paris University
1204	Crusaders sack Constantinople	
1208	Franciscan order founded	
1216	Dominican order founded	
1221		Birth of Bonaventure
1225		Birth of Aquinas
1227	Death of Genghis Khan	
1245		Albert and Aquinas at Cologne
1259	Foundation of Ottoman Empire	Bonaventure's *Itinerarium*
1264		Aquinas' *Summa contra gentiles*
1266	Giotto born	Aquinas' *Summa theologiae* begun
1268		Works of Roger Bacon
1271	Marco Polo in China	
1274		Aquinas and Bonaventure die
1290	Jews expelled from England	
1294	Boniface VIII becomes Pope	
1295		Scotus lecturing in Oxford
1302		Scotus lecturing in Paris
1305	Papacy moves to Avignon	
1308		Death of Scotus
1317		Ockham lecturing in Oxford
1321	Dante's *Divine Comedy*	
1324		Ockham called to Avignon
1337	Giotto dies	
1339	Beginning of Hundred Years War	
1347		Death of Ockham
1348	Black Death	
1353	Boccaccio's *Decameron*	
1360		Wyclif Master of Balliol
1374	Petrarch dies	
1377		Condemnation of Wyclif
1378	Great Schism begins	
1381	Peasants' Revolt in England	
1386		Death of Wyclif
1400	Death of Chaucer	
1414	Council of Constance begins	
1415	Battle of Agincourt	
1431	Joan of Arc burnt	
1439	Council of Florence	
1445	Birth of Botticelli	
1450	Gutenberg's Printing Press	
1453	Fall of Constantinople	
	Hundred Years War ends	
1472		Latin Aristotle printed
1475	Birth of Michelangelo	
1483	Birth of Luther	
1484		Ficino's Latin Plato

1492	Columbus to America	
1495		Greek Aristotle printed
1511	Raphael's *School of Athens*	
1512	Sistine Chapel ceiling painted	
1516	Erasmus' Greek Testament	
1517	Luther's Wittenberg theses	
1522	Luther's German Bible	
1531	Henry VIII breaks with Rome	
1532		Vitoria's *De Indis*
		Machiavelli's *The Prince*
1536	Calvin's *Institutes*	
1540	Foundation of Jesuits	
1543	Copernicus publishes	
1555	Peace of Augsburg	Ramus' *Dialectique*
1564	Shakespeare born	
1572	Massacre of St Bartholomew	Ramus dies
1578		Stephanus' Greek Plato
1580		Montaigne's *Essais*
1588	Defeat of Spanish Armada	Birth of Hobbes
1596		Birth of Descartes
1597		Suarez's *Disputationes*
1600		Giordano Bruno burnt
1603	Death of Elizabeth I	
1605	Gunpowder plot	Bacon's *Advancement*
1611	King James Bible	
1616	Death of Shakespeare	
1618	Thirty Years War begins	
1620	Pilgrim Fathers sail	Bacon's *Novum organum*
1628	Harvey's *De motu cordis*	
1632		Birth of Spinoza
		Birth of Locke
1633		Condemnation of Galileo
1636	Foundation of Harvard	
1637		Descartes's *Discourse*
1641		Descartes's *Meditations*
1642	English Civil War begins	
1644		Milton's *Areopagitica*
1648	Peace of Westphalia	
1649	Execution of Charles I	
1650		Death of Descartes
1651		Hobbes's *Leviathan*
1658	Death of Cromwell	
1662	Charter of the Royal Society	*Port Royal Logic*
1666	Great Fire of London	
1667	Milton's *Paradise Lost*	Locke's *Essay on Toleration*
1670		Spinoza's *Tractatus*
1672		Pufendorf's *De iure naturae*
1674		Malebranche's *Recherche*

1676		Leibniz invents calculus
1677		Death of Spinoza; *Ethics*
1679		Death of Hobbes
1681	Charter of Pennsylvania	
1682	Newton discovers gravity	
1685	Handel and J. S. Bach born	Berkeley born
1686		Leibniz's *Discourse*
1688	Expulsion of James II	
1690		Locke's *Essay*
1694	Bank of England founded	
1697		Bayle's *Dictionnaire*
1704	Battle of Blenheim	
1705		Leibniz's *New Essays*
1707	Union of England and Scotland	
1709		Berkeley's *New Theory*
1711		Birth of Hume
1713		Berkeley's *Dialogues*
1712	Pope's *The Rape of the Lock*	
1713	Treaty of Utrecht	
1714	Death of Queen Anne	Leibniz's *Monadology*
1715	Death of Louis XIV	
1726	Swift's *Gulliver's Travels*	
1738	Wesley founds Methodism	
1739		Hume's *Treatise*
1741	Handel's *Messiah*	
1745	Jacobite Rebellion	
1748	Peace of Aix-la-Chapelle	
1751		*L'Encyclopédie*
1753		Death of Berkeley
1755	Johnson's *Dictionary*	
1756	Seven Years War begins	
1759	British capture Quebec	
1769	Steam-engine patented	
1770	Birth of Beethoven	Birth of Hegel
1771	Cook in the Pacific	
1772	Partition of Poland	
1773	Suppression of Jesuits	
1774	Discovery of oxygen	
1776	American Declaration of Independence	Death of Hume
1778		Deaths of Voltaire, Rousseau
1779		Hume's *Dialogues* published
1781		Kant's first *Critique*
1783	Peace of Paris	
1785		Kant's *Groundwork*
1786	Mozart's *Figaro*	
1787	US Constitution	
1788	Gibbon's *Decline and Fall* completed	
1789	French Revolution	Bentham's *Principles*

1790	Galvanism discovered	
1791	Boswell's *Life of Johnson*	
1793	Execution of Louis XVI	
1794	Death of Robespierre	
1795		Fichte's *Wissenschaftslehre*
1797		Schelling's *Philosophy of Nature*
1798	*Lyrical Ballads*	
1799	Napoleon takes power	
1800	Beethoven's First Symphony	Schelling's *System*
	First electric battery	
1802	Turner joins Royal Academy	
1806		Hegel's *Phenomenology*
1812		Hegel's *Logic*
1814	Stephenson's Rocket	
1815	Battle of Waterloo	
1816	Austen's *Emma*	
1817		Hegel's *Encyclopedia*
1818		Schopenhauer's *World as Will*
1819	Byron's *Don Juan*	
1821		Hegel's *Philosophy of Right*
1824	British National Gallery opens	
1831		Death of Hegel
1832	Great Reform Act	
1840	Penny post founded	
1841		Feuerbach's *Christianity*
1843		Kierkegaard's *Either/Or*
		Mill's *System of Logic*
1846	Irish famine	
1847	Brontë's *Jane Eyre*	
1848	Year of Revolutions	Communist Manifesto
1850	Tennyson's *In Memoriam*	Marx's *German Ideology*
1852	Dickens's *Bleak House*	
1854	Crimean War	
1859		Darwin's *Origin of Species*
1865	American Civil War ends	
1867	Verdi's *Don Carlos*	Marx's *Das Kapital*
1869	First Vatican Council	
1870	Franco-Prussian War	Newman's *Grammar of Assent*
1871	Eliot's *Middlemarch*	
1874		Brentano's *Psychology*
1876	Victoria Empress of India	
1878	Tolstoy's *Anna Karenina*	
1879	Brahms's Violin Concerto	Frege's *Begriffsschrift*
1882	Wagner's *Parsifal*	
1884		Nietzsche's *Thus Spake Zarathustra*
1890		James's *Principles*
1895	Invention of wireless telegraphy	
1897	Discovery of the electron	Russell Fellow of Trinity

1899	Invention of the cinema	
1902		Croce's *Aesthetic*
1903	Invention of the aeroplane	Russell's Paradox
1906	Labour Party founded	
1907	Picasso's *Demoiselles*	Bergson's *Creative Evolution*
1908		Sorel on *Violence*
1910		Russell and Whitehead's *Principia*
1911	Stravinsky's *Rite of Spring*	
1913		Husserl's *Ideas*
1914	First World War begins	
1916		Einstein's General Theory of Relativity
1917	Russian Revolution	
1919	Treaty of Versailles	
1922	Eliot's *Waste Land*	Wittgenstein's *Tractatus*
1927		Heidegger's *Being and Time*
1928	Gropius's Bauhaus completed	Carnap's *Logische Aufbau*
1931		Gödel's Theorem
1933	Hitler comes to power	
1939	Second World War begins	
1940	Battle of Britain	Quine's *Mathematical Logic*
1942	Battle of Stalingrad	
1943		Sartre's *Being and Nothingness*
1945	First atom bombs used	
1949	Foundation of NATO	Ryle's *Concept of Mind*
1953		Wittgenstein's *Investigations*

FURTHER READING

1. ANCIENT PHILOSOPHY

THE VERY BEGINNING

Clastres, P., *Society against the State*, tr. R. Hurley (New York, 1977).

Cornford, F. M., *From Religion to Philosophy* (New York, 1957; first pub. 1912).

Frankfurt, H. and H. A., Wilson, J. A., and Jacobsen, T., *Before Philosophy* (Harmondsworth, 1949; first pub. 1942).

Lévi-Strauss, C., *The Savage Mind* (London, 1966).

Lloyd, G. E. R., *Magic, Reason and Experience* (Cambridge, 1979).

Ong, W. J. *Orality and Literacy* (London, 1982).

Onians, R. B., *The Origins of European Thought* (Cambridge, 1951).

Sahlins, M., *Stone Age Economics* (London, 1974).

—— *Culture and Practical Reason* (Chicago, 1976).

INSPIRED THINKERS

Barnes, J. (ed.), *Early Greek Philosophy* (Harmondsworth, 1987).

Dodds, E. R., *The Greeks and the Irrational* (Berkeley, Calif., 1951).

Heidegger, M., *Early Greek Thinking*, tr. D. F. Krell and F. A. Capuzzi (New York, 1984).

Kirk, G. S., Raven, J., and Schofield, M. (eds.), *The Presocratic Philosophers*, 2nd edn. (Cambridge, 1983).

O'Flaherty, W., *Dreams, Illusions and Other Realities* (Chicago, 1984).

Vernant, J. P., *Myth and Thought among the Greeks* (London, 1983).

West, M., *Early Greek Philosophy and the Orient* (Oxford, 1971).

THE SOPHISTIC MOVEMENT

Hussey, E., *The Presocratics* (London, 1972).

Kerferd, G., *The Sophistic Movement* (Cambridge, 1981).

Pirsig, R. M., *Zen and the Art of Motorcycle Maintenance* (London, 1974).

Renault, M., *The Last of the Wine* (London, 1956).

Vlastos, G., *Socrates: Ironist and Moral Philosopher* (Cambridge, 1991).

DIVINE PLATO

Crombie, I. M., *An Examination of Plato's Doctrines* (London, 1963).

Field, G. C., *Plato and his Contemporaries*, 3rd edn. (London, 1967).

Findlay, J. M., *Plato: The Written and Unwritten Doctrines*, 3rd edn. (London, 1967).

Irwin, T.H., *Plato's Moral Theory* (Oxford, 1977).

Taylor, A. E., *Plato* (London, 1936).

THE ARISTOTELIAN SYNTHESIS?

Ackrill, J. L., *Aristotle the Philosopher* (Oxford, 1981).

—— (ed.), *A New Aristotle Reader* (Oxford, 1987).

Barnes, J., Schofield, M., and Sorabji, R. (eds.), *Articles on Aristotle*, i–iv (London, 1975–9).

Grene, M., *A Portrait of Aristotle* (London, 1963).

Lloyd, G. E. R., *Aristotle: Growth and Development of his Thought* (Cambridge, 1968).

Sorabji, R., *Necessity, Cause and Blame* (London, 1980).

STOICS, EPICUREANS, AND WANDERING SAGES

Long, A. A., *Hellenistic Philosophy* (London, 1974).
—— and Sedley, D. (eds.), *The Hellenistic Philosophers* (Cambridge, 1987).
Mates, B., *Stoic Logic* (Berkeley, Calif., 1953).
Mitchison, N., *The Corn-King and the Spring-Queen* (London, 1931).
Sambursky, S., *Physics of the Stoics* (London, 1959).
Sandbach, F. H., *The Stoics* (London, 1975).

FROM DOUBT TO DOGMA

Annas, J., and Barnes, J., *The Modes of Scepticism* (Cambridge, 1985).
Armstrong, A. H. (ed.), *Classical Mediterranean Spirituality* (New York, 1986).
Dillon, J., *The Middle Platonists* (London, 1977).
Downing, G., *Jesus and the Idea of Freedom* (London, 1987).
Hengel, M., *Judaism and Hellenism*, tr. J. Bowden (London, 1974).
Wolfson, H. A., *Philo: Foundations of Religious Philosophy* (Cambridge, Mass., 1946).

THE PAGAN POSSIBILITIES

Armstrong, A. H., *An Introduction to Ancient Philosophy*, 3rd edn. (London, 1957).
—— (ed.), *The Cambridge History of Later Greek and Early Medieval Philosophy* (Cambridge, 1970).
Casey, M., *Kingfisher's Wing* (Crawley, 1987).
Chadwick, H. (ed.), *Origen: Contra Celsum*, 3rd edn. (Cambridge, 1980).
Dodds, E. R., *Pagan and Christian in an Age of Anxiety* (Cambridge, 1968).
Dombrowski, D. A., *The Philosophy of Vegetarianism* (Amherst, Mass., 1984).
Lamberton, R., *Homer the Theologian* (Berkeley, Calif., 1986).
Wallis, R. T., *Neo-Platonism* (London, 1972).
Wolfson, H. A., *Philosophy of the Church Fathers*, 3rd edn. (Cambridge, Mass., 1970).

2. MEDIEVAL PHILOSOPHY

GENERAL SURVEYS AND STUDIES OF PARTICULAR PERIODS

Armstrong, A. H. (ed.), *The Cambridge History of Later Greek and Early Medieval Philosophy* (Cambridge, 1970); covers the period through Anselm, including early Islamic philosophy.
Copleston, Frederick C., *A History of Philosophy*, ii and iii (Westminster, Md., 1950, 1953); clear and readable, yet admirably detailed and informative.
Gilson, Étienne, *History of Christian Philosophy in the Middle Ages* (New York, 1955); a classic and amazingly rich work.
Kretzmann, Norman, Kenny, Anthony, and Pinborg, Jan (eds.), *The Cambridge History of Later Medieval Philosophy* (Cambridge, 1982); contributions by many eminent scholars, especially good on logic and philosophy of language.

THE PATRISTIC PERIOD

Altaner, Berthold, *Patrology*, tr. Hilda C. Graef (Freiburg-im-Breisgau, 1960); a standard reference work for the patristic period.
Quasten, Johannes, *Patrology*, 4 vols. (Westminster, Md., 1950–88); an outstanding, detailed reference work.

AUGUSTINE

Gilson, Étienne, *The Christian Philosophy of Saint Augustine*, tr. L. W. Shook (New York, 1960); an excellent overview.
Kirwan, Christopher, *Augustine* (London, 1989); a philosophical study of major themes.

van der Meer, F., *Augustine the Bishop: The Life and Works of a Father of the Church*, tr. Brian Battershaw and G. R. Lewis (London, 1962); excellent for putting Augustine in context.

Nash, Ronald H., *The Light of the Mind: St Augustine's Theory of Knowledge* (Lexington, Ky., 1969); a clear and penetrating study of the theory of illumination.

BOETHIUS

Chadwick, Henry, *Boethius: The Consolations of Music, Logic, Theology and Philosophy* (Oxford, 1981); informative and authoritative.

Gibson, Margaret (ed.), *Boethius: His Life, Thought and Influence* (Oxford, 1981); a good collection of papers.

Gracia, Jorge J., *Introduction to the Problem of Individuation in the Early Middle Ages* (Munich, 1984; 2nd rev. edn., 1988); a detailed study of the problem through the twelfth century, with strong emphasis on Boethius.

JOHN SCOTTUS ERIUGENA

Marenbon, John, *From the Circle of Alcuin to the School of Auxerre: Logic, Theology and Philosophy in the Early Middle Ages* (Cambridge, 1981); discusses Eriugena and others from the Carolingian period.

ANSELM

Hopkins, Jasper, *A Companion to the Study of St Anselm* (Minneapolis, 1972); a useful handbook.

THE TWELFTH CENTURY

Dronke, Peter (ed.), *A History of Twelfth-Century Western Philosophy* (Cambridge, 1988); excellent essays by several scholars.

Evans, G. R., *Old Arts and New Theology: The Beginnings of Theology as an Academic Discipline* (Oxford, 1980); discusses changes in the style of philosophy and theology after Anselm.

Haskins, Charles Homer, *The Renaissance of the Twelfth Century* (Cambridge, Mass., 1927); a justly famous study.

PETER ABELARD

King, Peter, *Peter Abailard and the Problem of Universals in the Twelfth Century* (Ithaca, NY, forthcoming); a superb study, focusing on Abelard but discussing the entire history of the problem from Boethius to Abelard.

Luscombe, D. E., *The School of Peter Abelard* (Cambridge, 1969); a well-known study of Abelard's influences.

Sikes, J. G., *Peter Abelard* (Cambridge, 1932); still a helpful biography.

Tweedale, Martin M., *Abailard on Universals* (Amsterdam, 1976); a good, philosophically provocative study.

NEW DEVELOPMENTS IN LOGIC

De Rijk, L. M., *Logica Modernorum: A Contribution to the History of Early Terminist Logic*, 2 vols. in 3 (Assen, 1962–7); a monumental study, including many previously unpublished texts.

THOMAS AQUINAS

McInerny, Ralph, *Being and Predication: Thomistic Interpretations* (Washington, DC, 1986); a collection of several of the author's previously published papers on Aquinas and other philosophers in his milieu.

Weisheipl, James A., *Friar Thomas D'Aquino: His Life, Thought and Works* (Garden City, NY, 1974); a fascinating and authoritative biography, including a discussion of authentic works.

Wippel, John F., *Metaphysical Themes in Thomas Aquinas* (Washington, DC, 1984); an outstanding collection of several of the author's previously published papers on Aquinas.

BONAVENTURE

Gilson, Étienne, *The Philosophy of St Bonaventure* (New York, 1938; Paterson, NJ, 1965; first pub. in French, Paris, 1924); an older study, but still helpful.

Quinn, John Francis, *The Historical Constitution of St Bonaventure's Philosophy* (Toronto, 1973); a detailed and authoritative study.

JOHN DUNS SCOTUS

Wolter, Allan, *The Philosophical Theology of John Duns Scotus*, ed. Marilyn McCord Adams (Ithaca, NY, 1990); a collection of papers by an outstanding scholar of Scotus.

WILLIAM OF OCKHAM

Adams, Marilyn McCord, *William Ockham* (Notre Dame, Ind., 1987; repr. 1989); the best overall study of Ockham's philosophy.

LATE DEVELOPMENTS

Hudson, Anne, and Wilks, Michael (eds.), *From Ockham to Wyclif* (Oxford, 1987); a collection of essays including several on philosophical developments.

Kenny, Anthony, *Wyclif* (Oxford, 1985); a brief survey of main themes of Wyclif's philosophy and theology.

Maier, Anneliese, *On the Threshold of Exact Science: Selected Writings of Anneliese Maier on Late Medieval Natural Philosophy*, ed. and tr. Steven D. Sargent (Philadelphia, 1982); a collection of papers by the distinguished historian of late-medieval science.

Weinberg, Julius R., *Nicholas of Autrecourt: A Study in Fourteenth Century Thought* (Princeton, NJ, 1948; repr. New York, 1969); dated, but still a classic study.

3. DESCARTES TO KANT

GENERAL

Bennett, J., *Locke, Berkeley, Hume: Central Themes* (Oxford, 1971).
Copleston, F. C., *A History of Philosophy*, iv–vi (London, 1960).
Cottingham, John, *The Rationalists* (Oxford, 1988).
Russell, B., *A History of Western Philosophy* (London, 1961).
Woolhouse, R. S., *The Empiricists* (Oxford, 1988).

DESCARTES

Descartes, R., *Œuvres*, ed. C. Adam and P. Tannery, 12 vols. (Paris, 1897–1910).
—— *The Philosophical Writings of Descartes*, tr. John Cottingham, Robert Stoothoff, Dugald Murphy, and Anthony Kenny i–iii (Cambridge, 1985, 1991).
—— *Descartes' Conversation with Burman*, tr. with an introduction and commentary by J. Cottingham (Oxford, 1976).
Chappell, V., and Doney, W., *Twenty-Five Years of Descartes Scholarship 1960–1984* (New York, 1987).
Cottingham, J., *Descartes* (Oxford, 1986).
Frankfurt, H. G., *Demons, Dreamers and Madmen* (Indianapolis, 1970).
Gaukroger, S., *Cartesian Logic* (Oxford, 1989).
Kenny, A., *Descartes: A Study of his Philosophy* (New York, 1986; Bristol, 1993).
Schouls, P., *Descartes and the Enlightenment* (Montreal, 1989).
Sorell, T., *Descartes* (Milton Keynes, 1981).
Vrooman, J. R., *René Descartes: A Biography* (New York, 1970).
Williams, B., *Descartes: The Project of Pure Enquiry* (Harmondsworth, 1978).
Wilson, M., *Descartes* (London, 1978).

LOCKE

Locke, J., *An Essay Concerning Human Understanding* (1689), ed. P. H. Nidditch (Oxford, 1975).
—— *The Clarendon Edition of the Works of John Locke*, 15 vols. to date (Oxford, 1975–92).
Aaron, R. I., *John Locke*, 3rd edn. (Oxford, 1971).
Colman, J., *John Locke's Moral Philosophy* (Edinburgh, 1983).
Cranston, M., *John Locke: A Biography* (London, 1957).

Dunn, J., *John Locke* (Oxford, 1984).
Mackie, J. L., *Problems from Locke* (Oxford, 1976).
Woolhouse, R., *Locke's Philosophy of Science and Knowledge* (Oxford, 1971).
Yolton, J. W., *John Locke and the Way of Ideas* (Oxford, 1956).
—— *Locke and the Compass of Human Understanding* (Cambridge, 1970).

BERKELEY

Berkeley, G., *The Works of George Berkeley, Bishop of Cloyne*, ed. A. A. Luce and T. E. Jessop, 9 vols. (Edinburgh, 1948–57).
Armstrong, D. M., *Berkeley's Theory of Vision* (Melbourne, 1960).
Foster, J., and Robinson, H. (eds.), *Essays on Berkeley: A Tercentennial Celebration* (Oxford, 1985).
Pitcher, G., *Berkeley* (London, 1977).
Tipton, I. C., *Berkeley: The Philosophy of Immaterialism* (London, 1974).
Urmson, J. O., *Berkeley* (Oxford, 1982).
Warnock, G. J., *Berkeley*, 3rd edn. (Oxford, 1982).
Wild, J., *George Berkeley: A Study of his Life and Philosophy* (New York, 1962).
Winkler, K. P., *Berkeley: An Interpretation* (Oxford, 1989).

SPINOZA

Spinoza, B. de, *Spinoza: Opera*, ed. C. Gebhardt, 3 vols. (Heidelberg, 1925; repr. 1972).
—— *The Collected Works of Spinoza*, ed. and tr. E. Curley (Princeton, NJ, 1985).
Bennett, J., *A Study of Spinoza's Ethics* (Cambridge, 1984).
Curley, E. M., *Spinoza's Metaphysics* (Cambridge, Mass., 1969).
Delahunty, R. J., *Spinoza* (London, 1985).
Grene, M., *Spinoza: A Collection of Critical Essays* (South Bend, Ind., 1973).
Parkinson, G. H. R., *Spinoza* (Milton Keynes, 1983).
Scruton, R., *Spinoza* (Oxford, 1986).

LEIBNIZ

Leibniz, G. W., *Die philosophischen Schriften*, ed. C. I. Gerhardt, 7 vols. (Berlin, 1857–90; repr. Hildesheim, 1965).
—— *Philosophical Papers and Letters*, tr. L. Loemker, 2nd edn. (Dordrecht, 1969).
—— *New Essays on Human Understanding*, tr. and ed. P. Remnant and J. Bennett (Cambridge, 1981).
Brown, S., *Leibniz* (Brighton, 1984).
Frankfurt, H., *Leibniz: A Collection of Critical Essays* (New York, 1972).
Ishiguro, H., *Leibniz's Philosophy of Logic and Language* (London, 1972).
Mates, B., *The Philosophy of Leibniz: Metaphysics and Language* (New York, 1986).
Parkinson, G. H. R., *Logic and Reality in Leibniz's Metaphysics* (Oxford, 1965).
Rescher, N., *The Philosophy of Leibniz* (Englewood Cliffs, NJ, 1967).
Ross, G. M., *Leibniz* (Oxford, 1984).
Russell, B., *A Critical Exposition of the Philosophy of Leibniz* (London, 1900).
Woolhouse, R. S., (ed.), *Leibniz: Metaphysics and Philosophy of Science* (Oxford, 1981).

HUME

Hume, D., *An Enquiry Concerning Human Understanding*, ed. L. A. Selby-Bigge and P. H. Nidditch, 3rd edn. (Oxford, 1975).
——*A Treatise of Human Nature*, ed. L. A. Selby-Bigge and P. H. Nidditch, 2nd edn. (Oxford, 1978).
Anscombe, G. E. M., *Metaphysics and the Philosophy of Mind* (Oxford, 1981).
Ayer, A. J., *Hume* (Oxford, 1980).
Flew, A., *Hume's Philosophy of Belief* (London, 1961).
Kemp Smith, N., *The Philosophy of David Hume* (London, 1941).
Stroud, B., *Hume* (London, 1977).

KANT

Kant, I., *Gesammelte Schriften*, Prussian Academy of Sciences critical edn., 22 vols. (Berlin, 1902–44).
—— *Critique of Pure Reason*, tr. N. Kemp Smith (London, 1929; repr. 1973).
—— *Critique of Practical Reason*, tr. L. W. Beck (Chicago, 1949).
—— *Groundwork of the Metaphysic of Morals*, tr. H. Paton (London, 1955).
Allison, H., *Kant's Transcendental Idealism: An Interpretation and Defense* (New Haven, Conn., 1983).
Ameriks, K., *Kant's Theory of Mind: An Analysis of the Paralogisms of Pure Reason* (Oxford, 1982).
Bennett, J., *Kant's Analytic* (Cambridge, 1966).
—— *Kant's Dialectic* (Cambridge, 1974).
Bird, G., *Kant's Theory of Knowledge* (London, 1962).
Hacker, P. M. S., *Insight and Illusion* (Oxford, 1972).
Strawson, P. F., *The Bounds of Sense* (London, 1966).
Walker, R., *Kant* (London, 1979).

4. CONTINENTAL PHILOSOPHY FROM FICHTE TO SARTRE

GENERAL

This bibliography lists the works cited in the text, in available English translations, together with such other works of the philosophers considered as might interest the general reader. I have included no commentaries, since, in my view, all English-language commentaries that I have read in this field are invariably less accessible than the philosophers themselves.

FICHTE

Early Philosophical Writings, tr. and ed. Daniel Breazeale (Ithaca, NY, 1988).
The Science of Knowledge, with the first and second introductions, ed. and tr. Peter Heath and John Lacks (Cambridge, 1982); the *Wissenschaftslehre* in its most complete form, with useful addenda and commentary, in an up-to-date translation. Beware of nineteenth-century translations of this work.
The Vocation of Man, ed. with an introduction by Roderick M. Chisholm (New York, 1956); Fichte as a moralist.
Addresses to the German Nation, tr. R. F. Jones and G. H. Turnbull (London, 1922); Fichte as a political activist and rhetorician.

SCHELLING

Ideas for a Philosophy of Nature (1797), tr. Errol E. Harris and Peter Heath, with an introduction by Robert Stern (Cambridge, 1988).
System of Transcendental Idealism, tr. Peter Heath, with an introduction by Michael Vater (Charlottesville, Va., 1978); the principal source for Schelling's philosophical ideas.
Of Human Freedom, tr. with an introduction by James Gutmann (Chicago, 1936).
The Ages of the World, tr. with an introduction by F. de Wolfe Bolman, Jr. (New York, 1942); Schelling's influential philosophy of history.
The Philosophy of Art, tr. with an introduction by Douglas W. Scott, foreword by David Simpson (Minneapolis, 1989).

SCHILLER

On the Aesthetic Education of Man in a Series of Letters, ed. and tr. Elizabeth M. Wilkerson and L. A. Willoughby (Oxford, 1982).

HEGEL

Hegel translations and editions were hastily put together in the last century, and the hitherto authoritative versions finally published by T. M. Knox are now themselves giving way to newer versions, incorporating the more sober hopes entertained towards the Hegelian system by modern scholars. Technical terms are translated differently by different authors, but up-to-date translations should be used, and up-to-date editions of the posthumous writings.

Hegel's Science of Logic, tr. A. V. Miller, with a foreword by J. N. Findlay, 2 vols. (London, 1969).

Hegel's Logic: Part of the Encyclopedia, tr. William Wallace, 3rd edn. (Oxford, 1975).

The Phenomenology of Spirit, tr. A. V. Miller, with a foreword by J. N. Findlay (Oxford, 1977).

Elements of the Philosophy of Right, ed. Allen W. Wood, tr. H. B. Nisbet (Cambridge, 1991); this rearranges and also retranslates the text previously presented as *The Philosophy of Right* by T. M. Knox.

Aesthetics: Lectures on Fine Art, tr. T. M. Knox (Oxford, 1975).

Lectures on the Philosophy of History, tr. J. Sibree (London, 1890; reissued, New York, 1956).

FEUERBACH

Although out of the main stream, a brilliant writer who provides much food for thought.

The Essence of Christianity, tr. George Eliot, with an introduction by Karl Barth, foreword by H. Richard Niebuhr (New York, 1957); this classic translation has been frequently reissued since the famous novelist first introduced Feuerbach to the Victorian public.

The Fiery Book, tr. and ed. Zawar Hanfi (Garden City, NY, 1972); a selection from Feuerbach's writings.

MARX

Any attempt at a bibliography of Marx would have to be longer than this chapter. Few of his works were ever finished, and the heap of abandoned, unrevised, or unfinished writings is so vast that it is difficult to know where to begin. Fortunately the work has been done for us by three patient and intelligent editors, each of whom presents selections which include all that a reader needs in order to appreciate the impact of Marx on the history of thought.

Karl Marx: Selections, ed. David McLellan (Oxford, 1971).

Karl Marx: A Reader, ed. Jon Elster (Cambridge, 1986).

Marx: Selections, ed. Allen W. Wood (London, 1988).

SCHOPENHAUER

There are two translations of Schopenhauer's major work, with two different terms ('idea' and 'representation') used to translate Schopenhauer's 'Vorstellung'. 'Representation' is to be preferred, since Schopenhauer has another use for the term 'Idea'.

The World as Will and Idea, tr. R. B. Haldane and J. Kemp (London, 1906).

The World as Will and Representation, tr. E. F. J. Payne (India Hills, Colo., 1958).

There are many editions of Schopenhauer's shorter essays. The best is:

Parerga and Paralipomena: Short Philosophical Essays, tr. E. F. J. Payne (Oxford, 1974).

NIETZSCHE

Nietzsche is to be appreciated for his style and imagination, rather than his occasional pretences to a systematic argument. Hence he can best be approached through selections. The following are useful:

The Portable Nietzsche, ed. and tr. Walter Kaufmann (New York, 1954, 1968).

Basic Writings, tr. and ed. Walter Kaufmann (New York, 1992).

A Nietzsche Reader, tr. and ed. R. J. Hollingdale (Harmondsworth, 1977).

For the specific works referred to, see:

Twilight of the Idols and *The Antichrist*, tr. R. J. Hollingdale, with an introduction by Michael Tanner (London, 1990).

Beyond Good and Evil: Prelude to a Philosophy of the Future, tr. with an introduction by R. J. Hollingdale (Harmondsworth, 1973).

Thus Spake Zarathustra, tr. with an introduction by R. J. Hollingdale (Harmondsworth, 1969).

The Birth of Tragedy and *The Case of Wagner*, tr. with commentary by Walter Kaufmann (New York, 1967).

The Gay Science, tr. Walter Kaufmann (New York, 1974).

The Will to Power, tr. Walter Kaufmann and R. J. Hollingdale (New York, 1967); Nietzsche's posthumous writings, including some of his best aphorisms and paragraphs.

KIERKEGAARD

Either/Or: A Fragment of Life, tr. David F. Swenson and Lillian Marvin Swenson (Oxford, 1944).
Fear and Trembling and *Repetition*, ed. and tr. Howard V. Hong and Edna H. Hong (Princeton, NJ, 1983).
The Concept of Dread, tr. with an introduction by Walter Lowrie (Princeton, NJ, 1944).
Purity of Heart is to Will One Thing, tr. Douglas V. Steerer (New York, 1938).
The Sickness unto Death, tr. W. Lowrie (Princeton, NJ, 1941).
Concluding Unscientific Postscript, tr. David F. Swenson (completed by Walter Lowrie) (Princeton, NJ, 1941).
Selections from Kierkegaard, tr. Lee M. Hollander, rev. edn. (Garden City, NY, 1960).

BERGSON

Bergson's works exist in authorized English translations (Bergson was of partly English descent, and bilingual).
Creative Evolution, tr. Arthur Mitchell (London, 1911).
Time and Free Will: An Essay on the Immediate Data of Consciousness, tr. F. L. Pogson, 2nd edn. (London, 1912).
Matter and Memory, tr. Nancy Margaret Paul and W. Scott Palmer (pseud.) (London, 1912).
Laughter: An Essay on the Meaning of the Comic, tr. Cloudesley Brereton and Fred Rothwell (London, 1913); an interesting essay, and one of the few philosophical contributions to this subject apart from an essay by Schopenhauer and some ancient writings on comedy.

CROCE

Aesthetic, as Science of Expression and General Linguistic, tr. Douglas Ainslie (London, 1922).
My Philosophy, and Other Essays on the Moral and Political Problems of Our Time, selected by R. Klibansky, tr. E. F. Carritt (London, 1949).
Logic; or, The Science of the Pure Concept, tr. Douglas Ainslie (London, 1917).
The interested reader would be inspired and instructed also by:
Autobiography, tr. R. G. Collingwood (Oxford, 1927).
The Poetry of Dante, tr. Douglas Ainslie (New York, 1922).

BRENTANO

Psychology from an Empirical Standpoint, i–iii, ed. Oscar Kraus, tr. Margarete Schattle and Linda L. McAlister (London, 1973, 1980).
The True and the Evident, ed. Oscar Kraus, English edn. ed. and tr. Roderick M. Chisholm (London, 1966).
The Origin of the Knowledge of Right and Wrong, ed. and tr. Roderick M. Chisholm and Elizabeth H. Schneewind (New York, 1969).
Those interested in the work of Brentano's pupils might look at:
Christian Freiherr von Ehrenfels, *Cosmogony*, tr. Mildred Focht (New York, 1948).
Alexius Meinong, *On Assumptions*, tr. with an introduction by James Heanue (Berkeley, Calif., 1983).

HUSSERL

Logical Investigations, tr. J. N. Findlay, 2 vols. (London, 1970).
Ideas: General Introduction to Pure Phenomenology, tr. W. R. Boyce Gibson (London, 1931).
Cartesian Meditations: An Introduction to Phenomenology, tr. Dorion Cairns (The Hague, 1960).
The Crisis of the European Sciences and Transcendental Phenomenology: An Introduction to Phenomenological Philosophy, tr. David Carr (Evanston, Ill., 1970).

SCHLEIERMACHER

Hermeneutics: The Handwritten Manuscripts, ed. Heinz Kinmeste, tr. James Duke and Jack Forstman (Missoula, Mont. 1977).

DILTHEY

Introduction to the Human Sciences: An Attempt to Lay a Foundation for the Study of Society and History, tr. with an introduction by Ramon J. Betanzos (Detroit, 1988).

Pattern and Meaning in History: Thoughts on History and Society, ed. with an introduction by H. P. Rickman (New York, 1962).

Selected Writings, ed. and tr. with an introduction by H. P. Rickman (Cambridge, 1976).

HEIDEGGER

Being and Time, tr. John MacQuarrie and Edward Robinson (London, 1962).

For Heidegger's more relaxed essay-writing, see:

On the Piety of Thinking, tr. and ed. James G. Hart and John C. Maraldo (Bloomington, Ind., 1976).

SARTRE

Being and Nothingness: An Essay in Phenomenological Ontology, tr. with an introduction by Hazel Barnes (London, 1956).

Existentialism and Humanism, tr. with an introduction by Philip Mairet (London, 1948).

The following give a useful glimpse of Sartre's versatility:

The Emotions: Outline of a Theory, tr. Bernard Frechtman (New York, 1948).

What is Literature? And Other Essays (Cambridge, Mass., 1988).

Sartre's novels and plays are well known. Nothing that he wrote is more accomplished than his autobiography, *Les Mots* (Paris, 1964), which, however, loses everything in the English translation (*The Words*, tr. Bernard Frechtman (New York, 1964)).

5. MILL TO WITTGENSTEIN

GENERAL

Copleston, F. C., *A History of Philosophy*, vii and viii (London, 1966).

Passmore, J., *A Hundred Years of Philosophy* (London, 1957).

Warnock, G. J., *English Philosophy since 1900* (London, 1958).

Urmson, J. O., *Philosophical Analysis* (Oxford, 1956).

Kneale, W. and M., *The Development of Logic* (Oxford, 1962).

JOHN STUART MILL

Mill, J. S., *Collected Works of John Stuart Mill*, ed. F. E. L. Priestley, incomplete (Toronto, 1963–).

—— *A System of Logic* (repr. London, 1949).

—— *Autobiography*, ed. J. Stillinger (Oxford, 1971).

Anschutz, R. P., *The Philosophy of J. S. Mill* (Oxford, 1953).

Britton, K., *John Stuart Mill* (Harmondsworth, 1953).

Cranston, M., *John Stuart Mill* (London, 1958).

Packe, M. St John, *The Life of John Stuart Mill* (London, 1954).

Russell, B., *John Stuart Mill* (London, 1956).

Stephen, L., *The English Utilitarians*, iii (London, 1900).

FREGE

Frege, G. W., *Conceptual Notation and Related Articles*, ed. T. W. Bynum (Oxford, 1972).

—— *The Foundations of Arithmetic*, tr. J. L. Austin (Oxford, 1950).

—— *Collected Papers on Mathematics, Logic and Philosophy*, ed. B. McGuinness (Oxford, 1984).

—— *The Basic Laws of Arithmetic*, tr. M. Furth (Berkeley, Calif., 1967).

Anscombe, G. E. M., and Geach, P., *Three Philosophers* (Oxford, 1961).

Dummett, M., *Frege: Philosophy of Language* (London, 1973).
—— *The Interpretation of Frege's Philosophy* (London, 1981).
—— *Frege: Philosophy of Mathematics* (London, 1991).
Wright, C., *Frege's Conception of Numbers as Objects* (Aberdeen, 1983).

RUSSELL

Russell, B., *The Principles of Mathematics* (Cambridge, 1903).
—— *The Problems of Philosophy* (London, 1912).
—— *Mysticism and Logic* (London, 1918).
—— *Introduction to Mathematical Philosophy* (London, 1919).
—— *Logic and Knowledge*, ed. R. C. Marsh (London, 1956).
—— *Autobiography* (London, 1967).
Ayer, A. J., *Bertrand Russell* (London, 1972).
Hylton, P., *Russell, Idealism and the Emergence of Analytic Philosophy* (Oxford, 1990).
Pears, D. F., *Bertrand Russell and the British Tradition in Philosophy* (London, 1967).
Sainsbury, R. M., *Russell* (London, 1979).
Schilpp, P. A. (ed.), *The Philosophy of Bertrand Russell* (Evanston, Ill., 1946).

THE VIENNA CIRCLE

Ayer, A. J., *Language, Truth and Logic* (London, 1936).
—— (ed.), *Logical Positivism* (Glencoe, Ill., 1959).
Carnap, R., *The Logical Structure of the World*, tr. R. George (London, 1965).
Popper, K. R., *Logic of Scientific Discovery*, tr. J. and L. Freed (London, 1959).
Schlick, M., *General Theory of Knowledge*, tr. A. E. Blumberg (Vienna, 1974).
Waismann, F., *Ludwig Wittgenstein and the Vienna Circle*, ed. B. McGuinness, tr. J. Schulte and B. McGuinness (Oxford, 1979).
Bergmann, G., *The Metaphysics of Logical Positivism* (London, 1954).
Weinberg, R., *An Examination of Logical Positivism* (New York, 1936).

WITTGENSTEIN

Wittgenstein, L., *Tractatus Logico-Philosophicus*, tr. C. K. Ogden (London, 1922); tr. D. F. Pears and B. McGuinness (London, 1961).
—— *Philosophical Grammar*, ed. R. Rhees, tr. A. Kenny (Oxford, 1974).
—— *The Blue and Brown Books* (Oxford, 1958).
—— *Philosophical Investigations*, tr. G. E. M. Anscombe, 3rd edn. (London, 1958).
—— *Remarks on the Foundations of Mathematics*, ed. G. H. von Wright, R. Rhees, and G. E. M. Anscombe, 3rd edn. (Oxford, 1978).
—— *On Certainty*, ed. G. E. M. Anscombe and G. H. von Wright, tr. D. Paul and G. E. M. Anscombe (Oxford, 1969).
Anscombe, G. E. M., *An Introduction to Wittgenstein's Tractatus* (London, 1959).
Baker, G., and Hacker, P. M. S., *Scepticism, Rules and Meaning* (Oxford, 1984).
Hintikka, M. B., and Hintikka, J., *Investigating Wittgenstein* (Oxford, 1986).
Kenny, A., *Wittgenstein* (Harmondsworth, 1973).
Kripke, S., *Wittgenstein on Rules and Private Language* (Oxford, 1982).
Malcolm, N., *Nothing is Hidden* (Oxford, 1986).
Pears, D. F., *The False Prison*, i and ii (Oxford, 1988).
—— *Wittgenstein* (London, 1971).

6. POLITICAL PHILOSOPHY

Most of the philosophers discussed in this chapter appear also in earlier chapters, and further reading on them will be found there. This list offers supplementary reading specially devoted to their political philosophy. It also includes basic reading about philosophers not discussed elsewhere.

GREECE AND ROME

Barker, E., *Greek Political Theory* (London, 1918, 1960).
Sinclair, T. A., *A History of Greek Political Thought* (London, 1951).

PLATO

Annas, J., *An Introduction to Plato's* Republic (Oxford, 1981).
Popper, K., *The Open Society and its Enemies*, 4th edn., vol. 1 (London, 1963).
Saunders, T. J., *Plato's Penal Code* (Oxford, 1981).

ARISTOTLE

Aristotle, *The Politics*, ed. S. Everson (Cambridge, 1988).
Mulgan, R., *Aristotle's Political Theory* (Oxford, 1977).

STOICS, CICERO, AND SENECA

Reesor, M. E., *The Political Theory of the Old and Middle Stoa* (New York, 1951).
Cicero, *On the Commonwealth*, tr. and ed. G. H. Sabine and S. B. Smith (Indianapolis, 1976).
Wood, N., *Cicero's Social and Political Thought* (Berkeley, Calif., 1988).
Griffin, M. J., *Seneca: A Philosopher in Politics* (Oxford, 1976).

AUGUSTINE

Augustine, *The City of God*, tr. H. Bettenson (Harmondsworth, 1984).
Barrow, R. H., *Introduction to St Augustine, The City of God* (London, 1950).
Chadwick, H., *Augustine* (Oxford, 1986).
Deane, H. A., *The Political and Social Ideas of St Augustine* (New York, 1963).
Markus, R. A., *Saeculum: History and Society in the Theology of St Augustine* (Cambridge, 1970).

THE MIDDLE AGES

Burns, J. H., *The Cambridge History of Medieval Political Thought* (Cambridge, 1988).
McIlwain, C. H., *The Growth of Political Theory in the West* (London, 1932).
Murray, A., *Reason and Society in the Middle Ages* (Oxford, 1978).
Tierney, B., *Religion, Law and the Growth of Constitutional Thought 1150–1650* (Cambridge, 1982).
Ullmann, W., *A History of Political Thought in the Middle Ages* (Harmondsworth, 1965).

AQUINAS

Gilby, T., *The Political Thought of Thomas Aquinas* (Chicago, 1958).

DANTE, MARSIGLIO, AND OCKHAM

Dante, *De monarchia*, ed. G. Vinay (Florence, 1950).
——*Monarchy* and *Three Political Letters*, tr. D. Nicholl and C. Hardie (London, 1954).
Gilson, E., *Dante and Philosophy* (New York, 1963).
Holmes, G., *Dante* (Oxford, 1987).
Marsilius of Padua, *Defensor Pacis*, tr. A. Gewirth (New York, 1956).
McGrade, A. S., *The Political Thought of William of Ockham* (Cambridge, 1974).

WYCLIF

Daly, J., *The Political Theory of John Wyclif* (Chicago, 1962).
Kenny, A., *Wyclif* (Oxford, 1985).

THE MODERN WORLD

Macpherson, C. B., *The Political Theory of Possessive Individualism* (Oxford, 1966).
Plamenatz, J., *Man and Society*, 2 vols. (London, 1963).
Skinner, Q., *The Foundations of Modern Political Thought*, 2 vols. (Cambridge, 1978).

SIXTEENTH-CENTURY THOUGHT

Hexter, J. H., *The Vision of Politics on the Eve of the Reformation: More, Machiavelli, and Seyssel* (New York, 1973).
Skinner, Q., *Machiavelli* (Oxford, 1985).
Kenny, A., *Thomas More* (Oxford, 1983).
Hamilton, B., *Political Thought in Sixteenth-Century Spain: A Study of the Political Ideas of Vitoria, De Soto, Suarez and Molina* (Oxford, 1963).

SOVEREIGNTY AND NATURAL LAW

Edwards, C., *Hugo Grotius: The Miracle of Holland* (Chicago, 1981).
Franklin, J. H., *Jean Bodin and the Rise of Absolutist Theory* (Cambridge, 1973).
King, P., *The Ideology of Order: A Comparative Analysis of Jean Bodin and Thomas Hobbes* (London, 1974).
Bull, H., Kingsbury, B., and Roberts, A. (eds.), *Hugo Grotius and International Relations* (Oxford, 1992).

HOBBES

Hobbes, T., *Leviathan*, ed. C. B. Macpherson (Harmondsworth, 1968).
Gauthier, D., *The Logic of Leviathan* (Oxford, 1969).
Hampton, J., *Hobbes and the Social Contract Tradition* (Cambridge, 1986).
McNeilly, F., *The Anatomy of Leviathan* (London, 1968).
Peters, R. S., *Hobbes* (Harmondsworth, 1956).
Raphael, D. D., *Hobbes, Morals and Politics* (London, 1977).
Tuck, R., *Hobbes* (Oxford, 1989).

LOCKE

Locke J., *Two Treatises on Government*, ed. P. Laslett, 2nd edn. (Cambridge, 1968).
—— *Two Tracts on Government*, ed. Philip Abrams (Cambridge, 1967).
Dunn, J., *The Political Thought of John Locke* (Cambridge, 1969).
Seliger, M., *The Liberal Politics of John Locke* (London, 1968).

ROUSSEAU

Rousseau, J.-J., *The Social Contract* and *Discourses*, tr. G. D. H. Cole (New York, 1950).
Cobban, A., *Rousseau and the Modern State*, 2nd edn. (London, 1964).

PAINE AND GODWIN

Philp, M., *Paine* (Oxford, 1992).
Monro, D. H., *Godwin's Moral Philosophy* (Oxford, 1953).
St Clair, W., *The Godwins and the Shelleys* (London, 1989).

BURKE

Burke, E., *Reflections on the Revolution in France*, ed. C. C. O'Brien (Harmondsworth, 1969).
Kranmick, I., *The Rage of Edmund Burke* (New York, 1977).

Macpherson, C. B., *Burke* (Oxford, 1980).
O'Brien, C. C., *Burke's Great Melody* (London, 1992)

COLERIDGE

Coleridge, S. T., *On the Constitution of Church and State*, ed. J. Colmer (Oxford, 1976).
Calleo, D., *Coleridge and the Idea of the Modern State* (New Haven, Conn., 1966).
Colmer, J., *Coleridge: Critic of Society* (Oxford, 1959).

THE UTILITARIANS

Bentham, J., *The Works of Jeremy Bentham*, ed. J. H. Burns, J. R. Dinwiddy, and F. Rosen (London and Oxford, 1968–).
—— *An Introduction to the Principles of Morals and Legislation*, ed. J. H. Burns and H. L. A. Hart (London, 1982).
Dinwiddy, J., *Bentham* (Oxford, 1989).
Berger, F. R., *Happiness, Justice and Freedom: The Moral and Political Philosophy of John Stuart Mill* (London, 1984).

MARXISM

Avineri, S., *The Social and Political Thought of Karl Marx* (Cambridge, 1970).
Kolakowski, L., *Main Currents of Marxism*, 3 vols. (Oxford, 1981).
Popper, K. R., *The Open Society and its Enemies*, 4th edn., vol. 2 (London, 1963).
Singer, P., *Marx* (Oxford, 1981).
Lenin, V. I., *What Is To Be Done?* (Peking, 1975).
Femia, J., *Gramsci's Political Thought* (Oxford, 1981).

TOTALITARIANISM

Arendt, H., *The Origins of Totalitarianism* (New York, 1951).
Friedrich, C. J., and Brzezinski, Z., *Totalitarian Dictatorship and Autocracy* (Cambridge, Mass., 1965).
Hayek, F. A., *Road to Serfdom* (London, 1944).
Schapiro, L., *Totalitarianism* (London, 1972).
Zinoviev, A., *The Reality of Communism* (London, 1985).

ACKNOWLEDGEMENTS
OF SOURCES

The editor and publisher wish to thank the following, who have kindly given permission to
reproduce the illustrations on the following pages:

5   Mansell Collection, London
6   Landesmuseum, Trier
8   Giraudon
10 Mansell Collection, London
11 Mansell Collection, London
13 Rijksmuseum-Stichting, Amsterdam
14 Archiv für Kunst und Geschichte, Berlin
18 City of Bristol Museum and Art Gallery; photo: Bridgeman Art Library
23 Louvre, Paris; photo: Archiv für Kunst und Geschichte, Berlin
25 University of London/The Warburg Institute
29 Historical Museum of the City of Vienna
31 British Library, London: BL Royal 20Bxx 77^V
32 Vatican, Rome; photo: Archiv für Kunst und Geschichte, Berlin
34 Pisa, Italy; photo: Archiv für Kunst und Geschichte, Berlin
37 Private collection; photo: Christie's London
38 Louvre, Paris; photo: Archiv für Kunst und Geschichte, Berlin
41 British Library, London: BL Add 11912.2
44 Bodleian Library, Oxford
47 The Board of the Trustees of the Victoria and Albert Museum, London
50 Walker Art Gallery, Liverpool; photo: Mansell Collection, London
58 British Library, London: BL Add 10546 25^V
61 Chiesa d'Ognissanti, Florence; photo: Mansell Collection, London
64 Scientific American (Readings in Psychology, vol. II)

66 Hedlund & Rowley: Nelson, Atlas of the Early Christian World, p. 177 ill. 602
69 Private collection; photo: Christie's, London
71 Stadtsbibliothek, Bamburg
77 Bibliothèque Nationale, Paris (Cabinet des Médailles)
78 Vatican Apostolic Library: Vat. Lat. F32 219^V
81 Ancient Art and Architecture Collection, London
83 Musée Condé, Chantilly; photo: Giraudon
91 British Library, London
93 Giraudon
99 Bibliothèque Nationale, Paris
101 Gonville and Caius College, Cambridge: MS 464/571
103 Bodleian Library, Oxford
104 Krakow, Jagiellonian Library: MS 1771
108 Bodleian Library, Oxford: Byw c. 1 24
111 Uffizi Gallery, Florence; photo: Scala
114 The American Philosophical Society
115 Private collection, by kind permission of Madame Vieillard; photo: Ashmolean Museum, Oxford
118 Louvre, Paris; photo © R.M.N.
120 Archiv für Kunst und Geschichte, Berlin
122 Basilica S. Marco, Venice; photo: Alinari
123 Bodleian Library, Oxford
125 Archiv für Kunst und Geschichte, Berlin
127 Lolo Handke, Bad Berneck
128 Musée de l'Homme, Paris

131 Christ Church, Oxford
134 Ashmolean Museum, Oxford
141 Mansell Collection, London
146 Mansell Collection, London
148 Bodleian Library, Oxford: D. 4. 14. Art
152 Herzog Anton Ulrich Museum, Braunschweig; photo: Archiv für Kunst und Geschichte, Berlin
154 Archiv für Kunst und Geschichte, Berlin
156 Archiv für Kunst und Geschichte, Berlin
157 Giraudon
160 Private collection; photo: J. W. F. MacKenzie
164 Bridgeman Art Library
166 Archiv für Kunst und Geschichte, Berlin
170 Museo Bandini, Fiesole; photo: Archiv für Kunst und Geschichte, Berlin
174 Archiv für Kunst und Geschichte, Berlin
178 Bodleian Library, Oxford
182 Oskar Reinhart Foundation, Winterthur
188 British Library, London; photo: Bridgeman Art Library
194 Schiller National Museum, Marbach
195 University of Berlin; photo: Joachim Fisahn
198 Mansell Collection, London
199 Archiv für Kunst und Geschichte, Berlin
202 Hulton Picture Company
207 David King Collection, London
208 Phil Starling, London
210 Archiv für Kunst und Geschichte, Berlin

214 Schopenhauer Archiv, Stadt- und-Universitats-Bibliothek, Frankfurt am Main; photo: Archiv für Kunst und Geschichte, Berlin

215 Archiv für Kunst und Geschichte, Berlin

217 Archiv für Kunst und Geschichte, Berlin

219 Archiv für Kunst und Geschichte, Berlin

220 Archiv für Kunst und Geschichte, Berlin

222 Mansell Collection, London

223 Mansell Collection, London

224 Popperfoto

226 Popperfoto

229 Popperfoto

230 Balliol College, Oxford; photo: Nigel Frances

233 By kind permission of Freiburg University

235 Giraudon

237 Magnum, London

242 Image Select/Ann Ronan Picture Library

246 From *Judgements of Pure Thought* by Frege

247 Archiv für Kunst und Geschichte, Berlin

249 M. C. Escher/Cordon Art-Baarn- Holland

254 Camera Press, London

256 Magnum, London

258 Archiv für Kunst und Geschichte, Berlin

260 From *Protractatus*, an early version of *Tractatus Logico- Philosophicus* by Wittgenstein

263 Archiv für Kunst und Geschichte, Berlin

265 Archiv für Kunst und Geschichte, Berlin

268 Hulton Picture Company

271 Trinity College, Cambridge

278 Palazzo Pubblico, Siena; photo: Anderson

280 National Gallery, London

285 American School of Classical Studies at Athens

289 Museo Capitolino, Rome; photo: Archiv für Kunst und Geschichte, Berlin

290 Museo Nazionale Archeologico, Naples; photo: Archiv für Kunst und Geschichte, Berlin

293 Foto Fabbri

295 Musée de Bayeux; photo: Michael Holford

297 Badische Landesbibliothek

298 Private collection; photo: Christie's, London

300 Museo Petriano, Rome; photo: Anderson

302 Foto Fabbri

305 National Gallery of Art, Washington, DC: Samuel H. Kress Collection

306 San Silvestro, Rome; photo: Foto Fabbri

307 Foto Fabbri

311 Mansell Collection, London

315 Mansell Collection, London

316 British Library, London

320 National Portrait Gallery, London

322 Kunsthistorisches Museum, Vienna; photo: Archiv für Kunst und Geschichte, Berlin

327 Mansell Collection, London

330 Archiv für Kunst und Geschichte, Berlin

333 National Portrait Gallery, London

336 National Gallery of Ireland, Dublin

342 Mansell Collection, London

345 Mansell Collection, London

346 National Portrait Gallery, London

348 National Portrait Gallery, London

351 David King Collection, London

355 David King Collection, London

357 David King Collection, London

INDEX

Note: Page references in *italics* indicate illustrations and captions.

Abelard, Peter 82–5
  and Heloise *83*
  as teacher 85
  and universals 74, 82–4
Abraham, and sacrifice of Isaac 222, *223*
Absolute:
  in Hegel 201, 203, 206, 339, 341
  in Schelling 200
absolutism 277, 279, 327, 342
  and divine right of kings 308, 315–16, *315*, 319, 321, 323–4
  papal 301–3, 305–8
  of state 206, *316*
abstraction:
  in Boethius 74
  in Hegel 202–3
Academy, and Scepticism 45–6, 49
acquaintance:
  in Plato 65
  in Russell 255–7, 259, 261
Aegidius Colonna (Giles of Rome) 299, 301–3
aesthetics:
  in Croce 225–7
  in Hegel 216
  in Kant 169–71
  in Kierkegaard 221–2
  and modernism 354
  in Nietzsche 216
  in Schelling 200, 216
  in Schiller 200–1, 216
  in Schopenhauer 214–15, 216
  in Spengler 358
Alcibiades 281
Alcuin of York 74
Alexander I of Russia 323
Alexander of Aphrodisias 74
Alexander the Great:
  and Aristotle 30, *31*, 36
  empire 277, 281, 284, 286
alienation:
  in Fichte 198
  in Left Hegelianism 207
  in Marxism 201, 209–11, 360–1
  in Sartre 236
allegory, and Greek philosophy 9, 52
Althusius, Johannes 313–14, 317, 320
Ambrose of Milan, St:
  and Greek philosophy 57
  and state 291, 292
American Revolution, and Burke 337
Ammonius 49
analytic philosophy 239, 244, 276, 363–4, 365–6

  see also Frege, Gottlob; Russell, Bertrand; Wittgenstein, Ludwig
anarchism 224
Anaxagoras of Clazomenae 21
Anaximander of Miletus 6
Angst, in Heidegger 234
Anselm of Canterbury 59, 76–82, 87, 294
  Monologion 77–9
  ontological argument 79–82, 92, 187
  Proslogion 77, 80
  and reason 77–9
antinomianism, and Greek philosophy 20–1
antinomy of pure reason 182, 183–5
Antiochus of Ascalon 46
antipapalism 303–5
Antisthenes the Cynic 19, 22
anxiety, in Heidegger 234
Apollo, as intellect 218
appearance and reality 7, 14–17, 46
  in Fichte 196
  in Kant 169–71, 176–7, 180–1
apperceptions, in Kant 175–6, 177, 183, 204
appetition, in Leibniz 155
Aquinas, Thomas 88–92, *91*, *opp. 116*
  and Aristotle 30, 89, 91, 110, 299, 300–1
  and existence 90–2, 100
  and law 301, 304
  and plurality of forms 89–90
  and political philosophy 300–2
  and principle of identity 92, 97
  and theory of illumination 95
  and universal hylomorphism 89–90
  and universals 96
  see also God
Arcesilaus 45
argument, dialectic 181–3, 184–5
Arianism 48, 70
Aristippus of Cyrene 22
Aristo of Chios 40
aristocracy:
  in de Bonald 341
  in Greek city-states 279–81
  Roman 277–8, 288–9
  in Spinoza 319
  see also élites; oligarchy
Aristophanes, *The Clouds* 20
Aristotle 28–36, *29*, 46, 53, 204
  and beauty 27
  and categories 102, 172
  and change 60
  and earlier philosophers 7

  and knowledge 33–5, 65, 90
  and mathematics 17
  and medieval philosophy 30, 56–7, 89–90, 92–4, 100, 102–5, 279, 299, 300–1
  metaphysics 35
  and morality 5, 33, 36, 191
  and mythology 2
  and Plato 30, 32, 33, 286
  and political science 275, 323
  Politics 279, 284, 286, 299
  and qualities 34–5, 132, 133
  in Renaissance humanism *108*
  Sophistic Refutations 86
  translations 56–7, 70, 82, 86, 89, 299
  and universals 74, 97, 100
  see also explanation; logic; science; state; substance
arithmetic, *see* mathematics
Armitage, Edward *50*
Arnauld, Antoine 126, 153
Arnold, Matthew 276, 343
  and culture 343
art, *see* aesthetics
Athena *9*
Athens:
  as city-state 279
  fourth-century 18–19
atomism:
  in Democritus 12–14, *13*, 17
  empiricist 177–9
  in Epicurus 42
atomism, logical:
  in Russell 255
  in Wittgenstein 257–61, 264
Augustine of Hippo 55, 57–70, *66*
  City of God 282, 292, 299
  Confessions 60, 63
  and free will 62–3, 72
  and good and evil 60–2, 72
  and hierarchy of reality 59–62, 98
  and just-war theory 58
  and knowledge 63–5, 94
  and mutability of creatures 60, 67, 87, 90
  and Plato 57, 59
  and rhetoric 58–9
  and scepticism 63–5
  theory of illumination 76, 89;
    general 57, 63, 65–7, 69; problems 69–70, 94; special 67–9
Augustinian doctrinal complex 87–8, 89–90
authenticity, in Sartre 234
Avencibrol 87

Averroes (Ibn Rushd) 82
Avicebron 87
Avicenna (Ibn Sina) *81*, 82, 87, 90, 91
    and universals 98

Babeuf, François 224
Bacon, Francis 314
    and science 167, 347
    and secularization of philosophy *108*
Bakunin, Mikhail 354
Bauer, Bruno 207
Beauty:
    in Aristotle 27
    in Plato 22, 27
Beccaria, Cesare, Marchese de 327, 344
Beck, Jakob 193
behaviourism, and Wittgenstein 269
being:
    degrees of 59–60
    in Hegel 203–4
    and Thought 16, 75
belief, in Hume 161–2
Bentham, Jeremy 239
    and the Panopticon *345*
    political philosophy 319, 334, 343–4
    and utility 329, 343
Bergson, Henri 224–5, *224*, 356
    Time and Free Will 224–5
Berkeley, George 139–45, *141*, 180
    and abstract ideas 139–42, 158
    and existence of God 145
    qualities and ideas 142–4
    and religion 109
    and substance 136, 144–6, 240
    Three Dialogues 142–4
Bernstein, Eduard 352
Blackstone, Sir William 328, 343
Blum, Léon 362
Bodin, Jean:
    and contract theory 308
    and sovereignty 313
body:
    in Descartes 113, 119–20, 121–2
    in Platonism 52
    in Sartre 236–7
Boethius, Anicius Manlius Severinus
    56, 57, 70–4, *opp. 85*, 86, 294
    Consolation of Philosophy 70–1, 72
    and free will 72–3
    translations 70–1
    and universals 73–4, 84, 96, 100
Bolingbroke, Henry St John 321, 325,
    326, *327*, 343
Bonald, Louis de 341
Bonaventure, St 87, 92–6, *93*, *opp. 116*
    and Aristotle 89, 92–4
    and Augustine 89, 92
    and theory of illumination 94–6
Boniface VIII, Pope 299, *300*, 302
Bossuet, Jacques Bénigne 309, 319
Boswell, James, and Hume 158

Boyle, Robert 135
Bracton, Henry de 314
Bradley, F. H. 253, 341
Bradwardine, Thomas *148*
brain, split 136, *137*
Brentano, Franz 227–8
    *Psychology from an Empirical
        Standpoint* 227–8
British Library, reading room *208*
Buchanan, George 312
Buddhism, and substance 42
Bukharin, Nikolai Ivanovich 360
Buridan, Jean *104*, 105
    and impetus theory 103
Burke, Edmund 325, 334–7, *336*, 362
    and French Revolution 332, 334–7,
        342
Burley, Walter 96, 102
Butler, Joseph, and memory and
    consciousness 139
Byzantium:
    and Christianity 292
    and state 277, 291

calculus:
    infinitesimal 151
    predicate 39, 245
    propositional 39, 245
Calvin, John:
    and passive obedience 312
    and theocracy 292
Calvinism 311–12, 314
capitalism 209, 350–2, 355, 360
    and Fascism 356, 358–9
care, in Heidegger 234
Carlyle, Thomas 356
Carnap, Rudolf 262, 264
Carneades 45
Cassiodorus 84
categories:
    in Aristotle 102–3, 172
    deduction 172–4
    in Fichte 197
    in Kant 172–6, 180
    transcendental deduction 174–6
Catherine the Great of Russia 322
Cato the Censor 46
causation:
    in Descartes 60–1, 121
    and determination 165–6
    in Epicureanism 42
    in Fichte 197
    in Hume 162–6, *164*, 177, 179–80,
        273
    in Kant 175, 179–80, 182, 184–5,
        186–7, 189–90
    in Leibniz 155
    in J. S. Mill 241–3
    natural/free 186
    and necessary connection 162–3,
        165–7

in Spinoza 150
in Stoicism 39, 42
and time *170*
Chalcidius 56, 70
change:
    in Augustine 59–60
    in Burke 335–7
    in Comte 347
    in Kant 179–80
    in Marx 210–11, 350
    in Zeno of Elea 15
Charlemagne:
    and Carolingian Renaissance 74, 76
    and Holy Roman Empire 294–6,
        298
Charles I of England *315*, 317
Charles II of England, and Locke
    128–9, 321
Charles III of Spain 322
Charles the Bald, Emperor 74, 294
Chesterfield, Philip Dormer Stanhope,
    4th Earl 325
choice:
    in Aristotle 36
    in Epictetus 18
    in Kierkegaard 221–4
Chomsky, Noam 244
Christ Church, Oxford 128, *131*
Christian socialism 343, 356
Christianity 58
    and early modern philosophy 109
    in Kierkegaard 221–4
    and medieval philosophy 55, 56
    in Nietzsche 216, 219
    and paganism 49–52
    and political philosophy 277, 282,
        292–3
    and problem of identity 136–8
    see also Augustine of Hippo; church
        and state; papacy; Platonism
Christina of Sweden, Queen 126–7, *127*
Chrysippus 7, 39–40
church:
    national, in Coleridge 343
    positivist 224
church and state:
    in Aquinas 300–3
    in early Church 277, 288, 292–3
    in early modern world 308–9, 315–17
    in France 328
    and general Council 299, 303, 304,
        306, 307–8
    in Hobbes 318–19, 325
    in Locke 325
    in medieval philosophy 296–306
    in Reformation 310–12
    in Rousseau 330–1
Cicero 289
    and political philosophy 288–91,
        299
    and Stoicism 40–2, 57

citizenship:
  in Aristotle 285
  in Hegel 341
  in Locke 324
  in Stoicism 287
city-state:
  Greek 21, 276–7, 279–82, 284–6
  Italian 309, 310
  Roman 276–7, 281
civil society:
  in Greek philosophy 17, 51
  in Hegel 205–6, 340–1
  in Hobbes 317–19
  in Hume 326
  in Locke 325–6
  in Pufendorf 320
Civil War, English 317
class:
  in Aristotle 285
  in Fichte 339
  in Greek city-state 281, 295
  in Hegel 340–1
  logical 247–50, 252, 253
  in Marx 350–1
  in Plato 283–4
Cleisthenes 281, *285*
Clement V, Pope 302
Clement of Alexandria 4, 10, 43–5, 49
coexistence 180
cognition, intuitive 104
Coke, Edward 314
Cole, G. D. H. 361
Coleridge, S. T. *342*
  and conservatism 342–3
  influence 344
collectivism 353–4
Collingwood, R. G., on problems in
    philosophy 276
commitment:
  in Sartre 236–8
  to faith 221
communism:
  Soviet 353, 354–6
  Western 356
  see also Marxism
Comte, Auguste 224, 347
concepts:
  analytic of 171–4, 180, 196
  in Croce 225–6
  and existence 189
  in Frege 245
  in Hegel 202–4
  and images 140–2
  and judgement 172–6
  in Kant 225
  knowledge of 67–8
  in Moore 253
  of reason (ideas) 181–3
  transcendental deduction 174–6
consciousness:
  in Bergson 224–5

  in Brentano 228
  in Descartes 116, 117
  false 360
  in Hegel 205
  in Heidegger 233–4
  in Husserl 228
  in Kant 175–6
  in Locke 129, 138–9
  in Marx 209, 210
  and memory 139
  in Spinoza 150
consent, popular:
  in Cicero 289
  in early modern thought 312–13
  in Godwin 334
  in Hobbes 317–18
  in Hume 326
  in Locke 324, 349
  in medieval philosophy 299, 304,
    308–9
conservatism:
  post-Revolutionary 341–3
  see also Burke, Edmund
Constantine the Great 292, 296, 303,
    306
constitution:
  in Aristotle 285–6
  in Hegel 340
  in Paine 332
constitutionalism:
  in medieval philosophy 308, 316
  nineteenth-century 337–8, 341–3
contingents, future 72–3, 105
contract theory:
  in Democritus 17
  in early modern political
    philosophy 308, 309, 313–14
  in Greek philosophy 286–7
  in Hobbes 282, 308, 314, 318, 326–7,
    362
  in Hume 326
  in Kant 339
  in Locke 314, 320, 324–6, 362
  in Pufendorf 319–20
contradiction:
  in Hegel 202–3
  in Leibniz 153
  in Marx 211
  in Zeno of Elea 15
cosmology:
  in Aristotle *108*
  in Clement of Alexandria 43
Council of Constance 307, *307*
Counter-Reformation 109, 309
counterpositing, in Fichte 197
Crates of Thebes *37, 39, 52*
Critias 281
critical theory 360
criticism, in Nietzsche 217–18
Croce, Benedetto 225–7, *226*
  influence 361

Cromwell, Oliver 316–17, 321
culture 343, 353–4
  in Spengler 358
custom, and law 21, 288–9, 294, 313,
    314, 341
Cynics 36–9, 43
  and Christianity 48
  and political philosophy 287

Dante Alighieri:
  and antipapalism 299, 303–4, *305*
  on Aquinas 110
Darwin, Charles 338, 347–9
death:
  in Heidegger 234
  in Schopenhauer 214
deduction, in Kant 172–6
defence, and role of the state 279
democracy:
  in Bentham 344
  in de Maistre 341
  direct 281, 286
  and Fascism 356
  Greek 21, 281, 285
  liberal 353
  in J. S. Mill 345
  in Plato 283
  proportional representation 345
  representative 281, 332
  Roman 288–9
  in Rousseau 331–2, 362
  see also aristocracy; monarchy;
    oligarchy; tyranny
Democritus of Abdera 12, *13*, 14, 17
Descartes, René 36, 110–27, *118, 127, 128*
  and Cartesian circle 126–7
  and causation 60–1, 121
  Discourse on Method 110–12, 114, 122
  and doubt 114–16, *115*, 119
  and existence 116–20, 180
  and existence of God 122–6
  and Galileo 110, *111*
  and innate ideas 65–7, 68, 128–31
  and Kant 183
  and knowledge 64–8
  and light of nature 58
  and mathematics 110
  and matter 110, 145, 147
  Meditations 107, 114, 115–16, 117, *120*,
    124–6
  and mind and body 113, 119–20,
    121–2, *121, 122*, 147
  and ontological argument 79
  Passions of the Soul 121, 126–7
  and philosophical meditation *112*
  Principles of Philosophy 126, 147
  and qualities 132
  and religion 109
  and science 110–12, 113, 168, *opp. 181*
  and substance 147
  Treatise on Man 143

Descartes, René (*cont.*)
   and tree of knowledge *114*
descriptions, definite 253, 257
desire:
   in Hegel 204–6
   in Hobbes 317
   in Nietzsche 219
   in Schopenhauer 214–15
   sexual, in Sartre 236–7
   in Spinoza 150
   in Stoicism 287
despair, in Kierkegaard 222
despotism 277
   enlightened 321–3, 337, 344
   France 327–8
   tribal 353
Destiny, in early Greek philosophy 5
determinism:
   in Hume 165
   in Kant 186–7
   in Marx 352, 360
   in Western Marxism 360–1
dialectic:
   in Hegel 201, 202–6, 209, 339
   in Left Hegelianism 207
   in Marx 211, 350–2
   and Stoicism 46
   transcendental, in Kant 172, 181–2
   and Zeno of Elea 15
dialogue, in Dilthey 231
Diderot, Denis 322
Dilthey, Wilhelm 231–2
Diogenes the Cynic 36, 39, 43
Diogenes Laertius 4, 23, 45
Dionysus, as will 218
distinction:
   formal 99
   and unity 98, 99
dogmatism, and Fichte 196
Donation of Constantine 296, 303, *306*
doubt, methodological 114–16, 117, 119
dualism, in Descartes 113, 119, 121–2, 147
Duns Scotus, John 74, 98–100, *99*
   haecceity 100
   and theory of illumination 96
   and unity and distinction 99
duty, and good will 191–2

Earth Mother 3
Edict of Nantes *310*, 312, 319
education:
   aesthetic, in Schiller 200–1
   in Aristotle 286
   in Helvétius 329
   in J. S. Mill 345
   nineteenth-century growth 338
   in Plato 283, 284
   see also schools; universities
ego, in Husserl 229
Ehrenfels, Christian Freiherr von 227
Eikon Basilike 315

élites:
   in Burke 335
   in Fascism 356, 358
   in Hegel 340
   in Marxism 354
   in Milton 321
   in Pareto 357–8
   and the *philosophes* 329
   in Plato 283, 289, 340, 358
   in Saint-Simon 347
   and the Sophists 21
   in Spengler 358
   see also oligarchy
Elizabeth of the Palatine, Princess
   121–2, *123*, 126
emotions:
   in Hume 158
   in Spinoza 150–1
Empedocles of Agrigentum 7, 16, 19
empiricism:
   Greek 30–1
   in Hobbes 317
   in Hume 158–65
   and Kant 176, 185
   in Leibniz 151–8
   in Locke 128–39, 153, 326
   and Logical Positivism 261–2
   in Marx 209
   in J. S. Mill 239–43
   in Spinoza 147–51
Engels, Friedrich 211, 350, 352, 360
entelechies, in Leibniz 155
Epictetus 17–18, 36, 40, 47, 52, *242*
Epicureanism 40–3, 50
   political philosophy 286, 287
Epicurus 40–2, 286
Epimenides the Cretan 6
epistemology, *see* knowledge
equality:
   in modern political thought 317, 362
   in Stoicism 287, 288
Erastianism 296, 304
Eratosthenes 7
Eriugena, John Scottus 74–6, 294
   On the Division of Nature 76
Escher, M. C. 249
essence:
   and existence: in Aquinas 92–3; in
     Sartre 234–5, 364
   in Locke 135–6
ethics, *see* morality
Euclid:
   and Kant 171
   and J. S. Mill 243
   and Spinoza *148*
Europe, and medieval philosophy *96*
Eusebius of Caesarea 48
evil:
   in Augustine 60–3, 71–2
   in Boethius 72–3
   in Leibniz 156

   in Seneca 291
   see also free will
evolution:
   in Greek philosophy 6, 7
   and social science 347–9
   theory of 338
existence:
   in Aquinas 90–3, 100
   and causation 162–4
   in Descartes 116–20
   in Hegel 203–4, 232, 238
   in Heidegger 232–4, 236
   in Hume 161–4
   in Leibniz 153
   in Sartre 234–6
   in Schopenhauer 212–13
existentialism 363–4
   in Heidegger 232–4, 364
   in Kierkegaard 221
   in Sartre 234–6, 364
experience:
   in Aristotle 35
   in idealism 180, 200
   in Kant 175–6, 177, 179–81, 185, 338–9
   in J. S. Mill 243
   private 264
explanation:
   in Aristotle 7
   by cause/by reason 187
   and meaning 231
expression, and representation 225–7

faculties, in idealism 193
faith, and leap of faith 221, 222
fallacy, in Aristotle 86
falsifiability 262–3
family, in Hegel 206, 340
Fascism:
   and Nazism 358–60
   precursors 356–8
Ferguson, Adam 328
feudalism 210, 277, 294, 295
Feuerbach, L. 198, 201, 207
Fichte, J. G. 193, 194–8, *194*
   Addresses to the German Nation 195
   Critique of All Revelation 194
   and drama of the subject 197–8,
     204, 207, 211, 229, 238
   influence 211, 342
   and knowledge 197–8
   and positing of self 197–8, 204, 339
   and reason 339, 343
   Wissenschaftslehre 194–5
   see also nationalism; society
Ficino, Marsilio 56
Filmer, Sir Robert 309, 321, 323
foreknowledge, and free will 72–3
form and content:
   in Croce 226
   in Logical Positivism 262–4
form and matter 87–91, 169

forms:
  essential/accidental 91
  Platonic theory 248, 92–4
  plurality of 87, 88, 89–90
  substantial/accidental 89–90
Fortescue, Sir John 314
Fourier, Charles 350
Fox, Charles James *336*
franchise, extension 337
Franco, Francisco 353, 359
Frankfurt school 360
Frederick the Great of Prussia 322
free will:
  in Augustine 62–3, 72
  in Boethius 72–3
  in Hume 165–6
  in Leibniz 155–6
  and predestination 105
freedom:
  in Descartes 119
  in Fichte 197, 339
  in Hegel 205–6, 341
  in Kant 185–7
  in Leibniz 155–6
  in J. S. Mill 344–5
  in Milton 320
  in Paine 332
  in Sartre 234–8
  in Spinoza 150
  see also liberty
Frege, Gottlob *247*
  and analytic/synthetic propositions
    168
  and arithmetic 228
  Begriffsschrift 244, 245
  Grundgesetze der Arithmetik 244,
    245, 250–2
  Grundlagen der Arithmetik 244–6
  influence 239, 244, 258
  and mathematical logic 244–5, 255
  and philosophy of logic 245–6, 366,
    367
  and philosophy of mathematics
    246–52
  see also language
French Revolution:
  and Burke 332, 334–7
  and Kant 339
  and Rousseau 332
Freud, Sigmund 228

Galileo Galilei 34, 35, 109, 110, *111*, 319
  and qualities 132
Gassendi, Pierre 124, *125*
Gaunilo, and ontological argument
    80–2
Gelasius, Pope 303
geometry:
  in Frege *249*
  in Kant 171
  in J. S. Mill 243

  and Pythagoras 16
George I of Britain, and Leibniz 151–2
George III of Britain 323
Gerson, John 308
Gibbon, Edward 292
Giles of Rome (Aegidius Colonna)
    299, 301, 303
God:
  in Aquinas 90, 92, 158, 187, 190
  in Augustine 59–60
  in Berkeley 145
  in Boethius 72–3
  cosmological arguments for 187,
    189–90
  in Descartes 122–6, 157–8, 187, 190
  in Hebrew thought 9–12
  in Hellenistic philosophy 46–8
  in Kant 182, 187–90
  in Leibniz 156–9
  and nature 147
  ontological argument for 78–82, 92,
    122–6, 147–9, 187–90, 368
  physico-theological arguments for
    187, *188*, 190
  in Plato 27, 47
  in Pseudo-Dionysius 75–6
  as Pure Being 59–60
  in Schelling 200
  simplicity 67, 69, 87, 90
  in Spinoza 47, 147–9, 150–1
  in Stoicism 40, 43, 46–7
gods:
  in early mythology 2–4
  in Greek philosophy 5, 9–12, 24
Godwin, William 333–4, 342
Goethe, Johann Wolfgang von 217
good, in Augustine 60–2
Gorgias of Leontini 19
government:
  forms 284–6
  mixed 343
  representative 279
  resistance to 344
grace, and nature 70, 95
Gramsci, Antonio 361
Greeks:
  city-state 276, 277, 279–82, 284–6
  and early philosophy 4–5
  and Hellenistic philosophy 286–7
  inspired thinkers 9–17, 281
  and medieval philosophy 56–7
  in Nietzsche 216–18
  and religion 5–6
Green, T. H., on state 276, 331
Gregory I, Pope (the Great) 57
Gregory VII, Pope 296, *297*, 299
Gregory of Nyssa 52
Grosseteste, Robert 306–7
Grotius, Hugo 314, 317, 320
grounding principle, in Fichte 197
gymnosophists 39

haecceity:
  in Duns Scotus 100
  in Leibniz 153
Harrington, James, *Oceana* 321
Harvey, John 113
Hayek, Friedrich von 362, 375
Hegel, G. W. F. 193, 196, 198, 201–10,
    202
  and Absolute Idea 201, 203, 210,
    339, 360–1
  and aesthetics 216
  and being 203–4, 232, 236
  and civil society 206–10
  dialectic 201, 203–10, 339, 360–1
  Encyclopedia 201
  and Kant 201–2, 204, 206
  Lectures on Aesthetics 201
  and Marx 206–10
  and phenomenology 228
  Phenomenology of Spirit 201, 204
  Philosophy of Right 206
  political theory 340–1
  and reason 339, 356
  Science of Logic 202
  and universal history 201
  see also civil society; freedom;
    master and slave; morality;
    Schelling, Friedrich Wilhelm
    Joseph von; Schopenhauer,
    Arthur; spirit; state
Heidegger, Martin 198, 232–4, 364
  Being and Time 233–4
  and *Dasein* and *Existenz* 233–4, 236
  and Nazism 233
  and religion 234
  and time 225
Hellenism 45–8, 286–7
Helvétius, Claude-Adrien 327, 329,
    344
Henri IV of France *311*
Henry IV, Holy Roman Emperor,
  excommunication 296, *297*, 299
Heraclitus of Ephesus 12, 16, 17, 22,
  opp. 52
hermeneutics:
  in Germany 364
  in Schleiermacher 230
Hippocratic Corpus 30–1
history:
  in Fascism 359
  in Hegel 201, 209–10
  in Marx 210–11, 338, 350–3
  in Nietzsche 219–20
  in Schelling 209
  in Spengler 358
Hitler, Adolf 358–9
Hobbes, Thomas:
  and contract theory 282, 308, 314,
    318–19, 326–7
  Leviathan 316, 317–18
  and Locke 325

Hobbes, Thomas (*cont.*)
    on nation-state 277, 287, 362
Hölderlin, J. C. F. 216
holism, in Wittgenstein 259, 264–5
Holy Roman Empire, and papacy
        294–9, 298, 302–6
Hooker, Richard 314–16, 325
human nature:
    in Godwin 334
    in Kant 339
    in Locke 329
    in Wittgenstein 274
humanism, and medieval philosophy
        56
Hume, David 43, 158–66, *160*
    atheism 109, 158, 165
    and belief 161–2
    and causation 162–6, *164*, 177,
        179–80, 273
    contract theory 326–7
    *Dialogues Concerning Natural
        Religion* 158
    free will and determinism 165–6
    as historian 158
    and ideas and impressions 158–60,
        240, 259, 273
    political philosophy 326–7
    Treatise of Human Nature 158
    and utility 344
    see also meaning; memory
Hus, John 105
    and papacy 299, 308
Husserl, Edmund 228–32, *229*
    and Brentano 227, 228
    Cartesian Meditations 228, 229
    and Frege 244, *248*
    Ideas 228
    and intentionality 228
    and phenomenology 228–9, 231
    Philosophy of Arithmetic 228
    and science 229–30, 231
    and time 225
    Transcendental Phenomenology 229
hylomorphism, universal 87–8, 89,
        90

Iamblichus of Syria 6, 50, 52
Ibn Gabirol, Solomon 87
Ibn Rushd (Averroes) 82
Ibn Sina (Avicenna) *81*, 82, 87, 90, 91,
        98
ideas:
    abstract 139–42
    association of 162–3, 273
    as concepts of pure reason 181–3
    divine 67, 68, 69, 93, 94–5
    in Hobbes 317
    in Husserl 228–9
    and impressions 158–60, 161–2
    innate 65–7, 68, 128–32
    in Schopenhauer 213

simple/complex 159–60
sortal 135
Idea, Absolute:
    in Coleridge 342–3
    in Hegel 202–3, 206, 339
    in Schelling 200
ideal of pure reason 183, 187–90
idealism:
    in Berkeley 139–43, 180
    in Descartes 180
    in Fichte 196, 339, 342
    in Hegel 201–6, 210, 339
    neo-Hegelian 253
    refutation by Kant 180–2
    in Schelling 193, 198–200, 342
    in Schopenhauer 211–16
    transcendental 167–92, 196,
        198–200, 201–6, 211–16
identity of indiscernibles *154*
identity, principle of:
    in Aquinas 92, 97
    in Fichte 196–7
    in Locke 136–9
    in Schopenhauer 213
    in Wittgenstein 267, 272–3
ideology:
    in Marx 211
    in Pareto 357–8
illumination theory:
    in Augustine 57, 63, 65–7, 76, 87
    in Bonaventure 94–7
    general 65–7
    and knowledge 88, 89
    problems 68–70
    special 67–8
illusion:
    and scepticism 63–5, *64*
    and transcendental dialectic 181–3
images:
    and concepts 140–2
    and language 159–61
imagination:
    in Descartes 119
    and geometry *249*
    in Hume 159–61
    in Kant 176–7
imperative, categorical 191–2, 206
impressions, in Hume 158–60, 161–2,
        163, 259
inauthenticity:
    in Heidegger 234
    in Sartre 234, 236
India, gymnosophists 39
individual:
    in early modern philosophy 107–8
    in Fascism 358–9
    in modern philosophy 364
    and species 213
individualism:
    in Aristotle 35
    and collectivism 353

in de Maistre 341
in Spencer 347–9
individuation, problem of 97–8
    in Duns Scotus 100
    in Leibniz 213
    in Locke 135–6
    in William of Ockham 100–2
induction, in J. S. Mill 241–2
industrialism 337–8, 340, 349
    hostility to 343, 350, 361
inference:
    in Frege 245
    in Hume 273
    in Kant 181–2
    in J. S. Mill 240–1
infinity:
    in Bonaventure 94
    in Kant 184
    in Russell 252
intellect:
    in Aristotle 103
    in Duns Scotus 100
    in Nietzsche 218
    in Plotinus 48, 51–2
    in Schopenhauer 214
intentionality:
    in Brentano 227
    in Husserl 228
interpretation, in Schleiermacher 230
introspectionism, and Wittgenstein
        267–9
intuition 338
    in Aristotle 34–5
    axioms of 177
    in Bergson 356
    in Croce 225–7
    in Descartes 126
    and Fascism 356, 359
    intellectual 196–8
    in Kant 169–71, 175–7, 180–1, 196,
        225, 247
    in J. S. Mill 243–4
    of self 197
irrationalism, and political theory 356
Isidore of Seville 57
Islam, and medieval philosophy 55

Jakobson, Roman 365
James I, King of England 309, 314
Jaurès, Jean 361
Jefferson, Thomas 332
Jewish thought, early 49, 53
    idea of God in 9–12
Jews, medieval attitudes to 301, *302*
John Damascene 57
John the Evangelist 45
John of Paris 299, 303
John of Salisbury, *Policraticus* 299, 314
Johnson, Samuel 325
Joseph II of Austria 321–2, *322*
Jowett, Benjamin *230*

Judaism:
　and Hellenism 45
　medieval attitudes to 301, *302*
　and medieval philosophy 55
　and political philosophy 291–2
judgement:
　and concepts 172–6
　synthetic a priori 168, 175–7
　and understanding 175–6
Julian 'the Apostate' 49, *50*, 50–3
just-war theory 58, 314
justice 362
　in Cicero 291
　in Godwin 334
　in Plato 282–3
Justinian *opp.* 276
　codification of law 291
　and reconstruction of Roman
　　Empire 294

Kant, Immanuel 166–92, *167*
　as academic 108–9, 166
　analytic of concepts 171–4, 225
　analytic of principles 176–7
　analytic/synthetic judgements
　　167–9
　and categorical imperative 191–2,
　　206
　and contract theory 339
　Critique of Judgement 167, 200
　Critique of Practical Reason 167
　Critique of Pure Reason 167, 168,
　　174, 257
　and Descartes's theory of mind 113,
　　117
　and existence of God 187–90
　and Hegel 201–2, 204, 206
　and Hume 167
　influence 193, 194, 197, 339
　postulates of empirical thought
　　180–1
　a priori/a posteriori judgement
　　167–8, 169–71
　and religion 109
　and scholasticism 158
　and scientific method 167
　and synthetic a priori judgement
　　168–70, 172, 247
　and transcendental aesthetic 169–71
　and transcendental analytic 172
　and transcendental deduction of
　　categories 174–6
　and transcendental dialectic 172,
　　181–7
　see also intuition; mathematics;
　　morality; nature; noumena;
　　phenomena; reason;
　　Schopenhauer, Arthur; sensation;
　　understanding
Kautsky, Karl Johann 352
Kierkegaard, Søren 221–4, *223*, 365

and aesthetics 221–2
Concluding Unscientific Postscript
　221
Either/Or 221–2
Fear and Trembling 221, 222
and leap of faith 221, 222
see also morality
knowledge:
　a posteriori 130, 167
　a priori 130, 167–71, 172
　in Aristotle 33–4, 65, 90, 103
　in Augustine 63–70, 94–5
　in Bonaventure 94–6
　in Descartes 64–7, *114*, 116–17
　in Fichte 196–8
　in Hegel 202
　in Hobbes 317–18
　in Kant 167, 176, 181, 202, 212
　in Locke 128–30
　picture theory 361
　in Plato 65–7, 283
　and revelation 14, 70, 89, 94–5
　in Russell 255, 259–61
　in Schopenhauer 212
　and the Sophists 20
　tree of 113–4, *114*
　and universal hylomorphism 88
　and universals 73–4
　in Wittgenstein 269–70
　see also illumination theory

labour, alienation 201, 209–11, 360–1
labour theory of value 210–11, 351–2
Lambert, J. H., and phenomenology
　228
Lanfranc 76
language:
　and existence 90, 135–6
　in Frege 245–6, 365
　games 259, 264
　in Hume 161
　in Locke 135–6, 140
　and Logical Positivism 261
　picture theory 260–1, 270–4
　private 229, 267–70
　and rule-following 270–4
　in Russell 252–7, 261, 365
　and structuralism 365
　and thought 116, 367
　in Wittgenstein 229, 257–62,
　　267–74, 365
Laski, Harold 361
law:
　in Aquinas 301, 304
　in Aristotle 285
　common 314, 343
　divine 301, 304, 315
　in early Greek philosophy 5
　jus gentium 287, 313–14
　natural 288–9, 301, 313–18, 319–20,
　　324–6

in Plato 279, 283–4
in Roman Empire 287
statute 314
see also custom
Lebenswelt, in Husserl 229, 231
'Left Hegelians', and Marx 207
Leibniz, Gottfried Wilhelm 151–8, *152*
　and calculus 152, *156*
　and free will 155–6
　and God 155–7
　and identity of indiscernibles *154*
　and logic 153
　Monadology 153, 154–5
　and principle of individuation 213
　principle of sufficient reason 155
　Theodicy 153, *157*
leisure, in Hegel 205–6
Lenin, V. I. 354–5, *355*, 357, 358, 360
Leo III, Pope 298
Leo XIII, Pope 88
Levellers 317
liberation, in Spinoza 150–1
liberty 362
　in Hobbes 318
　in Locke 325
　in J. S. Mill 344
　in Montesquieu 328
　in Rousseau 331
　in Spinoza 319
　see also freedom
life, in Nietzsche 218–20
Locke, John 128–39, *131*, 362
　and abstract ideas 139–40, 158
　and contract theory 314, 320, 323–6,
　　362
　Essay Concerning Human
　　Understanding 129, 140
　and identity 136–9
　influence in France 327–8, 342
　and innate ideas 128–31
　political philosophy 323–6
　and primary and secondary
　　qualities 132–5, 142–4
　and state of nature 323–4, 327
　and substance 135–6, 138, 139
　Treatises on Government 129, 320,
　　323–4, 325
　see also consent; morality; property
logic:
　in Aristotle 31–3, 86, 245
　in Frege 244–50, 366, 367
　in Leibniz 151–3
　and linguistic analysis 252–7
　mathematical 171, 244–5
　in J. S. Mill 240–3, 262
　modal 245
　and philosophy 262
　philosophy of 245–6, 274
　and quantum theory 55
　in Russell 250–2, 255–7

logic (*cont.*)
  and Stoicism 39
  symbolic *246*
  tense 72–3, 245
  terministic 87
  transcendental 172
  truth-tables *260*
  and William of Ockham 102
  and Wittgenstein *260*, 262, 274, 367
Logical Positivism:
  and Verification Principle 262–3
  and Vienna Circle 262–4
  and Wittgenstein 262, 264
Louis XIV of France, and absolutism
    277, 309, 319
Louis XV of France 322, 327
love, in Schopenhauer 213
Lovejoy, A. O. 49
Lucretius, *The Nature of the Universe*
    41, 42, 287
Lukács, György 360
Luther, Martin:
  and passive obedience 292, 310
  and priesthood of all believers 304

Mach, Ernst 262
Machiavelli, Niccolò *opp. 277*, 304,
    309–10, 322
  Discourses 310
  The Prince 309–10
Maistre, Joseph Marie de 341
Malebranche, Nicolas, and theory of
    illumination 57
Manegold of Lautenbach *297*, 299
Manicheanism 57, 60
Marcus Aurelius *opp. 212*, 282, 287, 291
Marcuse, Herbert 360
Mariana, Juan de 312
Marius Victorinus 56
Marsiglio of Padua 299, 304, 306, 308
Marx, Karl 198, 206–11, *opp. 213*,
    349–53, *351*
  and aesthetics 216
  and base and superstructure 211,
    350–1
  Communist Manifesto 354–5
  edits *Rheinische Zeitung* 207, *207*
  and Hegel 206–10, 360
  and private property 209, 350
  and Schiller 201
  see also history; materialism
Marxism 363–4
  revisionist 352–3, 356
  Soviet 354, 356, 368
  Western 356, 360–2, 364, 368
  see also Marx, Karl
Masaryk, T. G. 227
master and slave, in Hegel 205, *opp.*
    213, 238
materialism:
  in Marx 209–11, 338, 350–2

monistic 40, 42
mathematics:
  as analytic 168
  in Frege 228, 244–5, 246–50
  and Greek philosophy 17, 26–7
  in Husserl 228
  in Kant 168, 247
  in medieval philosophy 103
  in J. S. Mill 168, 243, 247
  in Plato 283–4
  as a posteriori 168
  in Russell 168, 228, 252, 255
  as synthetic a priori 167, 171
  in Wittgenstein 274
matter:
  in Berkeley 144–5
  in Descartes 113, 147–9
  as extension in motion 113
  and form 87–8, 89–90, 91, 169
  in Hobbes 317
  in J. S. Mill 239–40
meaning:
  constancy 270–3
  and explanation 229–31
  in Hume 161
  and mind 266
  and reference 245–6
  and rule-following 270–4
  and structuralism 365
  and verification 262–3
medieval philosophy:
  dating 55–6
  decline in England 105
  and Greek philosophy 56–7, 277–8
  and theology 55, 77–9, 85, 92, 109,
    368
  as a tradition 107
Mediterranean, and early philosophy
    2, 2, 44
Meinong, Alexius 227, 253, 254
memory:
  in Bergson 225
  in Butler 139
  in Hume 160–1
Merleau-Ponty, Claude, and time 225
Merton Calculators *103*, 103, 105
metaphysics:
  and positivism 261–2
  transcendental 168
Mill, James 239, 319
  and utilitarianism 343
Mill, John Stuart 239–43, *242*
  and government 349
  and logic 240–3, 262
  and mathematics 168, 243, 246–7
  and the mind 239–40
  and names 240
  On Liberty 345
  On the Subjugation of Women 346
  Representative Government 345
  and social sciences 347

System of Logic 240–3, 347
  and utilitarianism *246*, 343, 344, 362
  see also tyranny, of the majority
Milton, John, political philosophy
    320–1
mind:
  in analytic philosophy 367
  in Augustine 63–70
  in Brentano 227
  in Descartes 117–21
  in Hobbes 317
  in Hume 158–62, 240
  and meaning of language 266
  in J. S. Mill 239–40
  in Spinoza 151
  and theory of illumination 68–9
  in Wittgenstein 266, 267–9, 270–4
  see also monism
modernism, and tradition 354
modernity, in Nietzsche 216, 219
monads, in Leibniz 154–5
monarchomachs 310–12
monarchy:
  in Aquinas 300
  constitutional 340
  in de Maistre 341
  and divine right of kings 309,
    315–16, *315*, 320–1, 323
  Germanic states 296–9
  in Harrington 321
  hereditary 277, 341
  mixed 321, 328
  national 308–9, 310
  right of resistance 299, 312–13,
    316–17
  and sovereign state 294
  see also absolutism; sovereignty
monism:
  materialist 40, 42
  in Spinoza 147–50
Montesquieu, Charles de Secondat,
    political philosophy 308, 328–9,
    339
Moore, G. E., and realism 253, *254*, 271
morality:
  in analytical philosophy 367
  in Aristotle 5, 33, 36, 191
  in Hegel 206, 236, 340
  in Helvétius 329
  in Kant 190–2, 339
  in Kierkegaard 221–4
  in Locke 325, 329
  in Nietzsche 218–19
  and politics 288–91
  and religion 221–4
  in Rousseau 331–2
  in Sartre 234–5, 236
  in Stoicism 5, 287
More, Sir Thomas 309, 310, 349
Morris, William 343, 361
Moses 48, 58

motion, impetus theory 103
music:
    in Kierkegaard 221
    and philosophy 215
    in Schopenhauer 215
    and Wagner 217–18
Musil, Robert 228
Mussolini, Benito 353, 357, 359
myth, in Sorel 356
mythology:
    and philosophy 9
    rise 1–3

Nagel, Thomas 369
names:
    in Frege 245–6
    in J. S. Mill 240
    in Russell 253, 255–7, 258, 259
    in Wittgenstein 258, 259–61, 270
Napoleon Bonaparte 323, 341
nation-state:
    emergence 294
    in Hegel 340–1
    in Hobbes 277
nationalism:
    and Fascism 356, 358–9
    and Fichte 195, 340, 343, 356, 359
    Islamic 353–4
    and Rousseau 331–2
nature:
    and God 147
    and grace 69–70, 94–5
    and individual 213
    in Kant 186–7, 200
    in Romanticism 338–9
    in Spinoza 147, 150
    state of 313, 317–18, 319–20, 324, 325,
        329
Nazism, and Fascism 358–60
necessity:
    in Boethius 72–3
    in Hume 162–5
    in Kant 167, 187–90
    in Marx 350
    in Spinoza 150–1
    see also truth, necessary
neo-Hegelianism 253
Neoplatonism 49–50
    and medieval philosophy 57, 60, 87,
        294
Neurath, Otto 262, 264
Newman, John Henry, and culture 343
Newton, Isaac 151, 328
Nicholas V, Pope 307
Nicholas of Autrecourt 104–5
Nicholas of Cusa 308
Nietzsche, Friedrich Wilhelm 216–21,
    217, 220
    Birth of Tragedy 216–18
    and eternal recurrence 219–20
    and Fascism 356

and Hegel 218
and intellect and will 218
Joyful Wisdom 218
and philosophy 218–19
Thus Spake Zarathustra 218
and *Übermensch* (Superman) *219,*
    219–20, 356, 359
see also morality; Schopenhauer,
    Arthur
nominalism 26
    and J. S. Mill 240
    in William of Ockham 100–2
    in Wittgenstein 270, 273
noumena, in Kant 180–1, 187, 229,
    338–9
numbers, natural:
    in Frege 248, 250
    in Russell 252

Oakeshott, Michael 362
obedience, passive 292, 297, 312, 315–17
object:
    in Fichte 197–8, 229
    in Frege 245
    in Hegel 232
    in Heidegger 232–4
    in Husserl 229
    in Marx 209
    in J. S. Mill 239
    in Russell 259–61
    in Sartre 234–8
    in Schopenhauer 212
    in Wittgenstein 258–61, 266–7, 270
objectification, in Marx 209
obligation, political 279, 312
    in Christianity 292
    in Hobbes 318, 362
    in Rousseau 362
    see also contract theory
obscenity, in Sartre 237
oligarchy:
    in Greek political philosophy 281,
        283–4, 286
    in Milton 320
    see also aristocracy; élites
opposition, in Fichte 197
Origen 49
Orwell, George 361
other, in Sartre 236–8
Owen, Robert 349–50

paganism and Christianity 48, 49–53
Paine, Thomas, *Rights of Man* 332, 333
Panaetius of Rhodes 288
pantheism, and identity principle 92
papacy:
    antipapalism 303–6, 308
    corruption 302, 306–8
    in de Maistre 341
    and Holy Roman Empire 295–300,
        297, 298, 302–6

paralogisms of pure reason 183
Pareto, Vilfredo 357–8
Parmenides *opp. 52*
    and being 76
    and change 59
    and truth 14–16
party, in communism 354–5, 361–2
patristics 57
perception:
    anticipations of 177
    in Berkeley 142–4
    in Descartes 119, *122,* 132–3
    in Leibniz 155
    in Locke 133–5, 142–3
Peripatetic School 30, 46
Petrarch (Francesco Petrarca) 313
Phaedo of Elis 22
phenomena:
    in Heidegger 232
    in Kant 180–1
    mental: in Brentano 227–8, 232; in
        Husserl 228
    in Schopenhauer 212
phenomenalism:
    in Berkeley 145
    and J. S. Mill 240
phenomenology:
    in Heidegger 232–4
    in Husserl 228–9, 231
    in Sartre 238
Philip the Fair, King of France 299,
    303
Philo of Alexandria *44,* 45, 46–9, 51
    and allegory 9
    and divine ideas 67, 92
Philo of Larisa 46
philosophy:
    analytic, *see* analytic philosophy
    Greek, *see* Greeks
    medieval, *see* medieval philosophy
    political, *see* political philosophy
    and science 269, 274, 366–7
    and theology, *see* theology
Pindar 9
Pitt, William 323
Plato 22–8, *23,* 44–5
    allegory of the cave 25
    and Aristotle 23, 30, *32,* 33–5
    and city-state 279
    and Democritus 12
    and the Earth 3
    Gorgias 282
    and the just ruler *280*
    Laws 23, 282, 283–4, 285
    in medieval philosophy 56, 279
    as moralizer 5
    and Parmenides 15
    Parmenides 28, 285
    Republic 279, 281, 282–4, 285, 310,
        349
    and the Sophists 18

Plato (*cont.*)
  Statesman 282, 283–4
  theory of forms 25–8, 92–4
  theory of reminiscence 65–7
  Timaeus 56, 70, 89
  see also Aristotle; Augustine;
    knowledge; mathematics;
    Socrates; soul; state; universals
Platonism 24–6
  and Christianity 44, 45, 48–50
  Pythagorean 16–17
play, in Schiller 200–1
Plekhanov, Georgi Valentinovich 211,
  354
Plotinus 26, 45, 46, 48, 49–53
  in medieval philosophy 56, 70
Plutarch, and early stories 9–10
Polemo 45, 46
political philosophy:
  definition 276–7
  problems in 278–9
  Western tradition 276–8
Pope, Alexander 140, 325
Popper, Karl 262–3, 363
Porphyry 26, 45, 49, 52, 53, 70
  and universals 73, 82–4, 97
Posidonius 39–40, 46
positivism:
  in Comte 224
  logical, *see* Logical Positivism
possibility:
  in Kant 187–9
  in Leibniz 155–8
post-structuralism 365
poverty:
  in Aquinas 301
  evangelical 303, 3-5
  and industrialization 347, 349–50
powers, separation of 33, 304, 324–5,
  339, 343
predestination, and free will 105
predication:
  in Abelard 84
  in Aristotle 74, 97, 172
  and plurality of forms 88, 90
prehistory, and earliest philosophy
  1–7
Price, Richard 334
principles, in Kant 172, 176–7, 180
process, time as 225
process philosophy 225
Proclus 55
production, relations of, in Marx
  209–11, 350–1, 354
progress:
  in Marx 211
  rejection of 358
  and social science 347
  in Whig history 5
proletariat:
  development 337–8

in Lukács 360
and Marxism 350–2, 355
property, private:
  in Aquinas 301
  in Aristotle 286
  church's right to 303, 305–6, 307–8
  in early modern thought 313
  in Fascism 358–9
  and growth of state 353
  in Hegel 209
  in Hume 326
  in Locke 324, 349
  in Marx 209, 350
  in Pufendorf 319
  in Seneca 291
  in Stoicism 39
propositions:
  analytic/synthetic 130, 167–71, 176,
    183, 187–9, 240
  existential 188–9
  mathematical 243
  in J. S. Mill 240–1, 243, 262
  necessary/contingent 153
  in Ockham 102
  a priori/a posteriori 167–8, 183
  in Russell 253–7
  verification 262–3
Protagoras 19, 20–1
Protestantism:
  and papacy 299
  and philosophy 109
  and political philosophy 292, 309,
    310–12, 314–16
  and religious association 304
Proudhon, Pierre Joseph 224, 350
Proust, Marcel, and time 225
Pseudo-Dionysius the Areopagite 70,
  75–6, 87
psychology:
  in analytic philosophy 366–7
  in Brentano 227
  empirical/rational 183, 227–8
  in Nietzsche 219
  in Plato 22–3
Pufendorf, Samuel 319–20
Pyrrho of Elis 22
Pythagoras of Samos 7, 14, 15–16, 26,
  opp. 52
  and mathematics 16, 17, 25
  and reform 17

quaestio format 85
qualities, primary/secondary 35, 132–5,
  142–4
quantification theory, in Frege 244–5
Questions of King Milinda 42

racism, and Fascism 359
rationalism:
  in Descartes 110–27, 128–9, 130
  in Hobbes 319

in Kant 166–92
in Leibniz 151–8
in Locke 325–6
and romanticism 182
universalistic 328
Raymond of Sauvetât 82
realism:
  and meaning 270, 273–4
  moderate 74, 96–7
  Platonic 26, 39
  strong 97
  and universals 74, 82–4, 87, 97, 102,
    105
reality:
  and appearance, *see* appearance and
    reality
  social, in Husserl 229
reason:
  antinomy of pure reason 182–5
  in Cicero 291
  in Greek philosophy 4–7, 15, 21, 43,
    51
  in Hegel 202–3, 356
  ideal of pure reason 181–2, 187–90
  in Kant 168, 181–7, 190–2, 202, 339
  metaphysical 339
  necessary 77–8
  paralogisms of pure reason 182–3
  and politics 347
  practical 190–2, 193, 212, 230
  and revelation 89, 94–5
  sufficient 155
  see also understanding
reasoning, deductive 241
recurrence, eternal 219–20
redistribution 334
reference, in Frege 246
Reformation:
  and political philosophy 309
  see also Protestantism
Reichenbach, Hans 262
religion:
  civic 331
  and Greek philosophy 5–6
  see also Christianity; Judaism
Renaissance 30, 306–7, 309, 310
renunciation, in Schopenhauer 213–16
representation:
  in Augustine 63–7
  in Croce 226
  in Nietzsche 218
  in Schopenhauer 213
representation, political, *see*
  democracy
republicanism:
  'crowned' 323, 356
  in Kant 339
  in Montesquieu 328
  in Paine 332
  Roman 281–2, 288
  in Sidney 321

resistance, right of 297–9, 312–14, 317–18, 324, 339, 344
ressentiment, in Nietzsche 219
revelation:
    and knowledge 15, 70, 89, 94–5
    and law 315
revolution:
    in Godwin 334
    in Kant 339
    in Lenin 354–6
    in Marx 211, 350–3, 360
    in Western Marxism 361, 362
Revolutions, Year of *210*, 338
Reinhold, Karl 193, 196
rhetoric 33, 58–9, 281
Ricardo, David, and Marx 209, 351
rights:
    civil 332
    human 288
    legal 344
    in Locke 324, 325–6
    natural 279, 318, 320–1, 332, 341, 344
    in Paine 332
    in Rousseau 331
Robespierre, M. M. I. de 224, *343*
Roman Empire:
    decline and fall 277–8, 292, 294
    and political philosophy 277–8, 281–2, 287–92, 300, 302
romanticism, German *182*, 223, 227, 229–30, 338–40
    see also Fichte, J. G.; Hegel, G. W. F.; Heidegger, Martin; Nietzsche, Friedrich Wilhelm; Schelling, Friedrich; Schopenhauer, Arthur
Rousseau, Jean-Jacques 329–32, *330*
    and civic religion 331
    and general will 329–32, 335
    and Hume 158
    and Plato 284
    and property 310, 326
    Social Contract 329–31, 339, 362
    see also morality
rule:
    and language use 270–3
    and mathematics 274
ruler, just *280*
Ruskin, John, and industrialism 343
Russell, Bertrand 256, 278, 365
    and Frege 244
    and linguistic analysis 252–7, 258
    and logical atomism 255
    and mathematics 168, 228, 250–2, 255
    'On Denoting' 253
    Paradox 250–2
    Principia Mathematica 250, 251
    and semantics 259
    and socialism 361
    and Spinoza *146*
    Theory of Types 255, 261

    see also logic; names
Ryle, Gilbert 268, *366*

Saint-Simon, C. H. de R. 209, 224
    and science 347, 349
Salome, Lou *220*
Sartre, Jean-Paul 234–8, *235*, *237*, 364
    Being and Nothingness 234–5
    Existentialism and Humanism 235, 236
    see also morality
Saussure, F. de 365
Scaevola, Mutius *134*
Scepticism:
    'Academic' 45–6, 48
    and Augustine 63–5
    and Cartesian doubt 114–16
    Pyrrhonian 7, 43, 46
Schelling, Friedrich Wilhelm Joseph von 193, 198–200, 342
    and aesthetics 200–1, 216
    and Hegel 200, 201
    and history 209
    positive and negative philosophy 201
    System of Transcendental Idealism 198
    and transcendental subject 198–200
Schiller, J. C. F. von 194, 199, 200–1, 209
    and aesthetics 200, 216
Schleiermacher, Friedrich Daniel Ernst 230–1, *230*
Schlick, Moritz 262, *263*, 264
Scholasticism 363–4
schools:
    cathedral 74, 82, 85
    monastic 74, 82, 83, 84–5, 107, 299
    see also education
Schopenhauer, Arthur 193, 197, 198, 211–16, *214*
    and aesthetics 214–15
    character 215–16
    and Hegel 211, 216, 356
    and Kant 212, 216
    and music 214–15
    and Nietzsche 216, 218
    pessimism 213–16
    and sexual love 213
    and will 212–16
    World as Will and Representation 212
Schutz, Alfred 232
science:
    and Aristotle 28–31, *34*, 35, 65, 105–6, 110
    'human' 231, 347–9
    and Husserl 230, 231
    and Logical Positivism 262–4
    and philosophy 269, 274, 366–7
    and politics 347–50

    and Schleiermacher 230
    and Wittgenstein 267, 274
science, cognitive 367
science, political 275
scripture, authority 109
self:
    in Hegel 204–6
    in Hume 240
    in Marx 209
    and not-self 197
    and other 205–6
self-consciousness:
    in Fichte 196–7, 204, 339
    in German romanticism 193
    in Hegel 204–6, 232
    in Heidegger 232–3
    in Husserl 228–9
    in idealism 196
    in Kant 175–6, 183, 196
    in Locke 138–9
    in Sartre 234–8
    in Schelling 198–202
self-determination:
    in Fichte 197–8
    in Hegel 205
    in Kant 186
Seneca, Lucius Annaeus:
    and Epicurus 40
    and medieval philosophy 56
    political philosophy *290*, 291
    and the Sophistic movement 17
sensation:
    in Augustine 63–4, 88
    in Berkeley 143–4, 239
    in Descartes 119, 121
    in Hobbes 317
    in Hume 158
    in Kant 169, 172, 177, 338–9
    in Locke 133–5
    in J. S. Mill 239–40
    in Wittgenstein 267–70
sense, in Frege 246
sensibility:
    and transcendental aesthetic 169–71
    and understanding 168–9, 172, 181, 212
sentence:
    in Frege 259
    in Russell 259, 261
    truth-value 246, 257
    in Wittgenstein 259–62, 264–6, 270
set theory, in Frege 245
Seven Sages *8*
Sextus Empiricus *8*
sexuality:
    in Sartre 236–7
    in Schopenhauer 213
Shaftesbury, Anthony Ashley Cooper, 1st Earl 129, 321
shame, in Sartre 236
Shaw, George Bernard 356, 361

Sidney, Algernon 321, 323–4
Sky Father 3, 9
slave and master, in Hegel 205–6, 238
slavery:
　in Aquinas 301
　in Aristotle 36, 284–5, 301
　in Bodin 313
　in Locke 324, 329
　in Montesquieu 329
Smith, Adam 158, 209, 362
social democracy 352, 354, 361–2
socialism:
　Christian 356
　development 337–8, 349–50
　evolutionary 352
　Fabian 356
　Guild 356
　and Marx 349–53
　and Saint-Simon 347
society:
　in Burke 335–7
　in de Maistre 341–2
　in Fichte 340
　mass 338
　in Paine 332
　in Rousseau 335, 340
　and the Sophists 17
　and state 313, 314
sociology:
　in French philosophy 224, 328
　phenomenological 232
Socrates 18–20, *opp. 21,* 36, 45–6, *opp. 52,* 281
　modern knowledge of 7
　and Nietzsche 218
　and Plato 18–19, 22–3, 282
solipsism, in Wittgenstein 266–70
Sophists 17–20, 281, 282
sophistry 17–18
Sorel, Georges 356–7, 359
Sorge (care), in Heidegger 234
soul:
　in Aquinas 90, 92
　in Augustine 59
　in Descartes 121–2, *122*
　immortality 92–5, 151
　and individuation 137
　in Kant 182, 183
　in Leibniz 155
　in Philo of Alexandria 51
　in Plato 25, 26, 65–7
　pre-existence 65–7
　in Spinoza 151
　and substance 88
sovereignty 279, 313–14
　of general will 329–31
　in Hobbes 318
　in Locke 325
　popular 325
　in Pufendorf 319–20
space, in Kant 169–70, 184

Spencer, Herbert:
　and evolutionary theory 338, *348,* 349
　and government 349
Spengler, Oswald 277, 328, 358
Spinoza, Baruch 146–51, *146,* 154, 203
　and emotions 150–1
　Ethics 107, 147, 149, 150, 151
　and God 45, 147–50, 151
　and liberation 150–1
　and monism 147–50
　and religion 109, 319
　and state 319
　Tractatus Theologico-Politicus 148
　see also nature; necessity
spirit:
　in Hegel 207, 209–10, 228, 341, 360
　universal 200, 209–10
Sprat, Thomas 7
Stalin, Josef 355, *357,* 358, 360–1
state:
　in Aristotle 33, 277, 284–6, 362
　collectivist 354, 361
　corporate 359
　in de Maistre 341
　dynastic 308–9
　in Epicureanism 287
　in Fichte 339
　forms 276–7
　functions 277
　in Hegel 206, 341
　in Hobbes 318–19, 362
　in Kant 339
　in Machiavelli 309–10
　in Marx 350
　in Montesquieu 328–9
　in Plato 279, 282–4, 362
　in political philosophy 276, *278,* 278–9
　in Rousseau 331–2
　in Spinoza 319
　see also church and state; contract theory; law; totalitarianism
statements, protocol 264
Stirner, Max, *The Self and its Own* 224
Stoicism 39–43, 45, 50
　ethics 39–40, 43, 45
　metaphysics 40, 43, 46
　and morality 5, 287
　and political philosophy 287, 288–9
　and truth 33
stories:
　oral 1–3, 5–7
　as 'philosophical' 9
　written 3–4
structuralism 365
Stuart, Charles Edward 323
Suarez, Francisco de 312–13
subject:
　in Sartre 234–8
　as self-conscious 193, 197–8, 204–6, 207–9, 232–3

transcendental 198–200, 212, 228–9
　in Wittgenstein 266–7
subjectivity, in Kierkegaard 221, 229
subordinationism 46
substance:
　in Aquinas 89–90, 92
　in Aristotle 35, 103
　in Berkeley 136, 144–6, 240
　in Descartes 110, 147
　in Epicurus 42
　in Kant 177–9
　in Leibniz 154–5
　in Locke 135–6, 138, 139
　in Spinoza 147–9
suicide:
　in Kant 192
　in Plotinus 53
　in Schopenhauer 214
Superman (*Übermensch*), in Nietzsche 218, 219, 356, 359
supposition, personal 102
surplus value theory 351–2
Swift, Jonathan 140, 325
syllogistic theory 86
Symmachus 70, *71*
syntax 245

Tawney, R. H. 361
taxation:
　in Bodin 313
　in Locke 324, 349
Thales of Miletus 10, 12, 26
theocracy 296
　in Judaism 292
　in Protestant Reformation 292, 312
theology:
　and early modern philosophy 109
　and Greek philosophy 12
　and medieval philosophy 55, 77–9, 85, 92, 109, 368
　natural, and Hume 160
Theophrastus 7
theory, political 275–6
　Greek 281
thought:
　and Being 15
　in Descartes 116–20, 183
　in Hegel 201–2, 204
　and language 113, 365–7
　in Locke 129
　and understanding 172
Thucydides 21
time:
　in Bergson 225
　and causation 170, 179–81
　and foreknowledge 72–3
　in Hegel 204
　in Kant 169–71, 177–80, 184
　in Spinoza 151
Tocqueville, Alexis de 345
tolerance, religious 319, 321

in Locke 324–5
totalitarianism:
    and growth of state 353
    and Rousseau 331–2
Toynbee, Arnold 277
tradition:
    in Burke 335
    and modernism 354
translation, and meaning 270–2
Trinity College, Cambridge 271
Trotsky, Leon 355
truth:
    in Augustine 64–5
    in Greek philosophy 7, 8, *11*, 12–24,
        26, 30, 33, 43, 46, 49–51
    in Kierkegaard 221
    necessary 153, 243, 262–3
    in Parmenides 14–16
tyranny:
    in Aquinas 301
    of the majority 331, 345
    in Plato 283–4
    and right of resistance 312

Ulpian (Domitius Ulpianus) 300
understanding:
    and experience 175, 180
    in hermeneutic school 364
    and judgement 176
    and reason 181, 231, 338–9, 342
    and sensibility 168–9, 172, 181, 212
unity:
    and distinction 97–9
    real minor 98–9
universalization, in William of
        Ockham 101
universals:
    in Abelard 74, 82–4
    in Aquinas 97
    in Aristotle 73–4, 97, 100
    in Avicenna 98
    in Boethius 73–4, 82–4, 97–8, 100
    in Duns Scotus 98–9
    in Plato 272
    in Porphyry 73, 82–4, 97
    and unity and distinction 97
    in William of Ockham 97, 101–2
    in Wyclif 105
universities, and medieval philosophy
        84–6, 107, 299
utilitarianism 343–6
    in Bolingbroke 325

in Godwin 334
in J. S. Mill *242*, 343, 345, 362
utility:
    in Helvétius 329, 344
    in Hobbes 326–7
    in Hume 344
    in J. S. Mill 345
Utopia, in More 311, 349

Valla, Lorenzo *306*
Verification Principle 262–3
Verstehen, in Dilthey 231
Vico, Giambattista 328
Vienna Circle 262–4
    and language 261–2
Vindiciae contra tyrannos 312, 320
virtue:
    cardinal 283
    civic 310, 328
    heroic 218–19, 356–7, 358
Voltaire, F. M. A. de 325
    Candide *157*, 159
    and church and state 328
    and enlightened despotism 322

Wagner, Richard 215
    and Nietzsche 216, 217, 218
    and Schopenhauer 216
Waismann, Friedrich 262
Walpole, Robert 325, 328
Weber, Max 232
welfare, and role of the state 277,
        332–4, 353–4, 362
Wells, H. G. 323, 356
Whitehead, A. N. 193, 225
    Principia Mathematica 250, 251
will:
    in Descartes 119
    general: in Kant 339; in Rousseau
        329–32, 339
    in Hegel 205–6
    in Hume 165–6
    in Kant 186–7, 190–2
    in Marx 209
    and morality 190–2
    in Nietzsche 218
    in Schelling 200
    in Schopenhauer 212–16
William III of England 129, 323
William of Champeaux 82–4, 85, 97
William of Ockham:
    and logic 102

and nominalism 101–2
and papacy 299, 302, 304–6, 314
and state 304–6
and substance and quality 102
and universals 97, 101–2
Winckelman, J. J. 217
Wittgenstein, Ludwig *opp. 244, 258,
        260, 265, 271*
    and analytical philosophy 239,
        365–7
    and Descartes's theory of mind 113
    and Frege 244, 246
    and holism 259, 264, 270
    and language-games 259, 271
    and Logical Positivism 262–4
    and meaning 270–2
    Philosophical Investigations 266,
        267, 272, 274
    and philosophy of mathematics 274
    and picture theory of language *260,
        260–1, 270*
    and private language 229, 267–70
    *Remarks on the Foundations of
        Mathematics* 274
    Thesis of Extensionality 261
    Tractatus Logico-Philosophicus
        257–62, *260*, 264–6, 269, 270–2
    see also mind; names; object; science
Wolff, Christian von 158
Wollstonecraft, Mary, on rights of
        women 346, *346*
women, in political thought 344, 346
Word, in Hellenistic philosophy 45–7
Wordsworth, William 337
writing, effect on early philosophy 3–4
Wundt, Wilhelm 227
Wyclif, John:
    and papacy 299, 306, 307–8, 314
    realism 105

Xenocrates 25, 45, 46
Xenophanes of Colophon, and
        mythology 10–12, 15
Xenophon 24

Zeno of Citium *38*, 39, 44, 288
Zeno of Elea 15
    paradoxes 16, 33
Zeus 5, *5*, 9

Index compiled by Meg Davies